INTRODUCTORY STATISTICS FOR PSYCHOLOGY

INTRODUCTORY STATISTICS FOR PSYCHOLOGY
THE LOGIC AND THE METHODS

GUSTAV LEVINE

Arizona State University

ACADEMIC PRESS

New York □ London □ Toronto □ Sydney □ San Francisco
A Subsidiary of Harcourt Brace Jovanovich, Publishers

The cartoons on pages 44, 59, 85, 153, 205, and 298 were drawn by Kerry Benson. The cartoons on pages 6, 24, 87, 155, 171, 179, 232, 272, and 279 were drawn by Abner Graboff.

Academic Press, Inc.
111 Fifth Avenue, New York, New York   10003

United Kingdom Edition published by Academic Press, Inc. (London) Ltd. 24/28 Oval Road, London NW1 7DX

ISBN: 0-12-445480-1
Library of Congress Catalog Card Number: 80-81254
Printed in the United States of America

CONTENTS

PREFACE

This just might be the world's most frequently rewritten text. I decided to write a statistics text because, in my ignorance, I was so pleased with the way in which I explained the topic. Expecting improved exam performance, I gave parts of the manuscript to my classes and examined them on the material. Unhappily, my explanations did not result in any better performance than when the students read equivalent sections in published texts. I persisted, rewriting the material and changing the organization until test performance improved. Surprisingly, the approach that made the difference was one that focused on vocabulary. This approach developed after I had listed all of the standard words and technical phrases that had to be learned in an introductory statistics course. I counted more than 200 such words and phrases. I determined to reconstruct my text so as to maximize the understanding and retention of the technical language and underlying concepts. What emerged was the format of this book.

Key statements concerning statistical logic, and definitions of new terms, are underlined. The underlined passages form their own coherent self-contained text within the larger text. The underlining has a dual function. It initially alerts the reader to the important material. It also offers a brief review text, which is embedded in the further clarification of the whole text. When students return to the underlined material for review, they are not restricted to the underlined material. If the material is not yet sufficiently clear, the further explanations, with concrete examples, are in the surrounding sentences.

A further component in this new format, which expedites learning of the underlined material, is a set of sentence completion items which are based only on the underlined passages. The sentence completions, found at the end of each chapter, offer an opportunity to rehearse the important material as well as a check on what has and has not been understood. The correct answers are given at the end of each set of sentence completions.

In keeping with the concern for the building of a technical vocabulary, each new word is set in bold face type at its first appearance, and is then included in a list of new words and concepts placed at the end of each chapter. Relevant page numbers accompany the list for ease in locating the text discussion of the concept.

Another major stumbling block to understanding statistics is the fact that most students entering an introductory statistics class are unfamiliar with the purposes and methods of psychological research. Since statistics is a tool of psychological research, the students are being taught to use a tool for a set of problems they have not yet recognized. The concepts of experimental design are therefore carefully interwoven with the statistical material. The first chapter is a discussion of experimental design, and briefly indicates the role of statistics. Independent and dependent variables are defined in this first chapter, and then identified in all future discussions of experimental questions. As another means of communicating the reasons for statistical analyses, the verbalization of conclusions to experiments is stressed. Proper conclusions from positive and negative results are illustrated, and conclusions from two-factor designs are thoroughly discussed. Alternative ways of stating the conclusions from a significant interaction are offered, along with a specification of the general form of such conclusions.

The three chapters on analysis of variance contain a little more material than is usually found in introductory statistics texts. Students have been able to handle this additional material because of the accompanying instructions in the use of double and triple subscripts, and the full use of subscripts in the latter portions of this text. Subscript notation simplifies the presentation of two-factor analysis of variance and computation of simple effects. It permits the use of clear tables summarizing the procedures. Most elementary texts minimize the use of subscript notation because beginning students are often dismayed or even intimidated by it. However, students have not been daunted by this text's presentation and have performed well on exams requiring the use of triple subscript notation.

In general, confrontations with mathematical formulas are not heartwarming experiences for students in the social and behavioral sciences. As a device for reducing potential discomfort, as well as for maximizing clarity, the presentation of each computational formula is accompanied by a table that offers a detailed example of the use of the formula. There are problems at the ends of the chapters offering practice in the use of the formulas. The answers are given in Appendix C, accompanied by computational details for the more difficult problems.

The topic of choosing the appropriate statistic is covered in every text, but seldom with adequate focus. In most texts, each chapter introducing a statistic indicates the conditions for the use of that particular statistic without ever contrasting and comparing the many choices. Few texts offer a summary of this widely dispersed material. Those texts that do summarize the bases for statistical choices offer a more complex picture than is necessary. This text offers four specific devices for enlightening students on statistical choice. First, as each statistic is introduced, it is compared and contrasted with all previously discussed statistics, both as to its purpose and the conditions for its use. Second, discussions of measurement scales have been avoided. There is controversy among psychologist-statisticians as to whether measurement scale type has relevance for the choice of a statistic. Mathematical statisticians appear to be unanimous in rejecting the relevance of measurement scales for statistical choice. The result is a clearer, less cluttered discussion of statistical choice. Therefore, in this text, consideration of levels of measurement have been omitted from the guidelines for choosing statistics.

The third device for aiding students in the choice of a statistic is a set of guidelines for an initial recognition of the appropriate statistic, prior to raising the issue of whether such assumptions as normality and independence have been met. These guidelines are summarized in a table in the final chapter. The table suggests the statistic that is most likely to be appropriate, and the student can then consider the more subtle issues concerning relevant assumptions. The page numbers of all earlier discussions of assumptions are listed in this chapter, for review and future use.

Finally, a set of 24 brief descriptions of experiments is included in the final chapter, for each of which the reader is to choose the appropriate statistic. Answers to this test are included.

The most gratifying result of my having finished this text (after six years of continuous rewriting and testing) has been a very different end-of-semester response. Prior to using this manuscript, I always heard the question, "But why do we need to learn this? I'm interested in people, not numbers." I still hear this question at the beginning of each semester, but it is no longer asked at the end of the semester.

I am grateful to the literary executor of the late Sir Ronal A. Fisher, F.R.S., to Dr. Frank Yates, R.R.S., and to Longman Group Ltd., London, for permission to reprint Tables III, IV, and VII from their book, *Statistical Tables for Biological, Agricultural and Medical Research,* 6th Edition (1974).

INTRODUCTION

Why should anyone who is interested in psychology want to read a book on statistics? The answer is that statistics is a tool for answering questions frequently asked by psychologists.

RELATIONSHIPS BETWEEN VARIABLES

Most of the questions asked by psychologists concern whether or not a relationship exists between some circumstance and behavior, or some inner state and behavior. For example: "Does frustration lead to aggression?"; "Does type of neighborhood affect self-esteem?"; or, "Does motivation affect reaction time?" Terms such as "frustration," "aggression," "type of neighborhood," and "self-esteem" are all **variables.** Psychological variables are behaviors, circumstances, states, and traits that can vary.

The question of whether frustration leads to aggression suggests that there are at least two different levels of the variable frustration (i.e., non-frustrated and frustrated). Aggression, hypothesized as varying due to frustration, is similarly presumed to be a potentially variable behavior, with different levels of aggression expressed at different times. In order to conclude that self-esteem is related to type of neighborhood, more than one neighborhood must be examined, and more than one level of self-esteem must be found.

A psychologist asks questions only about potentially variable circumstances and behaviors. The conclusion that the variables are related follows from observing that they vary together. If different levels of frustration are generally associated with different levels of aggression, the two variables are said to be related. Statistical techniques are usually required to determine whether or not the two variables covary.

Restricting Questions to Two Variables at a Time

Most variables are affected by a large number of other variables. For example, there are a great number of things that can affect the variable of self-esteem. The individual level of people's competence would probably affect their self-esteem. The neighborhood in which people are raised, along with other environmental variables, may also affect their self-esteem. However, it is often useful to initially examine the effects on a variable of just one other variable. For example, you might examine the relationship between variations in neighborhood and self-esteem in one study, and the relationship between variations in competence and self-esteem in another. It is also common practice to examine the relationship among three or even four variables within the same study. However, for the beginning student in statistics, it is important to first understand the simpler two-variable form for asking questions. Techniques for working with more than two variables at a time are introduced in Chapter 15.

It may be helpful to contrast questions about people that are sometimes asked by non-psychologists with those asked by psychologists. For example, a lay person might ask the question, "I wonder what makes people tick?" Such a question does not specify variables and does not suggest any context for answering the question. The questions asked by psychologists contemplating research always specify the variables: "Does frustration lead to aggression?" "Does type of neighborhood affect self-esteem?" Furthermore, such questions are asked with some research context in mind which has the potential for yielding answers.

A system for answering questions about relationships between variables has evolved. When the question is whether or not two variables are related, one variable is carefully controlled while the other variable is observed and measured (or otherwise classified).

Controlling a Variable A variable can be controlled by having it present for all members of one group, but absent for all members of another group. The group for which the controlled variable is absent is called the control group, and that for which the controlled variable is present is called the experimental group. The members of each group (either people or experimental animals) are called subjects.

In testing for a relationship between frustration and aggression, all the subjects in one group (the experimental group) are frustrated, while the subjects in another group (the control group) remain non-frustrated. Then, some measure of aggression is taken to see if aggression is different in the two groups. If it is, then we conclude that frustration and aggression are related.

A variable can also be controlled by having it present in different degrees in different groups. In this case, it must be present to a uniform degree within each group. For example, a study might be done with varying amounts of frustration in different groups to see if aggression varies at different levels of frustration. There would undoubtedly be many other differences among subjects in the groups besides their level of frustration. For example, people could vary in their energy levels or experiences just prior to entering the experimental situation; however, these would not be controlled differences between groups. It is expected that these uncontrolled differences will not exist consistently; that is, there is no reason to assume that everyone in one group will have a higher energy level than everyone in the other group. Rather, people should vary as much in energy levels between groups as within groups. The controlled variable, on the other hand, is controlled precisely in the sense of arranging for consistent differences between groups, and sameness within groups. Variables that are operating in the experiment (present to varying degrees), but are not controlled by the experimenter, are called **uncontrolled variables.**

We recognize two slightly different research contexts for answering questions about whether or not variables are related. The first involves experimental manipulation of the variations in the controlled variable to see if this manipulation results in changes in the observed variable.

Experimental Manipulation of the Controlled Variable

Experimental manipulation in psychological research consists of treating different groups of subjects differently. For example, this may mean offering different instructions to different groups, inducing different levels of frustration, or administering different dosages of a drug. The issue of whether aggression is related to frustration provides an example. An experimenter allows children in one group to play with some toys and then induces frustration by taking away a preferred toy—this is the experimental group. Another group is allowed to play without frustration—this is the control group. Do the children in the frustrated group break more toys and hit dolls more often than the children in the non-frustrated group? The children are observed and measured for the amount of aggression expressed by each child, and the measures from the different groups are compared. The general question is: "Does the differential treatment result in different sets of measurements on the observed variable?" If it does, then the conclusion drawn is that the two variables are related.

The context for answering such questions involves some deliberate manipulation of the situation so that it is different for the subjects in different groups. The children are experimentally manipulated to induce the controlled difference between groups and then are observed to see if the controlled and observed variables are related.

Classification of the Controlled Variable

There is a second research context for answering questions about relationships between variables which omits experimental manipulation of the controlled variable. Rather than treating subjects in different groups differently, the scientist asking the question merely differentiates groups on some preexisting basis of **classification.** The classes can be as simple as male and female, asking whether men and women are different with respect to some variable; or, as complex as socioeconomic class, involving a comparison of people in several complexly differentiated groups. For example, an experimenter might ask whether socioeconomic class is related to aggression. The experimenter would then classify people according to their socioeconomic class. In this way several socioeconomic groups would be defined, each group containing people of just one socioeconomic class. Children could be used as subjects, first being classified into socioeconomic classes, and then being allowed to play with toys. The children would be observed for aggressive behavior to see if more aggression occurs within one socioeconomic class than another. If the different groups express different amounts of aggression, it would be evidence in favor of the assertion that socioeconomic class is related to aggression. In such a study, socioeconomic class would be the controlled variable. It would not be controlled by variations in treatment of the subjects. It would be controlled by placing differently classified people in different groups. The observed variable would be some measure of the aggressive behavior of the children.

Independent and Dependent Variables
The word variable has been adopted from mathematics into experimental design and statistics. As an example, look at the function

$$Y = 5X + 2. \tag{1.1}$$

In this function, the value of Y waits upon the prior selection of a value for X. This function indicates precisely how Y is dependent upon X. If $X = 2$, then $Y = 12$, and if $X = 3$, then $Y = 17$. In the terminology of mathematics, Y is the

INDEPENDENT VARIABLE: PHYSICAL DISCOMFORT?
DEPENDENT VARIABLE: FREQUENCY OF HEADACHES?

dependent variable and X is the independent variable in Equation (1.1). In experimental design and statistics, the controlled variable is called the independent variable, and the observed variable is called the dependent variable. If the two variables are related, a subject's status on the independent variable will suggest the subject's status on the dependent variable. Variations in the independent variable would be associated with, and perhaps even be the cause of, variations in the dependent variable. The independent variable always defines the different groups in the experiment. The dependent variable is always the source of the recorded observations of the experiment (i.e., the data).

The Degree of Relationship Between Variables Only one goal was suggested in the prior discussion: obtaining an answer to the question of whether the two variables are related. A second goal in research is to obtain some estimate of the degree to which the two variables are related. Variables that are related can be strongly or weakly related. For example, you may find that socioeconomic class has some small relationship to aggression, but that frustration has one that is far stronger. Statistical techniques offer ways of measuring how strongly variables are related. The relationships between most psychological variables are probabilistic relationships. If frustration is related to aggression, then being frustrated increases the *probability* of being aggressive; it does not determine that a person will, with certainty, be aggressive. The stronger the relationship between variables, the greater the probability that changes in the independent variable will be associated with changes in the dependent variable. The concept of strength of relationship between variables is discussed in detail in Chapter 11.

The Goals of Psychological Research There are additional goals to research besides knowing whether or not variables are related, and to what degree. The overriding goal can be phrased as *understanding*. Understanding has many meanings in the context of psychological research. Understanding can mean that you know many of the relationships among a number of variables. For example, you may know that frustration sometimes leads to aggression, and also know that a person's self-concept helps to determine whether or not frustration leads to aggression. You may also know that other variables, such as type of neighborhood, can affect a person's self-concept, further increasing the circle of related variables. Research can lead to knowing about the relationships between ever-widening sets of variables. Understanding can be said to increase with the number of variables in the set of known relationships.

A further level of understanding is afforded by having a theory. A theory is an explanation of the network of relationships between the variables. A theory is considered to be a convincing explanation when it can be used to predict previously unknown relationships between variables. Research often consists of checking to see if the new relationships predicted by a theory exist.

The physical sciences have, from time to time, been successful in their theorizing, and so the overall testing of theories has been productive. In psychology, most of the theories are relatively undeveloped, with wide areas of ambiguity in predictions. But even the few well-developed psychological theories have been somewhat wanting in their power to predict. The powerful predictive functions of useful theories belongs more to psychology's future than to its past. At present, the field is still primarily testing the relationships between individual variables. When psychologists find that the variables in a set of variables are consistently related to each other in some fashion, a theory can be developed to explain the observed pattern of relationships. This often happens, and the psychological literature is filled with preliminary explanations that appear to have the potential for development into more fully-articulated theories. These primitive theories suggest some predictions. Observations are then collected to test whether the observations are consistent with, or contradict, the theory.

Unfortunately, findings of relationships between psychological variables have often tended to be inconsistent. Variables related in one study are sometimes found to be related differently, or not related at all, in other studies. This has retarded the development of theories. New psychological theories usually only appear reasonable for very short periods of time. It is likely that psychology still has to identify additional variables which will be more consistent in their relationships.

In the real world of psychological research, then, the vast majority of the work has been, and continues to be, testing whether or not variables are related, and to what degree they are related. Given these two goals, psychologists try to identify new variables to be observed, and new pairings of potentially related variables. When research techniques are employed to test for possible relationships between variables, statistical techniques are an essential part of the evaluation process.

THE PLACE OF STATISTICS IN PSYCHOLOGY

The place of statistics in answering questions about relationships can be better appreciated by contrasting questions involving physical variables with questions involving psychological variables.

In measuring the temperature at which water boils, the temperature is always 100°C, providing that the atmospheric pressure is 760 mm and that the water is perfectly pure. If the measuring instruments are perfect, an observer will always find the water beginning to boil at precisely 100°C.

Compare this physical example with the measurement of the point of frustration that might lead to aggression. Assume that an experimenter believes that frustration always leads to aggression, providing that the frustration reaches a specific, necessary point. To demonstrate that this is true, you must have knowledge of the conditions that can affect the frustration level at which aggressive behavior will occur. (This knowledge is analogous to the knowledge that the purity of water and atmospheric pressure both affect the boiling temperature of water.)

A very low point of frustration might lead to aggression when the frustrated individual has a long-standing dislike for the object of his or her aggression. Intangible things such as a person's self concept might affect the frustration level at which aggression will occur. For example, a person's perception of himself or herself as being a pacific individual who has found inner peace—or, by contrast, as a person who "never gets pushed around"—might result in different frustration points at which aggression will occur. Further, implicit social norms for behavior, and constraints on acting-out behavior, can also affect the frustration level which might lead to aggression. But not all people accept the same norms. There are many subcultures in the larger culture.

There is a large catalogue of psychological and social factors that can affect the point at which frustration will lead to aggression. But psychology is still too young to know all these relevant factors. (These are the potential new variables not yet recognized as relevant.) As a result, we must assume that many things are operating during experiments that cannot be controlled, because we do not know whether they are relevant, or even whether they exist. Each subject could conceivably have a different boiling point, based on unobserved influences (uncontrolled variables), in an experiment on frustration and aggression.

A further difficulty is that measurements of psychological variables, such as frustration and aggression, are very crude. The measurements will be far less exact than those of temperature or atmospheric pressure.

Psychological research, then, generally suffers from the presence of many uncontrolled and unknown variables, along with relatively unreliable measuring instruments. This does not mean that psychological research cannot be done. It merely means that psychological research has to incorporate special procedures to deal with all these unknown and uncontrolled influences on measurements. All social and behavioral sciences face this problem. All have solved it in a similar fashion, through the use of statistical techniques.

A simple example should serve to specify (in a preliminary way) the nature of the problems caused by these uncontrolled influences. Assume that the members of Psi Chi (the honor society for undergraduates interested in psychology) have been discussing a particular teacher. Some of the students believe that they would have done as well in their exams without attending the lectures; some other members of the society believe that the lectures were helpful.

This chapter of Psi Chi (we will pretend) is dedicated, whenever possible, to settling questions by experimental tests. They therefore decide to arrange for 20 members of the society who have not yet taken the course to now take it. Ten will attend the lectures and 10 will not, until the first exam. Thus, lecture attendance will be controlled, and will constitute the independent variable in the experiment. The first exam will offer the measurements for the dependent variable, indicating whether lecture attendance is related to exam performance. Table 1.1 offers the hypothetical data (hypothetical exam scores) of the Psi Chi members' experiment.

The two sets of scores in Table 1.1 are the not the same. On the average, the scores in the attending group are higher. Should this convince the students that attendance is useful? Groups of people always differ, at least to some small degree, on additional variables beside the variables being controlled. Individual differences in intelligence, in motivation, and in many other possible uncontrolled variables should have some effects on the scores. It is conceivable that the students in one group are just a little more intelligent, or a little less motivated, than the students in the other group. Therefore, these uncontrolled variables could be responsible for a difference between the two groups, even if lecture attendance was ineffective.

If some differences are possible when lecture attendance is ineffective, how could a difference between groups be used as a criterion of whether lecture attendance makes a difference? Clearly, what is needed is some criterion for when a difference signals an effective independent variable, and when it merely reflects the influence of uncontrolled variables.

TABLE 1.1
Exam scores for those attending and those not attending the lectures (hypothetical data).

Attending Lectures	Not Attending Lectures
100	95
80	90
90	90
95	70
85	75
70	80
100	75
75	85
90	65
90	80

Statistical techniques offer the needed criteria. Statistical tests generally use the source of the problem, variability, as the basis for the criteria. For example, many statistical techniques use some measure of the variability within single groups to estimate the variability that is only due to uncontrolled variables. This is possible since all subjects within a single group are treated identically on the independent variable, so the only influences for variability *within* a group can be assumed to be the uncontrolled variables. Consequently, variability within groups offers a measure of the variability that is only due to uncontrolled variables. Variability from group to group (between-group variability) has two possible sources. Between-group variability can follow from the effects of the controlled independent variable, as well as from the effects of uncontrolled variables. Therefore, the variability between groups is compared to the variability within groups. When variability between groups is found to exceed variability within groups, the best conclusion is that the controlled variable is adding something to the differences expected from uncontrolled variables. This would imply that the controlled independent variable does have an effect on the dependent variable. In this way, it is possible to identify a relationship between an independent variable and a dependent variable, even when uncontrolled variables are present.

Because of the importance of variability as a statistical concept, Chapter 5 is devoted to that topic. The concepts and formulas of Chapter 5 are then repeatedly referred to and used in the later chapters of this text.

DESCRIPTIVE STATISTICS There are other uses for statistics which are probably familiar to you. For example, statistics are used descriptively, as in describing a baseball player's batting average, or the average number of children in American families, or the average national income, and so on. A baseball player's batting average is a summary statement of all the results, over all the times that the player has come up to bat. All averages are brief summaries of large sets of numbers. A single listing of the number of children in each American family is too great for useful comprehension. The average is a way of summarizing all these numbers.

Descriptive statistics is concerned with the summarizing of information. Sometimes these summaries take the form of averages; sometimes they take the form of graphs. There are additional ways of summarizing information, all found in descriptive statistics.

The first six chapters of this text are exclusively concerned with discussions of descriptive statistics. Most of the concepts learned in these early sections are needed in the later discussions about the relationships between variables, which constitute the largest and most important part of this text.

In the example of the relationship between frustration and aggression in children, the question was asked with reference to all children, not just the small number of children exposed to the experimental manipulations. Most questions about relationships between psychological variables are asked with reference to the general population, or at least with reference to large sub–populations. Yet the task of collecting information from the complete general population is too great for most researchers. In practice, some limited, relatively small, and hopefully representative set of people provides the data, and then we draw inferences about the population as a whole from the limited set of available observations.

When a small group of subjects is examined to answer questions about people in general, researchers have to use some special techniques and some special logic. The explosion in the use of statistics is a direct result of the ingenious ways in which the problem of drawing inferences has been solved. Many statistical techniques have been developed which require a special and interesting form of logic for their application. The branch of statistics concerned with drawing inferences about large populations from relatively small numbers of observations is called **inferential statistics.**

The use of inferential statistics is an important part of the exploration of relationships between psychological variables. The techniques and logic required in inferential statistics are presented throughout the second half of this text.

**IMPORTANT
WORDS AND
CONCEPTS**

Variables (p. 3)
Controlled variable (p. 4)
Control group (p. 4)
Experimental group (p. 4)
Subjects (p. 4)
Uncontrolled variables (p. 5)
Experimental manipulation (p. 5)
Classification (p. 5)
Independent variable (p. 7)
Dependent variable (p. 7)
Descriptive statistics (p. 11)
Inferential statistics (p. 12)

**SENTENCE
COMPLETIONS**

The following incomplete sentences are taken from the underlined sentences in this chapter. Fill in the missing words and phrases and then correct them from the answers which follow.

1. The conclusion that variables are related follows from observing that the variables vary _____.
2. Statistical techniques are usually required to determine whether or not two psychological variables _____.

3. When only two variables are involved in research, one variable is carefully _____, while the other variable is _____.

4. A variable is controlled when it is _____ for all members of one group, but _____ for all members of another group. It is also controlled when it is _____ in different degrees in _____ _____.

5. Variables that are operating in the experiment but are not controlled are called _____ _____.

6. When a relationship between variables is investigated without the use of experimental manipulation, the groups are differentiated on some _____ _____.

7. The controlled variable is called the _____ variable, and the observed variable is called the _____ variable.

8. The _____ group is the group for which the independent variable is present, while the _____ group is the group for which it is absent.

9. When distinctions on the independent variable are based on some preexisting classifications, the subjects in the different groups are treated _____.

10. In a study involving experimental manipulation, the subjects in the different groups are treated _____. The basic question being asked is, does the _____ treatment result in _____? If it does, the conclusion drawn is that the variables_____ _____.

11. In order to know if the independent variable is related to the dependent variable, it would be necessary to know when an observed difference between groups is due to the independent variable, and when it is due to _____ _____.

12. Variability within groups offers a measure of the variability that is only due to _____ _____.

13. The branch of statistics concerned with the summarizing of information is called _____ statistics.

14. The branch of statistics concerned with drawing inferences about large populations from relatively small numbers of observations is called _____ statistics.

Answers 1. together (jointly) 2. covary (are related) 3. controlled; observed (measured) 4. present; absent; present; different groups 5. uncontrolled variables 6. preexisting classification 7. independent; dependent 8. experimental; control 9. identically 10. differently; different; different sets of measurements on the variable (different scores on the observed variable); are related 11. uncontrolled variables 12. uncontrolled variables 13. descriptive 14. inferential

THE AVERAGE

This chapter discusses two topics. The major focus is on the average, and three types of average are discussed and compared. A second purpose of this chapter is to introduce the summation sign, Σ, and its use.

In Chapter 1, the Psi Chi fraternity used some of their members as subjects in an experiment. Ten members were chosen to attend lectures, and 10 not to attend.

Suppose that the 10 students attending the lectures all find their attention waning at some point in the class, and that this prompts a discussion of ways to remain attentive in class. One student suggests drinking two cups of coffee before class as a solution to the problem. They elect to experiment on this question.

The students in the lecture-attending group decide that all 10 will continue to attend class, but five will have two cups of coffee before class, and the other five will not drink coffee at all before class. The 10 students all agree to keep stopwatches on their desks. The watches will be used to measure the amount of time that each student has remained continuously attentive from the start of the period. They want to see if the coffee group remains attentive longer than the non-coffee group. Coffee versus no coffee is the independent variable, and minutes of uninterrupted attention is the dependent variable.

Assume that the data appear as in Table 2.1, where the numbers represent minutes of uninterrupted attention. The simplest way to compare the two groups of scores is to compute the **average** of each group.

There are many different kinds of average. An average is always an attempt to summarize, or represent, a varied set of values with a single value. This is most generally done by identifying some central point around the middle of the complete set of values. This central point is then called the average. Therefore, the average is often described as a measure of **central tendency** for a set of values. However, there is more than one way to identify the central point of a set of values, sometimes resulting in different central points for the same set of scores. This difference in how and where the central point is located is what distinguishes most of the different

TABLE 2.1
Minutes of uninterrupted attention at the beginning of a lecture (hypothetical data)

Coffee	Non-coffee
10	10
20	20
30	30
40	40
100	50

definitions of average. The two most common definitions of average are called the mean and the median.

THE MEAN The **mean** is the best known definition of the average. It is simply the sum of all the scores in a group divided by the total number of scores in the group. The mean is symbolized as $\bar{X}$. The computation of the mean is shown in Equation (2.1):

$$\bar{X} = \frac{\Sigma X}{n} . \tag{2.1}$$

The letter X is a general symbol representing each score in the group of scores. It is not one constant score, but rather any one of many possible scores. The phrase "the sum of all scores" is replaced by "the sum of X," symbolically represented as ΣX. The symbol Σ is the upper-case Greek letter **sigma**, and is used to symbolize the addition operation. Consequently, ΣX implies that all the scores are to be added. The n is the number of X values (the number of scores). Thus $\Sigma X/n$ implies adding all the scores and then dividing by the number of scores, yielding the mean. For the coffee group in Table 2.1, the mean is

$$\bar{X} = \frac{\Sigma X}{n}$$

$$= \frac{10 + 20 + 30 + 40 + 100}{5}$$

$$= 40.$$

For the non-coffee group, the mean is

$$\bar{X} = \frac{10 + 20 + 30 + 40 + 50}{5}$$

$$= 30.$$

Thus, for the coffee and non-coffee groups, there are average initial attention spans of 40 and 30 minutes, respectively.

In the case of the non-coffee group, the average of 30 appears to be a reasonable value for representing the central tendency of the set of scores. That is, 30 conforms to an intuitive notion of a central point. (The other scores in the group are 10, 20, 40, and 50.) In the case of the coffee group, it is harder to obtain general agreement about what an intuitive central point is because of the one deviant score of 100. The middle is less easily identified.

Should the difference between the two groups in just the one highest score (100 versus 50) result in a pair of averages as different as 30 and 40? The difference in this example can only be due to the one deviant score of

100. This is an example of the general fact that <u>the mean is heavily influenced by deviant scores.</u> When there are deviant scores present, another definition of the average, the *median*, is considered.

THE MEDIAN   <u>The median is the middle score in a set of scores, in the sense of having as many scores above it in value as below it.</u> For example, in the non-coffee group of Table 2.1, the mean, 30, is also the median; that is, 30 is the middle value, being the score above 10 and 20, and below 40 and 50.

The concept of being the middle score assumes some listing of the scores in rank order. Thus, <u>it is necessary to **rank the scores** before deciding which score is the median.</u>

The Middle Rank and the Median   <u>The rank of a score is the score's relative position in an ordered listing of the scores. The scores are listed in order of decreasing values.</u> For example, in Table 2.2, the scores (values of X) are in ranked order. <u>The highest score is on the top, the next highest is next down, and so on to the lowest (smallest) score at the bottom of the list.</u>

The median, as the score with as many scores above it as below it, is the <u>score associated with the middle rank;</u> that is, if there are three scores, ranked one, two, and three, then two is the middle rank, and the score ranked second is the median. If there are five ranked scores, then the third score is the median. For larger sets of scores, the middle rank may not be so obvious. In that case, <u>a simple formula yields the middle rank.</u>

$$\text{Middle rank} = \frac{n + 1}{2} \qquad (2.2)$$

In Equation (2.2), n is the number of scores. For example, in Table 2.2, where there are seven scores, Equation (2.2) yields

$$\begin{array}{c} \text{Middle rank} \\ \text{for } n = 7 \end{array} = \frac{7 + 1}{2}$$

$$= 4.$$

TABLE 2.2
Ranked scores, with $n = 7$

Rank	Score
7	14
6	9
5	8
4	6
3	4
2	3
1	1

TABLE 2.3
Ranked scores, with $n = 6$

Rank	Score
6	80
5	70
4	60
3	50
2	40
1	30

Therefore, in any table with seven scores, the median is the score associated with a rank of 4. In Table 2.2 the median is 6.

When n is an even number, $(n + 1)/2$ will yield a value between two integers. For example, if $n = 6$, Equation (2.2) yields

$$\text{Middle rank for } n = 6 = \frac{6 + 1}{2}$$
$$= 3.5.$$

Table 2.3 offers a list of six ranked scores.

The computed middle rank of 3.5 is between the integer ranks of 3 and 4, associated with the scores 50 and 60. The computed middle rank is then most closely associated with *two* values in the table, both 50 and 60. When a set of scores has a middle rank that is between two integer ranks, the median is the mean of the two scores associated with the two adjacent ranks. For example, in Table 2.3, the median is the mean of 50 and 60. Recall that the mean of a set of scores is the sum of the scores divided by the number of scores. Thus, the mean of 50 and 60 is $(50 + 60)/2 = 55$. The median of the set of scores in Table 2.3 is 55.

In summary, to obtain the median, the following steps are taken.

1. List the scores in decreasing order of values, for ranking.
2. Apply Equation (2.2), $(n + 1)/2$, to obtain the middle rank.
3. If n is an odd number, then Equation (2.2) will yield the middle rank. The score associated with the middle rank is the median.
4. If n is an even number, Equation (2.2) will yield a point between two integer ranks. Take the mean of the two scores associated with the two middle integer ranks. The mean of these two scores is the median.

CHOOSING BETWEEN THE MEAN AND THE MEDIAN

In Table 2.4, the scores from the coffee and non-coffee groups (Table 2.1) are reproduced, with their ranks. In both sets of scores $n = 5$, so $(n + 1)/2$ yields a middle rank of three. The third ranked score in both sets of scores is 30, so 30 is the median for both sets.

TABLE 2.4

Scores of Table 2.1 ranked for computing the median

Coffee Group		Non-coffee Group	
Rank	Score	Rank	Score
5	100	5	50
4	40	4	40
3	30	3	30
2	20	2	20
1	10	1	10

Whereas the mean offers two different averages for these two sets of scores (40 and 30), the median yields the same average for the two sets of scores (30). This example is illustrative of three important points.

1. The same set of scores can sometimes yield different averages, depending on which definition of average is used.

2. The mean will yield an average that reflects the influence of the specific values of *all* scores, being very strongly influenced by deviant (extreme) scores. (The numbers 1, 2, 4, and 5 have a mean of $12/4 = 3$. The numbers 1, 2, 4, and 105 have a mean of $112/4 = 28$.)

3. The median will yield an average that does *not* reflect the influence of specific values of any extreme scores. (The median of 1, 2, 4, and 5 is 3. The median of 1, 2, 4, and 105 is 3.)

In choosing a particular form of average, the purposes to be served have to be considered. For example, suppose an experimenter is running an experiment using a single timer to measure each response. The scores, or times of the subjects in this hypothetical experiment, mostly range between 1 and 20 sec, but occasionally a score of 100 or more seconds appears. Assume that the experimenter becomes suspicious, wondering if the timer occasionally malfunctions, causing the occasional deviant scores. Given such a possibility, it is reasonable for the experimenter to give the extreme scores less influence. Therefore, the experimenter's choice of an average in this situation may be the median, rather than the mean.

As another illustration of the use of the median, assume a different pattern of events for the same experiment using a single timer. Assume that all the scores range between 1 and 20, none being greater than 20. Suppose that, after the experiment is run, it is discovered that the timer has been malfunctioning in the following way: Any time that the timer has to run for more than 20 sec, it stops on 20 sec. The result is that the data includes a number of instances in which the time for a subject's response is measured as 20 seconds, but in fact could have involved a response of more than 20 sec. Of course, after the experiment, there is no way to discover the true time for each response showing 20 sec on the timer.

In choosing an average to describe the average response time in this second example, the choice will again be the median. Since the inexact scores will all be at the extremes (20 or more seconds), the median would not be changed by substitution of the exact values (were they somehow known). The procedure for obtaining the median only requires identifying the score with as many scores above it as below it. The exact values of the extreme scores above or below the median will not influence the value of the median. By contrast, the mean *can not* be used if some of the X values are nonspecific numbers, because there is no way to get a specific value for ΣX.

In summary, the median is considered preferable to the mean under two conditions:

1. when there are extreme scores present whose influence needs to be minimized; and
2. when there are extreme scores of inexact value.

When neither point (1) nor (2) applies, the mean is generally used. In actual practice, the mean is the most often chosen form of average. The reason for the mean's popularity is that the mean is readily incorporated into most of the statistical techniques used to examine relationships between variables. There are some statistical techniques which incorporate the median rather than the mean, but these are less commonly used. For purely descriptive purposes, the mean or the median are both reasonable choices depending on the considerations summarized in points (1) and (2) above. But when more elaborate statistical analyses are planned, the mean is more often the choice of average. The uses of the mean with more elaborate statistical techniques will be illustrated and discussed later in this text.

As an example of the relative merits of choosing the mean or median for descriptive purposes, assume that there is a wage dispute between a union and a plant owner in a small plant with 75 workers. The union wants to be able to use a threat of a public boycott of the product, and the plant owner wishes to prevent such a boycott. Therefore, both sides wish to obtain public support for their respective positions.

The union informs the public, through the press, of their annual wages at the plant. They do this in order to support their claim that they require a raise. The union presents their current annual wages in the form of a mean, computed from the wages paid to all employees of the plant that year. The figure is $16,000.

In computing the average wage, the union included the wages of workers who had been laid off early in the year. Wages for workers who were employed all year ranged from $14,000 to $20,000. However, the union included the wages of some briefly employed workers whose wages ranged between $3000 and $5000 for the short period of their employment.

The briefly employed people obviously contributed deviantly small wages to the computation of the average wage. Their inclusion in the computation of the mean led to a misleadingly low summary statement of the average wage at the plant.

The employer, also anxious to give his side the best light, presented a different version of the mean. He computed a mean which included all employees who had been regularly employed all year, plus his own $150,000/year salary as company president. Thus he, too, used the mean in a way that could be misleading. His deviantly large salary will affect the mean and offer a misleadingly high figure as the annual wage at the plant.

If the employer must include his own salary, the company owner should use the median in computing the average annual wage. If the union must include the wages of the people only employed for a part of the year, they, too, should use the median.

Since the purpose of an average is to offer a single value that is representative of a set of values, the goal of achieving a representative figure should be kept in mind when selecting a form of average.

THE MODE The mode is defined as the most frequently occurring outcome in a set of outcomes, or the most frequently occurring score in a set of scores. For example, assume the following set of test scores: 90, 90, 95, 95, 95, 100. The mode is 95. If there is no single most frequent outcome, then there is no mode in the set of outcomes. There are no modes in the two sets of scores in Table 2.1

The mode is sometimes considered to be an average in that it is used as a single representation of a set of variable outcomes. However, it is not necessarily a representation of a central tendency. Rather, the mode is intended to give the most representative or most typical outcome, defined as being the single most frequent outcome.

The type of situation in which the mode is most likely to be useful is one in which the outcomes being represented are names or other non-quantified events. For example, people can be readily classified according to the state in which they were born. Another basis for non-quantitative classification is eye color. College attended is another example.

Non-quantitative classification of events is called nominal classification. Nominal classification has no numerical implication. The classes within the system are labels, usually verbal, with no necessary implication of quantity.

With nominal classification, it is possible to note the most frequently occurring event when there is one such class of events. The mode then becomes a possible basis for representing the set of events. In fact, for nominally classified sets of events, the mode is the only form of average that can be used.

As another example of the use of the mode, one sometimes sees a statement attempting to represent the predominant religious beliefs of a nation. It is not reasonable to ask for the mean or median of religious affiliation, but one can ask for the modal religious affiliation.

Unless there is one overwhelmingly frequent outcome of a survey or a test, the mode is not a very good representation. In addition, the mode is not incorporated into any other standard statistical procedure. This contrasts with the mean, which is readily incorporated into the most common statistical procedures, and the median, which can be incorporated into a few other statistical procedures.

SUMMARY COMPARISON

All three definitions of average are attempts to represent a set of scores (or outcomes) with a single score (or outcome). If the outcomes are non-quantitative (nominally classified), then there is no choice other than the mode. The mean is the best known and, in most circumstances, is the first to be considered. If there are a few deviant scores present, and/or some of the scores are indefinite in value, the median is generally considered as a possible choice of average.

The three averages discussed above are not the only available definitions of average, but they are the three most common.

THE SYMBOLS IN STATISTICAL FORMULAS

Statistical formulas are really instructions as to what numbers to add, what to multiply, what to divide, in what order, etc. For example, $\Sigma X / n$ is an instruction to first add all the numbers and then divide by the number of numbers. Since statistical formulas are a form of shorthand for the instructions, the more complex instructions can appear very busy and can sometimes look unintelligible at first meeting. But learning what the symbols mean, and learning the rules for their use, makes it possible and even easy to interpret the implicit instructions. In this and the following sections some definitions and general rules are given for the interpretation of the symbols used in statistical formulas.

The Variables X and Y

Any upper-case Latin letter can be used to symbolize individual numbers (individual scores) in a set of numbers. For example, ΣY is just as appropriate as ΣX if all the numbers to be summed are symbolized with a Y instead of an X.

The general symbol X (or Y), when representing a set of numbers, is called a **variable**, just as the behaviors and psychological characteristics discussed in Chapter 1 are called variables. Any outcome that has the potential of being more than one number or one class of events can be called a variable. Just as "amount of aggression" and "socioeconomic status" can be variables, so can X and Y. In fact, X and Y can, for example, respectively represent amount of aggression and socioeconomic status.

Subscripts for Variables There will be times when only some of the scores in a set of scores will be of interest, and only some of the scores should be added, or otherwise mathematically combined. How are individual scores on a variable to be differentiated from other scores on the variable? That is, how do you differentiate one X score from another?

The answer is that a second symbol is used, in the form of a subscript. Instead of using only the symbol X, the symbols X_1, X_2, X_3, etc. can be used. Any set of scores to be treated statistically are probably listed in a table of numbers in some order. The order can be the sequence in which the scores were gathered, or just the order in which they were randomly recorded by a research assistant. But the scores will be represented somewhere in some order, probably in a column or a row of numbers. The subscripts can be used to indicate each score's place in the listing. Thus each **subscripted variable** (X_1, X_2, X_3. . .) represents a specific score in the set.

Just as X is used as a general symbol for numerical scores, other letters are often used as symbols for numerical subscripts. The subscripted letter i is often used, as in X_i, to refer to a nonspecified numerical subscript. Thus X_i can stand for X_1, X_2, or X_3, etc. As an example, look at the following set of scores:

$$X_1 = 12$$
$$X_2 = 8$$
$$X_3 = 14.$$

In this set of scores,

$$X_i = X_1 = 12$$

or

$$X_i = X_2 = 8$$

or

$$X_i = X_3 = 14.$$

The symbol X_i, then, is just like the symbol X. It can stand for any score in the set of scores. The advantage of using X_i in place of just X is that X_i implies a potential for specificity. There will be times when you will want to refer to a specific subset of all the scores. For example, suppose that there is a set of five scores and you only want to add scores 2 through 4. This is expressed symbolically as

$$\sum_{i=2}^{4} X_i = X_2 + X_3 + X_4.$$

The symbolic statement $\sum_{i=2}^{4} X_i$ is verbalized as "the sum of X_i, from $i = 2$ through $i = 4$." The numerical subscript below sigma indicates the first term in the set of consecutive terms to be added, and the superscript above sigma indicates the last term in the set of consecutive terms to be added.

The set of scores for the coffee group in Table 2.1 can be restated as in Table 2.5.

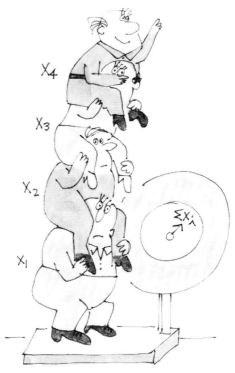

X_i = WEIGHT OF iTH PERSON

$\sum_{i=1}^{4} X_i$ = TOTAL WEIGHT OF THE FOUR PEOPLE

TABLE 2.5
Scores in the coffee group of Table 2.1, with
appropriate subscripts

Coffee Group
$X_1 = 10$
$X_2 = 20$
$X_3 = 30$
$X_4 = 40$
$X_5 = 100$

Suppose you wish to sum only the middle three scores in the coffee group. Symbolically, this is

$$\sum_{i=2}^{4} X_i = X_2 + X_3 + X_4$$

$$= 20 + 30 + 40$$

$$= 90.$$

If you want to sum all the scores in a set of scores, but wish to be specific in notation, the general expression will look like:

$$\sum_{i=1}^{n} X_i = X_1 + X_2 + \cdots + X_i + \cdots + X_n.$$

Note that the total number of scores is always symbolized as n.

When all the scores in a set are to be summed, it is not necessary to be specific about which scores are to be summed, suggesting the following symbolic equality:

$$\sum_{i=1}^{n} X_i = \Sigma X,$$

that is, <u>when no subscripts are indicated in a summation, as in ΣX, it implies that all the X scores are to be included in the summation.</u>

THE RULES OF SUMMATION There will be occasions when you will have to sum variables which have been combined through other mathematical operations. For example, you may have to obtain values such as $\Sigma(X+Y)$. Table 2.6 illustrates the meaning of $\Sigma(X+Y)$.

Sometimes you must follow the operation in parentheses first, before following the summation instruction from sigma. For example, perhaps you should add each value of X and Y in $\Sigma(X+Y)$, as in the last column of Table 2.6, before carrying out the summation implied by sigma; or perhaps you

TABLE 2.6
Illustration of the principle that summation distributes over addition, that is, $\Sigma(X+Y) = \Sigma X + \Sigma Y$.

i	X_i	Y_i	X_i+Y_i
1	2	3	5
2	4	5	9
3	1	2	3
	$\Sigma X = 7$	$\Sigma Y = 10$	$\Sigma(X+Y) = 17$

$$\Sigma X + \Sigma Y = 7 + 10$$
$$= 17$$

should first sum all the X and all the Y values, as in ΣX and ΣY, and *then* carry out the operation within the parentheses, that is, $\Sigma(X+Y) = \Sigma X + \Sigma Y$.

In the case of $\Sigma(X+Y)$, it can be done either way. The same result will be obtained either way. But this is not always the case with all combined operations. For example, in the case of $\Sigma(X+Y)^2$, different answers will occur, depending on whether the summation operation or squaring operation is applied first. The only correct way is to apply the squaring operation first.

Rules, then, are needed for how and when to apply sigma when sigma is used in formulas containing other mathematical operations. These rules for the use of sigma are called **the rules of summation**, and are presented below.

The rules of summation can be classified in a number of ways. In this text, the rules of summation are divided into just three major rules.

The First Rule of Summation

$\Sigma(X+Y) = \Sigma X + \Sigma Y$

Rule 1 states that sigma distributes over all terms that are being summed within the parentheses, that is, sigma distributes over addition and subtraction, analogously to the way that multiplication distributes over addition. For example,

$$a(b+c) = ab + ac.$$

Table 2.6 offers an example of Rule 1.

Since subtraction is simply the addition of negative numbers, sigma also distributes over subtraction, that is, according to Rule 1, the following is also correct:

$$\Sigma(X + Y - Z) = \Sigma X + \Sigma Y - \Sigma Z.$$

Sigma does *not* distribute over multiplication, that is,

$$\Sigma(X \cdot Y) \neq \Sigma X \cdot \Sigma Y.$$

TABLE 2.7
Illustration of the principle that summation does *not*
distribute over multiplication, that is, $\Sigma(X \cdot Y) \neq \Sigma X \cdot \Sigma Y$

i	X_i	Y_i	$X_i \cdot Y_i$
1	2	3	6
2	4	5	20
3	1	2	2
	$\Sigma X = 7$	$\Sigma Y = 10$	$\Sigma(X \cdot Y) = 28$
		$\Sigma X \cdot \Sigma Y = 7 \cdot 10$	
		$= 70$	

For example, look at Table 2.7, with the last column offering the products of paired scores (each $X_i \cdot Y_i$). The sum of the products is

$$\Sigma(X \cdot Y) = 6 + 20 + 2$$
$$= 28.$$

The product of the two sums, ΣX and ΣY, is

$$\Sigma X \cdot \Sigma Y = 7 \cdot 10$$
$$= 70.$$

Therefore,

$$\Sigma(X \cdot Y) \neq \Sigma X \cdot \Sigma Y.$$

There is an important exception to the rule that sigma distributes over addition and subtraction: Whenever an operation is indicated on the complete term in parentheses, that operation must be performed first, before distributing sigma. For example, in $\Sigma(X+Y)^2$, the squaring operation is indicated for the complete term $(X+Y)$. The squaring operation must be applied before sigma is distributed.

$$\Sigma(X + Y)^2 = \Sigma[(X + Y)(X + Y)]$$
$$= \Sigma(X^2 + 2XY + Y^2) \quad \text{[first squaring]}$$
$$= \Sigma X^2 + \Sigma 2XY + \Sigma Y^2 \quad \text{[distributing sigma].} \quad (2.3)$$

The same delay in the distribution of sigma applies to $\Sigma(X + Y - Z)^{-1}$, or $\Sigma[(X+Y)(X-Y)]$. In general, given any operation indicated on the whole term within parentheses or brackets, this operation precedes the distribution of sigma.

The Second Rule of Summation

$$\sum_{i=1}^{n} k = nk$$

Assume that, for some set of scores X, all the scores have the same value; that is, assume that for every value of i,

$$X_i = k,$$

where k is a constant. Further, suppose that it is necessary to obtain the sum $\sum_{i=1}^{n} X_i$ for the set of scores where X_i is a constant.

The second rule of summation states: If X is a constant, k, then

$$\sum_{i=1}^{n} X_i = X_1 + X_2 + \cdots + X_i + \cdots + X_n$$

$$= k + k + \cdots + k + \cdots + k$$

$$= nk.$$

Translated into words, the second rule of summation says that when summing a constant k, k should be repetitively added n times (equivalent to multiplying by n). Symbolically:

$$\sum_{i=1}^{n} k = nk$$

Equivalently, without subscripts:

$$\Sigma k = nk.$$

In summing a constant, then, simply multiply the constant by n.

The Third Rule of Summation

$\Sigma kX = k\Sigma X$

The third rule of summation is the simplest. Verbally, Rule 3 says that when a product of a constant value k and a variable value X are being summed over different values of X (as in ΣkX), the constant k can be placed *before* the summation sign (as in $k\Sigma X$). Rule 3 can be seen to be valid by simply spelling out ΣkX:

$$\Sigma kX = kX_1 + kX_2 + \cdots + kX_i + \cdots + kX_n$$

$$= k(X_1 + X_2 + \cdots + K_i + \cdots + X_n)$$

$$= k\Sigma X$$

Rule 3 only applies when the constant is a coefficient, as in ΣkX, where k is a coefficient of X. If the constant is the only term being added, as in Σk, then k must remain to the right of sigma, and only Rule 2 applies.

As an example of the use of Rule 3, Equation (2.3),

$$\Sigma(X+Y)^2 = \Sigma X^2 + \Sigma 2XY + \Sigma Y^2,$$

can be restated as

$$\Sigma(X+Y)^2 = \Sigma X^2 + 2\Sigma XY + \Sigma Y^2. \tag{2.4}$$

The next section offers an illustration of the use of the rules of summation.

The Sum of the Deviations from the Mean Equals Zero

It has been previously stated that the mean is a measure of central tendency. It was also stated that there are different ways in which a point of central tendency can be defined.

In the case of the mean, the point of central tendency is defined in the following way: If the score designated as the mean is subtracted from every score in the set of scores, the sum of all the differences [$\Sigma(X - \bar{X})$] will be zero; that is, take the score which has been designated as the mean, and subtract it from every other score in the set of scores. If the mean has been properly chosen, the sum of the deviations from the mean will equal zero. The formula for the mean, $\Sigma X/n$, always yields the only value for which the sum of the differences from that value is equal to zero.

Symbolically, this characteristic of the mean is stated as:

$$\Sigma(X - \bar{X}) = 0. \tag{2.5}$$

As an example, look at the set of numbers 4, 5, 6, 7, and 8. The mean is

$$\bar{X} = \Sigma X/n$$
$$= 30/5$$
$$= 6$$

If you take all the scores above the mean (each $X > \bar{X}$), and subtract the mean from each, this will sum to some positive number. In this example, $\Sigma(X - \bar{X})$ for all $X > \bar{X}$ yields

$$(8 - 6) + (7 - 6) = 2 + 1$$
$$= 3.$$

If you then take all the scores below the mean (each $X < \bar{X}$), and subtract the mean from each, this will sum to some negative number. In this example, $\Sigma(X - \bar{X})$ for all $X < \bar{X}$ yields

$$(4 - 6) + (5 - 6) = (-2) + (-1)$$
$$= -3.$$

In this case, as in every other case, you will find that the scores above the mean yield as much positive value as the scores below the mean yield negative value, when all the scores are subtracted from the mean. That is, the sum of the differences of scores above and below the mean cancel each other, leaving a total sum of the differences of zero. It is in this sense that the mean is a central point.

It has been stated that if the mean is defined as $\Sigma X/n$, then the sum of the differences from the mean, $\Sigma(X - \bar{X})$, always equals zero. How do we know that this is actually true? This claim is a theorem of mathematical statistics. A theorem is a statement which is believed to be provable through logic. How this particular theorem is proven is illustrated below.

In general, proofs are not offered in this text, but a few instructive exceptions have been included. The purpose of illustrating the proof of the mean's central tendency will be a dual one:

1. to underline the mean's specific definition of central tendency, that is, to underline the idea that the sum of the deviations from the mean equals zero; and
2. to offer an illustration of the use of the rules of summation.

It will be helpful in following the proof of

$$\Sigma(X - \bar{X}) = 0$$

if you appreciate the fact that for any one set of scores, the mean of that set of scores is a constant; that is, given the symbolic instruction $\Sigma\bar{X}$, Rule 2 of summation can be legitimately applied. For example, just as

$$\Sigma k = nk,$$

so

$$\Sigma\bar{X} = n\bar{X}.$$

Recall that we want to prove that the sum of the deviations from the mean defined as $\Sigma X/n$ is zero. What is required, then, to prove the theorem, is to substitute $\Sigma X/n$ for $\bar{X}$ in $\Sigma(X - \bar{X})$, and see if the result is an equality with zero. This is the logic underlying the following proof.

$$\Sigma(X - \bar{X}) = \Sigma X - \Sigma\bar{X} \qquad \text{[first rule of summation]}$$
$$= \Sigma X - n\bar{X} \qquad \text{[second rule of summation]}$$
$$= \Sigma X - n\left(\frac{\Sigma X}{n}\right) \qquad \text{[definition of the mean as } \bar{X} = \Sigma X/n]$$
$$= \Sigma X - \Sigma X \qquad \text{[algebraic equivalence, based on cancelling } n]$$
$$= 0 \qquad \text{[algebraic equivalence of } (\Sigma X - \Sigma X) \text{ and 0].}$$

The above proof began with the left side of Equation (2.5), and showed that an equality with zero is obtained when $\Sigma X/n$ is used as the definition of the mean.

The Logic and Purpose of a Proof The point of a proof is to show that the theorem follows logically from a set of accepted assumptions. The accepted assumptions in the above example are the rules of algebra and the rules of summation. When the accepted assumptions lead to a particular conclusion (such as the equivalence of Equation (2.5)), the conclusion is accepted. This is the sense in which Equation (2.5) was proven.

When a proof is presented, you should be careful not to lose sight of the fact that it is not the proof that is important. Rather, the theorem that has been proven is the fact of importance. The proof is just a guarantee of the theorem's validity. The theorem in this case is that the sum of the differences from the mean is zero.

SENTENCE
COMPLETIONS

The following incomplete sentences are taken from the underlined sentences in this chapter. Fill in the missing words and phrases and then correct them from the answers which follow.

1. An average is always an attempt to _____ or _____ a varied set of values with a single value. This is most generally done by identifying some _____ point around the _____ of the complete set of values.

2. The average is often described as a measure of _____ _____ for a set of values.

3. The formula for the mean is _____, where n is _____ .

4. Σ is the uppercase Greek letter _____ .

5. ΣX means that you should _____.

6. The mean is _____ by deviant scores.

7. The median is the _____ score in a set of scores, in the sense of _____ .

8. The rank of a score is _____ .

9. The median is the score associated with the _____ .

10. When n is an even number, $(n + 1) / 2$ will yield a value _____ .

*Where sigma does and does not distribute; exception to distribution over addition; summing a constant; changing the placement of a constant.

11. When a set of scores has a middle rank that is between two integer ranks, the median is the _____ associated with the two adjacent ranks.

12. The mean will yield an average that reflects the influence of the specific values of _____ scores, being very strongly influenced by _____.

13. The median will yield an average that _____ the influence of specific values of deviant (extreme) scores.

14. When there are inexact (nonspecific) scores, the _____ cannot be used to compute the average.

15. When more elaborate statistical analyses are planned, the _____ is most often the choice of average.

16. The mode is defined as _____ in a set of outcomes.

17. Non-quantitative classification of events is called _____ _____ .

18. For nominally classified sets of events, the _____ is the only form of average that can be used.

19. The _____ is the best known average and, in most circumstances, is the first to be considered.

20. If there are a few deviant scores present and/or some scores are indefinite in value, the _____ is generally considered as a possible choice of average.

21. Any _____ letter can be used to symbolize numbers (individual scores) in a set of numbers.

22. The general symbol X, when representing a set of numbers, is called a _____ .

23. The symbolic statement $\sum_{i=1}^{3} X_i$ is verbalized as _____ _____ .

24. The numerical subscript below sigma in $\sum_{i=i}^{n} X_i$ indicates the _____ _____ in the set of consecutive terms to be added, and the superscript above sigma indicates the _____ in the set of consecutive terms to be added.

25. When no subscripts are indicated in a summation, as in $\sum X$, it implies that _____ are to be included in the summation.

26. Rules for the use of _____ are called the "rules of summation."

27. Sigma distributes over _____ and _____ .

28. Sigma does *not* distribute over _____ .

29. There is an important exception to the distribution of sigma. Whenever an operation is indicated on the complete term in parentheses, _____ _____ .

30. In summing a constant, simply _____.
31. The expression ΣkX can be expressed as _____ .
32. It has been stated that if the mean is defined as $\Sigma X/n$, the sum of the differences from the mean, $\Sigma(X - \bar{X})$, equals _____.
33. The point of a proof is to show that the theorem follows logically from a set of _____ _____ .
34. The accepted assumptions for the proof that the sum of the deviations from the mean equals zero, are the rules of _____ and the rules of _____ .

Answers 1. summarize; represent; central; middle   2. central tendency   3. $\Sigma X/n$; the number of scores in the group   4. sigma   5. add all of the scores   6. heavily influenced   7. middle; having as many scores above it in value, as below it   8. the score's relative position in an ordered listing of the scores   9. middle rank   10. between two integers   11. mean of the two scores   12. all; deviant scores   13. does not reflect   14. mean   15. mean   16. the most frequently occurring outcome   17. nominal classification   18. mode   19. mean   20. median   21. uppercase Latin   22. variable   23. the sum of X_i, from $i = 1$ through $i = 3$ 24. first term; last term   25. all of the X scores   26. sigma   27. addition; subtraction   28. multiplication   29. that operation must be performed first, before distributing sigma   30. multiply the constant by n 31. $k\Sigma X$ 32. zero   33. accepted assumptions   34. algebra; summation

1. What is the median of the following set of scores? 8, 5, 7, 6, 10, 2, 6, 9, 9.
2. What is the median of the following set of scores? 20, 18, 10, 12, 10, 20, 9, 18, 16, 14.
3. What is the mode of the following set of scores? 100, 100, 98, 98, 100, 99, 100, 75, 85, 100.
4. Five subjects have taken two tests, test X and test Y. Their scores are as follows:

Subject	Test X	Test Y
1	4	7
2	3	6
3	1	4
4	5	3
5	2	5

(a) What is the mean for test X?
(b) What is the mean for test Y?
(c) Compute ΣX^2.
(d) Compute $(\Sigma X)^2$.
(e) Compute ΣY^2.
(f) Compute $(\Sigma Y)^2$.

(g) Compute $\displaystyle\sum_{i=2}^{4} X_i$

(h) Compute $\Sigma(X + Y)$.

(i) Compute $\Sigma(X + Y)^2$.

(j) Compute ΣXY. (Hint: Note that each value X_iY_i is a product of two values.)

(k) Compute $\displaystyle\sum_{i=2}^{3} X_iY_i$. (In answering this question, it will help to first list the X_iY_i values in order.)

5. Annual incomes of the staff and employer in the office of a small publisher are listed below:

Secretary	$9000
Bookkeeper	$12,000
Officeboy	$8000
Editor	$20,000
Office manager	$18,000
Owner of the firm	$60,000 plus 70% of the annual profit, which varies from year to year

Assume that the above data are all the information you can get. If you are asked to give the average income of the people listed above,

(a) what will be the appropriate measure of central tendency?

(b) If the owner decides to double his salary, which will this affect more, the mean or the median?

6. Assume that you have taken five exams in a course, and have received the grades 70, 80, 85, 90, and 100.

(a) What is the appropriate measure of central tendency, if you want to obtain your average grade over the five tests?

(b) Assume that there was a sixth test, but that you did not take it because you felt that you were not prepared. There was no make-up test. Suppose that the instructor includes a zero with your other grades because of the exam that you missed. What measure of central tendency will give the most representative picture of your test performance over the semester? (You are not being asked which definition of average is desirable or fair, but which one will give the most representative picture of your test performance, given that the zero is included in the computation of the average.)

t
h
r
e
e

FREQUENCY DISTRIBUTIONS

Recall the classroom instructor of the two previous chapters, the one who was having trouble keeping the attention of the Psi Chi members. Assume now that the instructor is sensitive to his lack of success as a lecturer, and that he attempts to confront his problem. Suppose he speculates that his own boredom is contagious, and wonders if a couple of cups of strong coffee before class may keep him more awake. He reasons that such an increase in his own alertness may be what the course needs. He decides to experiment. The instructor intends to compare two groups. With his Tuesday class he drinks two cups of coffee before class, but for his Wednesday class he does not drink any coffee before class. Therefore, the Tuesday class is his experimental group, and his Wednesday class is the control group.

The instructor takes special care to introduce material from his lectures into his final exam. The scores on the final exam will then offer a relevant measure of the class's attention, and serve as the dependent variable. At the end of the semester he compares the two groups, and the data for the 50 students in each class appear as in Tables 3.1a and 3.1b.

Note how difficult it is to distinguish any overall differences between Tables 3.1a and 3.1b, confronting so much data without any organization. Some method of organizing and summarizing the data is necessary.

A single value can be used, such as a mean or a median, to represent each set of scores. This, in fact, is what is often done. But the central tendency of a set of scores might not be the only interesting aspect of the data. An important piece of additional information is the pattern of relative frequencies of the scores. Two sets of scores can have the same average, but very different patterns of relative frequencies.

TABLE 3.1a
Experimental group, final exam scores

75	80	75	85	60	65	95	90	80	80
70	75	80	65	55	70	80	65	70	85
80	75	75	80	75	75	75	85	80	70
60	90	80	70	75	70	75	65	65	70
85	75	85	75	70	70	85	65	70	80

TABLE 3.1b
Control group, final exam scores

65	90	70	80	85	55	60	60	95	65
85	70	65	95	100	60	60	55	90	65
55	70	60	65	50	65	60	90	85	95
60	65	75	60	85	95	55	70	60	65
65	60	65	60	90	70	55	90	65	90

TABLE 3.2a
Final exam scores, experimental group, as a
frequency distribution

X	f
100	0
95	1
90	2
85	6
80	10
75	12
70	10
65	6
60	2
55	1
50	0

TABLE 3.2b
Final exam scores, control group, as a frequency
distribution

X	f
100	1
95	4
90	6
85	4
80	1
75	1
70	5
65	11
60	11
55	5
50	1

Any presentation of data which offers the frequency with which each score occurs is called a **frequency distribution**. Tables 3.2a and 3.2b are frequency distributions of the data in Tables 3.1a and 3.1b, respectively. Note that the highest score values are placed at the top of the listings in frequency distributions.

ADVANTAGES OF FREQUENCY DISTRIBUTIONS

By showing the frequency of each different score value, a frequency distribution allows a pattern of frequencies to be recognized. A second advantage is the economy of representation when there are frequent repetitions of values. For example, in Table 3.2b, scores of 60 and 65 each occur 11 times. Listing scores of 60 and 65 each 11 separate times is clearly inefficient. Listing a score X (such as 65), just once, adjacent to its frequency f (such as 11) is more efficient. Further, as seen in the next section, computations of descriptive statistics, such as the mean, are easier when a large set of scores is organized into a frequency distribution.

Computing the Mean of a Frequency Distribution To obtain the mean of a frequency distribution, a formula is used that is equivalent to the familiar formula

$$\bar{X} = \frac{\Sigma X}{n}.$$

(2.1)

The new version of the formula for the mean, like the old, requires the total of all scores to be divided by the number of scores. The total of all scores is simply stated differently when working with frequency distributions; that is, the total of all scores is expressed as ΣfX rather than as ΣX.

The product fX is seen in the third column of Table 3.3. The f represents the frequency of an X value, and fX is the product of the frequency of a value times the value. For example, for $X = 65$ in Table 3.3, $f = 11$, so that $fX = 11 \cdot 65 = 715$. The total sum of the scores, then, is ΣfX, as illustrated at the bottom of the third column in Table 3.3

Equation (3.1) presents the alternate formula for the mean when the data is in the form of a frequency distribution.

$$\bar{X} = \frac{\Sigma fX}{n}$$

(3.1)

The number of scores in the distribution is

$$n = \Sigma f.$$

TABLE 3.3
Computation of the mean for the data of Table 3.2b

X	f	fX		
100	1	100		
95	4	380		
90	6	540		
85	4	340	$\bar{X}$	$= \dfrac{\Sigma fX}{n}$
80	1	80		
75	1	75		
70	5	350		$= \dfrac{3565}{50}$
65	11	715		
60	11	660		
55	5	275		$= 71.3.$
50	1	50		
	$\Sigma f = n$	$\Sigma fX = 3565$		
	$= 50$			

Table 3.3 offers an example.

$$\bar{X} = \frac{\Sigma fX}{n}$$

$$= \frac{3565}{50}$$

$$= 71.3.$$

GRAPHS Table 3.2b offers a clear but undramatized listing of the frequency of each X value. A more dramatic picture of the relationship between the X values and their frequencies can be presented in a graph. A graph is another form of a frequency distribution.

All graphs have an X axis, sometimes called the **abscissa**.* The X axis is the horizontal line at the bottom of the graph, which indicates points on the scale of the variable of interest (such as the final exam scores in Table 3.2b). The X axis does not have to represent a quantitative variable. For example, the X axis can designate political parties in a graph indicating the size of voter registration in each party; or the X axis can designate astrological signs in a graph indicating the frequencies of people born under different signs.

There is also a Y axis, sometimes called the **ordinate**, which is placed vertically, perpendicular to the X axis.† In a frequency distribution presented in the form of a graph, the Y axis indicates the frequencies of the various points on the X axis.

The Y axis normally ranges over the frequencies encountered in the data. Similarly, the X axis ranges over the values of the variable that have occurred in the data. For purposes of comparisons with other graphs and other data, or in order to show zero points on the two scales, additional values can be added to either axis. Figure 3.1 offers graphs of the data in Tables 3.2a and 3.2b.

In a graph, a point (or circle or cross) is placed above each X axis value at some appropriate height on the Y axis. The points are usually connected, using straight lines between points, as in Figure 3.1. When the points are connected, the resulting figure is called a **frequency polygon**. In a frequency polygon, the ends of the graph touch the X axis to indicate the X-axis values at and beyond which there are no more frequencies (no more occurrences beyond a certain value). Two such dropped lines are shown in Figure 3.1b.

*Technically, an abscissa is an X axis coordinate of a single point on the graph. Hence, the X axis is properly designated the axis of abscissas. However, common usage favors the use of the single word abscissa to denote the X axis.

†The ordinate, like the abscissa, is an abbreviated term for the technically more correct axis of ordinates.

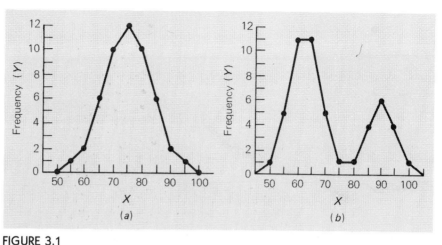

FIGURE 3.1
(a) A unimodal distribution (frequency polygon). Data from Table 3.2(a).
(b) A bimodal distribution (frequency polygon). Data from Table 3.2(b).

Frequency polygons have the advantage over tabled data of giving a quick overview of the relative frequencies of the different X-axis values. The relative heights of the segments of the graph indicate the relative frequencies of the entire distribution at a glance.

Modal Peaks When a particular point or interval of a graph towers above its neighboring points, the high point is called a **modal peak**. An example is the high point at X = 75 in Figure 3.1a. When there is one modal peak in a distribution, the distribution is called a **unimodal distribution**. In a unimodal distribution, then, a mode is readily identified.

When there are two modal peaks the distribution is called a **bimodal distribution**. For example, in Figure 3.1b there is a modal peak at X = 90, and another one that extends over two points, 60 and 65.

There can be more than two peaks, in which case we have a multimodal distribution, or there can be a distribution with no modal peaks. A distribution with no modal peaks and identical Y axis heights all along the X axis is a **rectangular distribution**. A rectangular distribution has uniform frequencies, and is therefore sometimes called a uniform distribution. Figure 3.2 is a graph of an approximately rectangular distribution.

Slight increases in frequency above neighboring points are not considered to be modal peaks. For example, the slight increases above neighboring points in Figure 3.2 are not modal peaks.

More often than not, distributions will be unimodal or bimodal. For example, in grading a large class, it is often expected that the scores will form a

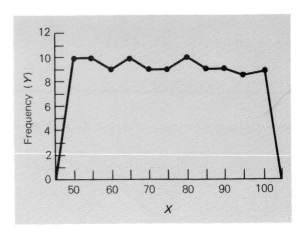

FIGURE 3.2
An approximately
rectangular distribution

unimodal distribution with the modal peak approximately in the center of the distribution, as in Figure 3.1a. All scores in the neighborhood of the modal peak receive the average grade, that is, a C. Fewer people receive B and D as grades, and still less A and F.

As an example of a bimodal distribution of exam scores, consider the case of a course which is reasonably easy, provided that the students study the material. The group that studies will do well, having their own modal peak on the higher end of the scale of scores, with similar scores distributed around that modal peak located on the right-hand end of the X axis. A second group of students, those who do not study, will do poorly, with a modal peak concentrated around a low score, which will be the center of a sub-section of the graph located nearer to the left-hand end of the X axis. Figure 3.1b offers a graphic illustration of such a distribution. In the example of the teacher who did not create interest in his class, many of the students may not have been motivated to study or attend class, resulting in the larger proportion of the class doing poorly, as implied in Figure 3.1b.

Skewness   A distribution with a modal peak in the middle of the distribution has very different implications than a distribution with a modal peak of approximately the same height, but at one of the ends of the distribution. Compare, for example, the symmetric distribution in Figure 3.1a with the two distributions in Figure 3.3.

The instructor whose class performed as in Figure 3.3a may conclude that his exams were too difficult, or that his students were not as good as he would wish, or that he had failed as a teacher. The opposite conclusions are suggested to the teacher whose class performed in accordance with the graph of Figure 3.3b.

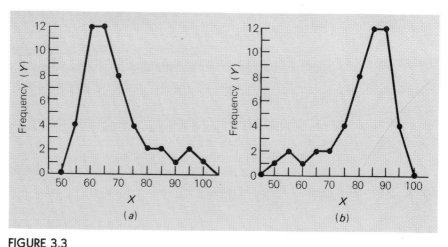

FIGURE 3.3
(a) A unimodal distribution, skewed to the right.
(b) A unimodal distribution, skewed to the left.

A distribution which has a modal peak that is off to one side of the distribution, with the remainder of the distribution being relatively shallow, is called a **skewed distribution**. Figures 3.3a and 3.3b are both skewed distributions.

The word skew means slanting. When the decline from the modal peak is to the right, it is slanted to the right, and is described as skewed to the right. The distribution in Figure 3.3a is skewed to the right. Similarly, a distribution with a modal peak to the right, with the distribution trailing off at a lower level to the left, is skewed to the left (see Figure 3.3b). The direction of skewness is sometimes confused, because it is natural to focus on the modal peak, without which there would not be any skew. Remember that the direction of skewness is defined by the direction in which the distribution slants away from the modal peak. The numbers on a graph's X axis increase to the right, and decrease to the left. When a graph is skewed to the right, it is therefore sometimes described as **positively skewed**. Similarly, **negatively skewed** implies that the curve trails off (slants) to the left.

Continuous Distributions A continuous distribution is one where for any two values that have been indicated, there is another value that can be identified between the two; and there is still another value between even these more closely placed values; and so on, indefinitely; that is, in a continuous distribution, the values along the X axis increase and decrease by infinitely small amounts. Stated another way, the distance between adjacent values on the X axis approaches zero.

As an example, people's heights are measured to the nearest half inch or quarter inch, or nearest centimeter or half centimeter. But some people actually differ by smaller amounts than a quarter inch or a half centimeter. A limit is recognized to our abilities to discriminate differences with a ruler that are smaller than some value. For any difference in heights that can be measured, a smaller difference can be named. Therefore, there is a realistic limit to the number of values that can be usefully indicated on the X axis. A graph of people's heights, therefore, appears as a finite distribution. But it represents an underlying continuous distribution. It is in this sense that an obtained finite distribution can be considered as representing an underlying continuous distribution.

Most psychological traits, educational abilities, and aptitudes are continuous variables, and so have underlying continuous distributions. For example, although IQ tests give people integer IQ scores (such as 99, 100, and 101), it can be assumed that smaller differences exist between some people, even when the smaller differences cannot be measured. Whenever a characteristic being measured can (theoretically) include infinitely small differences, a test of that characteristic is thought of as measuring a continuous trait.

When the points on a graph of a frequency distribution are connected to form a frequency polygon, a continuous distribution is implied, that is, the lines between the points suggest intervening frequencies for intervening X-axis values. When it is clear that the distribution is discontinuous, another form of graph, called a histogram, is generally used.

Histograms A histogram, or bar graph, is a graph in which the heights (the Y-axis values) are represented by vertical bars above the X-axis values, as in Figure 3.4, which represents the number of students from each of various states, majoring in psychology, at some college.

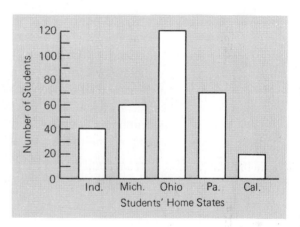

FIGURE 3.4
A histogram of the frequencies for a discontinuous variable

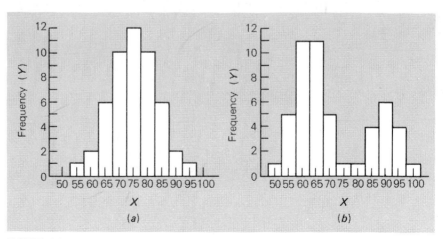

FIGURE 3.5
(a) A unimodal distribution and (b) a bimodal distribution, drawn as histograms

Although histograms usually represent discontinuous data, they can be used to represent continuous distributions. When the variable on the X axis is considered continuous, it is customary to have the bars touching each other, as in Figure 3.5. These two graphs are representations of the same sets of data that are graphed with frequency polygons in Figure 3.1. When the variable is discontinuous, the bars usually (though not necessarily) are kept separate, as in Figure 3.4.

In commercial presentations of data, such as in advertising copy, histograms are frequently used because of their more dramatic nature. The differences among the heights of the bars emphasize the differences in Y axis values.

Improper Uses of Graphs Ocassionally, improper uses of graphs occur. For example, assume that a manufacturer wishes to show that in a survey of physicians, the manufacturer's product (brand A) is preferred more frequently than the competing products. However, if the preference is actually slight, as in Figure 3.6a, the difference can be given an inflated appearance by omitting part of the Y axis, as in Figure 3.6b. The break in the Y axis in Figure 3.6b indicates that the graph has been cut. If the Y axis values are omitted, the possibilities of misleading the reader are enhanced.

A cut graph is not necessarily improper. It depends on the purpose to which it is put, and whether it has been made clear that the graph has been cut.

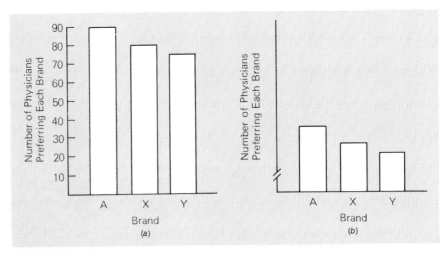

FIGURE 3.6
(a) Hypothetical comparison of three brands, with an intact graph.
(b) Figure (a) with the Y axis cut

This chapter is devoted mainly to frequency distributions. The graphs discussed have all been graphs of frequency distributions. However, there are other uses for graphs. For example, you may wish to depict the results of an experiment checking the relationship between level of frustration and amount of aggression, where the two variables were measured over a range of values. Subjects would have been subjected to varied (measured) levels of frustration, and their aggression then measured on some continuous scale. The average level of aggression, at each level of frustration, would have been computed for this set of subjects. If the results of the experiment were graphed, the results might look like Figure 3.7 which graphically makes three points: the lack of increases in aggression as low frustration levels are increased; the steep rise in aggression for any increases in frustration at a middle range; and an asymptotic level of aggression (a limiting value beyond which aggression does not increase).

Different researchers using different means of frustrating subjects, and different measures of aggression, may have varied results. But if the general form of the curves are similar, a **theoretical curve** can be drawn, as in Figure 3.8. Theoretical curves summarize the general form of the relationship assumed or found between two variables, and are usually presented as smoothed curves. When graphing relationships between variables, the independent variable is represented on the X axis, and the dependent variable on the Y axis.

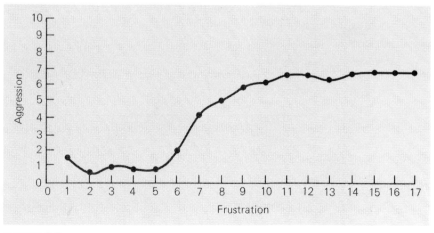

FIGURE 3.7
A graph of the relationship between two variables. (Hypothetical data from a hypothetical experiment. The levels of aggression that have been graphed are the average levels hypothetically found at each level of frustration.)

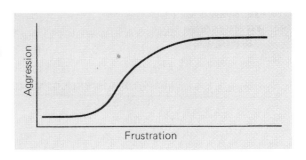

FIGURE 3.8
A theoretical curve of the relationship between two variables (using a hypothetical relationship between frustration and aggression as a specific example)

GROUPED DATA When distributions of exam scores were presented in Table 3.2, there were only 11 score values listed. They ranged from 50 to 100, in multiples of five. Actually, it is not unusual to have exam scores or other measurements that are not multiples of five, such as 78 and 83. It also happens that measurements go well beyond the limits of 50–100. Under the conditions of wider variability of numerical values, a list of values and their frequencies can be unmanageably long.

A long listing of values can be avoided by listing intervals of values. A frequency distribution that lists intervals, and presents the frequencies of values within each interval, is called a **grouped frequency distribution**. Frequency distributions that list the frequency of each individual value are called **regular frequency distributions**. Up to this point in this chapter, the distributions discussed and pictured have been regular frequency distributions. In this section, grouped frequency distributions are discussed. An example of a grouped frequency distribution is given in Table 3.4a.

Since the size of the intervals that are used in grouped frequency distributions vary, a definition of interval sizes is useful.

TABLE 3.4a
A grouped frequency distribution

X	f
66–70	16
61–65	30
56–60	48
51–55	27
46–50	8
41–45	3
36–40	2
31–35	2
26–30	1
21–25	2

In Table 3.4a, there is a bottom interval of 21–25. Immediately above that interval is the interval 26–30. There is no apparent provision for the occurrence of a score of, say, 25.2, or 25.3, or 25.2561. In cases where a continuous distribution of scores is assumed, there will be some scores that are not contained in any interval.

To avoid the problem of excluded scores, the intervals can be redefined so that they overlap, that is, the limits of each interval are extended. The extended limits of the intervals are called the real limits.

The **real limits of an interval** are the points midway between adjacent intervals. More specifically, the **upper real limit of an interval** is the point midway between the top of the interval and the bottom of the next higher interval. The **lower real limit** of the same interval is the point midway between the bottom of the interval and the top of the adjacent lower interval. Each interval is extended, for the real limits, to the points midway between intervals. Therefore, the upper real limit of an interval is identical to the lower real limit of the next higher interval. For example, the real limits of the interval 26–30 in Table 3.4a are 25.5–30.5. The next higher interval has the real limits 30.5–35.5. Table 3.4a is restated in Table 3.4b, with the real limits listed.

A grouped frequency distribution is usually presented in the form of Table 3.4a, that is, the real limits are *not* shown in the table. The real limits are just assumed to exist, extending midway between the **overt limits** appearing in the table.

The **size of an interval** is usually defined in terms of the real limits. The size of an interval is the difference between the top and bottom values of the real limits. Thus, in Table 3.4a, the size of each interval is equal to five. For example, 20.5 to 25.5 is five, as is 25.5 to 30.5. If you wanted to compute the interval size from the overt limits of Table 3.4a, you would have to add 1 to obtain the interval size. For example, 21 to 25 is four, plus one equals five.

TABLE 3.4b

A grouped frequency distribution with the real limits expressed

X	f
65.5–70.5	16
60.5–65.5	30
55.5–60.5	48
50.5–55.5	27
45.5–50.5	8
40.5–45.5	3
35.5–40.5	2
30.5–35.5	2
25.5–30.5	1
20.5–25.5	2

The Range of a Distribution The range of the entire distribution is usually computed as the difference between the top of the highest real limit and the bottom of the lowest real limit in the distribution. In Table 3.4a, the range of the distribution is:

$$\text{Range} = 70.5 - 20.5$$
$$= 50.$$

Using the overt limits, the range can be stated as:

$$\text{Range} = 70 - 21 + 1$$
$$= 50.$$

We will use the range in the next section when we choose the size and number of intervals that we use for a given distribution.

Choosing the Size and Number of Intervals In discussing the choice of the size and number of intervals when setting up a grouped frequency distribution, it is helpful to have a specific set of data. Table 3.5 provides a set of data for that purpose.

The decision as to the size of the intervals is related to the number of intervals desired, and the range of the distribution. The larger the size of the intervals, the smaller the number of intervals for a given range.

The lowest and highest intervals should contain the lowest and highest scores, respectively. In Table 3.5, the respective values are 45 and 98. Therefore, for the data in Table 3.5, the lowest and highest real limits are 44.5 and 98.5. The range of the grouped frequency distribution will be, at least:

$$\text{range} = 98.5 - 44.5$$
$$= 54$$

or, using overt limits,

$$\text{range} = 98 - 45 + 1$$
$$= 54.$$

Knowing the range of the distribution, it is possible to explore the number of intervals resulting from each possible choice of interval size, that is,

$$\text{number of intervals} = \frac{\text{range}}{\text{interval size}}.$$

TABLE 3.5
Hypothetical set of raw data

71	49	67	71	66	79	64	59	93	79
70	87	75	54	85	93	86	71	61	45
72	75	49	76	55	63	56	65	75	69
66	79	72	62	67	74	79	72	76	98

As an example, an interval size of six can be tried for the data of Table 3.5. Since the range is 54, an interval size of six yields:

$$\text{Number of intervals} = \frac{54}{6}$$
$$= 9.$$

A distribution of the data of Table 3.5, with an interval size of six, is presented in Table 3.6a.

Table 3.6b presents a distribution of the same raw data from Table 3.5, but with an interval size of five. The number of resulting intervals is:

$$\text{Number of intervals} = \frac{54}{5}$$
$$= 10.8.$$

Thus, an interval of size five yields 11 intervals.

TABLE 3.6a
Grouped frequency distribution with an interval size of six

X	f
93–98	3
87–92	1
81–86	2
75–80	9
69–74	9
63–68	7
57–62	3
51–56	3
45–50	3

TABLE 3.6b
Grouped frequency distribution with an interval size of five

X	f
95–99	1
90–94	2
85–89	3
80–84	0
75–79	9
70–74	8
65–69	6
60–64	4
55–59	3
50–54	1
45–49	3

TABLE 3.6c
Grouped frequency distribution with an interval size
of five

X	f
94–98	1
89–93	2
84–88	3
79–83	4
74–78	6
69–73	8
64–68	6
59–63	4
54–58	3
49–53	2
44–48	1

Note that it is not necessary to begin the lowest interval with the lowest score as the bottom of the interval, nor is it necessary to end the highest interval with the highest score as the top of the interval. The highest score in Table 3.5 is 98, but the top interval of Table 3.6b is 95–99. The range of listed intervals can be extended a bit to accommodate different interval sizes. This can be done as long as each top and bottom interval includes the highest and lowest scores obtained. As another example, the same set of data can again be presented in 11 intervals of size five, but with a different value for the bottom of the lowest interval, as in Table 3.6c.

The size of the interval, or the point at which you begin the lowest interval, is a matter of personal choice.* One particular interval size, or a particular initial value for the lowest interval, may obscure some interesting aspects of the data which an alternative interval selection may reveal. For example, Tables 3.6a–c are all grouped frequency distributions of the same set of raw data listed in Table 3.5. However, only the grouping of Table 3.6c reveals a perfectly symmetrical distribution.

The purpose of grouping data is to reduce the size of the listing so that you can scan the data effectively. It is then hoped that the data will in some way make sense, or offer a discernible pattern, as in Table 3.6c. Some texts suggest 8–15 intervals as reasonable limits to the number of intervals. Others suggest 10–20. However, the goals of effective scanning and making sense out of the data should be the ultimate guides. There is really no commonly accepted correct or incorrect number of intervals. Select the number of intervals and interval size that will help the data to appear comprehensible.

*Many texts suggest that the bottom of the lowest interval should always be a multiple of the interval size. In that case, Table 3.6b would be correct, since 45 is a multiple of 5. Table 3.6c would be incorrect. However, there is no rationale for this rule, and it is not universally followed.

Zero Frequencies Intervals with zero frequencies are normally omitted when they are the highest or lowest intervals. Thus, the distributions generally begin and end with nonzero frequencies. Intervening intervals with zero frequencies are almost always listed.

The exception to the practice of beginning and ending with nonzero frequencies generally involves a comparison between two or more different distributions. When comparing different sets of data, the different data sets are generally organized into the same intervals. If one distribution has a zero frequency at the lowest interval, but the other does not, that interval is included in both distributions to make the comparison clear. An example using a regular (non-grouped) frequency distribution, is found in the earlier comparison of Tables 3.2a and 3.2b.

Unequal Intervals It is common to try to maintain equally sized intervals throughout a grouped frequency distribution, but only if it makes sense for that particular situation.

An example in which unequal intervals may be desirable is in exam scores. It is not unusual, with exam scores, to have 90–100 (interval size 11) equal to A, 80–89 (interval size 10) equal to B, 70–79 (interval size 10) equal to C, etc. It makes sense in a listing of the exam results to maintain intervals that correspond to grades, even though the top (A) interval is unequal to the others.

As another example, suppose that a shy woman, who participated very little in high school, has just entered college. She decides to try to participate more in her college classes. Out of curiosity, she keeps a record in all 40 of her college courses of the number of times that she participates in class by making comments or asking questions. This hypothetical set of data is presented in Table 3.7, where the X values represent the number of

TABLE 3.7
Number of participations per semester in each of 40 courses (hypothetical data)

X	f	X	f	X	f
24	1	15	0	7	2
23	0	14	3	6	0
22	0	13	2	5	2
21	1	12	4	4	1
20	0	11	3	3	3
19	1	10	2	2	0
18	1	9	0	1	0
17	1	8	2	0	9
16	2				

participations in an individual course. The frequencies (*f* values) are the number of courses in which a particular number of participations was recorded. For example, in Table 3.7, $X = 14$ and $f = 3$ means that in three of her courses she participated 14 times during a semester.

Assume that the student wants to restate the data as a grouped frequency distribution. The range in Table 3.7 is $24.5 - (-.5) = 25$. Dividing by three, for an interval of size three, yields eight and a fraction, suggesting nine intervals. The grouped frequency distribution will then look like the data in Table 3.8a. Note that Table 3.8a is a bimodal distribution, having modal peaks at intervals 0–2 and 12–14.

Suppose that further thought has brought the student to the realization that courses in which there was no participation may in reality represent a different category than all the rest. Grouping zero frequencies with other frequencies (such as one and two in the interval 0–2) may not be advisable. The zero frequency may indicate no interest in the course. Such courses

TABLE 3.8a
Grouped frequency distribution of data in Table 3.7, with equal intervals

X	f
24–26	1
21–23	1
18–20	2
15–17	3
12–14	9
9–11	5
6–8	4
3–5	6
0–2	9

TABLE 3.8b
Grouped frequency distribution of data in Table 3.7, with unequal intervals

X	f
22–24	1
19–21	2
16–18	4
13–15	5
10–12	9
7–9	4
4–6	3
1–3	3
0	9

should perhaps be listed separately from the rest, within the table. For this alternative arrangement, the scores may be grouped as in Table 3.8b.

There is another type of instance in which unequal sizes of intervals may be desirable. Suppose that you are doing an experiment in which you are measuring how many trials are required by each subject before they learn some task. This can be an experiment in which you are comparing two sets of instructions for the same task or two different methods for teaching a skill. You test each subject until some criterion of errorless performance is reached, that is, you have some consecutive number of correct responses without errors, which is the definition of a subject's having learned the task. You will eventually compare the number of trials required for learning the task (to reach the criterion of errorless performance) for each group. For example, you will compare one group with one set of instructions to another group with another set of instructions, to see if more trials are required under one set of conditions.

But how many trials will you report for a subject who simply never learns the task? Sometimes a subject will continue to occasionally make errors, never reaching a criterion of errorless performance. You will eventually have to dismiss the subject. There is generally a limit to the patience of a subject, and to the time that she or he can spend. Thus, a number of trials is set before the experiment as the number of trials after which a subject will be dismissed, even if the task has not been mastered. Assume that for the experiment under discussion you dismiss a subject after "more than 50 trials." The highest interval in Table 3.9 indicates a way of handling this problem.

A subject's performance is measured as being over 50 when the subject has not learned by the fiftieth trial. But if the experiment had continued, the subject might have learned at any subsequent time, or perhaps never. Thus

TABLE 3.9
Use of an open interval

X	f
Over 50	2
46–50	2
41–45	4
36–40	10
31–35	15
26–30	19
21–25	23
16–20	28
11–15	22
6–10	11
1–5	8

the top interval in Table 3.9 has a nonspecific upper limit. An interval that has a nonspecific upper limit is sometimes called an **open interval**. All subjects not learning during an experiment with a limited number of trials contribute to the open interval.

Graphing Grouped Data In graphing grouped data, there can be a question of how to indicate the values for the X axis, since there may not be sufficient room for stating the complete interval at each focused point on the X axis. In those instances, the midpoints of the intervals are generally stated on the X axis, although there is no rule against presenting the complete interval if there is room.

The same procedure is followed for histograms as with frequency polygons. However, with histograms the X-axis values are located below the appropriate bars, with the X-axis points placed in the middle of the bars, as in Figure 3.5.

Computing the Mean with Grouped Data Whenever grouped data are used, a certain amount of information is lost. The frequencies indicate the number of occurrences of scores that fall within an interval, but the specific value of each of these scores is lost. In computations using grouped data, the midpoints of the intervals represent each score. Consequently the computation of statistics, such as the mean or the median with grouped data, introduces the possibility of some inaccuracy. Nevertheless, there are times when such computations may be desirable. Under such conditions, the mean is computed in the same way as with ungrouped data, but with the midpoint of each interval used as the X value in equation (3.1).

Applying Equation (3.1) to the data of Table 3.7 as grouped in Table 3.8a, a mean of 9.025 is obtained (see Table 3.10 for the computations). Apply-

TABLE 3.10
Computation of the mean from grouped data

X	f	Mid point	fX	
24–26	1	25	25	
21–23	1	22	22	
18–20	2	19	38	
15–17	3	16	48	Mean $= \dfrac{\Sigma fX}{n}$
12–14	9	13	117	
9–11	5	10	50	$= \dfrac{361}{40}$
6–8	4	7	28	
3–5	6	4	24	$= 9.025$
0–2	9	1	9	
	$\Sigma f = n$		$\Sigma fX = 361$	
	$= 40$			

ing the same equation to the same data, but this time as grouped in Table 3.8b, a mean of 8.825 is obtained. This is the actual mean of the data, as computed from the original ungrouped data in Table 3.7. As can be seen in this example, the mean will not always be distorted when computed from grouped data. Generally, the distortions will not be large, but there is a greater likelihood of the distortion being larger when the intervals are wider.

CUMULATIVE FREQUENCY DISTRIBUTIONS It is often useful to know the number of scores (and from this the percentage of scores) that have fallen above or below a particular value of the distribution. This information, when desired, is added to a frequency distribution in the form of an additional column, called a **cumulative frequency** column, and headed *cf,* as in Tables 3.11a and 3.11b. These two tables are identical

TABLE 3.11a
Experimental group, with cumulative frequency column

X	f	cf
100	0	50
95	1	50
90	2	49
85	6	47
80	10	41
75	12	31
70	10	19
65	6	9
60	2	3
55	1	1
50	0	0

TABLE 3.11b
Control group, with cumulative frequency column

X	f	cf
100	1	50
95	4	49
90	6	45
85	4	39
80	1	35
75	1	34
70	5	33
65	11	28
60	11	17
55	5	6
50	1	1

to Tables 3.2a and 3.2b, with the addition of the cumulative frequency column.

The cumulative frequency column begins at the bottom, with the frequency of the lowest value in the distribution. As the column moves upward it cumulates, that is, it adds the frequency of each higher score value in the distribution. The final cumulative total at the highest score value in the distribution will equal the total number of scores in the distribution.

The cumulative frequency column can only remain the same, or increase, at each higher score value. (It remains the same when there is a frequency of zero for a particular score, as at $X = 100$ in Table 3.11a.)

Graphs of Cumulative Frequency Distributions The graph of a cumulative frequency distribution can only increase or remain the same, moving from left to right. A graph that can only change in one direction is called a **monotonic distribution**. A graph of a monotonic distribution can be **monotonic increasing** or **monotonic decreasing**. The graph of a cumulative frequency distribution is said to be monotonic increasing. Figures 3.9a and 3.9b are graphs of the cumulative frequency columns in Tables 3.11a and 3.11b, respectively.

The cumulative frequency column, in a tabled frequency distribution, is used in the computation of percentiles. The meaning and computation of percentiles are given in Chapter 4.

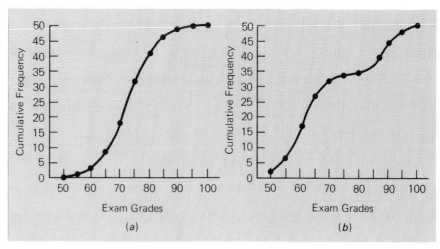

FIGURE 3.9
Cumulative frequency graphs of experimental group (a) and control group (b)

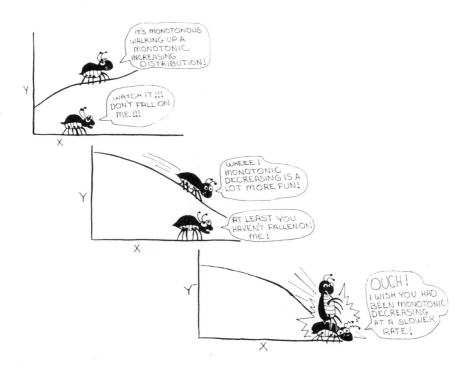

SENTENCE COMPLETIONS The following incomplete sentences are taken from the underlined sentences in this chapter. Fill in the missing words and phrases and then correct them from the answers which follow.

1. Any presentation which offers the frequency with which each score occurs is called a _____ _____ .

2. In frequency distributions, the _____ score values are placed at the top of the listings.

3. In a frequency distribution, the total sum of the scores can be symbolized as _____ .

4. The X axis is sometimes called the _____.
   It is the _____ line, placed _____
   _____ .

5. The Y axis is sometimes called the _____ . It is
   the _____ line, placed_____
   _____ .

6. In a frequency distribution presented in the form of a graph, the Y axis indicates the _____ of the various points on the X axis.

7. When the points of a graph are connected, the resulting figure is called a
   _____ _____ .

8. In a frequency polygon, the ends of the graph_____ .

9. When a particular point or interval of a graph towers above its neighboring points, the high point is called a_____ _____ .

10. When there is one modal peak in a distribution, the distribution is called a _____ distribution.

11. When there are two modal peaks in a distribution, the distribution is called a _____ distribution.

12. A distribution with no modal peaks and identical Y axis heights all along the X axis is a _____ distribution.

13. A rectangular distribution is sometimes called a_____ distribution.

14. A distribution which has a modal peak that is off to one side of the distribution, with the remainder of the distribution being relatively shallow, is called a _____ distribution.

15. The direction of skewness is defined by _____
_____ .

16. The numbers on a graph's X axis increase to the_____ .

17. _____ skewed implies that the curve slants to the left.

18. In a continuous distribution, the values along the X axis increase by infinitely _____ amounts.

19. A graph of people's heights appears as a finite distribution, but it represents an underlying _____ _____.

20. Another name for a bar graph is a _____.

21. Theoretical curves summarize the general form of the relationship between _____ _____, and are usually presented as _____ curves.

22. When graphing relationships between variables, the_____ variable is represented on the X axis, and the _____ variable on the Y axis.

23. A frequency distribution that lists intervals, and presents the frequencies of values within each interval, is called a_____ frequency distribution. Frequency distributions that list the frequency of each individual value, are called_____ frequency distributions.

24. The real limits of an interval are the points_____ _____ adjacent overt intervals.

25. The size of an interval is the difference between the top and bottom values of the_____ _____ .

26. The range of the entire distribution is usually computed as the difference between _____
_____ .

27. The purpose of grouping data is to_____
_____ .

28. An interval that is nonspecific as to its upper limit is sometimes called
_____ .

29. In histograms, the X axis values are located below the appropriate bars, with the X axis points placed_____
_____.

30. The computation of statistics, such as the mean and median, with grouped data, introduces the possibility of some _____ .

31. The cumulative frequency column begins at the bottom of the frequency of the lowest value in the distribution. As the column moves upward, it
_____ .

32. In a cumulative distribution, the final cumulative total at the highest score value equals _____
_____.

33. The cumulative frequency column can only remain the same or _____ at each higher score value.

34. A graph that can only change in one direction is called a _____ .

35. A graph of a cumulative frequency distribution is said to be monotonic _____ .

PROBLEMS

1. The following scores show the number of errors for each student in a class, following a 20-item quiz. 18, 14, 17, 18, 16, 11, 19, 14, 19, 20, 13, 12, 18, 18, 17, 15, 17, 18, 13, 19, 16, 20, 15, 15, 10, 16, 17, 18, 19, 18, 18, 19, 18, 17, 18.
   Place these scores into a regular frequency distribution, adding a cumulative frequency column.

2. Plot a frequency polygon for the frequency data in Problem 1.

3. Is the distribution in Problem 1 unimodal or bimodal?

4. Is the distribution in Problem 1 skewed? If so, in which direction?

5. Compute the mean of the distribution in Problem 1, using Equation (3.1).

6. Compute the mean of the frequency distribution in Table 3.2a.

7. Assume that you wish to appeal to a religious organization for funds for your college. You present a verbal appeal and then, to impress upon them the extent of the use of the school by members of that religious group, you present a graph, indicating the religious affiliations of the students at the school. Assume that there are four different faiths represented in the student population. The religious organization to which your appeal is addressed is represented in the hypothetical data below by the Roman numeral IV.

Religious affiliation	Number at school
I	60
II	20
III	20
IV	300

What type of graph will you use? Draw the graph.

8. What is the interval size of the following grouped frequency distribution?

X	f
39–41	1
36–38	3
33–35	2
30–32	6
27–29	14
24–26	9
21–23	2
18–20	6
15–17	12
12–14	4
9–11	1

9. (a) Draw the grouped frequency distribution of problem 8 as a frequency polygon.
   (b) Draw the grouped frequency distribution of problem 8 as a histogram.
10. Compute the mean of the distribution in Problem 9.
11. (a) What is the range of the following distribution? 70, 41, 37, 42, 56, 41, 33, 63, 44, 51, 36, 31, 32, 47, 41, 39, 68, 43, 52, 38, 60, 35, 59, 36, 40, 48, 41, 40, 57, 65, 51, 40, 53, 41, 66, 35, 37, 46, 54, 42, 63, 45, 50, 38, 44, 43, 39, 47.
    (b) If the interval size is 2, how many intervals will result?
    (c) What will be the size of the intervals if you want to have precisely 14 intervals?
    (d) Set up the frequency distribution, with 14 intervals, for this data.
12. Subjects are given a series of concept formation problems to solve. There are up to five dimensions that can be included and made to vary: color, shape, size, placement, and orientation of stimulus figures. Only one dimension is relevant to the solution of each problem. The sub-

ject's task is to identify the relevant dimension in each problem. The number of dimensions incorporated in the stimulus figures constitutes the independent variable. The dependent variable is the number of trials to solve each problem.

The following table lists the average number of trials needed, for each number of dimensions in a problem, as found in this hypothetical experiment.

Number of dimensions per problem	Average number of trials
1	2
2	3
3	4
4	8
5	9

Draw the graph of the relationship between the two variables as found in this hypothetical experiment.

PERCENTILES

Some people act in an angry manner, but when asked, deny any awareness of being angry. It is possible that they are not really angry, but just have an aggressive or antagonistic personality style. However, there do seem to be occasions when people are genuinely angry, yet manage to relabel or otherwise deny their anger to themselves. Competitive feelings, needs for power, sexual desires, etc., are all occasionally experienced in one sense, but denied being experienced in another, by the same person.

Assume that someone has developed a test of self-awareness—i.e., measuring the degree to which people are in contact with their own feelings. Assume that you take this self-awareness test and score a 6. What does a score of 6 mean?

One way in which a score can be given meaning is if the highest and lowest scores are known. If the test scores range from 0 to 7, you will have a different impression of your performance than if they range from 0 to 20. Your score has even more meaning if it tells you the percentage of people who have obtained a score equal to or less than yours. For example, when you have performed on a test at a level equal to or better than 90% of the people taking the test, you will probably believe that you have done quite well.

A means of reporting scores so that they instantly offer an indication of their relative standing is to present them in terms of the percentage of scores they have equaled or surpassed. The percentage of scores equaled or surpassed by a raw score is the **percentile rank** of a raw score; that is, a percentile rank of a score X is the percent of scores at or below the raw score X. PR $(X) = 20$ means that X equals or surpasses 20% of the scores. This gives the score instant meaning on a scale of relative performance.

The raw scores themselves are usually called **percentiles** when they are identified with a specific percentile rank. A percentile is a raw score associated with a specified percentile rank. A percentile is symbolized P_{perc}, where the subscripted perc refers to the percentage equaled or surpassed. $P_{20} = 35$ means that a score of 35 equals or surpasses 20% of the scores. Allowing for differences due to rounding percentile ranks, finding $P_{20} = 35$ implies PR(35) $\approx$ 20.

For example, assume 1000 scores obtained on an examination of 1000 people. Suppose that someone wishes to know which score divides the bottom 20% of the scores from the top 80%. (Perhaps any score within the bottom 20% constitutes failure.) This is asking for the 20th percentile, symbolized P_{20}. The percentile is some specific score, such as $P_{20} = 35$.

Whereas a percentile is always a score, a percentile rank of some score X is always a percentage. For example, PR(35) = 20 means that 20% of the scores fall at or below a score of 35, so 20 is the percentile rank of a score of 35. The percentile is sometimes called the percentile point. This helps to distinguish the percentile as a specific score on some scale, rather than as a percentage.

If you have a set of scores and want information about percentages at or below the scores, you ask for percentile ranks. But if the problem is discovering which raw scores equal or surpass specified percentages, then you ask for percentiles.

COMPUTING PERCENTILE RANKS OF RAW SCORES

It will be helpful to identify three percentages in a distribution: the percentage below, the percentage at, and the percentage above some raw score X.

Suppose that Table 4.1 represents the performance of 200 people, including the reader, who have taken the self-awareness test alluded to in the opening paragraph of this chapter. The table lists 200 scores expressed as a regular frequency distribution. If you scored a 6, then you may be interested in the percentage of people who also scored a 6. In other words, what percentage of the scores are equal to 6? The frequency column in Table 4.1 indicates that eight people obtained a score of 6. Since there are 200 scores, the percentage of scores equal to 6 is:

$$\text{Percentage at } X = \frac{\text{number at } X}{\text{total number of scores}} \times 100 \qquad (4.1)$$

$$= \frac{\text{number at } 6}{\text{total number of scores}} \times 100$$

$$= \frac{8}{200} \times 100$$

$$= 4.$$

Thus, 4% of the scores are equal to 6, your hypothetical score.

TABLE 4.1
Frequency distribution for a hypothetical test of self-awareness (higher scores imply greater self-awareness)

X	f	cf
10	4	200
9	16	196
8	24	180
7	12	156
6	8	144
5	4	136
4	20	132
3	44	112
2	42	68
1	22	26
0	4	4

68   Percentiles

But what percentage of the scores obtained are below 6? The percentage of scores below any score X is obtained from the cumulative frequency column. The cumulative frequency column gives the number of occurrences of scores up to the value X. At $X = 6$, the cumulative frequency column gives the number of scores of 6 or less. At $X = 5$, the cumulative frequency column gives the number of scores of 5 or less. To obtain the frequency of scores *below* 6, you consult the cumulative frequency column at $X = 5$. In Table 4.1, the cumulative frequency column indicates that 136 scores were below 6. For the *percentage* of scores below 6, a formula is used that is analogous to Equation (4.1):

$$\text{Percentage below } X = \frac{\text{number below } X}{\text{total number of scores}} \times 100 \qquad (4.2)$$

$$= \frac{\text{number below } 6}{\text{total number of scores}} \times 100$$

$$= \frac{136}{200} \times 100$$

$$= 68.$$

Thus, 68% of the scores are less than 6. The two percentages obtained so far are the percentages below 6 and at 6. These are 68 and 4, respectively, which yield 72% when added together. This implies that 72% of the scores are at or below a raw score of 6, and that 28% of the scores are higher than 6 $(100 - 72 = 28)$.

The above analysis identifies three percentages (below, at, and above). But a percentile associated with a percentile rank is usually defined as a dividing point, dividing the distribution into two portions: the percentage of scores at or below a score of X (the percentile rank), and the percentage of scores at or above a score of X. This division into just two percentages is accomplished by dividing the percentage of scores *at* X in half, and attributing half of that percent to the scores at or below X, and half to the scores at or above X. This enables the percentile to be defined as a dividing point in the distribution, with the lower percentage defining the percentile rank.

For example, a score of 6 from the distribution in Table 4.1 has a percentile rank of $68\% + \frac{1}{2}(4\%) = 70\%$. Thus a score of 6 is equal to or higher than 70% of the scores in the distribution. At the same time, $X = 6$ is a score that is equal to or below $28\% + \frac{1}{2}(4\%) = 30\%$ of the scores; that is, a score of 6 is properly described as being in the top 30%, and also as being in the bottom 70%. It is, in fact, at the top of the bottom 70%, and at the bottom of the top 30%.

A percentile rank of a score X was defined as that percentage of the scores at or below a score of X. In Table 4.1, the percentage of scores at or below a score of 6 is 70%. Therefore, in the distribution of Table 4.1, the percentile rank of 6 is 70. If higher implies better, a score of 6 is equal to or better than 70% of the scores.

The steps in computing a percentile rank for a score X can be summarized as follows.

1. Set up a cumulative frequency distribution.
2. Identify the number of scores *below* X by looking in the cumulative frequency column adjacent to the score that is just *below* a score of X.
3. Convert the number of scores below X into a percentage with Equation (4.2):

$$\text{Percentage below } X = \frac{\text{number below } X}{\text{total number of scores}} \times 100.$$

4. Identify the number of scores *at* X by looking in the frequency column adjacent to X.
5. Convert the number of scores at X into a percentage, with Equation (4.1):

$$\text{Percentage at } X = \frac{\text{number at } X}{\text{total number of scores}} \times 100.$$

6. Add half the percentage at X to the percentage below X, to obtain the percentile rank of X.

The above steps are summarized in Equation (4.3).

$$PR(X) = \text{percentage below } X + \frac{1}{2}(\text{percentage at } X) \tag{4.3}$$

$$= \frac{\text{number below } X}{\text{total no. of scores}} \times 100 + \frac{1}{2}\left(\frac{\text{number at } X}{\text{total no. of scores}} \times 100\right)$$

$$= \left[\text{number below } X + \frac{1}{2}\left(\text{no. at } X\right)\right] \frac{100}{\text{total no. of scores}}.$$

Using Equation (4.3), the percentile rank of a score of 7 in Table 4.1 is

$$PR(7) = \left[144 + \frac{1}{2}(12)\right]\frac{100}{200}$$

$$= 150\frac{100}{200}$$

$$= 75.$$

Equation (4.3) is designed for regular frequency distributions. For grouped frequency distributions, a slight change is required.

Grouped frequency distributions do not reveal the frequencies of individual score values, only those of intervals. Therefore, the formula for computing percentile ranks in grouped frequency distributions requires a replacement of X with an interval in Equation (4.3). Specifically, the terms number at X and number below X are replaced with the terms number in the **critical interval** and the number below the critical interval, where the critical interval is the interval containing X. If these were the only changes, the formula in Equation (4.3) would be restated as in Equation (4.4):

$$PR(X) = \left[\text{no. below crit int} + \frac{1}{2} (\text{no. in crit int}) \right] \frac{100}{\text{total no. of scores}}. \quad (4.4)$$

However, Equation (4.4) suggests that half the scores in the critical interval should contribute to the percentile rank of X. This is not necessarily so. The raw score X could be at the bottom of the critical interval, or at the top, or anywhere in between. The further up into the interval that X is, the larger the proportion of scores in the critical interval that should contribute to the percentile rank of the score X; that is, a score higher in the critical interval should have a higher percentile rank than a score at the bottom. Therefore, the fraction of the scores surpassed by X within the critical interval is used in place of ½ in Equation (4.4). This fraction is

$$\text{fraction of scores surpassed by } X \text{ in critical interval} = \frac{X - \begin{array}{c}\text{lower limit of}\\\text{critical interval}\end{array}}{\text{interval size}},$$

which, if used in place of ½ in Equation (4.4), yields Equation (4.5).

TABLE 4.2
Grouped frequency distribution for a set of
hypothetical scores. (Note that the critical interval,
when computing the percentile rank, is the interval
containing X.)

X	f	cf	
60–64	4	112	
55–59	5	108	
50–54	8	103	
45–49	10	95	
40–44	12	85	
35–39	12	73	
30–34	13	61	
25–29	16	48	← Critical interval for PR(26)
20–24	10	32	
15–19	8	22	
10–14	8	14	
5–9	6	6	

$$PR(X) =$$

$$\left[\left(\begin{array}{c}\text{no. below}\\\text{crit int}\end{array}\right) + \left(\dfrac{X - \begin{array}{c}\text{lower limit}\\\text{of crit int}\end{array}}{\text{interval size}}\right)\left(\begin{array}{c}\text{no. in}\\\text{crit int}\end{array}\right)\right]\dfrac{100}{\text{tot. no. of scores}} \qquad (4.5)$$

Using Equation (4.5), we can find the percentile rank of a score of 26 in the grouped frequency distribution of Table 4.2:

$$PR(26) =$$

$$\left[\left(\begin{array}{c}\text{no. below}\\\text{crit int}\end{array}\right) + \left(\dfrac{26 - \begin{array}{c}\text{lower limit}\\\text{of crit int}\end{array}}{\text{interval size}}\right)\left(\begin{array}{c}\text{no. in}\\\text{crit int}\end{array}\right)\right]\dfrac{100}{\text{tot. no. of scores}}$$

$$= [32 + \left(\dfrac{26 - 24.5}{5}\right)16]\dfrac{100}{112}$$

$$= 36.8\,\dfrac{100}{112}$$

$$= 32.86$$

$$\approx 33$$

Note that a percentile rank is rounded to the nearest whole number. Percentile ranks are defined as one of 100 successive classes into which scores may fall. Therefore, percentile ranks are only defined as integers, which in practice range from 1 to 99. The top ranked scores are in the 99th percentile, since this simultaneously places them in the top 1%.

The Use of Percentile Ranks   It is often helpful to abandon the raw scores themselves and offer only percentile ranks when people wish to know the results of a test. It may be kinder to tell the parent of a child who has scored 85 on an IQ test, for which the average score is 100, that the child has scored "equal to or better than 25% of children his age"; or that the child "has scored in the top 75%" (assuming that these percentages are correct for the specific IQ test).

A major reason for using percentile ranks to represent test performance is that they allow comparisons of test performance when dealing with different tests. A student may receive a grade of 80 on the first exam of the semester, and a grade of 70 on the second exam. Before deciding that the student's performance has declined, we may want to know how the other students performed. All exams are not equally difficult. The second exam may have been more difficult than the first, and a score of 70 may have been a far better score on the second exam than a score of 80 on the first. We are interested in how this student stands in relation to other students, on both exams.

Percentile ranks express a student's relative standing on an exam in units that do not change their implication from exam to exam, as long as the same or equivalent students are being examined. The percentile ranks, ranging from 1 to 99 on every test, always represent the same information—the percentage of the obtained scores that the person's score equals or surpasses.

When changing reference groups, the evaluative implication of percentile ranks can change. For example, assume a test of abstract ability. Among a group of people with superior intelligence, a percentile rank of 80 is impressive. Among a group of people with below average intelligence, the same percentile rank is less impressive. A person's percentile rank on an exam in one class can be compared to her percentile rank on an exam in another class—but only if it can be assumed that the two classes are equivalent in ability.

It is not advisable to use percentile ranks unless you are dealing with a large number of scores, preferably more than 100, since a percentile rank implies a division of the scores into 100 consecutive intervals. The meaning is distorted when the comparison is spread over fewer than 100 scores. Further, with a small class, an instructor may have an entire class of unrepresentative students, for example, all below-average. In this case, the relative class standings offered by percentile ranks can give misleading impressions as to the ability of the students.

The Use of Percentiles   A common use of percentiles is for cutoff scores. For example, in a particular school, the top 10% of the students (in terms of grade point average) may be placed on the dean's list. What grade point average is the cutoff point for getting on the dean's list?

The school has a listing of all the students' grade-point averages in the form of a frequency distribution. The cutoff score for the top 10% is the 90th percentile. The question is, what grade point is the 90th percentile?

Percentiles are used with many other measurements besides test scores. For example, before the imposition of a national speed limit of 55 mph in 1973, percentiles were used in the determination of speed limits for new highways. The speeds of cars on a new highway were measured by radar and placed into a frequency distribution. Then that speed which was the 85th percentile became the speed limit for that highway (rounded to the nearest multiple of 5).

A check of actual speeds of cars on speed-posted Arizona highways before the 55-mph mandatory speed limit, and for two years after, showed that the new limit reduced the 85th percentile by 10 mph. On rural interstate highways, the 85th percentile went from 75 mph in 1973 to 65 mph in the subsequent two years. On urban interstate highways, the 85th percentile went from 65 mph to the legal limit of 55 mph. Therefore, on urban highways in Arizona, 85% of the cars observed the new limits, traveling at or below 55 mph.

In general, <u>when it is important to identify which score is the dividing point for some specified *relative* level of performance, the procedure for identifying percentiles is used.</u>

DECILES   It is sometimes useful to divide the scores of a distribution into 10 equal frequency classes, <u>each class containing 10% of the scores. The points at which the scores are divided into 10 equal parts are called **deciles**.</u> The first decile is equivalent to the 10th percentile, the second to the 20th percentile, and so on through the ninth decile, which is equivalent to the 90th percentile.

QUARTILES   It is sometimes useful to divide the scores of a distribution into four equal frequency classes, <u>each class containing 25% of the scores. The points at which the scores are divided into four equal parts are called **quartiles**.</u> The first quartile is equivalent to the 25th percentile, the second quartile is equivalent to the 50th percentile (which is also equivalent to the fifth decile), and the third quartile is equivalent to the 75th percentile.

COMPUTING PERCENTILES   Percentiles are those scores that are the dividing points between the 100 adjacent segments defining percentile ranks. Yet there may be less than 100 integer values in the scores of the distribution. For example, in Table 4.1, with 200 scores, there are only 11 integer values in the distribution (0–10). Therefore, some of the 99 percentiles ($P_1, P_2, \ldots, P_{99}$), each being a different value ranging from 0 to 10, must be non-integer score values. Where are the non-integer score values in Table 4.1?

When discussing grouped frequency distributions, a distinction was made between overt and real limits. This distinction can also apply to a regular frequency distribution. For example, Table 4.1 can be re-expressed with the real limits visible, as in Table 4.3, which illustrates a regular frequency distribution interpreted as a grouped frequency distribution, where the interval size is 1. It also suggests how the distribution can be treated as a continuous distribution, despite the restriction to integer valued scores in the data. You simply recognize the real limits. <u>In finding percentiles within regular frequency distributions, we use the real limits.</u> Thus, an integer such as 8 is treated implicitly as 7.5–8.5.

Suppose we want to obtain the 85th percentile in Table 4.4. The scores are ranked. We want to know which score is 85% of the way up in the

TABLE 4.3

Table 4.1 re-expressed with real limits visible

X	f	cf
9.5–10.5	4	200
8.5–9.5	16	196
7.5–8.5	24	180
6.5–7.5	12	156
5.5–6.5	8	144
4.5–5.5	4	136
3.5–4.5	20	132
2.5–3.5	44	112
1.5–2.5	42	68
0.5–1.5	22	26
−0.5–0.5	4	4

rankings of the cumulative frequency column. This desired cumulative frequency is obtained by multiplying the total number of scores (200 in Table 4.4) by the desired percentage (in this case, 85%).

$$\text{Desired cumulative frequency} = \text{percentage of total} \qquad (4.6)$$
$$= 85\% \times 200$$
$$= 170.$$

Thus, the 170th score is 85% of the way up the cumulative frequency column in Table 4.4. What we ultimately want is the score which is 170th in rank. Therefore, we need the value on the X side of the table, which is associated with 170 on the cumulative frequency side.

The desired cumulative frequency of 170 is not listed in the cumulative frequency column of Table 4.4. The closest values listed are 156 and 180.

TABLE 4.4

Frequency distribution for a hypothetical test of self-awareness (higher scores imply greater self-awareness)

X	f	cf	
10	4	200	
9	16	196	
8	24	180	←Critical interval for P_{85}
7	12	156	←Critical interval for P_{75}
6	8	144	
5	4	136	
4	20	132	
3	44	112	
2	42	68	
1	22	26	
0	4	4	

Since the desired cumulative frequency is above 156, the desired X value must be at least equal to the top of the interval adjacent to 156. The value 7 adjacent to 156 implies an interval of 6.5–7.5. Therefore, X equals at least 7.5 in this example, and so is within the next higher interval, 7.5–8.5. It is convenient to identify the interval containing X, 7.5–8.5 in this example, as the critical interval.

When computing a percentile, the first task is to identify the critical interval containing the needed value of X. The critical interval is identified through the desired cumulative frequency, computed with Equation (4.6), where the critical interval is the one adjacent to the desired cumulative frequency, or its closest higher value. Note that in computing percentiles, the critical interval is defined via the cumulative frequency column. In computing percentile ranks, the critical interval is defined via the column of X-value intervals.

In the above example, how much of the critical interval is below a cumulative frequency of 170? That is, how far into the interval 7.5–8.5 should we go to find the 170th score? We have seen that a cumulation of 156 is equivalent to 7.5. The difference between the desired cumulative frequency, 170, and 156 is $170-156 = 14$.

What *proportion* of the critical interval 7.5–8.5 is 14 scores? It depends on the number of scores within the interval. In this example, the number of scores in the critical interval is 24 (as seen in the frequency column of Table 4.4). The proportion of the critical interval belonging to the scores between 156 and 170 in Table 4.4, therefore, is $14/24 = .58$. This suggests that .58 of the interval 7.5–8.5 belongs with the cumulation of scores up to the 170th score in rank.

The computation of the proportion of the critical interval is summarized in Equation (4.7):

$$\begin{aligned}\text{Proportion of critical} \atop \text{interval to be added} &= \frac{\begin{matrix}\text{desired} \\ \text{cum freq}\end{matrix} - \begin{matrix}\text{cum freq below} \\ \text{critical interval}\end{matrix}}{\text{frequency in critical interval}} \times \text{interval size} \qquad (4.7)\\[2em] &= \frac{\text{perc of total} - \begin{matrix}\text{cum freq below} \\ \text{critical interval}\end{matrix}}{\text{frequency in critical interval}} \times \text{interval size}\\[2em] &= \frac{85\% \times 200 - \begin{matrix}\text{cum freq below} \\ \text{critical interval}\end{matrix}}{\text{frequency in critical interval}} \times 1\\[2em] &= \frac{170 - 156}{24} \times 1\\[1em] &= .58.\end{aligned}$$

Equation (4.7) indicates how much should be added to the bottom of the critical interval to yield the percentile value. Therefore, the 85th percentile, which extends to the 170th score in rank, is 7.5 + .58 = 8.08. That is, 8.08 is the 85th percentile in Table 4.4. Equation (4.8) summarizes the complete computation.

$$P_{perc} = \frac{\text{lower limit of}}{\text{crit interval}} + \frac{\overset{\text{perc}}{\underset{\text{of total}}{}} - \overset{\text{cum freq below}}{\underset{\text{crit interval}}{}}}{\text{freq in crit interval}} \times \text{interval size} \quad (4.8)$$

$$P_{85} = 7.5 + \frac{(85\% \times 200) - 156}{24} \times 1$$

$$= 7.5 + \frac{170 - 156}{24} \times 1$$

$$= 7.5 + .58$$

$$= 8.08.$$

As another example, suppose we want to find the 75th percentile in Table 4.4. First, the desired cumulative frequency is computed, using Equation (4.6) to locate the critical interval. Applying Equation (4.6) indicates that 75% of 200 is 150. Table 4.4 shows that 150 surpasses the listed cumulative frequency of 144, but is less than the listed cumulative frequency of 156. Since 156 is the closest higher cumulative frequency, it identifies the critical interval. The critical interval, therefore, is 6.5–7.5. This suggests that the 75th percentile is at least 6.5. Applying Equation (4.8) yields the actual 75th percentile:

$$P_{75} = \frac{\text{lower limit of}}{\text{crit interval}} + \frac{(75\% \times 200) - \overset{\text{cum freq below the}}{\underset{\text{critical interval}}{}}}{\text{freq in crit interval}} \times \text{interval size}$$

$$= 6.5 + \frac{150 - 144}{12} \times 1$$

$$= 7.0.$$

Note that Equation (4.8), for computing some P_{perc}, always requires the prior determination of the critical interval. The desired cumulative frequency (equal to percent of total), or its closest higher value in the cumulative frequency column, determines the critical interval.

Equation (4.8) is constructed so that it is equally applicable to both grouped and regular frequency distributions. With regular frequency distributions the interval size is always 1. With grouped frequency distributions the interval size depends on how the data are grouped. Table 4.5 is a grouped frequency distribution with an interval size of 5.

TABLE 4.5
Grouped frequency distribution for a set of
hypothetical scores

X	f	cf	
60–64	4	112	
55–59	5	108	
50–54	8	103	
45–49	10	95	
40–44	12	85	
35–39	12	73	
30–34	13	61	
25–29	16	48	←Critical interval for P_{40}
20–24	10	32	
15–19	8	22	
10–14	8	14	
5–9	6	6	

Using Equation (4.8), we can find the 40th percentile in the grouped
frequency distribution of Table 4.5:

$$P_{40} = \begin{array}{c}\text{lower limit of}\\\text{crit interval}\end{array} + \frac{(40\% \times \text{tot}) - \begin{array}{c}\text{cum freq below}\\\text{crit interval}\end{array}}{\text{freq in crit interval}} \times \text{interval size}$$

$$= \begin{array}{c}\text{lower limit of}\\\text{crit interval}\end{array} + \frac{(40\% \times 112) - \begin{array}{c}\text{cum freq below}\\\text{crit interval}\end{array}}{\text{freq in crit interval}} \times \text{interval size}$$

$$= 24.5 + \frac{(44.80 - 32)}{16} \times 5$$

$$= 24.5 + 4.00$$

$$= 28.5.$$

The above computations indicate that 28.5 is the 40th percentile in Table
4.5.

Computing the Median as the 50th Percentile The median is the score with as many scores ranked below as above it in
value. This also defines the 50th percentile (50% below and 50% above).
This suggests that <u>the median can be computed by computing the 50th</u>
<u>percentile.</u>

As an example of this approach to computing the median, the 50th
percentile is computed for the distribution in Table 4.5:

$$\text{Median} = P_{50}$$

$$= \begin{array}{c}\text{lower limit of}\\\text{crit interval}\end{array} + \frac{(50\% \times \text{tot}) - \begin{array}{c}\text{cum freq below}\\\text{crit interval}\end{array}}{\text{freq in crit interval}} \times \text{interval size}$$

$$= \frac{\text{lower limit of}}{\text{crit interval}} + \frac{(50\% \times 112) - \frac{\text{cum freq below}}{\text{crit interval}}}{\text{freq in crit interval}} \times \text{interval size}$$

$$= 29.5 + \frac{(56 - 48)}{13} \times 5$$

$$= 29.5 + 3.08$$

$$= 32.58.$$

The above computations indicate that the median of the distribution in Table 4.5 is 32.58.

The same procedure can be used for a regular frequency distribution with an interval of 1. For example, the median for the distribution in Table 4.4 is:

Median $= P_{50}$

$$= \frac{\text{lower limit of}}{\text{crit interval}} + \frac{(50\% \times 200) - \frac{\text{cum freq below}}{\text{crit interval}}}{\text{freq in crit interval}} \times 1$$

$$= 2.5 + \frac{(100 - 68)}{44} \times 1$$

$$= 2.5 + .73$$

$$= 3.23.$$

In Chapter 2, a simpler method was provided for computing the median with a regular frequency distribution. The scores were simply ranked, and the score with the middle rank was designated as the median. Looking at Table 4.4, you might recognize that the simple method does not work when there are many repetitions of scores in the middle ranks. Under such conditions, the method of finding the 50th percentile, presented in this chapter, is the way to obtain the median. When dealing with grouped frequency distributions, or with any distribution containing multiple frequencies, the method of finding the 50th percentile, illustrated here, is usually the most accurate procedure.

The following incomplete sentences are taken from the underlined sentences in this chapter. Fill in the missing words and phrases and then correct them from the answers which follow.

1. The percentile rank of a score is _____
   _____.

2. Raw scores are usually called _____when they are identified with a specific percentile rank.

3. Whereas a percentile rank is always a _____,
   a percentile is always a _____ .

4. The _____is defined as a dividing point in the distribution with the _____ _____ defining the percentile rank.

5. Percentile ranks are a way of expressing a student's relative standing on an exam in units that do not change their implication from exam to exam, as long as _____
   _____ .

6. When it is important to identify just which score is the cutoff score for some relative level of performance, you compute the _____.

7. The points at which the scores are divided into 10 equal parts are called
   _____ .

8. The points at which the scores are divided into four equals parts are called _____ .

9. When you have the score and need to identify a percentage (equaled or surpassed), you compute _____.

10. The median can be computed by computing the _____.

11. In computing a percentile, the critical interval is the interval _____
   _____
   _____.

12. In computing percentile ranks, the critical interval is _____
   _____.

13. In computing percentiles, the column used to determine the critical interval is the column containing _____ _____.

14. A _____ _____is rounded to the nearest whole number, but this is not necessary for a _____.

Answers 1. the percentage of scores equaled or surpassed (the percent of scores at or below the raw score X) 2. percentiles 3. percentage; score 4. percentile; lower percentage 5. the same or equivalent students are being examined 6. percentile 7. deciles 8. quartiles 9. the percentile rank 10. 50th percentile 11. adjacent to the desired cumulative frequency, or its closest higher value 12. the interval containing X 13. cumulative frequencies 14. percentile rank; percentile

PROBLEMS	X	f	cf
	10	10	500
	9	10	490
	8	30	480
	7	60	450
	6	80	390
	5	100	310
	4	60	210
	3	50	150
	2	40	100
	1	40	60
	0	20	20

1. Compute the percentile rank for a score of 8, for the above frequency distribution.
2. Compute the 70th percentile for the above frequency distribution.
3. Compute the percentile rank for a score of 4 for the above frequency distribution, using both Equations (4.5) and (4.3), to see how they are equivalent with a regular frequency distribution.

Use the following distribution for the remaining problems in this chapter.

X	f	cf
39–41	8	160
36–38	20	152
33–35	40	132
30–32	24	92
27–29	20	68
24–26	16	48
21–23	12	32
18–20	8	20
15–17	4	12
12–14	4	8
9–11	4	4

4. Compute the percentile rank for a score of 10 in the above grouped frequency distribution.
5. Compute the percentile rank for a score of 20 in the above grouped frequency distribution.
6. (a) Compute the median for the above grouped frequency distribution.
   (b) Compute the remaining two other quartiles for the above grouped frequency distribution. (Recall that P_{50} is the 50th percentile, the fifth decile, the median, and the second quartile.)

VARIABILITY

Most psychological phenomena vary from measurement to measurement of the same person, and are even more variable when measuring different people. An angry man is not always angry or, at the least, is differently angry from time to time; a confident person varies in confidence; an intellectually acute woman is differently acute from time to time. Thus, differences in and among people are a constant source of variability in test scores, and in most other measurements of people.

A second source of variability is the variability caused by imperfections in our measuring instruments. For example, assume that you wish to check diet A against diet B for weight loss. During the first month you follow diet A, weighing yourself at the beginning and end of the month on your bathroom scale. Your scale indicates that you lost five pounds under diet A. You return to your favorite foods for a couple of weeks while you build up the courage to go on diet B. With diet B you again follow the procedure of weighing yourself at the beginning and end of the month. After diet B your bathroom scale tells you that you have lost four pounds, one pound less than with diet A.

But how accurate is your scale? Does your scale vary somewhat from day to day? Or, if you simply stand on two different places on the scale (say, dead center, and then closer to the edge), will the scale register a little differently?

What is suggested is that measuring instruments contribute their own variability so that the same item measured more than once may yield different measurements. If this is the case with your bathroom scale, you will not know whether the difference in weight loss reflects a difference in the effectiveness of the diets or is simply an example of variability contributed by your measuring instrument.

Tests are measuring instruments. But they measure less tangible qualities such as intelligence, acquired information, and ability. Verbal test items are sometimes misread, or interpreted differently at different times. The result is potential variability in the scores of a single person, even if the person is unchanged in the trait or ability, from time to time.

Educational and psychological tests, such as IQ tests, personality tests, and course examinations are far less reliable (less consistent) than physical devices such as scales and rulers. Any set of psychological or educational measurements can be expected to include variability due to measurement inconsistency, differences between people, and changes in a person from time to time.

POPULATIONS VERSUS SAMPLES

Suppose an association has been formed by men to combat what they describe as "the more extreme positions of the feminist movement." Their convention meets in Atlantic City, and they select a name. They call themselves "Males Against Liberation Extremists" (the acronym being MALE). They commission a series of studies on similarities and differences between the sexes that they believe will be helpful. They begin with an attempt to find out whether men are superior to women when dealing with abstract materials, as is sometimes assumed. They are quite prepared to learn that the converse is true. They simply want the facts.

MALE would like to test every living man and woman to determine if there is a difference between men and women in abstract ability. To do this, they would have to construct a test in every different language, and the test would have to take into account all cultural differences. This is too difficult, if not impossible, so they agree to limit their testing to the English-speaking **population.**

The word population has a broader meaning in the statistical literature than in vernacular usage. The word population as used by statisticians refers to any collection of items that all share some specified characteristic. The items can be people or other living things, and their common characteristic can be a language or geographical boundary. But the items can also be inanimate objects. They can, for example, be all the screws being manufactured by a particular machine in a particular factory. A statistician may be asked to estimate the expected number of defective screws that will be produced by that machine. All the screws that will ever be produced by that machine will be the population. The statistical question may be phrased as: "What proportion of the population is expected to be defective?"

The machine may function for 20 years before being replaced. Clearly, it will not be useful to simply count the defective screws for 20 years. By the time the question is answered the machine will have been replaced. Rather, the statistician will take a small subset of the machine's current production. This limited number of screws will be used to draw conclusions about the population of screws.

The members of MALE wish to compare the population of all English-speaking women and the population of all English-speaking men. Here, too, the reasonable approach to the problem is to take a small subset of each of the defined populations.

A small subset of a population which is examined in order to learn about the entire population is called a **sample.** Reference to a sample always implies that there is a larger population in which we are interested. A sample is obtained in order to facilitate conclusions about the population from which the sample is drawn.

Infinite Populations Psychological research generally deals in measurements of personality variables, intellectual variables, response times, error rates, etc. The actual

population of interest is generally very large. Since there is usually variability in measurement, it may be desirable to re-measure. But how many times? The only limits are the time and patience of the subjects and experimenter. Consequently, <u>the potential number of measurements is, in many cases, infinite. Therefore, it is necessary to settle for just a sample of the population of potential measurements.</u> More often than not we use a single measurement of each member of a relatively small sample of a large population.

Parameters Versus Statistics Suppose that the organization MALE selects a sample of men and a sample of women, and conducts their study. Assume that they find means for the samples of men and women on an abstract abilities test. These sample means can be symbolized as $\bar{X}_m$ (for men) and $\bar{X}_w$ (for women).

The two sample mean values are **statistics**. There is more than one meaning to the word statistics. In this context, statistics are summarizing values associated with particular samples. A statistic can summarize the central tendency of scores in a sample in the form of a mean or in the form of a median. These are just two examples of statistics. A statistic can also summarize other quantitative characteristics of samples. More often than not, interest in the statistics of samples centers around measures of central tendency and measures of variability.

Recall, however, that the eventual interest goes beyond samples, and is really directed toward populations. The statistics of samples constitutes information used to draw conclusions about the populations from which the samples are obtained.

Just as the quantitative characteristics of samples are called statistics, there is a name for the measures of the characteristics of populations. The quantitative characteristics of individual populations are called **parameters**. The mean of a population is a parameter of that population. The mean of a population is symbolized with the Greek letter mu, μ. In general, Greek letters are used to symbolize parameters and Latin letters to symbolize statistics. Statistics are estimates of population parameters. A sample mean, $\bar{X}$, is an estimate of some population mean, μ.*

In the study conducted for the organization MALE, the researchers obtain a sample mean for women ($\bar{X}_w$) and a sample mean for men ($\bar{X}_m$) on the same test of abstract abilities. They had hoped that these two mean values, obtained as two statistics of two samples, would indeed represent the parameter values in the two populations that were sampled; that is, in comparing $\bar{X}_w$ with $\bar{X}_m$, they would like to believe that they are comparing μ_w with μ_m.

Different samples can yield different values when sampled from the same population. For this reason, a researcher or other observer cannot have confidence that any one sample statistic truly represents the desired population parameter. But it is desirable to know if the sample estimates are at least likely to be close to the true population values.

It turns out that it is possible to know something about how close the sample estimates will be. It has been indicated above that when using a

---

*The sample mean $\bar{X}$ was seen, in Equation (2.1), to be computed as

$$\frac{\Sigma X}{n} = \bar{X},$$

where summation is over all the scores in the *sample*. The population mean μ is similarly computed as

$$\frac{\Sigma X}{n} = \mu,$$

the difference being that in computing μ, the summation extends over all the scores in the *population*.

statistic to estimate a parameter, variability in measurement causes error in the estimates. In these instances, knowledge of the extent of variability can help to approximate the degree of error in the estimates of parameters. Thus, variability is often measured in order to anticipate the degree of potential error in the estimates of parameters.

An important precondition for estimating potential errors is that the samples must be randomly selected. **Random samples** are defined below.

Random Samples A sample is a random sample when it has been obtained according to two criteria: (1) Each member of the population has an equal chance of being in the sample. (2) Every combination of n members of the population has an equal chance of being in a sample containing n members.

The second criterion can be best understood with an example. Assume that a supermarket is giving away two turkeys for Thanksgiving. Every person shopping in the store fills out a slip and puts it in a box at the front of the store. (To simplify matters, assume that only one slip per family is permitted.) Two names are then randomly selected from the box, and both families receive free turkeys. The population being randomly sampled is every family that shops at the supermarket. The size of the sample is $n = 2$.

To meet the second point of the definition of random, the sample that is drawn must be just as likely to include John Doe and his next door neighbor, as it is likely to include John Doe and a family several houses away, as it is likely to include the two neighbors on either side of John Doe, and so on (assuming they all shop at the supermarket). If the sample size is $n = 2$, every combination of two members of the population must have an equal chance of being in the sample. The first criterion of random selection is satisfied if no one slip is placed in a favored position in the box.

Note that if only one member of the population is to be selected, the second criterion is not needed, since it becomes identical to the first criterion. The meaning of the second criterion is that when more than one member of the population is to be selected, the selection of each member is to be independent of any other. For example, assume an attempt to identify the average IQ in a school through the testing of a small random sample. We can randomly select, say, 25 students and give them each an IQ test. But assume that a lazy psychologist decides to only randomly select one person, and asks that one person to bring along 24 school friends to also be tested. Such a sample is less likely to be representative of the school than a sample in which every combination of 25 students has a chance of being included in the sample.

Let us return to the free turkey example, with a change in assumptions. Suppose there is no limit to the number of slips a family can put in the box. Each time a person shops he or she gets a slip to put into the drawing box. Different families shop with different frequencies, so some families have a better chance of winning a turkey than others. In fact, one family may conceivably win both turkeys. However, the sample drawn is still a random sample of slips, if every slip has an equal chance of being selected, and if every combination of two slips has an equal chance of being selected.

The general point to be understood about random sampling is that <u>a random sample is a reference to a sampling procedure. Random sampling does not refer to a type of outcome (such as a fair outcome).</u> If the two criteria for random sampling are observed in doing sampling, then, regardless of the outcome, the sample is called a random sample.

In reaching decisions about population values and differences, statistical theory uses the assumption that all samples are random samples. Therefore, it is important to use random samples in collecting data. (Random samples are assumed in all examples throughout this text.)

A simple way to insure a random sample is to identify every member of a population by a number, then select the sample from a table of random numbers. Table II in Appendix B is a table of random numbers. The table can be entered at any point, and any prearranged procedure can be followed. For example, you can go up or down the columns. When finishing a column, you can return to the top of the next column or go up from the bottom of the next column, however you have previously decided to proceed. To insure that the table is initially entered randomly, some procedure—such as pointing to the page with a pencil, eyes averted—is generally used. This then offers a starting point that itself varies randomly each time the table is used.

MEASURES OF VARIABILITY FROM THE COMPLETE POPULATION Consider two related measures of variability. One measure can be obtained from the variability within a sample. A second obvious source is the variability as measured in the complete population of values (when the complete population is available).

Sometimes, when gathering data, the interest is in only a small population, such as the students in a particular class or a particular school. In this case, the population is small enough for complete measurement. There are several measures of variability that can be computed in a population. In this section, different measures of variability are discussed under the assumption that the entire population is available for measurement.

The Range The range is one indication of the extent of variability. The range of a grouped frequency distribution is the difference between the higher real limit of the highest interval in the distribution and the lower real limit of the lowest interval.

As indicated in Chapter 3, the real limits of adjacent intervals in a grouped frequency distribution are the points midway between the intervals. When the distribution is a regular frequency distribution, the implicit real limits are the values between the X values. Given sequentially valued integers, as in Tables 5.1a and 5.1b, the real limits are obtained by the addition and subtraction of .5 for each listed integer. Therefore, to obtain the range of the distribution in Table 5.1a, the lower real limit of the lowest value ($10 - .5 = 9.5$) is subtracted from the higher real limit of the highest value ($16 + .5 = 16.5$), yielding

$$\text{range} = 16.5 - 9.5$$
$$= 7.$$

For the distribution in Table 5.1b,

$$\text{range} = 16.5 - 2.5$$
$$= 14.$$

The distributions in Tables 5.1a and 5.1b are almost identical, yet they have ranges 7 and 14, respectively. The range ignores the bulk of the scores, responding only to the two most extreme scores in the distribution.

TABLE 5.1a
Hypothetical distribution of scores

X	f
16	9
15	13
14	16
13	20
12	19
11	14
10	8

TABLE 5.1b
Hypothetical distribution of scores

X	f
16	9
15	13
14	16
13	20
12	19
11	14
10	7
3	1

If one of the extreme scores is far from the bulk of the distribution (as in the case of 3 in Table 5.1b), the range can be a misleading index of variability. Therefore, the range is used only for rough, informal indications of variability.

The Mean Deviation One of the major statistics for representing distributions is the mean. Given a distribution in which the mean is a representative measure of central tendency, a reasonable statement of variability can be the degree of dispersion around the mean. Specifically, all the differences between each score and the mean can be summed. Then the average of these differences, $\Sigma(X - \mu)/n$, can be computed. However, in Chapter 2 it was shown that the sum of the differences from the mean is always equal to zero. Therefore, the sum of the differences from the mean cannot be used to differentiate variability among different distributions.

One way of getting around this problem is to sum the absolute values of the differences from the mean, rather than summing their algebraic values. An absolute value is one in which the algebraic sign is disregarded. For example, the absolute value of $|5 - 3| = |3 - 5|$, although the algebraic difference of $(5 - 3) \neq (3 - 5)$; that is, $(5 - 3) = 2$, whereas $(3 - 5) = -2$.

The average of the absolute differences from the mean is called **the mean deviation**:

$$\text{Mean deviation} = \frac{\Sigma |X - \mu|}{n}.$$

In Table 5.2 a distribution is presented with a range of 9 and a mean deviation of 2.40. The mean of the distribution is 4.

TABLE 5.2
Hypothetical distribution of scores, with a comparison of the computations of the range, mean deviation, variance, and standard deviation

	X	$|X - 4|$	$(X - 4)^2$
Mean = $\frac{20}{5}$ = 4.			
Range = 9.5 − 0.5 = 9.	9	5	25
	5	1	1
Mean deviation = $\frac{\Sigma|X - 4|}{5}$	3	1	1
	2	2	4
$= \frac{12}{5}$	1	3	9
	$\Sigma X = 20$	$\Sigma|X - 4| = 12$	$\Sigma(X - 4)^2 = 40$
$= 2.40.$			

$$\text{Variance} = \frac{\Sigma(X - 4)^2}{5} = \frac{40}{5} = 8.$$

$$\begin{array}{l}\text{Standard}\\\text{deviation}\end{array} = \sqrt{\frac{\Sigma(X - 4)^2}{5}} = \sqrt{\frac{40}{5}} = \sqrt{8} = 2.83$$

The mean deviation is rarely used, for although it is a reasonable measure of variability, it is not usable in conjunction with most statistical techniques, which require consistence with the laws of algebra. Ignoring the signs of numbers violates the laws of algebra. Instead of the mean deviation, a similar measure that is consistent with the laws of algebra and easily used with a variety of statistical techniques has become the major measure of variability. This measure is called **the variance**. Both the variance and its square root, called **the standard deviation**, are discussed at length in the remainder of this chapter.

The Variance The variance is the average squared deviation from the mean, as symbolized in Equation (5.1).

$$\sigma^2 = \frac{\Sigma(X - \mu)^2}{n}. \tag{5.1}$$

The symbol σ is the lowercase Greek letter sigma. With the superscript 2, σ^2 is the symbol for the variance.

For the distribution in Table 5.2, the variance is obtained by subtracting the mean from each score and squaring each difference. The average of these squared differences, for the data in Table 5.2, is

$$\sigma^2 = \frac{(9 - 4)^2 + (5 - 4)^2 + \cdots + (1 - 4)^2}{5}$$

$$= \frac{40}{5}$$

$$= 8.$$

Because the differences in Equation (5.1) for the variance are squared, the variance is of a different magnitude than the mean deviation. The square root of the variance offers a value that is of the same general magnitude as the mean deviation. The square root of the variance, like the variance itself, is useful in conjunction with other statistics. The square root of the variance is called the standard deviation.

The Standard Deviation The standard deviation (σ), being the square root of the variance (σ^2), is symbolized by the same Greek letter as the variance, but without the superscript 2. Symbolically, the standard deviation is

$$\sigma = \sqrt{\sigma^2} \tag{5.2}$$

$$= \sqrt{\frac{\Sigma(X - \mu)^2}{n}} .$$

For the distribution in Table 5.2, the standard deviation is

$$\sigma = \sqrt{8}$$

$$= 2.83.$$

Note that as a result of the square root operation the standard deviation is similar in magnitude to the average absolute difference from the mean (the mean deviation).

SAMPLE ESTIMATES OF VARIABILITY When a population parameter is estimated with a sample. statistic, individual estimates can be in error. However, it is often possible to obtain an estimate for which the average of an endless number of sample estimates will not be in error. This is called an **unbiased estimate**; that is, an unbiased estimate is one for which the long-run average of sampled statistics from a population will accurately reflect the value of the population parameter. It is the formula for the statistic that is or is not biased.

An example of an unbiased estimate is the formula in the equation for the mean, Equation (2.1):

$$\bar{X} = \frac{\Sigma X}{n}$$

An average of an endless number of random sample estimates of the mean from a single population, each computed with $\Sigma X/n$, equals the population parameter μ. (It is because this is only true for random samples that random samples are required.)

An example of a biased estimate is the formula for the variance in Equation (5.1),

$$\sigma^2 = \frac{\Sigma(X - \mu)^2}{n},$$

if it is used to estimate the population variance from sample data. Using sample data, the population mean will not be available, so $\bar{X}$ *replaces* μ in Equation (5.1), yielding $\Sigma(X - \bar{X})^2/n$. Statisticians have shown that the use of $\bar{X}$ in place of μ increases the likelihood of obtaining a smaller value for the variance; that is, sample estimates of the variance, computed with $\Sigma(X - \bar{X})^2/n$, are biased in the direction of underestimates. Therefore, Equation (5.1) has to be slightly altered when using sample data to estimate the population variance. The difference is in the denominator, where $n - 1$ replaces n. Thus, whereas $\Sigma(X - \bar{X})^2/n$ offers a biased sample estimate, $\Sigma(X - \bar{X})^2/(n - 1)$ offers an unbiased sample estimate of the variance in the population.

A concept that will be helpful in understanding the required change in Equation (5.1) is the concept of **degrees of freedom**. We will need the concept of degrees of freedom at several points in the text. This concept is discussed at this point, using the estimation of the variance to show the application of the concept of degrees of freedom.

Degrees of Freedom The number of scores that are free to vary independently in estimating a parameter with a statistic are called the degrees of freedom for that statistic. For example, in estimating the mean of a population, the n scores in the sample are all added, each of which can vary independently of the others. Any one score that is drawn has no effect on any other score. Any one score gives no information about the values of previous or subsequent scores in the sample. Also, no subset of the sampled scores gives any information about any other subset of the sampled scores.

In summary, a set of scores is independent if none of the outcomes predicts or affects any of the other outcomes in the set. Degrees of freedom are the number of independent scores used in the estimate of a parameter. The estimated mean is an estimate obtained from n independent scores. The estimate of the mean is therefore defined as having n degrees of freedom.

By contrast with the mean, the estimate of the variance has only $n-1$ degrees of freedom, since, as shown immediately below, the estimate of the variance is constructed from only $n-1$ independent scores.

It will be helpful to first restate Equation (5.1) for the variance with the implicit subscripts overtly expressed.

$$\sigma^2 = \frac{\sum_{i=1}^{n} (X_i - \mu)^2}{n}.$$

Assume a sample of only two scores, with which it is intended to estimate the variance of the complete population. Assume that the sample scores are $X_1 = 10$ and $X_2 = 8$. Given a sample, the population mean, μ, is not available, so it is necessary to estimate the population mean with the same sample data that will be used to estimate the variance. For this example, the sample mean is:

$$\bar{X} = \frac{\sum X}{n}$$

$$= \frac{10 + 8}{2}$$

$$= 9.$$

In this example, then, $X_1 = 10$, $X_2 = 8$, and $\bar{X} = 9$.

But suppose all that is known is $\bar{X}$ and X_1, with X_2 unknown. As is shown in the following equalities, given only $\bar{X}$ and X_1, the value of X_2 is implied; that is, it is not free to vary.

$$\frac{\sum X}{n} = \bar{X},$$

so

$$\frac{X_1 + X_2}{2} = \bar{X},$$

$$X_1 + X_2 = 2\bar{X},$$

$$X_2 = 2\bar{X} - X_1.$$

Given $\bar{X} = 9$ and $X_1 = 10$,

$$X_2 = 2(9) - 10$$

$$= 8.$$

Thus, given the value of the mean and one score in a two-score sample, the other score is fixed. If there are three scores, X_1, X_2 and X_3, and all but one, say X_3, are known, then X_3 can be determined from the other values if the mean is known.

$$\frac{X_1 + X_2 + X_3}{3} = \bar{X}$$

$$X_1 + X_2 + X_3 = 3\bar{X}$$

$$X_3 = 3\bar{X} - X_1 - X_2$$

Therefore, given a three-score sample, only two of the three scores are free to vary once the value of the mean is set by the sample estimate.

In general, for any number of scores, given the mean and all the scores except one, the last score is determined (is not independent). Therefore, only $n-1$ of the scores are independent, once the mean has been established from a sample of scores.

It has been shown that an estimate of the variance from a sample requires the prior estimate of the mean. Thus, there are $n-1$ independent scores when estimating the variance from a sample.

Recall that the definition of degrees of freedom is the number of independent values used in an estimate. Therefore, the estimate of the variance has $n-1$ degrees of freedom.

The Estimate of the Variance If the degrees of freedom are used as the denominator in the formula for the variance, the estimate of the variance will be unbiased. In the preceding section, it was seen that the estimate of the variance has $n-1$ degrees of freedom. The sum of the squared deviations from the mean of a sample, therefore, is divided by $n-1$ rather than by n.

The estimate of the variance from a sample is symbolized by s^2. The correct formula for s^2, implicit in the preceding discussion, appears in Equation (5.3).

$$s^2 = \frac{\Sigma(X - \bar{X})^2}{n-1} \tag{5.3}$$

Assume an infinite number of random samples of s^2, using Equation (5.3) to repeatedly estimate the value of σ^2. The long-run average of these sample values of s^2 will equal the value of σ^2 in the population; that is, when Equation (5.3) for s^2 is applied to a sample, it yields an unbiased estimate of the population variance, σ^2.

Some texts use $\hat{\sigma}^2$ when referring to an estimate of the variance, rather than s^2. However, this text will continue to use the common rule of symbolizing statistics (sample estimates) with Latin letters, such as $\bar{X}$ and s^2, reserving Greek letters, such as μ and σ^2, for parameters of populations.

The Estimate of the Standard Deviation In the previous section, the estimate of the variance was defined with Equation (5.3) above. Equation (5.2) defines the standard deviation as the square root of the variance. The square root of Equation (5.3) is therefore used to define the estimate of the standard deviation from a sample, as in Equation (5.4). Like the estimate of the variance, the estimate of the standard deviation has $n-1$ degrees of freedom.

$$s = \sqrt{\frac{\Sigma(X - \bar{X})^2}{n-1}}. \qquad (5.4)$$

COMPUTATIONAL FORMULAS FOR VARIANCE AND STANDARD DEVIATION The previously offered formulas for the variance and standard deviation can be called defining or intuitive formulas. These formulas are mathematical definitions of the statistics. The operations in the equations are equivalent to the verbal definitions. For example, the population variance is defined as "the average squared deviation from the mean," and so Equation (5.1) presents precisely that mathematical operation, that is,

$$\sigma^2 = \frac{\Sigma(X - \mu)^2}{n}.$$

But carrying out Equation (5.1) with a body of data means first computing the population mean, then subtracting that mean from each score, then squaring each such value, summing all those values, and then dividing by n. This procedure is tedious and prone to arithmetic errors. There is an equivalent but simpler formula that will yield the same values for the population variance. This **computational formula** for the population variance is presented as Equation (5.5):

$$\sigma^2 = \frac{\Sigma X^2 - (\Sigma X)^2/n}{n}. \qquad (5.5)$$

Since the standard deviation is the square root of the variance, the variance is always computed on the way to obtaining the standard deviation; that is, if the population standard deviation is desired, Equation (5.5) is used to compute the variance, and then its square root is taken.

The computational formula for the standard deviation, then, is just the square root of the computational formula for the variance, as summarized in Equation (5.6):

$$\sigma = \sqrt{\frac{\Sigma X^2 - (\Sigma X)^2/n}{n}} \qquad (5.6)$$

The computational formulas are less prone to errors and easier to use than the defining formulas. (This is because the computational formulas do not require the summing of differences.)

The above computational formulas have only three terms: n, ΣX^2, and $(\Sigma X)^2$. The latter two terms should be carefully differentiated, that is,

$$\Sigma X^2 \neq (\Sigma X)^2.$$

ΣX^2 means that each score should be individually squared, before summing. For example, using the data in Table 5.2,

$$\Sigma X^2 = 9^2 + 5^2 + 3^2 + 2^2 + 1^2$$
$$= 120.$$

For the term $(\Sigma X)^2$, all the scores must be summed *before* squaring, that is,

$$(\Sigma X)^2 = (9 + 5 + 3 + 2 + 1)^2$$
$$= (20)^2$$
$$= 400.$$

The computational formulas are illustrated in Table 5.3.
It will always be true that

$$\Sigma X^2 \geqslant \frac{(\Sigma X)^2}{n}.$$

The reason is that the numerators of Equations (5.1) and (5.5) imply the following equivalence

$$\Sigma X^2 - \frac{(\Sigma X)^2}{n} = \Sigma (X - \mu)^2,$$

and the sum of squared values cannot be negative. Thus, <u>you cannot have a negative variance,</u> whether computed by the computational or defining formulas.

TABLE 5.3
Hypothetical distribution of scores, illustrating the use of the computational formulas for the variance and standard deviation [Equations (5.5) and (5.6)]

		X	X^2	
σ^2 = variance		9	81	σ = standard deviation
		5	25	$= \sqrt{\sigma^2}$
$= \dfrac{\Sigma X^2 - (\Sigma X)^2/n}{n}$		3	9	$= \sqrt{8}$
		2	4	$= 2.83$
$= \dfrac{120 - (400)/5}{5}$		$\Sigma X = \overline{20}$	$\Sigma X^2 = \overline{120}$	
	$(\Sigma X)^2 = 400$			
$= \dfrac{120 - 80}{5}$				
$= 8$				

Equations (5.1) and (5.5) are mathematically equivalent:

$$\frac{\Sigma(X - \mu)^2}{n} = \frac{\Sigma X^2 - (\Sigma X)^2/n}{n}$$

It will be instructive to pause here, to prove the equality of the defining and computational formulas of the variance. All that is required is some simple algebra and the three rules of summation presented in Chapter 2.

To prove the equality of these equations which appear so different, we need only prove the equality between the numerators, since both equations have the same denominator (n). Therefore, we want to prove that

$$\Sigma(X - \mu)^2 = \Sigma X^2 - \frac{(\Sigma X)^2}{n}. \tag{5.7}$$

The proof follows.

$\Sigma(X - \mu)^2 = \Sigma[(X - \mu)(X - \mu)]$	(by definition)
$= \Sigma(X^2 - 2X\mu + \mu^2)$	(algebraic equivalence: carried out the multiplication)
$= \Sigma X^2 - \Sigma 2X\mu + \Sigma \mu^2$	(first rule of summation: distributed sigma)
$= \Sigma X^2 - 2\mu\Sigma X + \Sigma \mu^2$	(third rule of summation: placed constants to the left of sigma)
$= \Sigma X^2 - 2\mu\Sigma X + n\mu^2$	(second rule of summation: sum of a constant equals n times that constant)
$= \Sigma X^2 - 2\left(\dfrac{\Sigma X}{n}\right)\Sigma X + n\left(\dfrac{\Sigma X}{n}\right)^2$	(definition of the mean: $\mu = \dfrac{\Sigma X}{n}$)
$= \Sigma X^2 - 2\dfrac{(\Sigma X)^2}{n} + \dfrac{(\Sigma X)^2}{n}$	(algebraic equivalence: restated the second term and cancelled one n in the numerator and denominator of the third term)
$= \Sigma X^2 - \dfrac{(\Sigma X)^2}{n}$	(algebraic equivalence: added and subtracted as indicated in the previous step).

The proof begins with $\Sigma(X - \mu)^2$ and ends with $\Sigma X^2 - (\Sigma X)^2/n$, having only applied operations of equivalence (from algebra and the laws of summation). This proves the equivalence of the two terms.

The previous proof can be restated beginning with $\Sigma(X - \bar{X})^2$, which is the term that is used with samples [see Equations (5.3) and (5.4)]. The steps of the proof and the results are identical, since both $\bar{X}$ and μ are transformed to $\Sigma X/n$ in the proof. The result is Equation (5.8):

$$\Sigma(X - \bar{X})^2 = \Sigma X^2 - \frac{(\Sigma X)^2}{n} \tag{5.8}$$

The difference between Equations (5.7) and (5.8) is only in their applications (to populations and samples, respectively). The operations are identical.

Computational Formulas for Samples Equation (5.8) allows the transformation of Equations (5.3) and (5.4) into equations (5.9) and (5.10), respectively.

$$s^2 = \frac{\Sigma X^2 - (\Sigma X)^2/n}{n-1}, \tag{5.9}$$

$$s = \sqrt{s^2} \tag{5.10}$$
$$= \sqrt{\frac{\Sigma X^2 - (\Sigma X)^2/n}{n-1}}.$$

Equations (5.9) and (5.10) are the computational formulas for obtaining the estimates of the variance and standard deviation from samples.

TABLE 5.4
Summary of variance and standard deviation formulas

		Defining Formulas	Computational Formulas
Population Value	Variance (σ^2)	$\dfrac{\Sigma(X - \mu)^2}{n}$	$\dfrac{\Sigma X^2 - (\Sigma X)^2/n}{n}$
	Standard deviation (σ)	$\sqrt{\dfrac{\Sigma(X - \mu)^2}{n}}$	$\sqrt{\dfrac{\Sigma X^2 - (\Sigma X)^2/n}{n}}$
Sample Estimate	Variance (s^2)	$\dfrac{\Sigma(X - \bar{X})^2}{n-1}$	$\dfrac{\Sigma X^2 - (\Sigma X)^2/n}{n-1}$
	Standard deviation (s)	$\sqrt{\dfrac{\Sigma(X - \bar{X})^2}{n-1}}$	$\sqrt{\dfrac{\Sigma X^2 - (\Sigma X)^2/n}{n-1}}$

Contrasting Defining and Computational Formulas At this point, you may be somewhat overwhelmed by the appearance in this chapter of eight related formulas. Table 5.4 is an attempt to clarify the relationship among the eight formulas. To appreciate the uses of the various formulas, look at Table 5.5, where there is some hypothetical data (four scores, where $X = 1, 2, 3,$ and 4).

TABLE 5.5
Hypothetical data treated with some of the formulas of Table 5.4

X	X²		
		$\sigma^2 = \dfrac{\Sigma X^2 - (\Sigma X)^2/n}{n}$	$s^2 = \dfrac{\Sigma X^2 - (\Sigma X)^2/n}{n-1}$
1	1		
2	4	$= \dfrac{30 - (10)^2/4}{4}$	$= \dfrac{30 - (10)^2/4}{3}$
3	9		
4	16	$= 1.25$	$= 1.67$
$\Sigma X = 10$	$\Sigma X^2 = 30$	$\sigma = \sqrt{1.25}$	$s = \sqrt{1.67}$
$n = 4$		$= 1.12$	$= 1.29$

There are eight formulas in Table 5.4, but only four formulas have been applied to the data of Table 5.5, because only four of the formulas are computational formulas. The defining formulas help in understanding what the variance and standard deviation are, but for computational purposes, only the computational formulas should be used.

The choice then, is between either of two pairs of computational for-mulas: σ^2 and σ, or s^2 and s. The choice depends on whether you are computing parameters directly from the complete population, or comput-ing statistics (estimating parameters with samples). If the data are sam-ple data, you use s^2 and s to compute the statistics. If the data consist of the complete population of values, you use σ^2 and σ to compute the parameters.

TABLE 5.6
Computing the variance without first forming a frequency distribution

X	X²	
7	49	
7	49	
6	36	
6	36	$\sigma^2 = \dfrac{\Sigma X^2 - (\Sigma X)^2/n}{n}$
6	36	
5	25	$= \dfrac{297 - (51)^2/9}{9}$
5	25	
5	25	$= .89$
4	16	
$\Sigma X = 51$	$\Sigma X^2 = 297$	
$n = 9$		

Tables 5.3 and 5.5 offer distributions where each score occurs only once. What if you want to obtain the variance of a set of scores as presented in Table 5.6? In the table, many of the scores recur repeatedly. In Chapter 3 it was indicated that the mean can sometimes be more readily computed when the data is first put into the form of a frequency distribution.

The computational formulas for the variance and standard deviation can also be restated to incorporate multiple frequencies of scores. These additional versions of the variance and standard deviation formulas are used when the data is stated as a frequency distribution. Table 5.6 is restated as a frequency distribution in Table 5.7.

TABLE 5.7
Computing the variance from a frequency distribution

X	f	fX	X^2	fX^2	
7	2	14	49	98	$\sigma^2 = \dfrac{\Sigma fX^2 - (\Sigma fX)^2/n}{n}$
6	3	18	36	108	
5	3	15	25	75	$= \dfrac{297 - (51)^2/9}{9}$
4	1	4	16	16	
	$n = 9$	$fX = 51$		$\Sigma fX^2 = 297$	$= .89$

In comparing Tables 5.6 and 5.7, we can see that

$$(\Sigma X)^2 = (\Sigma fX)^2 \tag{5.11}$$

and

$$\Sigma X^2 = \Sigma fX^2. \tag{5.12}$$

Note that

$$fX^2 = f \cdot X^2$$

but

$$fX^2 \neq (fX)^2,$$

a common error.

In summary, in computing the variance or the standard deviation (or their estimates), it is advisable to use the frequency distribution versions when working with frequency distributions. Equations (5.11) and (5.12) are the only substitutions that are necessary in the formulas that were previously given. Table 5.8 is an expanded version of Table 5.4, and includes the formulas for working with frequency distributions.

TABLE 5.8
Summary of variance and standard deviation formulas, including use of frequencies

		Defining Formulas	Computational Formulas	Computational Formulas Incorporating Frequency
Population Value	Variance (σ^2)	$\dfrac{\Sigma(X - \mu)^2}{n}$	$\dfrac{\Sigma X^2 - (\Sigma X)^2/n}{n}$	$\dfrac{\Sigma fX^2 - (\Sigma fX)^2/n}{n}$
	Standard deviation (σ)	$\sqrt{\dfrac{\Sigma(X - \mu)^2}{n}}$	$\sqrt{\dfrac{\Sigma X^2 - (\Sigma X)^2/n}{n}}$	$\sqrt{\dfrac{\Sigma fX^2 - (\Sigma fX)^2/n}{n}}$
Sample Estimate	Variance (s^2)	$\dfrac{\Sigma(X - \bar{X})^2}{n-1}$	$\dfrac{\Sigma X^2 - (\Sigma X)^2/n}{n-1}$	$\dfrac{\Sigma fX^2 - (\Sigma fX)^2/n}{n-1}$
	Standard deviation (s)	$\sqrt{\dfrac{\Sigma(X - \bar{X})^2}{n-1}}$	$\sqrt{\dfrac{\Sigma X^2 - (\Sigma X)^2/n}{n-1}}$	$\sqrt{\dfrac{\Sigma fX^2 - (\Sigma fX)^2/n}{n-1}}$

IMPORTANT WORDS AND CONCEPTS

Sources of variability (p. 83)
Populations (p. 84)
Samples (p. 84)
Statistics (p. 86)
Parameters (p. 86)
Random samples (p. 87)
The range (p. 89)
The mean deviation (p. 91)
The variance (p. 91)
The standard deviation (p. 91)
Unbiased estimates (p. 92)
Degrees of freedom (p. 93)

SENTENCE COMPLETIONS

The following incomplete sentences are taken from the underlined sentences in this chapter. Fill in the missing words and phrases and then correct them from the answers which follow.

1. Any set of psychological or educational measurements can be expected to include variability due to _____,
   _____ , and _____
   _____ .

2. The word population as used by statisticians can refer to any collection of items that _____ .

3. A small subset of a population examined in order to _____
   _____ is called a sample.

4. A sample is obtained to facilitate conclusions about the _____
   _____

5. Given an infinite number of potential measurements, it is necessary to settle for a _____ of the _____.

6. The quantitative characteristics of _____ are called parameters. The mean of a population is a _____ of that population. Greek letters are used to symbolize _____, Latin letters to symbolize _____.

7. Statistics are _____ of population parameters. A sample mean, $\bar{X}$, is an _____ of some population mean, μ.

8. A sample is a random sample when it has been obtained according to two criteria: (1) _____

   _____.

   (2) _____

   _____.

9. A random sample is a reference to a sampling _____.

10. The _____ of a grouped frequency distribution is the difference between the higher real limit of the highest interval in the distribution and the lower real limit of the lowest interval.

11. The square root of the _____ is called the

   _____ _____ .

12. An _____ estimate is an estimate for which the long-run average of sampled statistics from a population will accurately reflect the value of the population parameter.

13. An example of a (an) _____ estimate is the formula in the equation for the mean.

14. An example of a (an) _____ estimate is the formula for the variance $\Sigma(X - \bar{X})^2/n$ if it is used to estimate the variance from sample data.

15. A set of scores are _____ if none of the outcomes predict or affect any of the other outcomes in the set. Degrees of freedom are the number of _____ scores used in the estimate of a parameter.

16. The estimate of the variance has _____ degrees of freedom.

17. If the degrees of freedom are used as the denominator in the formula for the variance, the estimate of the variance will be _____.

18. The long-run average of sample values of s^2 will equal the value of

   _____ .

19. You cannot have a _____ variance.

20. If the data are considered to be sample data, you use _____ and _____ to compute the variance and standard deviation, respectively. If the data are considered to be the complete population of values, you use _____ and _____ to compute the parameters. (Use the correct symbols.)

Answers 1. measurement inconsistency; differences between people; changes from time to time in the same person   2. all share some specified characteristic   3. learn about the entire population   4. population from which the sample was drawn   5. sample; population   6. populations; parameter; parameters; statistics   7. estimates; estimate   8. (1) Each member of the population has an equal chance of being in the sample. (2) Every combination of *n* members of the population has an equal chance of being in a sample containing *n* members.   9. procedure   10. range   11. variance; standard deviation   12. unbiased   13. unbiased   14. biased   15. independent; independent   16. *n*-1   17. unbiased   18. σ^2 (or, the population variance)   19. negative   20. s^2; s; σ^2; σ

PROBLEMS

1. Compute the variance of the following set of scores, using a computational formula. 2, 4, 6, 8.

2. Compute the standard deviation of the following set of scores, using a computational formula. 1, 2, 2, 3.

3. The standard deviation of the following set of scores is 2.45. The scores are 1, 2, 2, 6, 7, 8, 7, 8, 8, 7, 6, 7, 8, 8, 7, 9, 10. What is the variance? Think before proceeding on this one.

4. The variance of the following set of scores, computed with the formula

$$\sigma^2 = \frac{\Sigma(X - \mu)^2}{n},$$

is 12.14. The scores are 1, 2, 4, 4, 6, 6, 8, 8, 12, 12, 10, 9. What will be the variance, computed with

$$\sigma^2 = \frac{\Sigma X^2 - (\Sigma X)^2/n}{n}?$$

Think before proceeding on this one.

5. The following set of scores is a sample from a larger population. Give the best estimate of the standard deviation of the population of scores from which these four scores were sampled: 1, 3, 6, 10.

6. There are 10 students in a small class, and the teacher wants the mean and variance for the set of scores that they obtained on an exam.
   (a) What is an appropriate computational formula for the teacher to use for the variance?
   (b) What is the appropriate computational formula if the teacher wants the standard deviation?
   (c) If the teacher considers the students in the class to be a random sample from a much larger population (from all the students through the years in the class, rather than just these few students in this year's class), what is a correct computational formula for the estimate of the variance of this *larger population*? (Remember that the teacher will only have available the scores for the students in this year's class.)

z SCORES AND EFFECTS OF LINEAR TRANSFORMATIONS

The recent changeover in the United States to the metric system of measurement has probably created some awareness of the arbitrariness of most systems of measurement. The conversion from the Fahrenheit temperature scale to the Celsius scale may have had the same effect.

In psychological measurement, the arbitrary nature of most scales of measurement has always been obvious. For example, if you obtained a score of 17 on a test of hostility, what would that mean? Without more information about the average of all the scores, and some indication of the variability among the scores, you could not make sense out of the number 17. In Chapter 4 it was shown that converting a score to a percentile rank provides information about the meaning of a score. Therefore, percentile ranks are given, at times, rather than the raw scores.

When a set of scores is changed to some new scale according to some consistent rule applied to each score, the scores are said to be transformed. The rule for conversion from Celsius to Fahrenheit, for example, is

$$\text{degrees Fahrenheit} = \frac{9}{5}(\text{degrees Celsius}) + 32.$$

The conversion of raw scores to percentile ranks, given in Equation (4.3), is a little more cumbersome than the temperature conversion, but it is nonetheless an example of a transformation. There is another common transformation for psychological scores besides percentile ranks, which has many uses in statistics. This is the **transformation of scores** to z scores.

A **z score** converts a raw score X to a statement of its distance from the mean of the distribution, μ; that is, there is a distance (difference), $X - \mu$. The distance of X from the mean is re-expressed in terms of numbers of standard deviations by dividing $X - \mu$ by the standard deviation, σ:

$$z = \frac{X - \mu}{\sigma}. \tag{6.1}$$

For example, if the average score of a distribution of IQ test scores is 100, and the standard deviation is 16, a score of 132 will be two standard deviations from the mean; that is, 132 is two steps from 100 if each step is equal to 16. In the form of Equation (6.1),

$$z = \frac{132 - 100}{16}$$
$$= 2.$$

If a person scores 68 on the IQ test, he or she will be below the mean of the distribution, yielding, a negative z score. Specifically, from Equation (6.1),

$$z = \frac{68 - 100}{16}$$
$$= -2.$$

A person with a z score of 0 would be a person with the mean score of 100.

$$z = \frac{100 - 100}{16}$$

$$= 0.$$

Positive z scores are above the mean and negative z scores are below.

Equation (6.1) is the formula for transforming a raw score X to a z score. For the converse transformation of a z score to a raw score, Equation (6.1) can be rearranged in the following way.

$$\frac{X - \mu}{\sigma} = z,$$

$$X - \mu = \sigma z,$$

$$X = \mu + \sigma z. \qquad (6.2)$$

Thus, if $\sigma = 16$ and $\mu = 100$, the raw score equivalent of a z score of 2 is:

$$X = \mu + \sigma z$$

$$= 100 + 16(2)$$

$$= 132.$$

A z score of -2 yields:

$$X = 100 + 16(-2)$$

$$= 68.$$

A z score of zero yields the original raw score mean:

$$X = 100 + 16(0)$$

$$= 100.$$

This equivalence of a z score of zero and the mean of the raw scores is true regardless of the raw score mean and the raw score standard deviation; that is, from Equation (6.2),

$$X = \mu + \sigma z$$

$$= \mu + \sigma(0)$$

$$= \mu.$$

This raises an important question. If the mean of the raw scores has an equivalent z score of zero, is the mean of the z score distribution then zero (when all the scores in the distribution have been converted to z scores)? Related questions of importance are, what happens to the variance and standard deviation when all the scores are converted to z scores? These questions are answered in the remainder of this chapter.

This chapter has two purposes. One is to introduce the transformation between z scores and raw scores in the form of Equations (6.1) and (6.2). This has been accomplished above. The second purpose is to prove that the mean of a distribution of z scores is always equal to 0; and the variance and standard deviation of a distribution of z scores are always equal to 1.

The transformation of z scores with Equation (6.1) involves two operations: the numerator operation of subtraction (or addition by a negative number) in $(X - \mu)$, and the denominator operation of division (or multiplication by a reciprocal) in $(X - \mu)/\sigma$. The second goal of this chapter will therefore be pursued by first isolating the effects of addition and subtraction on the mean, variance, and standard deviation, and then by isolating the effects of multiplication and division on the mean, variance, and standard deviation.

ADDING A CONSTANT VALUE TO THE SCORES OF A DISTRIBUTION

It will be demonstrated that if a constant value a is added to every score in a distribution, the mean of that distribution will increase by precisely that amount a.

The mean of a distribution of scores is

$$\frac{\Sigma X}{n} = \mu.$$

If each X in the distribution is changed to $X + a$, the result of adding all the scores and dividing by the number of scores will be

$$\frac{\Sigma(X + a)}{n} = \mu_{new}.$$

Using the rules of summation and some simple algebraic equivalences, it is possible to determine just what the new mean will be. The procedure follows.

$$\frac{\Sigma(X + a)}{n} = \frac{\Sigma X + \Sigma a}{n} \quad \text{(rule 1 of summation)}$$

$$= \frac{\Sigma X}{n} + \frac{\Sigma a}{n} \quad \text{(algebraic equivalence)}$$

$$= \mu + \frac{\Sigma a}{n} \quad \text{(definition of the mean)}$$

$$= \mu + \frac{na}{n} \quad \text{(rule 2 of summation, since } a \text{ is a constant)}$$

$$= \mu + a \quad \text{(algebraic equivalence).}$$

The preceding steps leading from $\dfrac{\Sigma(X + a)}{n}$ to $\mu + a$ constitute a proof* of the assertion that adding a constant value to every score in a distribution increases the mean by that amount. Symbolically,

$$\frac{\Sigma(X + a)}{n} = \mu + a. \qquad (6.3)$$

If a in Equation (6.3) is a negative value, then the mean decreases by that amount.

An example of the use of Equation (6.3) would be a teacher deciding that an exam was too difficult, and therefore increasing every student's grade by 25 points. If the original mean of the distribution was 50, the new mean would be 75.

The Variance and Standard Deviation Are Unchanged by Addition of a Constant The variance does not change at all when the individual scores are changed by addition or subtraction. When each score is increased or decreased by some value a, the mean is also increased or decreased by that same amount a, according to Equation (6.3). The variance is the average squared difference between the individual scores and the mean. But these differences between individual scores and the mean are not changed when the individual scores and the mean all change by the same amount. Therefore, the variance remains unchanged by the addition (or subtraction) of a constant to the scores of the distribution.

Recall that the variance, from Equation (5.1), is

$$\sigma^2 = \frac{\Sigma(X - \mu)^2}{n}.$$

The lack of sensitivity of the variance to the addition of a constant is expressed symbolically in Equation (6.4).

$$\frac{\Sigma[(X + a) - (\mu + a)]^2}{n} = \frac{\Sigma(X - \mu)^2}{n} \qquad (6.4)$$

$$= \sigma^2.$$

The form of the left-hand expression in Equation (6.4) is due to the fact that not only is the value a added to each value X, changing X to $(X + a)$, but, from Equation (6.3), it is implied that adding the constant a creates a new mean $(\mu + a)$.

The proof of Equation (6.4) does not require the rules of summation. It

---

*As discussed in Chapter 2, a proof is merely a demonstration that some accepted assumptions logically lead to a particular conclusion. The assumptions used here are the rules of summation and algebra, and the definition of the mean.

merely requires simplifying the numerator in the left-hand expression of the equation, that is,

$$\Sigma[(X + a) - (\mu + a)]^2 = \Sigma(X + a - \mu - a)^2$$
$$= \Sigma(X - \mu)^2,$$

which is the unchanged sum of squares in the numerator of the original variance.

The standard deviation has the same insensitivity to the addition (or subtraction) of a constant. The standard deviation is merely the square root of the variance, so if the variance is unchanged by a transformation, so is the standard deviation.

The sensitivity of the mean to the addition of a constant, while the variance and standard deviation are unaffected, is an important point. It will be discussed again and used in Chapter 13, as well as in the remainder of this chapter.

A specific example of the effects of adding a constant to the scores of a distribution is given in Table 6.1 where the constant $a = 4$.

TABLE 6.1
Example of the effects on the mean, variance, and standard deviation of adding a constant, $a = 4$, to the scores of a distribution

X	X^2	$(X + 4) = Y$	Y^2
10	100	14	196
8	64	12	144
6	36	10	100
4	16	8	64
2	4	6	36
$\Sigma X = 30$ $\quad$ $\Sigma X^2 = 220$		$\Sigma Y = 50$ $\quad$ $\Sigma Y^2 = 540$	

$$\frac{(\Sigma X)^2}{n} = \frac{(30)^2}{5} \qquad\qquad \frac{(\Sigma Y)^2}{n} = \frac{(50)^2}{5}$$
$$= 180 \qquad\qquad\qquad = 500$$

$$\sigma^2 = \frac{\Sigma X^2 - (\Sigma X)^2/n}{n} \qquad \sigma^2 = \frac{\Sigma Y^2 - (\Sigma Y)^2/n}{n}$$

$$= \frac{220 - 180}{5} \qquad\qquad = \frac{540 - 500}{5}$$

$$= 8 \longleftarrow \text{Identity} \longrightarrow = 8$$

$$\mu = \frac{\Sigma X}{n} \qquad\qquad\qquad \mu = \frac{\Sigma Y}{n}$$

$$= \frac{30}{5} \qquad\qquad\qquad = \frac{50}{5}$$

$$= 6 \longleftarrow 6 + 4 = 10 \longrightarrow = 10$$

MULTIPLYING THE SCORES OF A DISTRIBUTION BY A CONSTANT

If every score in a distribution is multiplied by a constant b, the new mean will be b times the old mean, expressed:

$$\frac{\Sigma bX}{n} = b\mu. \tag{6.5}$$

The proof of Equation (6.5) is very simple, taking only two steps:

$$\frac{\Sigma bX}{n} = \frac{b\Sigma X}{n} \quad \text{(third rule of summation)}$$

$$= b\mu \quad \text{(definition of the mean as } \Sigma X/n).$$

Changes in the Variance and Standard Deviation

If every score in a distribution is multiplied by a constant value b, the new variance is b^2 times the old variance:

$$\frac{\Sigma(bX - b\mu)^2}{n} = b^2\sigma^2. \tag{6.6}$$

The form of the left-hand expression in Equation (6.6) is due to the fact that not only is the value b multiplied times each score X, but from Equation (6.5) it is seen that this creates a new mean, $b\mu$.

The proof of Equation (6.6) requires only algebraic simplification and the third law of summation:

$$\frac{\Sigma(bX - b\mu)^2}{n} = \frac{\Sigma[b(X - \mu)]^2}{n} \quad \text{(algebraic equivalence)}$$

$$= \frac{\Sigma b^2(X - \mu)^2}{n} \quad \text{(algebraic equivalence)}$$

$$= \frac{b^2\Sigma(X - \mu)^2}{n} \quad \text{(third law of summation)}$$

$$= b^2\sigma^2 \quad \text{(definition of the variance).}$$

The standard deviation will always be the square root of the variance, which means that if the variance is changed to $b^2\sigma^2$, the new standard deviation is

$$\sqrt{b^2\sigma^2} = b\sigma.$$

Restating the above effects of transformations, if every score of a distribution is multiplied by a constant value b, the standard deviation is transformed in the same way as the mean; that is, the new standard deviation will be b times the old standard deviation, and the new mean will be b times the old mean. The new variance will be the square of the constant times the old variance. These changes are summarized in Table 6.2.

TABLE 6.2

Summary of the effects of multiplying the scores in a distribution by a constant b

	Old	New
Mean	μ	$b\mu$
Standard deviation	σ	$b\sigma$
Variance	σ^2	$b^2\sigma^2$

Table 6.3 compares a distribution with and without a constant, $b = 5$, multiplied times each score.

TABLE 6.3

Example of the effects on the mean, variance, and standard deviation of multiplying the scores of a distribution by a constant, $b = 5$

X	X^2	$Y = 5X$	Y^2
10	100	50	2500
8	64	40	1600
6	36	30	900
4	16	20	400
2	4	10	100
$\Sigma X = 30$	$\Sigma X^2 = 220$	$\Sigma Y = 150$	$\Sigma Y^2 = 5500$

$$\frac{(\Sigma X)^2}{n} = \frac{(30)^2}{5} \qquad\qquad \frac{(\Sigma Y)^2}{n} = \frac{(150)^2}{5}$$
$$= 180 \qquad\qquad\qquad = 4500$$

$$\sigma^2 = \frac{\Sigma X^2 - (\Sigma X)^2/n}{n} \qquad \sigma^2 = \frac{\Sigma Y^2 - (\Sigma Y)^2/n}{n}$$
$$= \frac{220 - 180}{5} \qquad\qquad = \frac{5500 - 4500}{5}$$
$$= 8 \longleftarrow 5^2(8) = 200 \longrightarrow = 200$$

$$\sigma = \sqrt{\sigma^2} \qquad\qquad\qquad \sigma = \sqrt{\sigma^2}$$
$$= \sqrt{8} \qquad\qquad\qquad = \sqrt{200}$$

$$= 2.828 \longleftarrow 5(2.828) = 14.140 \longrightarrow = 14.140$$

$$\mu = \frac{\Sigma X}{n} \qquad\qquad\qquad \mu = \frac{\Sigma Y}{n}$$
$$= \frac{30}{5} \qquad\qquad\qquad = \frac{150}{5}$$
$$= 6 \longleftarrow 5(6) = 30 \longrightarrow = 30$$

EFFECTS OF z SCORE TRANSFORMATIONS Early in this chapter the transformation to a z score was recognized as involving two mathematical operations: The operation of subtraction (addition of a minus value) in $(X - \mu)$, and the operation of division (multiplication by a reciprocal) in $(X - \mu)/\sigma$. Transformations affected through addition and/or multiplication of the scores are called **linear transformations**. The previous sections, therefore, illustrated the general effects of linear transformations, rather than just the specific effects of the particular linear transformation, the transformation to z scores, accomplished through Equation (6.1).

In this section, the specific operations of a z score transformation (subtraction of the mean from each score, and division of each such result by the standard deviation) are examined. The z score transformation, Equation (6.1),

$$z = \frac{(X - \mu)}{\sigma},$$

suggests that first the mean is to be subtracted from each score in the form $(X - \mu)$. Subtracting any constant a from every score changes the mean by the amount a, yielding a new mean $(\mu - a)$. When $a = \mu$, the mean is changed to $(\mu - \mu) = 0$. The variance and standard deviation are not affected by the addition or subtraction of a constant. Thus, after subtraction of the mean from every score, the new mean will be $\mu_{new} = 0$, and the variance and standard deviation will remain σ^2 and σ, respectively.

The second operation is multiplication of the new scores, each $(X - \mu)$, by the reciprocal of the standard deviation, $1/\sigma$. Multiplying each score by a value $1/\sigma$ changes the mean to $(1/\sigma)\mu$. But the mean in this case is the new μ, where $\mu_{new} = 0$, and $(1/\sigma)0 = 0$. Therefore, the mean remains zero when the scores are transformed to z scores. The variance and the standard deviation, on the other hand, are changed when the scores are multiplied by $1/\sigma$. Specifically, from Table 6.2, the new variance following from any transformation bX is

$$\sigma^2_{new} = b^2\sigma^2.$$

Therefore, when $b = 1/\sigma$, the new variance changes to

$$\sigma^2_{new} = \frac{1}{\sigma^2}\sigma^2$$

$$= 1.$$

The standard deviation, being the square root of the variance, is also equal to 1. Put another way,

$$\sigma_{new} = \frac{1}{\sigma}\sigma$$

$$= 1.$$

In summary, <u>when a set of scores is transformed to z scores, the new distribution of z scores always has a mean of 0 and a variance and standard deviation both equal to 1.</u>

Symbolically,

$$\mu_z = 0,$$
$$\sigma_z^2 = 1,$$
$$\sigma_z = 1.$$

The earlier sections of this chapter simply proved that the above three equalities are true.

Figure 6.1 offers a graph of a distribution in terms of both the raw and equivalent z scores. The figure demonstrates that <u>the values on the X axis do not change their ordinal relationship to each other when transformed to z scores. The points on the X axis are simply relabelled.</u> Further, the relative frequencies do not change for equivalent raw scores and z scores; that is, <u>the shape of the distribution of scores is unchanged by a transformation to z scores.</u> The only change is in the labels of the scores on the X axis.

This new system of labels results in an interesting advantage. <u>Simply by knowing if a z score is positive or negative, we know whether the score is above or below the mean. The larger the absolute value of a z score, the further that score is from the mean.</u> Given a distribution like that in Figure 6.1, z scores close to zero are common or typical scores. The larger the absolute value of a z score, the more unusual (rarer) that score is in the distribution.

No matter what the original set of raw score values, the new set of transformed scores always has the same mean of 0 and the same standard deviation of 1. A z score of 2 has the same relative place in two similarly shaped distributions, regardless of the scale of the original raw scores. <u>$z = 2$ always means that the score is two standard deviations above the mean.</u> Thus, all sets of scores, after having been transformed to z scores,

FIGURE 6.1
Graph of a distribution with a mean of 80 and a standard deviation of 5.

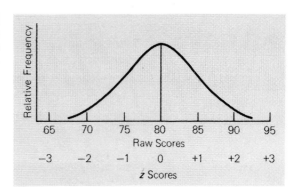

can be talked about in equivalent terms. The one requirement for being able to discuss all sets of scores in the same frame of reference when transformed to z scores is that the raw scores must all come from similarly shaped distributions.

The z score is generally used with a commonly obtainable distribution, the normal distribution, discussed in Chapter 9. Therefore, the advantage of a universal scale for different sets of scores is often realizable. After scores have been transformed to z scores, they are frequently called **standard scores**. Standard scores will be discussed again in Chapter 9 in the context of the normal distribution.

<table>
<tr><td>IMPORTANT
WORDS AND
CONCEPTS</td><td>Transformation of scores (p. 107)
z score (p. 107)
Linear transformations (p. 114)
Standard scores (p. 116)</td></tr>
</table>

SENTENCE COMPLETIONS
The following sentences are taken from the underlined sentences in this chapter. Fill in the missing words and phrases, then correct them from the answers which follow.

1. When a set of scores is changed to some new scale according to some consistent rule applied to each score, the scores are said to be

_____ .

2. A z score converts a raw score X to a statement of its _____ from the mean of the distribution. The _____ of X from the mean is re-expressed in terms of numbers of _____

_____ .

3. Positive z scores are _____ the mean and negative z scores are _____ the mean.

4. A raw score equal to the mean of the raw scores has a z score of ____.

5. Assume a mean of a distribution equal to 12. If 6 is added to each score in the distribution, the new mean will be _____ .

6. Assume a variance of 16 and a standard deviation of 4, in some distribution. If 8 is added to each score in the distribution, the new variance is _____ and the new standard deviation is _____.

7. Assume a distribution with a mean of 50, a variance of 4, and a standard deviation of 2. If every score is multiplied by 3, the new mean will be _____ , the new variance _____ , and the new standard deviation _____.

8. When a set of scores is transformed to z scores, the new distribution of z scores always has a mean of _____, and a variance and standard deviation equal to _____ .

9. The values on the X axis (do, do not) change their ordinal relationship to each other when transformed to z scores. The shape of the distribution is _____by a transformation to z scores.

10. By knowing if a z score is, respectively, _____ or _____ , we know whether the score is above or below the mean.

11. The _____ the absolute value of a z score, the further that score is from the mean.

12. A z score of 2 is always _____ above the mean.

13. z scores are also called _____ _____.

14. Transformations affected through addition and/or multiplication of the scores are called _____ _____.

Answers 1. transformed 2. distance; distance; standard deviations 3. above; below 4. 0 5. 18 6. 16; 4 7. 150; 36; 6 8. 0; 1 9. do not; unchanged 10. positive; negative 11. larger 12. two standard deviations 13. standard scores 14. linear transformations

PROBLEMS

1. A distribution of raw scores has a mean of 50 and a standard deviation of 7.
   (a) What is the z score equivalent of a raw score of 60.5?
   (b) What is the z score equivalent of a raw score of 39.5?
   (c) In this same distribution, a person has a score of 64. How many standard deviations away from the mean is this score?
   (d) What is the z score equivalent of a raw score of 64?
   (e) Generalizing from the answers to (c) and (d), what is the relationship between standard deviations and z scores?

2. A distribution of raw scores has a mean of 40 and a standard deviation of 6.
   (a) What is the raw score equivalent of a z score of 3?
   (b) What is the raw score equivalent of a z score of −2?

3. In Chapter 5, the computational formula for the standard deviation of a set of scores was given as

$$\sigma = \sqrt{\frac{\Sigma X^2 - (\Sigma X)^2/n}{n}}$$

For the following set of scores, compute the z score equivalent of a raw score of 7, carrying out the computations to two decimal places: 1, 2, 4, 4, 6, 6, 7.

seven

PROBABILITY

Whenever the physical or psychological characteristics of people are observed, variability is seen. Variability is present even when examining the same people at different times. This variability is further exaggerated by the instruments used in psychological measurement. Yet, as research psychologists, counselors, educators, and citizens trying to live successfully in the world, we wish to predict human behavior. How do we predict when the only certainty is variability? The answer is that we deal in probabilities.

Informally, the word probability is used similarly to the word likelihood. A probable event is considered to be a likely event. An improbable event is an unlikely event. Unless you are a scientist, gambler, or T.V. weatherman, you are not too likely to actually be assigning numbers to events to specify the degree of likelihood when discussing probabilities. Yet the notion of probability becomes most useful when specific values can be associated with specific events.

Mathematicians have constructed a theory of probability which allows for a quantitative discussion of probability. This same quantitative theory of probability offers the logical underpinnings for statistical techniques. The theory has three axioms (assumptions) that are used together with the operations and logic of other areas of mathematics to derive a host of theorems (laws) for the theory of probability. These axioms and theorems can be used to draw conclusions about the probabilities of particular events.

THE SAMPLE SPACE In probability theory, the focus is on the relative likelihood of potential outcomes. The totality of potential outcomes in a given situation is called the **sample space**, symbolized S. *There are two different designations for* individual potential outcomes: **events** and **sample points**.

Events and Sample Points Any potential outcome can be called an event. Only certain events can be called sample points. The simplest unambiguously definable and mutually exclusive individual outcomes are called sample points. The occurrence of any one sample point precludes the occurrence of any other. For example, in tossing a coin, the sample space consists of two sample points, a head and a tail. A head and a tail are mutually exclusive, since only one can occur on any one toss. Additionally, they are unambiguously defined. Consequently, a head and a tail qualify as sample points in the sample space of outcomes from a coin toss.

The complete listing of all the sample points in a given sample space is called an **exhaustive listing.** For example, all possibilities are exhausted when you have mentioned a head and a tail, given an impending single toss of a coin.

The term event is used to describe a subset of the sample space involving one or more sample points. It is a more inclusive term than sample point, and is equivalent to what is generally meant by outcome. The event of being wrong in a five-option multiple choice question is an event composed of four sample points. The event of being right consists of a single sample point. Thus, a sample point is also an event, but an event is not necessarily a sample point. An event is an outcome defined by one or more sample points.

Whereas sample points are, by definition, mutually exclusive, events do not have to be mutually exclusive; that is, different events can have sample points in common. When they do, they are not **mutually exclusive events,** since when a sample point common to two events occurs as an outcome, both events are defined as having occurred. For example, a restaurateur has 20 dinner items on his menu, and he records the frequencies with which different items are ordered. Eventually, he states the probability of a particular dish being ordered. The different items on the menu are different sample points in the sample space of orders. The sample points are clearly mutually exclusive, since each customer orders only one dinner. But the menu is divided into many different events (subsets of sample points) that are not mutually exclusive. For example, the restaurateur wants to know the probability that someone will order a seafood, as opposed to a meat dinner. He also wonders about the probability of someone ordering an expensive meal, or a dish that will take extra time to prepare. Each of these events is probably defined by a number of different items on the menu. There are probably several expensive dishes, several seafood dishes, and several dishes that take some extra time to prepare. But often seafood items are also expensive items, and dishes that take extra time to prepare are also expensive items. For example, the sample point "Maine Lobster" is common to both the event "sea food item" and the event "expensive item." Thus, events, which can sometimes have sample points in common, are not necessarily mutually exclusive.

THE AXIOMS OF PROBABILITY The first **axiom of probability** states that a probability value for some future outcome, be it an event or a sample point, must be between 0 and 1, inclusive. Symbolically, given an event E_j with a probability $P(E_j)$,

$$0 \le P(E_j) \le 1. \tag{7.1a}$$
$$\text{(Axiom 1)}$$

Given a sample point S_j, with a probability $P(S_j)$,

$$0 \le P(S_j) \le 1. \tag{7.1b}$$

Although the first axiom states that events can have a probability of 0 and 1 as well as the values in between, the focus is usually on events with a probability *between* 0 and 1; that is, the primary interest in statistical questions is in uncertain events. A probability of 0 implies that the event will not occur, and a probability of 1 implies that the event will occur.

Probability as a Closed System The second axiom of probability states that the sum of the probabilities of all the sample points in a sample space must equal 1. Symbolically,

$$P(\mathbb{S}) = 1, \qquad \text{(Axiom 2)}$$

where $\mathbb{S}$, the sample space, is the complete set of all possible outcomes. Alternatively, this second axiom of probability is expressed symbolically in Equation (7.2).

$$P(S_1) + P(S_2) + \cdots + P(S_j) + \cdots + P(S_n) = 1, \qquad (7.2)$$
$$\text{(Axiom 2)}$$

where S_j is the jth sample point of n sample points in a sample space containing just these n sample points. (Any sample point can be designated as the jth sample point.)

The second axiom also holds for any set of *mutually exclusive* and exhaustive events, that is,

$$P(E_1) + P(E_2) + \cdots + P(E_j) + \cdots + P(E_n) = 1, \qquad (7.3)$$

where E_j is the jth event of n *mutually exclusive* and exhaustive events.

Axiom 2 implies that if the probability of one event in a sample space increases, then the probability of some other event must decrease.

If one horse hurts his leg before a horse race, the chances of the other horses winning, and therefore their individual probabilities of winning, will be increased to the extent that the injured horse's were decreased.

Equal Probabilities, Theoretically Assigned The question arises as to where one would obtain a probability value. Probabilities can be assigned on the basis of any one of many sets of theoretical assumptions or, empirically, on the basis of past events.

One basis for theoretical assignments is the assumption that every one of n sample points in a sample space has the same probability of occurrence. Axiom 2 says that all the probabilities in a sample space must sum to 1. The only way to have n equal probabilities sum to 1 is to assign each probability a value of $1/n$. Thus, if S_j is the jth or any one of n sample points in a sample space, then

$$P(S_j) = \frac{1}{n}. \qquad (7.4)$$

For example, the sample space of outcomes for the tossing of a coin has two sample points: a head and a tail. For a fair coin, the probability of a

121   The Axioms of Probability

head equals the probability of a tail, that is, 1/2. Equations (7.2) and (7.4) are both satisfied.

Assume a sadistic professor, who gives multiple choice questions, and selects the correct answer to each question randomly. Assume further that he offers five alternatives for each question, and that the questions are so ambiguous that the students are neither misled nor aided by their knowledge of the subject. Each answer then has a probability of $1/5 = .2$ of being correct, according to Equation (7.4).

Complementary Events When a sample space can be defined as containing just two mutually exclusive events, E_1 and E_2, the event E_2 is called the complement of the event E_1, symbolized with a bar over E_1. $P(\bar{E}_1)$ signifies the probability of E_1 not occurring. Given a sample space containing just two events, E_1 and E_2, the following equivalence is implied:

$$P(E_2) = P(\bar{E}_1).$$

The second axiom of probability, Equation (7.3), indicates that for two mutually exclusive and exhaustive events,

$$P(E_1) + P(E_2) = 1,$$

which implies that

$$P(E_1) + P(\bar{E}_1) = 1.$$

Subtracting $P(E_1)$ from both sides yields Equation (7.5), the probability of a **complementary event**.

$$P(\bar{E}_1) = 1 - P(E_1). \tag{7.5}$$

When the probability of being right is

$$P(E_1) = .2,$$

as in the randomly correct multiple choice questions discussed above, the probability of being wrong (the probability of the complementary event), is

$$P(\bar{E}_1) = 1 - P(E_1)$$
$$= 1 - .2$$
$$= .8.$$

There is another way to obtain the value .8 for the probability of being wrong, which offers an example for the third axiom of probability.

Summing Mutually Exclusive Events ("Or Relations") The third axiom of probability states: <u>Given a subset of mutually exclusive events, the probability of any one among them occurring is the sum of their individual probabilities.</u> For only two mutually exclusive events,

$$P(E_1 \text{ or } E_2) = P(E_1) + P(E_2). \qquad \text{(Axiom 3)}$$

If the probability of a fair die coming up 1 in a single throw is

$$P(E_1) = \frac{1}{6}$$

and the probability of the same fair die coming up 2 is

$$P(E_2) = \frac{1}{6},$$

then the probability of the die coming up either a 1 or a 2 in the single throw is

$$P(E_1 \text{ or } E_2) = P(E_1) + P(E_2)$$
$$= \frac{1}{6} + \frac{1}{6}$$
$$= \frac{1}{3}.$$

For several mutually exclusive events, Axiom 3 can be symbolized as in Equation (7.6).

$$P(E_1 \text{ or } E_2 \text{ or...or } E_j \text{ or...or } E_n) = \qquad\qquad (7.6)$$
$$P(E_1) + P(E_2) + \cdots + P(E_j) + \cdots + P(E_n) \quad \text{(Axiom 3)}$$

Since sample points are mutually exclusive events, Equation (7.6) also holds for sample points.

In the case of the probability of being wrong in the multiple choice question with five alternatives, there are four sample points that are wrong and that together constitute the event of being wrong. The student chooses only one answer, so all four ways of being wrong are mutually exclusive. Therefore, from Equation (7.6), the probability of being wrong is the sum of the respective probabilities of the ways of being wrong. Symbolizing the four ways of being wrong as E_1, E_2, E_3, and E_4,

$$P(E_1 \text{ or } E_2 \text{ or } E_3 \text{ or } E_4) = .2 + .2 + .2 + .2$$
$$= .8,$$

so that the probability of being wrong is .8.

Given several mutually exclusive and exhaustive events, E_1, E_2,..., E_j,..., E_n, the probability of any one of the events E_j *not* occurring is the sum of the probabilities of all the *other* events. In equation form, this is

$$P(\bar{E}_j) = P(E_1) + P(E_2) + \cdots + P(E_i) + P(E_k) + \cdots + P(E_n), \qquad (7.7)$$

where $P(E_j)$ has been specifically excluded from the right-hand side of Equation (7.7).

As seen when discussing Equation (7.5) for complementary events, summing all the probabilities for all the alternative events may not be necessary. We can state the probability that E_j has not occurred as the probability of a complementary event; that is, we can define a pair of complementary events, where one event is the excluded event and the other is the set of all other outcomes. To obtain the probability of a nonoccurrence of the excluded event, subtract its probability from one. $P(\bar{E}_j)$ signifies the probability of event E_j *not* occurring. If the probability of the correct answer is $P(E_j) = .2$, then the probability of the wrong answer is $P(\bar{E}_j) = 1 - .2 = .8$.

It can be helpful to think of Equation (7.5) for the probability of a complementary event as an equation for the **not relation**; that is, whenever you want the probability that some event will not occur, you take the probability of the complementary event.

Another verbal equivalent to the equations in this chapter can be found for Equation (7.6), the equation for the probability of any one of many mutually exclusive events. It can be helpful to think of equation (7.6) as the appropriate equation when an **or relation** is discussed; that is, when you wish to know the probability of any one *or* another event occurring, you add their individual probabilities of occurrence (assuming that they are mutually exclusive events).

Joint Events ("And Relations") Suppose a student is taking the random-answer multiple choice question described above. What is the probability that this student will answer all of the questions correctly (assuming 10 questions on the test)?

The answer is obtained with the help of a theorem of probability for **joint events** that are independent of each other. (Independence was defined in Chapter 5.) In the present context, two events are independent if knowledge of the occurrence of one does not affect the estimate of the probability of the other. For example, assume that a student is guessing on the multiple choice quiz. Assume further that the fact that the student guesses correctly on any one question does not change the probability of his or her guessing correctly on any other question. The answers on each of the different questions are independent of each other.

The probability of a joint event, with **independent events**, is the product of the probabilities of the individual events.

For two independent events, E_1 and E_2, with respective probabilities $P(E_1)$ and $P(E_2)$, the probability of both E_1 and E_2 occurring is $P(E_1) \times P(E_2)$.

For any number of events, say n events,

$$P(E_1 \text{ and } E_2 \text{ and....and } E_j \text{ and...and } E_n)$$
$$= P(E_1) \times P(E_2) \times \cdots \times P(E_j) \times \cdots \times P(E_n) \qquad (7.8)$$

when every event E_j is independent of every other event.

Specifically, the probability of 10 events in succession occurring, where each has a probability of .2 of occurring individually, is $(.2)^{10} =$ .0000001024. Thus, if a student is only guessing on 10 multiple choice questions, each with five choices, the probability of getting all 10 correct is less than one in a million.

Equation (7.8) has a verbal equivalent, just as Equations (7.5) and (7.6) have verbal equivalents. Equation (7.8) can be thought of as being usefully invoked when considering an "and relation." An "**and relation**" is one where the question concerns the probability of several events all occurring. Assuming that they are all independent of each other, the probability is obtained from the product of the individual probabilities of occurrence.

If the probability of a particular lightning bolt striking a particular spot is $1/1,000,000$, and the probability of your being in that spot at that moment is $1/1,000,000$, then the probability of your being struck by that lightning bolt in that spot is $(1/1,000,000) \times (1/1,000,000)$.

Table (7.1) summarizes the axioms and theorems of probability that have been discussed above.

TABLE 7.1
Summary of the three axioms of probability (numbers 1–3) and two theorems of probability. Number 3 is the "or relation;" number 4 is the "not relation;" and number 5 is the "and relation."

1. If $P(E_j)$ is the probability of any event E_j, then
$$0 \leq P(E_j) \leq 1.$$

2. If $E_1, E_2, ..., E_j, ..., E_n$ is a set of mutually exclusive and exhaustive events in a sample space, then
$$P(E_1) + P(E_2) + \cdots + P(E_j) + \cdots + P(E_n) = 1.$$

3. If $E_1, E_2, ..., E_j, ..., E_n$ are mutually exclusive events in a sample space, then
$$P(E_1 \text{ or } E_2 \text{ or } ... \text{ or } E_j \text{ or } ... \text{ or } E_n)$$
$$= P(E_1) + P(E_2) + \cdots + P(E_j) + \cdots + P(E_n).$$

4. If E_1 and E_2 are mutually exclusive and exhaustive events in a sample space, then
$$P(E_2) = 1 - P(E_1).$$

Equivalently, recognizing E_2 as the complement of E_1,
$$P(\bar{E}_1) = 1 - P(E_1).$$

5. If $E_1, E_2, ..., E_j, ..., E_n$ are independent events in a sample space, then
$$P(E_1 \text{ and } E_2 \text{ and } ... \text{ and } E_j \text{ and } ... \text{ and } E_n)$$
$$= P(E_1) \times P(E_2) \times \cdots \times P(E_j) \times \cdots \times P(E_n).$$

COMPARING THEORETICAL AND EMPIRICAL PROBABILITIES

Recall the previous example of multiple choice questions, each with five alternatives. Suppose that the teacher was not really being sadistic, as was assumed above. Suppose that he was doing an experiment to see whether, when people guess from among the five choices on a test, they in fact have a position preference in their answers. For example, people may more often tend to select the middle answer (when they do not know the answer), or the first answer, etc. If there is no preference operating, then all positions will be chosen approximately equally often when there is no way of knowing the correct answer. Put another way, the expectation is for one of two outcomes: A rectangular probability distribution, which, in this example, represents chance (random) selection of answers, or some other probability distribution, representing preferences for one or more answer positions.

Experimenters generally arrange experimental situations so that both chance and non-chance happenings can be identified. The occurrence of non-chance events usually signals some relationship between variables. The details of this logic are presented in the following chapters. Of particular importance are the various probability distributions for chance events, several of which will be presented later in this text. Each such probability distribution, like the rectangular distribution in the above example, offers *expected* probability values for outcomes when only chance is operating. Sometimes it is necessary to derive probability values from experimental outcomes, rather than from assumptions. Probability estimates based on actual outcomes are called **empirical probabilities**.

EMPIRICAL BASIS OF PROBABILITY

There is a psychological maxim that can serve as well for statistics. "The best predictor of future behavior is past behavior." In the spirit of this advice, the probability of events (that is, their future relative frequencies of occurrence) is taken from the relative frequency of these events in some finite number of past trials, which offers a sample of what will happen with infinite sampling. That sampled relative frequency becomes the empirical definition of probability. (Often the sampled trials are the trials of an experiment.)

The probability, then, of an event E_j is empirically defined as

$$P(E_j) = \frac{m}{n},\qquad(7.9)$$

where m is the number of times that event E_j has occurred in a series of n trials. The larger that n is, the more reliable this definition of probability will be; that is, the larger that n is, the more confidence we have that the sample proportion reflects the true population proportion, and therefore a correct statement of probability. By true population proportion we mean the proportion of times that event E_j would occur in an infinite number of trials.

For example, assume a random sample of 10 adults ($n = 10$) and an observation of the proportion that are employed. Suppose that five of the observed people are employed ($m = 5$). The best bet as to the probability of employment [$P(E)$] in the sampled population is

$$P(E) = \frac{m}{n}$$

$$= \frac{5}{10}$$

$$= .5.$$

Now assume that another sample of 10 adults is taken, and then another, and still another. The second sample yields $4/10 = .4$, the third $7/10 = .7$, and so on. The long-run average of all these estimates represents the true population proportion; that is, given enough of these samples, the average will be equal to the proportion of employment in the entire population of adults.

But the n in the example, 10, is small, so it is not appropriate to have much confidence in the estimate of the proportion from any one of the samples. But if n were large, say 5000, any one random sample would be expected to be close to the true population proportion. Therefore, as n gets larger in Equation (7.9), there is more confidence in the empirical estimate of probability.

The following incomplete sentences are taken from the underlined sentences in this chapter. Fill in the missing words and phrases and then correct them from the answers which follow.

1. The first axiom of probability states that a probability value for some future outcome must be between _____ and _____ , inclusive.

2. The term _____ is used to describe a subset of the sample space involving one or more sample points.

3. The second axiom of probability states that the sum of the probabilities of all the sample points in a sample space must _____ _____ . If the probability of one event in a sample space increases, then the probability of some other event must _____.

4. The only way to have n equal probabilities sum to 1 is to assign each probability a value of _____ .

5. When dealing with mutually exclusive dichotomous events, one event is called the _____ of the other.

6. The third axiom of probability states that, given a subset of mutually exclusive sample points or events, the probability of any one among them occurring is _____ _____.

7. Given several mutually exclusive and exhaustive events, $E_1, E_2, ..., E_j, ...,$ E_n, the probability of any one of the events, E_j, *not* occurring is _____ _____of all the other events.

8. Whenever you want the probability that some event will not occur, you take the probability of the _____ event.

9. When you wish to know the probability of any one *or* another event occurring, you _____their individual probabilities of occurrence (assuming they are mutually exclusive events).

10. Two events are independent if _____ _____ _____ _____.

11. The probability of **a** joint event, with independent events, is _____ _____.

12. An "and relation" is one where the question concerns the probability of _____ . Assuming that the events are all independent of each other, the probability of an "and relation" is obtained from _____ _____.

13. The empirically based probability of future events is taken from _____ _____ _____.

14. The _____ that n is, the more confidence we have that the sample proportion reflects the true population proportion. By true population proportion, we mean _____
_____
_____.

PROBLEMS

1. The six possible outcomes with a standard die are independent, mutually _____ outcomes. Each of the six possible outcomes is a sample _____ in the sample space of outcomes from the tossing of a die. Suppose that you play a game where the appearance of a 3 makes you lose, but every other outcome means that you win. This dichotomizes the sample space into two mutually exclusive _____.
The event of winning is the _____ of the event of losing.
   The probability of a 2 or a 3 coming up is equal to _____.
If the die is thrown twice, the probability of a 3 coming up both times is equal to _____.

2. During the month of March in a particular city, it rains on approximately one third of the days. This March, it has rained on the first, second, and third Thursdays of the month. If the probability of it raining on any one day is independent of it raining on any other day, the probability of it raining next year on all four Thursdays in March is _____.

3. You toss two fair coins, a penny and a nickel, once each. The probability of two heads is _____. The probability of a head with the nickel and a tail with the penny is
_____.
The probability of a tail with the nickel and a head with the penny is __.
The probability of one head and one tail is _____.

4. A T.V. quiz program asks mostly easy questions. The average contestant can answer about 60% of the questions correctly. There is a bonus of $1000 if a contestant can correctly answer six consecutive questions. If a contestant is only asked six questions, what is the chance of that contestant winning the bonus?

5. Each contestant picks a category, and then a question is selected from that category. A random selection device picks one of five questions within the category. One of the questions is a hard question, and the other four are easy. The easy questions have the following probabilities of being selected: .30, .15, .05, and .20.

(a) What is the probability of selecting an easy question?

(b) What is the probability of selecting a hard question ?

6. Assume that two urns each contain thousands of marbles. In urn number 1, 80% of the marbles are white and 20% are red. In urn number 2, 90% of the marbles are white and 10% are red. The marbles are randomly dispersed in each urn. A blindfolded person picks up one marble from urn number 1 and one marble from urn number 2.

(a) What is the probability of obtaining two red marbles?

(b) What is the probability of obtaining a red marble from urn number 1 and a white marble from urn number 2?

(c) What is the probability of obtaining a white marble from urn number 1 and a red marble from urn number 2?

(d) What is the probability of obtaining a red and a white marble?

(e) What is the probability of obtaining at least one red marble?

THE BINOMIAL DISTRIBUTION

Assume that you and a friend have jointly purchased a car. You are accustomed to doing things together, so you both assume that there will be little conflict in the use of the car. However, you have decided to prepare in advance for any such difficulties. In case you both need to go in different directions with the car, you will simply toss a coin. When it comes up heads, your friend will use the car. When it comes up tails, you will use it.

Over a period of months there have now been six occasions when you both needed to use the car to go in separate directions. Each time your friend tossed the coin. Each time it came up heads. Given a fair coin fairly tossed, six heads in six tosses would appear to be an unlikely outcome, though not an impossible outcome. Should you be suspicious?

REACHING CONCLUSIONS FROM UNLIKELY EVENTS Suppose your friend tosses the coin 1000 times and it always comes up heads. You will probably assume something like a two-headed coin. On the other hand, if your friend tosses the coin only twice and it comes up heads both times, you will not be inclined toward any suspicion of dishonesty. An issue of interest is, at just what other points, between two and 1000, should you conclude that something has interfered with chance? For example, would six heads in a row be such a point? When an outcome occurs that is extremely unlikely on the basis of chance, you can begin to wonder whether chance alone was all that was operating.

The first step is to try to obtain specific estimates of just what the probability is of any particular outcome, that is, just what percentage of the time will the questionable result occur if only chance is operating?

One way to determine the probability of chance happenings is to set up a situation where only chance is operating, under whatever conditions were originally assumed. For example, in the case of the agreement with your friend, the assumed conditions were a fair coin fairly tossed six times.

An Empirical Model of Chance It would be a simple (though boring) task in this case to simply toss a coin six times, and then continue to do this over and over again, recording the number of heads for each six tosses. In this way, a frequency distribution can be recorded. This will offer an empirically based distribution of the relative frequencies of events. An empirical distribution is one based on observations. Suppose you recorded the results of such an effort, as in Table 8.1, which records the number of heads that occurred in each of 1000 hypothetical repetitions of tossing a coin six times. The second column gives the frequency of each possible number of heads and the third column gives the proportions. Assume that these are the same proportional results that you would get with infinite tossing of a coin. For example, six consecutive heads occurred only 10 times in the 1000 repetitions of the coin tossing

TABLE 8.1

Hypothetical frequency of heads in six tosses of a coin, hypothetically repeated 1000 times

Event (No. of Heads)	Frequency (per 1000)	Probability
0	10	.01
1	100	.10
2	240	.24
3	300	.30
4	240	.24
5	100	.10
6	10	.01

procedure. You therefore conclude that your best estimate of the probability of six heads occurring in six tosses of a coin is

$$\text{Probability (6 heads in 6 tosses)} = \frac{10}{1000}$$

$$= .01$$

as shown in the third column of Table 8.1.

Rejecting Initial Assumptions In the above coin tossing example, a fair coin fairly tossed was taken as a set of initial assumptions about the conditions operating in the situation. Then a probability distribution, given in Table 8.1, was constructed by examining the implications of the assumptions (observing the relative frequencies with a fair coin). Therefore, the probability distribution of Table 8.1 is now included in the initial assumptions. These assumptions indicate that six heads in six coin tosses are not to be expected, except as a rare event; that is, six heads in six coin tosses can be classed as an unlikely event.

When an unlikely event occurs, there are two options. It can be concluded that a rare event has been witnessed, or it can be concluded that the initial assumptions about the situation are incorrect. For example, perhaps your friend was not tossing a fair coin. This would be an example of interference with the operation of chance. You can recognize or at least suspect this interference when an event occurs that is unlikely, given chance. Table 8.1 is the picture or model of chance for this example.

In general, in statistical inference, when an unlikely event occurs, the initial assumptions that make the event unlikely are rejected. The probability distribution associated with those assumptions is rejected.

If we can reject our initial assumptions, then we can usually draw some alternative conclusion of interest. For example, if you conclude that the sampled outcome is not one that would be likely to result from a fair coin fairly tossed, you will probably conclude that your friend was cheating.

The Null Hypothesis When we plan to check the validity of some initial assumptions, we call the set of initial assumptions our **null hypothesis.** When the assumptions lead to a probability distribution, the probability distribution is then part of our null hypothesis.

The term null hypothesis comes from the word nullify, which means to negate, and the word hypothesis, which refers to a tentative assumption. A null hypothesis, then, is a tentative assumption that there may be reason to nullify. In the car agreement, the null hypothesis is that a fair coin has been fairly tossed. The **null hypothesis distribution** is always a probability distribution of chance events. A distribution of chance events is identified so as to offer a contrast with some possible non-chance outcome. Given interference with chance, events that are not likely outcomes under the null hypothesis may become likely. Experiments are generally run to see if the outcomes nullify the assumption that a chance distribution is operating.

Hypotheses and assumptions in everyday life are notions about what is expected and what appears to be true. But the statistical concept of a null hypothesis is generally a set of assumptions under suspicion. When a null hypothesis is rejected, it is a confirmation of underlying doubts about the assumptions.

In the coin tossing example, the coin's status as a fair coin is under suspicion. The null hypothesis is that the coin is fair. The probability distribution for the null hypothesis is the distribution for a fair coin. The experiment is the six coin tosses by your friend. The finding of six heads is the experimental outcome. The experimental outcome is tested against the probability distribution of the null hypothesis. The answer (fair coin or not) depends on whether the experimental outcome appears to have been an unlikely event.

In order to reject a null hypothesis, we must be able to identify unlikely events. For this reason, tests of statistical hypotheses always begin by specifying a probability distribution that is implied by the initial assumptions. The probability distribution will specify the probability of every possible event.

For most purposes it is not necessary to derive the distribution empirically. For example, we do not need to toss coins endlessly. Rather, the probability distributions can generally be derived mathematically from the initial assumptions. Probability distributions that are mathematically derived from initial assumptions are called **theoretical probability distributions.** In the next section, the derivation of a theoretical probability distribution for coin tossing is illustrated.

You will not have to derive theoretical probability distributions in order to use statistical procedures. The most frequently used probability distributions have already been developed by mathematical statisticians. Therefore, most statistical procedures simply require selecting the correct probability distribution for expected outcomes, for any specific set of initial assumptions. The probability distribution is then used to identify unlikely outcomes, and can serve to signal interference with chance. But it will be helpful for you to follow the development of a probability distribution from initial assumptions in at least one instance. It merely entails applying the axioms and theorems of probability that were presented in the preceding chapter on probability.

A THEORETICAL PROBABILITY DISTRIBUTION FOR COIN TOSSING In this section, the theoretical probability distribution for the outcomes from the fair tossing of a fair coin are developed. This will serve as a demonstration of the mathematical derivation of a probability distribution from some initial assumptions. The assumptions here are those of a fair coin fairly tossed. This means that the probability of a head, p, equals the probability of a tail, $1-p$, which equals .5. The outcome of every toss is independent of every other toss.

Given these simple assumptions of $p = 1-p = .5$, and every toss independent of the outcome of every other toss, what is the probability of two heads in a row? or three heads? or six heads?

The occurrence of several events (two or more) was described in the chapter on probability as a joint event. It was simultaneously described as an "and relation." The probability of a joint event, when it involves events which are independent of each other, is the product of the individual probabilities [expressed mathematically in Equation (7.8)]. Thus, the probability of two heads occurring on two consecutive tosses is $p \cdot p = (.5)^2 = .25$. The probability of three consecutive heads occurring is $p^3 = (.5)^3 = .125$. The probability of two heads and then a tail is $p^2(1-p) = (.5)^2(.5) = (.5)^3$, which again is .125. The probability of six heads occurring on six consecutive tosses is $p^6 = (.5)^6 = .015625$. The probability of three consecutive tails, followed by three consecutive heads, is $p^3(1-p)^3 = (.5)^3(.5)^3 = (.5)^6$, which again equals .015625.

It should be clear by now that the probability of any specific sequence of coin toss outcomes, for a fair coin, is always $(.5)^n$, where n is the number of times that the coin is tossed. Thus, any single sequence resulting from six tosses has a probability of $(.5)^6 = .015625$. All of the possible sequences from three tosses of a coin are listed in the first column of Table 8.2. The second column indicates that any single sequence resulting from three tosses has a probability of $(.5)^3 = .125$. Think of each sequence as a sample point in the sample space of outcomes from three coin tosses, each with a probability of .125.

TABLE 8.2

Probabilities for sequences of heads and tails, and for specified numbers of heads, from three tosses of a fair coin. The sequences of H's and T's represent the different possible sequences of heads and tails. The fourth column is the probability of a specified number of heads, requiring the addition of the probabilities of all the sequences through which a specified number of heads can occur.

Sample Points (Sequence)	Probability of Sample Points (Sequence)	Events (Number of Heads)	Probability of Events (Probability of Specified Number of Heads)
TTT	.125	0	Prob. 0 heads = .125
HTT	.125	1	
THT	.125	1	Prob. 1 head = 3(.125) = .375
TTH	.125	1	
		3 sequences	
HHT	.125	2	
HTH	.125	2	Prob. 2 heads = 3(.125) = .375
THH	.125	2	
		3 sequences	
HHH	.125	3	Prob. 3 heads = .125

Table 8.2 has another (third) column, labeled Events. An event refers to a specified number of heads. For example, HTT, THT, and TTH are three sequences (sample points), all qualifying as the same event of one head. The event of one head occurs when *any* of these three sequences (sample points) occurs. This is clearly an "or relation," since any one or the other of these three sequences qualifies as the event of one head. Therefore, Equation (7.6), the third axiom of probability, is used to obtain the probability of one head.

$$P(\text{one head in three tosses}) = P(\text{HTT}) + P(\text{THT}) + P(\text{TTH}) \qquad (8.1)$$
$$= .125 + .125 + .125$$
$$= 3(.125)$$
$$= .375.$$

Equation (7.6) is also used to obtain the probability of two heads. Both of these computations are summarized in the last column of Table 8.2. Where only one sequence qualifies as a particular outcome, the probability of that sequence and the event are the same. This is seen in the last column for the events of zero and three heads.

Summarizing, the theorem for joint events ["and relations," Equation (7.8)] is used to obtain the probability of any individual sequence, and the third axiom of probability ["or relations," Equation (7.6)] is additionally incorporated to obtain the probability of any event attainable through more than one sequence.

The last column of Table 8.2 is a mathematically derived probability distribution for the outcomes of three tosses of a fair coin. The preceding section described how the theorem for joint events [Equation (7.8)] and the third axiom of probability [Equation (7.6)] generated the desired probabilities. These two components of the theory of probability can be incorporated within a single equation for computing the probability of a specified number of heads. Equation (8.2a) offers the formula for the tossing of three coins.

$$\text{Probability of } X \text{ heads} \atop \text{(in three tosses)} = \left(\begin{matrix} \text{number of ways that } X \text{ heads} \\ \text{can occur in three tosses} \end{matrix}\right)(.5)^3 \quad (8.2a)$$

When computing the probability of one head in three tosses, the verbal part of the formula in Equation (8.2a) becomes the number 3,

$$\begin{aligned} \text{Probability of one head} && \\ \text{(in three tosses)} &= 3(.5)^3 \\ &= 3(.125) \\ &= .375, \end{aligned}$$

as detailed in column 4 of Table 8.2.

Equation (8.2a) can be expressed more generally for any number of coin tosses, as seen in Equation (8.2b).

$$\text{Probability of } X \text{ heads} \atop \text{(in } n \text{ tosses)} = \left(\begin{matrix} \text{number of ways that } X \text{ heads} \\ \text{can occur in } n \text{ tosses} \end{matrix}\right)(.5)^n \quad (8.2b)$$

Earlier in this chapter, a probability distribution for six coin tosses was needed. It was suggested that tossing six coins 1000 times would yield the needed probability distribution. Table 8.1 was the hypothetical result of this assumed coin tossing project. Now it can be seen that Equation (8.2b) could be used, rather than going through such a coin tossing procedure.

In applying Equation (8.2b), a problem arises when dealing with larger numbers of coin tosses. The verbal phrase in the formula is "number of ways that X heads can occur in n tosses." This number was easily obtained for three coin tosses. Every possible arrangement of H and T was listed, given the three positions to be filled (as in the first column of Table 8.2). But when dealing with more than three or four coin tosses, the number of possible outcomes becomes very large. For example, for six coin tosses, there are 64 different sequences of heads and tails that can occur. Simply listing all the possible sequences (as in the first column of Table 8.2) is not only cumbersome, but will probably lead to omissions and duplications of sequences. Fortunately, there is a formula for obtaining the "number of ways that X heads can occur in n coin tosses." The formula is symbolized as $\binom{n}{X}$, and is called the **binomial coefficient.** The literature on the binomial coefficient generally discusses the binomial coefficient as the number of ways of obtaining X successes in n trials (where, in coin tossing examples, heads usually constitute successes, and the number of coin tosses constitutes the number of trials).

The Binomial Coefficient The formula for the binomial coefficient is given in Equation (8.3).

$$\binom{n}{X} = \text{number of ways that } X \text{ successes can occur in } n \text{ trials.} \quad (8.3)$$

$$\binom{n}{X} = \frac{n!}{(n-X)!\,X!}$$

The $n!$ in Equation (8.3) is called n factorial, and

$$n! = n(n-1)(n-2)\cdots 1$$

For example,

$$3! = 3\cdot 2\cdot 1$$
$$= 6$$

and

$$4! = 4\cdot 3\cdot 2\cdot 1$$
$$= 24.$$

If $n = 6$ and $X = 2$, the binomial coefficient is computed from

$$n! = 6!$$
$$= 6\cdot 5\cdot 4\cdot 3\cdot 2\cdot 1$$

and

$$X! = 2!$$
$$= 2\cdot 1$$

and

$$(n-X)! = (6-2)!$$
$$= 4!$$
$$= 4\cdot 3\cdot 2\cdot 1.$$

Applying Equation (8.3) to $\binom{6}{2}$,

$$\binom{6}{2} = \frac{6!}{(6-2)!2!}$$

$$= \frac{6 \cdot 5 \cdot 4 \cdot 3 \cdot 2 \cdot 1}{4!2!}$$

$$= \frac{6 \cdot 5 \cdot 4!}{4!2!}$$

$$= \frac{6 \cdot 5}{2!}$$

$$= 15.$$

It was stated above that the binomial coefficient, $\binom{n}{X}$, gives the number of ways of obtaining X heads in n coin tosses. More generally, the binomial coefficient gives the number of ways of obtaining X successes and $n - X$ failures in n trials. Equivalently, the binomial coefficient gives the number of ways in which X items can be selected from among n items, or X people from among n people, and so on. (Each person, analogously to a coin, undergoes a trial in which the person does or does not succeed in being selected.) For example, suppose an officer has to select two out of six soldiers to go on a dangerous mission. How many different selections are possible? That is, how many different combinations of two men can be selected from six men? The binomial coefficient, Equation (8.3), computes that value from $\binom{6}{2}$ as 15.

As another example, suppose you take an exam and have to guess on six of the questions. You later find out that you guessed correctly on just two of the six questions, but you were not told which ones. The binomial coefficient $\binom{6}{2}$ = 15 tells you that there are 15 different possible combinations of two successes in six trials. Therefore, there are 15 different ways that you could have gotten a total of two out of six questions correct.

Continuing to apply Equation (8.3), you would find that

$$\binom{6}{1} = 6,$$

$$\binom{6}{3} = 20,$$

etc.

In working out the value of $\binom{6}{0}$ you may have some difficulty, since the value of 0! in

$$\binom{6}{0} = \frac{6!}{(6-0)!0!}$$

has not yet been defined. We define 0! as

$$0! = 1,$$

so that

$$\binom{6}{0} = \frac{6!}{(6-0)!0!}$$

$$= \frac{6!}{6!0!}$$

$$= \frac{6!}{6!1}$$

$$= 1.$$

Substituting the more general n for the specific value of 6,

$$\binom{n}{0} = \frac{n!}{(n-0)!0!}$$

$$= \frac{n!}{n!1}$$

$$= 1.$$

A verbal equivalent of

$$\binom{n}{0} = 1$$

is that there is only one arrangement of zero successes in n trials (or only one sequence with zero heads in n coin tosses).

It should now be possible for you to appreciate how the statement, "number of ways that X heads can occur in n tosses" can be replaced with the binomial coefficient. This transforms Equation (8.2b),

$$\text{Probability of } X \text{ heads (in } n \text{ tosses)} = \left(\begin{array}{c}\text{number of ways that } X \text{ heads}\\ \text{can occur in } n \text{ tosses}\end{array}\right)(.5)^n,$$

into Equation (8.4):

$$\text{Probability of } X \text{ heads (in } n \text{ tosses)} = \binom{n}{x}(.5)^n. \tag{8.4}$$

Specifically, for six coin tosses, equation (8.4) will appear as Equation (8.5).

$$\text{Probability of } X \text{ heads (in 6 tosses)} = \binom{6}{x}(.5)^6 \tag{8.5}$$

Table 8.3 offers the theoretical probability distribution for six tosses of a fair coin, calculated from Equation (8.5).

TABLE 8.3

Probability distribution for six tosses of a fair coin

Number of Heads	Probability	Calculated as Shown
0	.0156	$\binom{6}{0}(.5)^6 = 1(.5)^6$
1	.0936	$\binom{6}{1}(.5)^6 = 6(.5)^6$
2	.2344	$\binom{6}{2}(.5)^6 = 15(.5)^6$
3	.3125	$\binom{6}{3}(.5)^6 = 20(.5)^6$
4	.2344	$\binom{6}{4}(.5)^6 = 15(.5)^6$
5	.0936	$\binom{6}{5}(.5)^6 = 6(.5)^6$
6	.0156	$\binom{6}{6}(.5)^6 = 1(.5)^6$

THEORETICAL ANALYSIS OF THE BINOMIAL DISTRIBUTION

The logic used in developing Equation (8.4)

$$\frac{\text{Probability of } X \text{ heads}}{(\text{in } n \text{ tosses})} = \binom{n}{x}(.5)^n$$

employed the probability theorem for joint events [multiplying the probabilities of independent joint events in $(.5)^n$] and the third axiom of probability [adding the $\binom{n}{x}$ probabilities of mutually exclusive events]. The use of the particular probability of $p = .5$ per trial was not required by the theorem for joint events. The probability of a single trial's success was taken as .5 because the fair tossing of a fair coin was assumed as the physical model.

Suppose a different physical model was used. Suppose there is an urn containing marbles of two colors, red and white. A blindfolded person reaches into the urn and pulls out one marble. After each trial the selected marble is placed back into the urn. The urn is then thoroughly mixed before the next trial. In this way the outcomes of successive trials are independent of each other.

Each selection of a marble is called a trial. With coin tossing, the possible outcomes are a head or a tail. With marbles in an urn, the possible outcomes from individual trials are different colored marbles.

What is the probability of a red marble on each trial? If half the marbles are red, the probability of selecting a red marble is ½, yielding precisely the same analysis, and the same probability distribution, as for heads in coin tossing.

Suppose that only 30% of the marbles in an urn are red, and 70% are white, with red representing success. The probability of a success is then .3, with the probability of a failure .7. These respective probabilities for success and failure can be symbolized as $p = .3$ and $(1 - p) = .7$ (the latter being the complement of the former). Assume that there are 10 trials (10 marbles selected from the urn, in the manner described above). What is the probability of four successes followed by six failures?

Each success (red marble) occurs with a probability of $p = .3$. Four such joint occurrences will have a probability of $(p)^4 = (.3)^4$. Six remaining trials with failures (white marbles), each occurring with a probability of $(1-p) = .7$, will have a joint occurrence probability of $(1-p)^6 = (.7)^6$. The probability of the specific sequence will therefore be

$$(p)^4(1-p)^6 = (.3)^4(.7)^6.$$

Again suppose four successes and six failures, but occurring in a different sequence. For example, suppose the first two trials are successes, as well as the last two trials, with the intervening six trials all failures. The probability of this sequence is

$$(p)^2(1-p)^6(p)^2 = (p)^4(1-p)^6$$
$$= (.3)^4(.7)^6,$$

yielding the same probability as for the other sequence containing the same number of successes. We can make the more general statement that when a sequence has X successes and $n-X$ failures, however ordered, the probability of each sequence is the same.

$$\begin{array}{l} \text{Probability of a single sequence} \\ \text{yielding } X \text{ successes in } n \text{ trials} \end{array} = p^X(1-p)^{n-X}.$$

As in the case of the coin tossing equation, it is necessary to determine the number of ways in which a particular event can be realized. There are a number of sequences that can yield four successes and six failures in 10 trials. As in the case of the coin tossing equation, the binomial coefficient is used to determine the number of ways in which X successes can be obtained in n trials. Assuming $\binom{n}{X}$ different ways for X successes, the equation for the probability of X successes in n trials is given by Equation (8.6).

$$\begin{array}{l} \text{The probability of } X \text{ successes} \\ \text{in } n \text{ trials} \end{array} = \binom{n}{X}(p)^X(1-p)^{n-X}. \qquad (8.6)$$

Equation (8.6) is the equation for a frequently occurring probability distribution, called **the binomial distribution.** The equation for the binomial distribution is symbolized by $B(X; n, p)$, allowing for the specification of the number of successes (X), the number of trials (n), and the probability of a single success (p). Using this symbol, Equation (8.6) is restated as Equation (8.7).

$$B(X; n, p) = \binom{n}{X}(p)^X(1-p)^{n-X} \qquad (8.7)$$

The earlier equation for coin tossing, Equation (8.4), is just a special case of the more general equation for the binomial distribution expressed in Equation (8.7). When $p = (1-p) = .5$, Equation (8.7) equals Equation (8.4). Specifically,

$$B(X; n, .5) = \binom{n}{x}(.5)^x(1-.5)^{n-x}$$
$$= \binom{n}{x}(.5)^n.$$

Assumptions of the Binomial Distribution Our interest in the binomial distribution was motivated by the need to find the probabilities of events, given some initial assumptions about the situation yielding the outcomes. It was stated that the initial assumptions would offer the basis for generating (or selecting) the appropriate probability distribution. The assumptions of the examples used in this chapter were found to generate the binomial distribution [Equation (8.7)]. These assumptions are now formally stated.

There are four assumptions necessary for the binomial distribution to accurately model the probabilities of events in a given situation. The assumptions are:

1. We must be able to dichotomize the outcome of every trial. In this context, dichotomize means to divide the possible outcomes of any trial into two mutually exclusive alternatives. Some examples are success versus failure, head versus tail, and right versus wrong.
2. The probability of success (and, of course, failure) must be constant over trials (that is, p must be a constant value).
3. Each trial must be independent of every other trial.
4. There must be a specified number of trials (n).

THE BINOMIAL DISTRIBUTION AS A MODEL OF SURVIVAL IN ILLNESS Suppose the probability of survival from some very serious illness is .3. Assume that there is reason to count the survivals of 10 people at a time in checking on the deadliness of the disease. (For example, a particular hospital ward isolating this illness may have room for 10 patients at a time.) In any one group of 10 patients there can be any number of survivors, up to 10. In looking at many groups of 10 patients, some sort of frequency distribution of numbers of survivors is expected. Given many repetitions of the examination of the survival rate among new groups of 10 patients, there is a certain frequency of zero survivors; another frequency of one out of 10 survivors; another frequency of two out of 10 survivors, etc. This set of frequencies from zero to 10 survivors constitutes the frequency distribution of survival from that illness.

Note that in this situation the outcomes can be dichotomized as success or failure (survival or death). Also, there is a constant probability of success (survival), which is $p = .3$. It is likely that each person's survival is independent of any other person's, and there is a specific number of trials (that is, 10 patients checked for each survival count). Thus, the assumptions for a binomial distribution of the number of survivors have been met.

What does it mean when the assumptions of a particular distribution have been met? It means that the actual distribution of outcomes is expected to match the theoretical probability distribution whose assumptions have been met. In this example, it is expected that the relative frequency of different numbers of survivors (over many years of observing the patients 10 at a time) will be close to the binomial distribution, where $n = 10$ and $p = .3$.

In Equation (8.8) the formula for the binomial distribution is re-expressed with $n = 10$ and $p = .3$.

$$B(X; 10, .3) = \binom{10}{X}(.3)^X(.7)^{10-X}. \qquad (8.8)$$

Using Equation (8.3) for the binomial coefficient, $\binom{n}{X}$, the values of $\binom{10}{0}$, $\binom{10}{1}$, $\binom{10}{2}$, $\cdots$, $\binom{10}{10}$ equal 1, 10, 45, $\cdots$ 1, respectively. The probability of zero successes (survivors) is

$$B(0; 10, .3) = \binom{10}{0}(.3)^0(.7)^{10-0}$$

$$= 1(1)(.0282)$$

$$= .0282.$$

The probability of one success is

$$B(1; 10, .3) = \binom{10}{1}(.3)^1(.7)^{10-1}$$

$$= 10(.3)(.0404)$$

$$= .1211,$$

etc.

Using the values derived from Equation (8.8) as X goes from zero to 10 yields the probabilities in the second column of Table 8.4.

TABLE 8.4
The binomial distribution for $B(X; 10, .3) = \binom{10}{X}(.3)^X(.7)^{10-X}$

Success	Probability	Cumulative Probability
0	.0282	.9999[a]
1	.1211	.9717
2	.2335	.8506
3	.2668	.6171
4	.2001	.3503
5	.1029	.1502
6	.0368	.0473
7	.0090	.0105
8	.0014	.0015
9	.0001	.0001
10	.0000	.0000

[a]Rounding error prevents the cumulative probability distribution from reaching 1.0000.

Assume that a pharmacologist has developed a drug that she believes will improve a person's chances of surviving the illness. Ten volunteers are found who have the illness and are willing to take the new drug.

The logic here is similar to that used in questioning the honesty of the coin tosser in the car example. The null hypothesis is not something which is believed, but something which is doubted. There is probably some reasonable expectation that the drug will work, or it would not be tested. But the null hypothesis is that the drug will *not* work. There is an advantage in assuming an ineffective independent variable as the null hypothesis. By assuming an ineffective independent variable, we know what to expect if the drug does not work. Table 8.4, derived from the equation for the binomial distribution, spells out the probabilities of all the possible survival outcomes, given that the drug does not have any effect. If an **unlikely event** (an unusual number of survivors) occurs among the 10 patients given the drug, it can be recognized by referring to Table 8.4, where the specific probability of any outcome is given. For example, if 10 out of 10 patients survive, Table 8.4 indicates that this event will occur *less* than once in 10,000 such tests, if the drug has no effect. (Carried to six decimal places, the bottom row in Table 8.4 would show a probability of .000006 for 10 survivors.)

Given such a rare event, we are faced with the conclusion that a very rare event has occurred, or else that the assumed binomial distribution, $B(X; 10, .3)$ is not accurate. Perhaps the drug *is* effective, changing the probability of survival for those receiving the drug. Then $p = .3$ is the wrong value for p in $B(X; n, p)$. Which is more likely? The occurrence of an event that is expected to occur less than one time in 10,000 times, or an effective drug?

The above argument suggests that given 10 survivors among a group of 10 patients who have received the drug, there is reason to draw a conclusion contrary to the null hypothesis. We can conclude that the drug is effective. Further, the probability of being wrong after having drawn such a conclusion is specifiable. The probability obtained with $B(10; 10, .3)$ indicates the probability of a false conclusion (the probability of 10 survivors with an ineffective drug).

In summary, the pharmacologist, like any other experimenter, has set up a null hypothesis of an ineffective independent variable. If the evidence discredits the null hypothesis, a contrary conclusion (of an effective independent variable) will have been reached.

CRITICAL VALUES It was indicated that an especially unlikely outcome, such as 10 survivors among 10 patients in the drug example, would have clearly allowed the pharmacologist to reject the null hypothesis (and thus conclude that the drug was effective). It is possible to incorporate more than one possible result into the class of unlikely outcomes. For example, "nine or 10 survivors" could be defined as the class of unlikely outcomes. The probabilities of both nine and 10 survivors, as given in Table 8.4, could both be added; that is, when incorporating more than one possible event into the class of unlikely outcomes, axiom 3 of probability theory (for "or relations") must be followed. This has been done in the third column of Table 8.4, where the probabilities of events are cumulated upward beginning with 10 successes. In the third column, we see that nine or 10 survivors is an outcome that will only occur about once in 10,000 times, given the normal course of the disease (and an ineffective drug). Thus, the null hypothesis can reasonably be rejected with nine as well as 10 survivors. Continuing up the third column of Table 8.4, "seven or more survivors" is an outcome which is expected to occur only about once in 100 times, given an ineffective drug. If being wrong on the average of once every 100 times in such decisions is an acceptable probability of error, seven or more survivors is an acceptable criterion for rejecting the null hypothesis.

If seven or more survivors are selected as the definition of an unlikely event, then 7 is called the **critical value**. The critical value is the least extreme value included in the set of possible events that leads to rejection of the null hypothesis. Reaching or surpassing the critical value signals the rejection of the null hypothesis.

Type I Errors   If 6 is taken as the critical value in Table 8.4, the third column of the table indicates that it will be erroneously concluded that the drug was effective 5% of the time. Five percent of the time a true null hypothesis will be believed to be false. Using 7 as the critical value, a true null hypothesis will only be erroneously rejected 1% of the time (as seen in the third column).

The type of error that is made in erroneously rejecting a true null hypothesis is called a **Type I error**. The probability of a Type I error is often symbolized by the Greek letter alpha (α), and so is sometimes called the alpha error.

Since the Type I error consists of erroneously rejecting a true null hypothesis, it can only be made when the null hypothesis is true, but the critical value is nonetheless reached or surpassed. In the above drug example, the null hypothesis is true if the pharmacologist is testing an ineffective drug.

It may be helpful to illustrate the concept of a Type I error with a story. In the heart of the Amazon region of South America, there are a number of widely separated Indian villages whose inhabitants share a common language and customs. Their remote ancestors all lived together in one village. But at the point in time of this story, the different villages had little contact with each other. In fact, their only contact was the rare occasion when an ostracized native was forced to leave a village and seek a new home in another village. Of course, expatriates were always greeted with suspicion in a new village, and were never accepted unless they could prove their usefulness with some needed skill.

In the village of Shokum there was a young man who constantly followed the village shaman, hoping to learn the secrets of his magic, so that he himself could someday be a shaman. The shaman, for his part, was afraid to have his secrets learned, so he contrived to turn the villagers against the young aspirant. The young man, whose Indian name translates as "thin twig" or "skinny," eventually had to leave the village.

When Skinny left, he determined to come to some new village as a shaman. The problem was to offer some proof of magical abilities. All that he had been able to learn from watching the old shaman were some authoritative mannerisms, some standard ceremonies, and some incantations. He instinctively knew that these things would be enough to maintain the role of shaman, if only the new villagers believed that he had the powers of an authentic shaman. What he needed was some impressive initial indication of powers that would assure him of acceptance by the new villagers.

Skinny found the way. Although he could not personally label his inspiration in our terms, he intuitively understood that he could use a Type I error to appear to possess magical powers. He recognized that a patient man could use a rare event to suggest a miracle.

In this area of the Amazon, there is a type of three-leaf clover which offers an omnipresent outdoor carpet. There is a mutant strain, evenly mixed throughout the ground cover of clover, which has four leaves. The natives in all the villages consider the finding of such a four-leaf clover an omen of good fortune.

The now homeless Skinny had hoped to improve his own fortunes by finding as many four-leaf clovers as he could, carrying them with him in his search for a new village. In the process of searching for these four-leaf clovers, he got the impression that approximately one out of every 20 clovers was a four-leaf clover. He checked and rechecked this initial impression, and eventually became confident that this was true. At this point his mind grasped the insight of a Type I error and, with this in mind, he set out for his first village.

He entered the village and was first met by village elders and young children. Other adults who were momentarily idle joined the curious crowd. Skinny spoke of his magic powers and all that he might do for those he favored. Then, suddenly, he touched one of the children on the shoulder and said, "When you next stoop to pick up a clover, it will be a four-leaf clover." Eagerly, the child bent down and, frowning, held up a three-leaf clover. The elders and other onlookers laughed the would-be shaman out of the village.

Skinny then went on to the next village. He again repeated the routine. Again a selected child picked up a clover, and again it was a three-leaf clover. Again the expatriate was laughed out of the village.

Eventually, after many such attempts, patience gave him the desired rare event. He had barely finished his promise of a four-leaf clover, when a childish shriek of delight raised the hair on the backs of ancient necks. The child was dancing up and down with his tightly clutched four-leaf clover, while the elders were calling to all who had not been present. Told the story, all crowded forward to touch the new shaman, prepared to believe all that he would thenceforth say. Their new medicine man had been born of a Type I error.

From the point of view of the Amazon villagers, there was only one sample, and it consisted of only one trial. The conclusion of a "miracle" (controlled production of a rare event) was based on a single event of a four-leaf clover. There was no opportunity for the selection of a more extreme critical value in the miniature experiment at each village. But suppose that Skinny had been afraid of some cynical villagers, and had determined to make his miracle the occurrence of an even more unlikely event. He could have repeated his promise of a four-leaf clover twice in each village. If he had done this, the villagers would have had an option of accepting him as a miracle worker only if he had produced two four-leaf clovers, or they could possibly have accepted him with only one four-leaf clover in two tries. This would have been an example of a choice of critical values. What would have been the null hypothesis probability distribution if there were two trials in each village? Table 8.5 gives the probability distribution for zero to two successes in two trials, with a probability of a success in a single trial being one in 20 ($p = .05$).

As seen in Table 8.5, where $B(2; 2, .05) = .0025$, Skinny would have been homeless for a long time if the villagers insisted on two out of two four-leaf clovers. Note that, given an option, the people in a village could have protected themselves against a Type I error by using a higher critical value, that is, the more stringent test. Similarly, in the drug example, greater protection against acceptance of an ineffective drug would be obtained through higher critical values (as illustrated in the prior discussion of Table 8.4).

TABLE 8.5

Probability distribution for finding zero to two four-leaf clovers in two trials, where $p = .05$, in $B(X; 2, .05)$

Number of Four-Leaf Clovers	Probability	Cumulative Probability
0	$\binom{2}{0}(.05)^0(.95)^2 = .9025$	1.000
1	$\binom{2}{1}(.05)^1(.95)^1 = .0950$	.0975
2	$\binom{2}{2}(.05)^2(.95)^0 = .0025$	.0025

It may seem advisable to always use the most extreme critical value possible (such as 10 in Table 8.4). Unfortunately, there is another type of error, a **Type II error**, which can be made. As the probability of a Type I error is made smaller by changing the critical value, the probability of a Type II error is made larger.

Type II Errors   A Type II error is made whenever we fail to reject a false null hypothesis. For example, a Type II error is made if we fail to recognize that a new and powerful drug has healing powers. Whereas Type I errors are erroneous rejections of the null hypothesis, Type II errors are erroneous failures to reject it. A Type II error, then, can only be made with an effective independent variable, and when the critical value has not been reached. The probability of a Type II error is often symbolized by the Greek letter beta (β), and so is sometimes called the **beta error**.

In making statistical decisions, we generally decide on the probability of a Type I error that we are willing to risk. This, in turn, determines the critical value to be used in making the decision. The Type II error probabilities are related to the Type I error probabilities. But the relationship is not a simple one. We generally do not know the specific probability of making a Type II error.

Just as Type I errors can be made only when the null hypothesis is true, Type II errors can be made only when an **alternative distribution** is the correct distribution (and not recognized as such). For example, a new drug may improve survival from .3 to .5, or to .7 or to 1.0 (if the drug cures everyone). Higher average survival rates mean that the two distributions are further apart. Figure 8.1 shows two binomial distributions, where the only difference is in the p values [$B(X; 10, .3)$ and $B(X; 10, .7)$]. The further apart the null hypothesis distribution and the alternative distribution, the more likely that the null hypothesis will be recognized as false. This is because more of the true alternative distribution is beyond the critical value being used. A higher proportion of samples from the alternative distribution will yield values beyond the critical value as defined on the null hypothesis distribution.

If we know the probabilities of the alternative distribution, we can be specific about the probability of obtaining values that are beyond the critical value. It would then be possible to be specific about the probability of rejecting the null hypothesis when an alternative distribution is the correct distribution.

Unfortunately, we never know the probability values within the alternative distribution. Only the null hypothesis distribution can be specified (from the initial assumptions about how chance operates in the experimental situation).

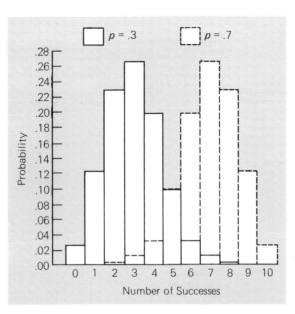

FIGURE 8.1
Two overlapping binomial distributions, where the only difference is in the p values; $p = .3$ versus $p = .7$

However, your understanding of Type II errors will be enhanced by our pretending to know the alternative distribution in a hypothetical situation. Specifying a true alternative distribution enables us to estimate the probability of a Type II error, giving the concept greater specificity. Therefore, we will pretend to know the alternative distribution in one example. The major purpose of the unrealistic assumption and following discussion is to clarify the important relationship between Type I and Type II errors.

Assume again that a scientist is testing a new drug. Further, assume that the drug actually increases the probability of survival from .3 to .7. This means that the null hypothesis that the drug is ineffective is incorrect. The probability of survival is therefore not represented by the null hypothesis distribution, which in this case has $p = .3$, but by the binomial distribution for which $p = .7$. Table 8.6 presents the probabilities and cumulative probabilities for both probability distributions, with $n = 10$, assuming again that there are 10 trials (10 patients) in the experiment.

The first three columns of Table 8.6 are simply a restatement of Table 8.4 for the binomial distribution with $n = 10$ and $p = .3$. The last two columns are the probabilities and cumulative probabilities, respectively, for the binomial distribution with $n = 10$ and $p = .7$. The second column of Table 8.6, then, offers the null hypothesis distribution, and the fourth column offers the alternative distribution for this example.

TABLE 8.6

Contrast of a null hypothesis distribution, $B(X; 10, .3)$, and an alternative distribution, $B(X, 10, .7)$

Successes (Survivors)	Null Hypothesis Distribution		Alternative Distribution	
	Probability with $p = .3$	Cumulative Probability	Probability with $p = .7$	Cumulative Probability
0	.0282	.9999[a]	.0000	.9999[a]
1	.1211	.9717	.0001	.9999
2	.2335	.8506	.0014	.9998
3	.2668	.6171	.0090	.9984
4	.2001	.3503	.0368	.9894
5	.1029	.1502	.1029	.9526
6	.0368	.0473	.2001	.8497
7	.0090	.0105	.2668	.6496
8	.0014	.0015	.2335	.3828
9	.0001	.0001	.1211	.1493
10	.0000	.0000	.0282	.0282

[a]Includes rounding error.

Suppose the critical value chosen by the scientist was 7. According to the null hypothesis distribution ($p = .3$), the critical value of 7 is reached or surpassed only 1% of the time (.0105 in the row for seven successes in the third column of Table 8.6). But we are now assuming that the drug is effective, so $p = .3$ no longer correctly describes the survival rate. We assume instead that (unknown to the scientist) the new distribution has $p = .7$. A value of 7 has a probability of .6496 of being reached or surpassed, when $p = .7$. Thus, given an effective drug which improves survival probability from .3 to .7, and a critical value of 7 survivors, the probability of recognizing the drug as effective is about .65. The probability of not reaching the critical value (the probability of obtaining a value less than 7) is the probability of a Type II error. When the critical value is 7, the probability of a Type II error is the probability of *not* having an outcome of 7 or more. This being a "not relation," the probability of a Type II error is 1.00 − .65 = .35. The probability of the Type II error can be reduced by reducing the critical value. For example, the critical value of 6 is expected to be reached or surpassed about 85% of the time, as seen in the fifth column (which shows .8497 as the cumulative probability in the row for 6 successes). The probability of a Type II error will then be 1.00 − .85 = .15. Thus, in reducing the critical value from 7 to 6 in this example, the probability of a Type II error is reduced from .35 to .15.

In summary, the choice of a critical value sets both the Type I and Type II error probabilities. The critical value, however, is usually selected to set the

Type I error at a predetermined level. For the drug example, this is done by consulting the third column in Table 8.6, finding the row of the desired Type I error level, and using the survival number in that row as the critical value. Although the Type II error also follows from this choice, the fourth and fifth columns of Table 8.6 are not normally available to the researcher. Therefore, the specific probability of the Type II error associated with any critical value is not known. All that is known is that <u>the larger (more extreme) the critical value that is selected in controlling the probability of a Type I error, the larger the resulting probability of a Type II error.</u>

Later, another way of adjusting Type I errors to minimize Type II errors will be discussed. This appears in Chapter 9 under the topic of one- versus two-tailed tests of significance. Also, in Chapter 10 it will be shown how increasing the sample size will reduce the probability of a Type II error.

Table 8.7 summarizes the relationship between the true state of the null hypothesis and which error, if any, has been made, as a function of whether or not the critical value has been reached. The key to this three-way relationship is the true state of the null hypothesis (indicated in the left-hand margin of Table 8.7).

TABLE 8.7
Relationship between the true state of the null hypothesis, and which error, if any, has been made, as a function of whether or not the critical value has been reached

	Reached Critical Value	Did Not Reach Critical Value
When the Null Hypothesis Is True	Type I error	No error
When the Null Hypothesis Is False	No error	Type II error

We can only know if there has been an error if we know the true state of the null hypothesis. But we never really know the true state of the null hypothesis. When the null hypothesis is rejected, it is rejected with some probability of a Type I error. When it is not rejected, this decision, too, entails the probability of error (the Type II error). Whatever our conclusion, there is always some probability of error. We cannot know with certainty whether or not the null hypothesis is correct. The discussion of types of error, then, is really a theoretical discussion. It concerns the kinds of error that can be made, and the way in which the selection of a critical value affects the probabilities of these errors. But we can never know in a specific statistical test whether or not we have actually made an error in our decision.

Statistical Significance When the critical value has been reached or surpassed, it is common practice to say that **statistical significance** has been obtained. Statistical significance is not synonymous with social significance, or meaningfulness, although it is often associated with meaningful findings. Statistical significance is an expression which is equivalent to stating that the critical value has been reached or surpassed. It then implies that the null hypothesis has been rejected. In terms of more specific conclusions, statistical significance signifies the acceptance of some relationship between the variables. For example, assume that statistical significance is obtained in a study of the effect of a drug on an illness. This is synonymous with the conclusion that the drug has an effect on the course of the illness.

Controlling the Probability of Being Wrong

An important contribution of statistical techniques is that the probability of being wrong in drawing conclusions about relationships between variables can be controlled. The statistician or experimenter decides on a Type I error probability and sets the critical value accordingly. The Type I error probability tells the experimenter the percentage of time that ineffective variables will be erroneously classified as effective (that is, percentage of time that true null hypotheses will be rejected as false). In the drug example, a Type I error level of .05 means that 5% of useless drugs will be classified as useful.

When statistical significance is not reached, a Type II error is possible. A drug can be useful but not be recognized as such. Therefore, some percentage of the time, when working with useful drugs, they will not be recognized as useful. However, we generally cannot be specific about the probability of missing the fact that an effective drug is, in fact, effective. As discussed above, there are a number of factors influencing the probability of failing to recognize a true alternative distribution. For example, it depends on how effective the drug is. This lack of specificity about the probability of a Type II error removes one of the important advantages to statistical decisions. Saying that you may be wrong, while not knowing the probability of being wrong, is not saying very much.

An important difference, then, between Type I and Type II errors is that we can be specific about the probability of Type I errors, but we usually lack that specificity for Type II errors.*

In summary, the main advantage of statistically developed conclusions is that we can control the probability of being wrong in our conclusions. We control Type I error probabilities by selecting critical values in keeping with the Type I error probability we are willing to accept. This, in turn, affects the Type II error probability. The Type II error probability is inversely related to the Type I error probability when the Type I error probability is changed through adjustment of the critical value. But we are usually unable to specify the resulting probability of the Type II error.

Verbalizing Statistically-Based Conclusions When we may be making a Type I error (that is, when we have statistical significance), we are free to state our conclusions with almost no qualifications. For example, in our drug example we would say, "The drug appears to be effective," or, "The evidence indicates that the drug increases the chances of survival from the illness." We may be wrong, but we do not have to express this possibility in our statement. The Type I error probability used in selecting the critical value is always reported with the research. The Type I error probability specifies the probability of our having incorrectly classified an ineffective variable as effective.

On the other hand, if we do not have statistical significance (suggesting the possibility of a Type II error), we do *not* state that the evidence suggests that the drug is *in*effective. Lack of specificity about the probability of a Type II error limits the usefulness of a statement about ineffectiveness. Therefore, given lack of statistical significance, we hedge and say something like, "There is no evidence that the drug is effective."

In summary, when we reach or exceed our critical value, achieving statistical significance, we can draw conclusions from our research. When we do not have statistical significance, we generally suspend judgment.†

---

*There are some assumptions and considerations that can yield some estimates of the Type II error. These are described, with many very helpful tables, in an excellent book on the topic of Type II errors: *Statistical Power Analysis for the Behavioral Sciences, Revised Edition,* by Jacob Cohen (New York: Academic Press, 1977).

†An article presenting arguments in favor of acceptance of the null hypothesis under some conditions of nonsignificance, rather than suspending judgment, is: Greenwald, Anthony G. "Consequences of Prejudice Against the Null Hypothesis." (*Psychological Bulletin,* 1975, *82,* 1–20.) An article that discusses the way in which problems in experimental design can lead to incorrect acceptance of the null hypothesis is presented in the "History of the Sleeper Effect: Some Logical Pitfalls in Accepting the Null Hypothesis." by Thomas D. Cook, et al. (*Psychological Bulletin,* 1979, *86,* 662–679.)

SENTENCE COMPLETIONS

The following incomplete sentences are taken from the underlined sentences in this chapter. Fill in the missing words and phrases and then correct them from the answers which follow.

1. When we plan to check the validity of some initial assumptions, we call the set of initial assumptions our _____ _____.

2. In statistical inference, when an unlikely event occurs, we _____ our initial assumptions. Then we can usually draw some _____ conclusion.

3. A null hypothesis is a tentative _____ that we may have reason to nullify.

4. In order to reject our null hypothesis, we need to be able to identify unlikely events. Therefore, we need a _____ _____.

5. It is our statement of initial assumptions that will allow us to develop or select the appropriate _____ _____.

6. We use the _____ _____ to determine the number of ways in which we obtain X successes in n trials. Each potential sequence of X successes in n trials has a probability of $(p)^x(1-p)^{n-x}$. Assuming $\binom{n}{x}$ different ways for X successes, the equation for the probability of X successes in n trials is given by $B(X; n, p) = \binom{n}{x}p^x(1-p)^{n-x}$. This is called the equation for the _____.

7. There is a set of sample values (outcomes) that will cause us to reject our null hypothesis. The least extreme value leading to rejection of the null hypothesis is called the _____ value.

8. The type of error that is made in erroneously _____ the null hypothesis is called a Type I error.

9. We can only make the Type I error when the null hypothesis is _____ but we have nonetheless reached or surpassed the critical value.

10. We generally do not know the probability of our making a Type _____ error.

11. If we use a more extreme critical value, we _____ the probability of a Type I error. At the same time, we _____ the probability of a Type II error.

12. A Type II error is made whenever we fail to reject a _____ null hypothesis.

13. A Type II error can only be made when
    a. the _____   _____ has not been reached;
    b. the independent variable is _____; and
    c. the null hypothesis is _____.

14. The Type I error is sometimes called the _____ error, and the Type II error is sometimes called the _____ error.

15. Discussions of Type I and Type II errors are always with reference to probabilities. In any specific instance, we _____ _____ whether or not we have made an error.

16. Statistical significance is an expression which is equivalent to stating that the critical value _____.

17. Statistical significance implies that the null hypothesis has been _____ .

18. Statistical significance signifies the _____ of a relationship between variables.

19. An important contribution of statistical techniques is that the probability of being wrong in drawing conclusions about relationships between variables _____.

20. An important difference between Type I and Type II errors is that we can be specific about _____, but _____ _____.

21. When we achieve _____   _____ , we can draw conclusions from our research. When we _____ , we generally suspend judgment.

PROBLEMS

1. There are four assumptions necessary for the binomial distribution to accurately model the outcome probabilities in a given situation. What are these four assumptions?

2. $4! =$

3. $0! =$

4. If $n = 9$ and $X = 6$, $\binom{n}{X} =$

5. If $n = 5$ and $X = 3$, $\binom{n}{X} =$

6. If $n = 5$ and $p = .3$, the probability distribution for $B(X; n, p)$ is

X	Probability
0	_____
1	_____
2	_____
3	_____
4	_____
5	_____

7. What is the probability of four or more occurrences of success in the distribution of problem 6?

8. Assume that you have a room containing hundreds of urns, each filled with both red and white marbles. In the different urns the red and white marbles are in different proportions.

   You pick out one marble from one urn, and then put it back. You then mix up all the marbles in that urn, and again reach into that same urn, taking out a second marble. You do this repeatedly, until you take out five marbles.

   The label has been removed from the urn, so that you cannot be sure of the proportions of red and white marbles in that particular urn. You are interested in testing whether this is the urn in which there are $p = .3$ white and $(1-p) = .7$ red marbles. You therefore select $B(X; 5, .3)$ as your null hypothesis distribution. You want to see if your empirical results allow you to reject your null hypothesis.

(a) If this is the urn for which $p = .3$, what is the probability of your obtaining four or more white marbles out of your five randomly selected marbles?

(b) Assume that you decide that four or more white marbles is your critical value. Further, assume that the null hypothesis ($p = .3$) is in fact true. What is the probability of your making a Type I error?

9. Given an unlikely outcome from a set of assumptions, we can conclude that we have witnessed an unusual event. What other conclusion can we reach?

10. A man claims to have extrasensory perception (ESP). To test his claim, five cards are made up, each of which contains one number from 1 to 5. The cards are shuffled, and one is drawn while kept from the man's view. He then guesses which card was drawn (guessing which number was on the card). This procedure is repeated 10 times, so that the man makes a total of 10 guesses.

   If the man were only guessing, he would have a probability of $1/5 = .2$ of being correct on any one trial. Since the cards are shuffled before each trial, each trial (each guess) is independent of any other, and the probability of being correct, $p = .2$, is a constant value. We have met the assumptions for the binomial distribution, with $n = 10$ and $p = .2$ (if the man does not have ESP and is only guessing). The probability distribution for the binomial distribution with $n = 10$ and $p = .2$ is given below.

Success	Probability	Cumulative Probability
0	.1074	1.0000
1	.2684	.8926
2	.3020	.6242
3	.2013	.3222
4	.0881	.1209
5	.0264	.0328
6	.0055	.0064
7	.0008	.0009
8	.0001	.0001
9	.0000	.0000
10	.0000	.0000

Probability distribution $B(X; 10, .2)$.

(a) Assume a critical value of 5, and $B(X; 10, .2)$. Can we determine the probability of a Type I error? If so, what is the probability of a Type I error?

(b) Can we determine the probability of a Type II error? If so, what is the probability of a Type II error?

11. Assume that the man in the ESP experiment (Problem 10) guesses six cards correctly, and we wish to test the man's claim of ESP.
    (a) We have the probability distribution $B(X; 10, .2)$, a critical value of 5, and an empirical value of 6. Have we enough evidence to reject the null hypothesis?
    (b) Do we have statistical significance?
12. Assume now that it is desirable to decrease our Type II error probability, and we do this by increasing our Type I error probability from .03 to .12. What is the new critical value?
13. Assume now that the man really does have extrasensory perception, and that it helped him in his guessing task. In fact, it helped him enough so that, although any ordinary person only has a .2 probability of being correct, he has a .5 probability of being correct on any guess. He is going to all the universities in the country to demonstrate his ESP. The probability distribution for the binomial with $n = 10$ and $p = .5$, including the cumulative probabilities, is given in the table below.

Success	Probability	Cumulative Probability
0	.0010	1.0001
1	.0098	.9991
2	.0439	.9893
3	.1172	.9454
4	.2051	.8282
5	.2461	.6231
6	.2051	.3770
7	.1172	.1719
8	.0439	.0547
9	.0098	.0108
10	.0010	.0010

Probability distribution $B(X; 10, .5)$

If a particular university used a critical value of 5 in evaluating the man's claims of ESP, what is the probability of that university recognizing his ESP talents?

THE NORMAL DISTRIBUTION

In Chapter 8, the binomial distribution was presented as a model of outcome probabilities. The conditions were given under which the binomial distribution is appropriate as an assumption of outcome probabilities. The outcomes can only be whole numbers from zero to n. An example is the tossing of a coin 10 times, where the only possible outcomes are the numbers 0–10 (heads, or tails).

There will be times when other distributions will be appropriate. For example, what if a continuous distribution of outcomes, such as people's heights, is being sampled? The outcomes can be any real numbers, including values *between* whole numbers.

The normal distribution is a continuous, unimodal, symmetric distribution, loosely described as a bell-shaped curve. In this chapter, the normal distribution is discussed. A graph of the normal distribution is presented in Figure 9.1.

The tails of the normal distribution never actually touch the X axis. This implies that outcomes defined on even the most extreme intervals of the X axis are possible (though improbable). Many of the real-life events that are otherwise approximately normally distributed violate this assumption. That is, they do not have the possibility of infinitely large or small values. An example is the variable graphed in Figure 9.1, which is a graph of heights from a hypothetical population of men. There are no men in any population who are, for example, 610 centimeters (20 feet) tall. This one violation of the normal distribution's assumptions is frequently disregarded. Distributions are considered to be normally distributed even if the X axis does not extend from $-\infty$ to $+\infty$.

Continuous distributions were defined in Chapter 3. This chapter begins with a review of the concept of continuous distributions. The problems of stating probabilities of outcomes in continuous distributions, and the solu-

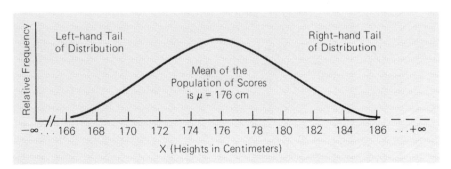

FIGURE 9.1
Graph of a normal distribution. This is a distribution of heights of men in a hypothetical population.

tions to these problems, are discussed. The equation for the normal distribution is also briefly examined.

When the probabilities of outcomes are desired, a table which is derived from the equation for the normal distribution is used. The use of this table is discussed in detail here, since it is an important table. The use of the normal distribution as it relates to statistical inference is stressed in this chapter. This involves using the normal distribution to determine when an independent variable (some experimental treatment, for example) has been effective.

DEFINING PROBABILITIES IN CONTINUOUS DISTRIBUTIONS
The distribution of the heights of people offers a continuous distribution and is generally normally distributed. Let us begin, then, with a discussion of a distribution of heights, using Figure 9.1 as an example.

In stating people's heights there can be decimal values, and there is no limit to the number of different possible values. For any two values that can be named (for example, 173 cm and 174 cm)*, other values can be named which conceivably can occur between the two values previously named (for example, 173.2 and 173.3 cm). For any two such intervening values, additional values can be named that are between the intervening values (for example, 173.25 cm). Endless intervening values can be named at finer and finer degrees of potential measurement, using more and more decimal places. For distributions of heights, between any two points (defined by any specific number of decimal places) there is always another point (defined by still more decimal places). Therefore, distributions of heights are continuous distributions, containing an infinite number of potential heights. This implies that in any distribution of heights there is an infinite number of mutually exclusive events possible, each with some theoretical possibility of occurring; that is, in measuring some new individual's height, there is an infinite number of potential outcomes of the measurement process.

In a continuous distribution, then, any point on the X axis can be defined by endless decimal places (some or all of which can be zeros). In continuous distributions, when we think of the probability for a particular value on the X axis, we think of the probability of a point defined by endless decimal places. Intuitively, the probability of that exact point occurring seems very small. For example, 173.00000100..., 173.00001100..., and 173.123123400... cm are all possible points on an X axis of men's heights. Yet the probability of a particular man being exactly any one of these precise heights is so unlikely as to have almost no probability at all. Given an interval, such as 173–174 cm, there is a specifiable probability greater

*A height of 173 cm is equivalent to 68.11 inches and a height of 174 cm is equivalent to a height of 68.50 inches.

than zero. But for any exact point on the *X* axis (definable only by infinite decimal places) the probability approaches zero.

In the case of a continuous distribution, there is an infinite number of possible events, and the probability of each event approaches zero. The question then arises of how to present a probability distribution for events that have a continuous distribution.

The problem of too many events can be solved by grouped frequency distributions; that is, for continuous distributions, the probabilities of intervals of *X* values can be listed.

The intervals in a continuous distribution can be presented as in Chapter 2, dividing the *X* axis into an arbitrary number of equal intervals, as for grouped frequency distributions. For example, heights can be presented in centimeter intervals such as 160–164, 165–169, and 170–174, with real limits 159.5–164.5, 164.5–169.5, and 169.5–174.5, as discussed in Chapter 2. But it is most often advantageous to use a cumulative interval, coupled with cumulative probabilities for the cumulatively grouped outcomes. This was illustrated in Chapter 8 for the binomial distribution of outcomes from coin tosses. For the binomial distribution, taking 10 heads as the most extreme event possible from 10 tosses, the events were cumulated so that the next outcome possible was nine or more, the next eight or more, etc. The probability for each succeeding cumulatively defined event is the sum of the probabilities for all events in the cumulated set.

As an example of cumulated probabilities with a continuous distribution, look again at Figure 9.1, which extends from an infinitely small value on the left to an infinitely large value on the right, with the bulk of the occurrences of scores between 166 and 186 cm. Table 9.1 presents some representative values of *X*, with their probabilities cumulated downward in the second column, beginning with $-\infty$ in the left-hand tail of Figure 9.1. Each probability in the second column is a probability of having a height of *X* or less. For example, in this distribution there is a probability of .0062 that a person has a height of 166 cm or less. Farther down in the second column there is a probability of .9938 that a person has a height of 186 cm or less, but only a probability of .5000 that a person in this distribution has a height of 176 cm or less.

There can also be a need for probabilities cumulated from the largest value in the population. This offers the probability of a height of *X* or greater. Representative values, summing from the right-hand side of Figure 9.1, are given in the third column of Table 9.1, cumulating upward. For example, the probability of a person being at least 166 cm tall (that is, the probability of being 166 cm tall or taller) is .9938. The probability of being 186 cm tall or taller has a probability of .0062.

If you have not studied calculus, you may wonder how you can add an infinite number of values, each approaching zero, and come up with a

TABLE 9.1

Cumulated probabilities of Figure 9.1, cumulated from left to right (second column), and right to left (third column)

Heights on the X Axis in Fig. 9.1	Cumulative Probabilities	
	From Left-Hand Tail to Height X	From Right-Hand Tail to Height X
$-\infty$	.0000	1.0000
.	.	.
.	.	.
.	.	.
166	.0062	.9938
167	.0122	.9878
168	.0228	.9772
.	.	.
.	.	.
175	.4013	.5987
176	.5000	.5000
177	.5987	.4013
.	.	.
.	.	.
185	.9878	.0122
186	.9938	.0062
.	.	.
.	.	.
$+\infty$	1.0000	.0000

meaningful number (as in Table 9.1). The technique of integration in infinite calculus is the appropriate method. Integration has many applications, including the solution to the problem of measuring areas under segments of curves.

You probably recall that the area of a rectangle is the width times the height. In measuring areas under curves, imaginary rectangles are identified in the areas being measured. For example, in Figure 9.2(a) two vertical lines have been drawn to mark off an interval of the distribution. A rectangle can be seen in the segmented area of the curve in Figure 9.2(b). The area of the rectangle gives an approximate measure of the area in the interval under the curve. The black area above the curve constitutes the error in the measurement. Several rectangles can be superimposed on the segment, as in Figure 9.3(a), and their areas summed. This reduces the error by reducing the area above the curve. By increasing the number of rectangles, as in Figure 9.3(b), we reduce the error in measurement of the area within an interval under the curve. Finally, the widths of the rectangles can be made infinitely small (making the area of each rectangle infinitely small), providing room for an infinite number of rectangles. The result is an

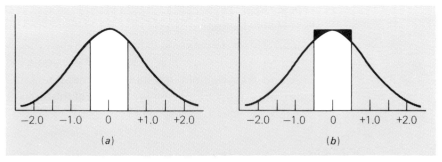

FIGURE 9.2
(a) Graph of a normal distribution, with z scores indicated on the X axis. A center section has been marked off for estimation of the area in the segment.
(b) Reproduction of (a), with the implicit rectangle made explicit. The black areas reflect the error in measurement of the segment under the curve, if a single rectangle is recognized within the segment.

infinite number of infinitely small values to add, which is accomplished through the calculus of integration.

The analogy between measuring an infinite number of infinitely small areas and summing an infinite number of infinitely small probabilities is a useful one. The analogy permits us to equate areas with probabilities, so that when we know the area of a segment under the curve, we also know the probability of an outcome defined as any event within that segment. The identity is made possible by considering the total area of the curve as equal to one. Then segments of the curve are identified as having areas between zero and one. In Figure 9.1, a height of 176 cm on the X axis divides the area of the curve in half, so that half of the area is below 176 cm. Thus the *area* is given a value of .5000. Analogously, the *probability of an outcome* of 176 cm or less is .5000.

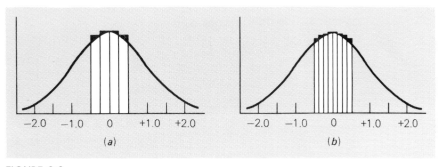

FIGURE 9.3
(a) Restatement of Figure 9.2(b), with four rectangles replacing the one rectangle.
(b) Restatement of Figure 9.2(b), with eight rectangles replacing the one rectangle. Black areas represent error in measurement of the segment under the curve.

The conceptual basis for specifying a probability for an interval in a continuous distribution has been described. The technique of integral calculus is used to measure the area under the curve within an interval. You will not have to use calculus, however. The calculations have already been done, and are available in a table which appears in Appendix B as Table III. Its use is described in a later section of this chapter.

The Defining Equation for the Normal Distribution You may remember that the binomial distribution, described in Chapter 8, was generated by Equation (8.7). For any value of X, this equation yields a probability.

$$B(X; n, p) = \binom{n}{x} (p)^x (1-p)^{n-x} \qquad [8.7]$$

In a graph of the binomial distribution, the values of $B(X; n, p)$ are represented as values on the Y axis, changing as X changes. The binomial distribution is a finite probability distribution, so each value on the X axis is an integer value and has a specific probability [graphed as $Y = B(X; n, p)$]. For example, the probability distribution presented in Chapter 8 as Table 8.4 has been restated as a graph in Figure 9.4. Table 8.4 and Figure 9.4 were generated by the binomial distribution with $n = 10$ and $p = .3$, presented here as Equation (9.1).

$$B(X; 10, .3) = \binom{10}{x}(.3)^x(.7)^{10-x} \qquad (9.1)$$

The graph of Equation (9.1) is presented in Figure 9.4 as a histogram, since the X axis is composed of discrete values. When dealing with theoretical continuous distributions, it is correct to use smoothed frequency polygons, as in Figures 9.1–9.3, which are all graphs of the normal distribution. The normal distribution is generated by Equation (9.2).

FIGURE 9.4
Graph of Equation (9.1). Probabilities of each X value are listed in Table 8.4.

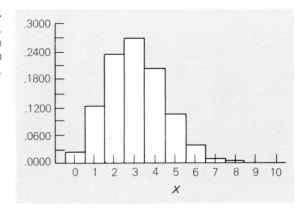

$$Y = \frac{1}{\sqrt{2\pi\sigma^2}} e^{-(X-\mu)^2/2\sigma^2} \tag{9.2}$$

Equation (9.2) defines the normal distribution. The verbal statements about the normal distribution (unimodal, symmetric, bell shaped) follow from the equation, which establishes the shape of the distribution. Equation (9.2) indicates just what Y-axis values (what variations in the curve) should be associated with each X-axis value in a graph of the normal distribution. Equation (9.2) looks imposing. It will look less imposing if the equation is looked at carefully, with the help of the discussion in the next paragraph.

There are five symbols in Equation (9.2): e, π, X, μ, and σ^2. The first two, e and π, are actually constants (approximately 2.72 and 3.14, respectively). The symbol X is the value whose Y-axis value is to be found through Equation (9.2). Therefore, X changes with each use of the equation. The values μ and σ^2 are the mean and variance of the set of X values whose respective Y-axis values are to be found through Equation (9.2). Therefore, μ and σ^2 are constants for any set of X values. Thus, for any set of X values, every symbol in this equation has some constant numerical value, except X (which can represent any value in the set).

Assume a set of intelligence test scores, with a mean of $\mu = 100$ and a variance of $\sigma^2 = 256$. Equation (9.2) for this distribution looks like:

$$Y = \frac{1}{\sqrt{2(3.14)(256)}} (2.72)^{-(X-100)^2/2(256)}.$$

If we now look at a similar set of intelligence test scores, but this time for a group of honor students, we may find a higher average and smaller variance (because the group is intellectually more homogeneous). Assume that the new mean is 120, and the new variance is 200. Applying Equation (9.2) to this new set of scores, we only have to change the mean and variance. Attempting to find the respective Y-axis values of different X scores from this new brighter population, Equation (9.2) looks like:

$$Y = \frac{1}{\sqrt{2(3.14)(200)}} (2.72)^{-(X-120)^2/2(200)}.$$

The normal distribution is a continuous distribution, so that the X-axis values in Equation (9.2) can take on any real number values, including endless decimal places. A continuous distribution cannot have probabilities appreciably different than zero for individual X-axis values. Therefore, the Y in Equation (9.2) does not represent specific probability values for specific X values, just relative positions for the graph. But the relative positions (heights on the Y axis) are not arbitrary. The integration (sum) of the Y values in any interval on the X axis will yield the probability of obtaining an outcome within that interval.

The X-axis values in Figures 9.2–9.3 are standard scores; that is, they represent the number of raw-score standard deviations from the raw-score mean, through Equation (6.6).

$$z = \frac{X - \mu}{\sigma}.$$ [6.6]

As discussed in Chapter 6, if the original X values (raw scores) are normally distributed, then the z scores are normally distributed. As is the case with any set of z scores, a normal distribution of z scores has a mean of $\mu_z = 0$, with $\sigma_z^2 = 1$ and $\sigma_z = 1$ as the variance and standard deviation, respectively.*

As seen in Equation (9.2), the formula for the normal distribution is

$$Y = \frac{1}{\sqrt{2\pi\sigma^2}} e^{-(X-\mu)^2/2\sigma^2}.$$

When the scores (X values) are transformed to z scores, the variance σ^2 is replaced by 1, the mean μ by 0, and the raw score X by the z score, yielding Equation (9.3).

$$Y = \frac{1}{\sqrt{2\pi 1}} e^{-(z-0)^2/2\cdot 1},$$ (9.3)

$$Y = \frac{1}{\sqrt{2\pi}} e^{-z^2/2}.$$

When the X-axis values are transformed to z scores, the graph does not change its shape. Only the values on the X axis are changed. Figure 9.1 is reproduced below, as Figure 9.5, with z scores indicated on the X axis, along with the original raw scores. A score that is two standard deviations above the mean of the raw scores will always have a z score of +2, whatever the scale of the original raw scores. z scores are always located in the same place in a normal distribution. Only the values of the raw scores change, with changes in the scale of the scores.

A table of probabilities within a normal distribution (Table III in Appendix B) has been prepared which offers the probabilities of intervals under the normal curve. To make the table useful for all scales of scores, it is presented in terms of z scores. Therefore, in order to use the prepared table for determining the probabilities within a normal distribution, the raw scores must be transformed to z scores. The z score in question is first located in the table. Adjacent to the z score is the probability of a score within an interval that begins with that z score. The table includes the probability of all scores in the interval beginning with that z score and

---

*The mean and variance, μ_z and σ_z^2, are subscripted to emphasize that it is *the distribution of z scores* that has a mean of $\mu_z = 0$ and variance of $\sigma_z^2 = 1$, not the original raw-score distribution.

extending over all greater scores. It also includes the probability of all scores equal to or less than that z score. The following section offers a detailed discussion of the use of the table.

Using the Table of Probabilities Under the Normal Curve Because the normal distribution is a symmetric distribution, <u>corresponding intervals on both sides of the mean have the same probabilities</u> (same proportion of outcomes). For example, in Figure 9.5 scores in the interval from $-\infty$ to $z = -2.5$ have the same probability as scores in the interval from $+2.5$ to $+\infty$. Similarly, scores ranging from 0 to -1.0 have the same probability as scores ranging from 0 to $+1.0$. This means that in presenting the probabilities for outcomes from a normal distribution, it is only necessary to present the probabilities for one side of the distribution. For this reason, most tables of the probabilities for normal distributions save space by only presenting the right half of the X axis (the positive z scores).

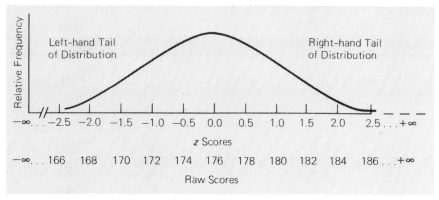

FIGURE 9.5

Graph of a normal distribution (Figure 9.1), with both z scores and raw scores (in centimeters) indicated on the X axis. The mean of the population of scores is $\mu = 176$ cm, and the standard deviation is $\sigma = 4$.

$$z = \frac{(X - \mu)}{\sigma} = \frac{(X - 176)}{4}$$

A z score of zero represents the mean. This centrally placed zero point (see Figure 9.5) can be used as the beginning of the right half of the distribution. Tables of normally distributed probabilities usually begin with a z score of $z = 0.00$, and increase at the second decimal place. For example, such a table might begin as in Table 9.2, in which the probability of a score of z or less is in the second column.

Since z scores are really distance from the mean [$z = (X - \mu)/\sigma$], many tables present the probability of an outcome in the interval between the mean and each z score, as exampled in Table 9.3. The second column in Table 9.3 presents probabilities of the occurrence of outcomes within intervals, where one end of each interval is the mean ($z = 0.00$), and the other end is the listed z score. Table 9.3 is taken from the larger, more complete Table of Probabilities Under the Normal Curve (Table III in Appendix B), which has four columns. Column 1 of Table III lists z scores. Column 2 lists probabilities of outcomes between the mean and the listed z score. Column 3 lists the probabilities of a score of z or less (from $-\infty$ to z) and column 4 lists the probabilities of a score of z or greater (from z to $+\infty$).

You should, at this point, use Table III in Appendix B to identify the probabilities associated with specific values of z. For example, go down column 1 to a z score of 1.00. Column 2 indicates that the probability of a score between the mean ($z = 0.00$) and $z = 1.00$ is .3413. That is, .3413 is the proportion of outcomes in the population that lie between 0.00 and 1.00. Since the normal distribution is a symmetric distribution, the probability of a score between $z = -1.00$ and 0.00 is also .3413. Recall that a z score of

TABLE 9.2
Areas from $-\infty$ to selected z scores

z Score	Area from $-\infty$ to z
0.00	.5000
0.01	.5040
0.02	.5080
0.03	.5120

TABLE 9.3
Areas from mean to selected z scores

z score	Area from mean to z
0.00	.0000
0.01	.0040
0.02	.0080
0.03	.0120

1.00 (and -1.00) is one standard deviation from the mean. Suppose you want to know the probability of a score being within one standard deviation of the mean, without regard to its being either above or below the mean. This is (from column 2 of the table)

$$\text{Probability } (-1 \leq z \leq +1) = .3413 + .3413$$

$$= .6826.$$

Restating this with a concrete example, suppose there is a test measuring assertiveness. Further, suppose that the mean score on this test within some population is 50, and that the standard deviation is 5. If the population of assertiveness scores is normally distributed, it means that approximately 68% of the population will have scores between 45 and 55 ($50 - 5 = 45$, and $50 + 5 = 55$).

Recall that column 3 lists the probabilities for scores of z or less. Column 3 indicates (adjacent to $z = 1.00$) that approximately 84% of any normally distributed population has a score equal to or less than one standard deviation above the mean. If the population is the group of people who have taken the hypothetical assertiveness test, approximately 84% of the population will have scores equal to or less than 55. Column 4, which gives the probabilities of scores of z or *greater,* indicates that approximately 16% of the population have scores equal to or greater than 55. Stated another way, people scoring at or above 55 are in the top 16% of assertiveness in this hypothetical population. Figure 9.6 shows the area relationship between a z score of 1.00 and the columns of Table III.

What is the probability of a score lying within two standard deviations of the mean? Entering Table III at $z = 2.00$ and consulting the second column, the probability of a score lying between the mean and a z score of 2.00 is .4772. Therefore,

$$P(-2.00 \leq z \leq +2.00) = P(-2.00 \leq z \leq +0.00) + P(0.00 \leq z \leq +2.00)$$

$$= .4772 + .4772$$

$$= .9544,$$

that is, approximately 95% of the scores in a normal distribution lie within

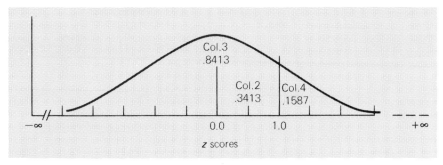

FIGURE 9.6
Relationships between a z score of 1.00 and columns of Table III in Appendix B. The values given are the proportions of the area within each segment.

two standard deviations of the mean. In a commonly used IQ test, the mean is 100 and the standard deviation is 16. Since $100 - 2(16) = 68$, and $100 + 2(16) = 132$, approximately 95% of the population have scores ranging between 68 and 132. Because the distribution is symmetric, this means that close to 2½% of the population have scores above 132, and close to 2½% have scores below 68.

What is the probability of a score lying between $z = +2.00$ and $+1.00$? Look at the second column of Table III at the interval from the mean to $z = 1.00$, and the interval from the mean to $z = 2.00$. For the latter interval, there is a probability of .4772, which is the proportion of the area between the mean and $z = 2.00$. The desired answer requires that this area be reduced to that between $z = 1.00$ and 2.00. The area between the mean and $z = 1.00$, which is .3413, must be subtracted from .4772. Symbolically,

$$P(1.00 \leq z \leq 2.00) = P(0.00 \leq z \leq 2.00) - P(0.00 \leq z \leq 1.00)$$
$$= .4772 - .3413$$
$$= .1359.$$

Figure 9.7 presents the relationships in visual form.

Most commonly, Table III is used to obtain the probability associated with reaching or surpassing a particular z score. This means a frequent use of column 4. For example, what is the probability of obtaining a z score of at least $+1.64$? Column 4 indicates that the probability is .0505. What is the probability of reaching or surpassing a z score of $+1.96$? Column 4 indicates that the probability is .0250.

It is sometimes useful to go from the probabilities listed in the body of the table to the associated z scores, that is, you may have a particular probability in mind and have to find the z score. For example, suppose a class has taken an exam, and you wish to know which exam score is the cutoff point signifying the top 10% of the class' performance. You do not have a z score

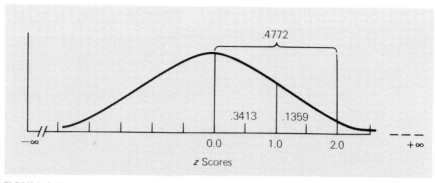

FIGURE 9.7
Areas between $z = 0.00$ and $z = 1.00$; between $z = 1.00$ and $z = 2.00$; and between $z = 0.00$ and $z = 2.00$.

specified, but rather have a percentage (10%). You use the percentage to obtain the associated z score, and then convert that z score to a raw score which is the desired cutoff score.

If assuming a normally distributed population, the z score associated with the top 10% can be found via column 4 of Table III. Column 4 lists the percent of the area above a particular point, so you move down the column looking for a probability value closest to 10%. The table lists decimal values to four decimal places, so you seek the value closest to .1000. The closest value listed in the table is .1003, found at $z = 1.28$. Another way to find the same z score is to move down column 3, which lists the proportion of the area below each z score. The z score dividing the top 10% from the bottom 90% is adjacent to .9000, or some closest value, in column 3. Here again, the closest tabled value (.8997) is found at a z score of 1.28.

In summary, the z score equivalent of the cutoff score for the top 10% and bottom 90% is 1.28. But we want the raw score associated with the top 10%. In this example, what raw score is equivalent to a z score of 1.28? To obtain a specific raw score, the raw score mean, μ, and the standard deviation, σ, are required. Equation (6.2), restated here as Equation (9.4), is used to obtain X from μ, σ, and z. Assume, in this example, that $\mu = 80$ and $\sigma = 10$.

$$X = \mu + \sigma z \qquad (9.4)$$

The desired value of X (the raw-score equivalent of $z = 1.28$) is

$$X = \mu + \sigma z$$
$$= 80 + 10(1.28)$$
$$= 92.80.$$

Since exam scores are usually only reported in integer values, a score of 93 is used as the cutoff score signifying the top 10% of the class.

175 Defining Probabilities in Continuous Distributions

Marking on a Curve College students often hear of professors who mark on a curve. The method for doing this is to assume a normal distribution and then look for the scores associated with various cutoff points. For example, if a professor assumes that 10% of the class always deserve an A, and 10% always deserve to fail, he will find the cutoff point for the top 10% as we did in the last section. In the preceding example, with a mean of 80 and a standard deviation of 10, 93 was found to be the cutoff score for the top 10%. Thus, those scoring 93 or above receive an A. The procedure is similar for identifying the bottom 10% due to fail. The difference is that negative z scores are used in Equation (9.4). Specifically,

$$X = \mu + \sigma z$$
$$= 80 + 10(-1.28)$$
$$= 80 - 12.80$$
$$= 67.20.$$

Thus, 67 is the cutoff score for a failing grade. For intervening grades, the professor may decide that 15% below the top 10% generally are B students. He may similarly conclude that 15% above failing should receive a D, and the remaining 50% in the middle should receive a C. To obtain the cutoff score for the B group, the professor looks for the cutoff score for the top 25% (15% below the top 10%), which column 4 of Table III places at $z = .67$. Incorporating this z value into Equation (9.4), the raw score is

$$X = 80 + 10(.67)$$
$$= 86.70.$$

Thus, a z score of B is given to those students scoring between 87 and 92.

The major argument in favor of marking on a curve is that exams are not generally that accurate as absolute measures of performance. One exam may be hard and another easy, and some professors just have a tendency to give either hard or easy exams. By marking on a curve, it is relative performance within the class taking the exam that determines a person's grade. If the class is large enough, it might be assumed that the class has the same percentages of good, bad, and indifferent students in it as the general population. We might conclude from experience at a particular school that, for example, 10% of the students at the school are superior, and 15% are good but not classifiable as superior. Then we give these same percentages grades that are appropriate to such evaluations. The problem with marking on a curve is that very few classes are large enough to offer a representative sample of the general population of students at the school. The use of constant proportions of the different grades can therefore be inappropriate.

SAMPLE MEANS AS ESTIMATES OF POPULATION MEANS

To this point in this chapter, the discussion has centered on distributions of individual scores. Most scientific questions concern means of groups of scores, rather than the individual scores. Therefore, it is important to discuss probability distributions of means. The distribution of individual scores in a population and the distribution of sample means from that population are closely related. In this and the following section, distributions of means and their relationship to distributions of individual scores are discussed.

Suppose that in the course of a semester you have a total of 50 exams in all your classes (all graded on a scale of 0–100). Assume further that you have obtained an overall average of 90. However, your test scores varied somewhat, offering a distribution like that given in Table 9.4.

Assume now that a prospective employer, or a relative considering financial support, or some other person of importance in your life needs to be impressed by your scholarship. Suppose the only information that this person has is one randomly selected exam score out of 50 scores, and you do not know which exam score it is.

Clearly you would be worried. You would not feel secure that the one score represents you fairly. A single random score is an unreliable sample of performance, since it varies greatly with different random samples.

Suppose this person with your fate in his or her hands has not seen one, but rather five, out of the 50 exams. Assume that your benefactor used the mean of the five exams in the sample to estimate your scholarship. You will feel better than with only a single score, but you may still be worried about the sample mean.

Now suppose that 15 of the 50 exam scores were used to compute the sample mean. You are likely to feel a little more secure in the belief that your performance is being fairly represented.

In the above example, the set of 50 exam scores is a population with a mean $\mu = 90$, which is being sampled. It was suggested that your confi-

TABLE 9.4

Distribution of hypothetical exam scores

Score	Frequency
100	10
95	12
90	13
85	7
80	3
75	2
70	2
65	1

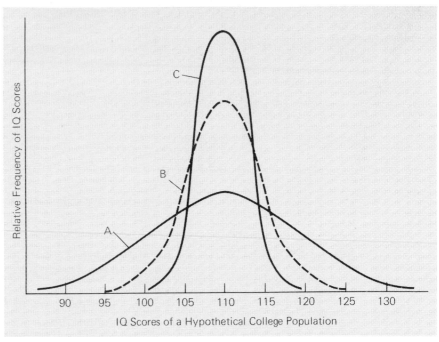

FIGURE 9.8

Illustration of the law of large numbers. The distribution of individual IQ scores (distribution A), is lower and wider than the distributions of means. As sample size is increased (from distribution B, with sample size of $n = 4$, to distribution C, with sample size of $n = 10$), the means of samples from the hypothetical college population are less widely dispersed around the population mean of $\mu = 110$.

dence in the estimate of the population mean would increase as the sample size increased; that is, for a small sample you would worry that $\bar{X}$ is possibly widely discrepant from μ. With a large sample, however, the value of $\bar{X}$ is expected to be closer to μ. Symbolically, as n increases, the expectation of the difference $(\bar{X} - \mu)$ gets progressively smaller.

This intuitively reasonable picture of increasing confidence with increased sample size can be proven to be a correct expectation. The expected value of $(\bar{X} - \mu)$ does decrease as n increases. This is a theorem of mathematical statistics, and is called the **law of large numbers.**

The law of large numbers says that as the sample size is increased, the means of samples, $\bar{X}$, are expected to be grouped more closely around the population mean, μ. [This is the meaning of a decrease in expectation of $(\bar{X} - \mu)$]. Figure 9.8 illustrates the law of large numbers.

Distribution A, the lowest and widest distribution in Figure 9.8, is the distribution of individual IQ scores from a hypothetical college population with an average IQ of 110. Distribution B is the distribution of means

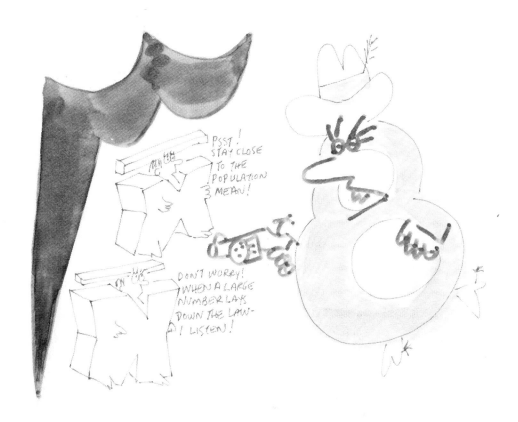

randomly sampled from the same population as distribution A, with sample size of $n = 4$. Distribution C, the tallest and most narrow of the distributions, is a distribution of means, but with a sample size of $n = 10$, from the population represented by distribution A.

The Standard Error of the Mean In Figure 9.8, the lowest and widest curve, distribution A, was drawn with a standard deviation for samples of individual scores of $\sigma = 10$. The two taller and narrower curves represent distributions of samples of means, rather than of individual scores. The standard deviation of sample means is called **the standard error of the mean** and is symbolized with a subscripted mean, as $\sigma_{\bar{x}}$. The law of large numbers states that larger samples (larger values of n) result in sample means that are closer to the population mean; that is, the sampled means will vary less with larger n, all being closer to the same value, μ. In Figure 9.8, as n increases (from 1 to 4 to 10), the distributions cluster more closely around $\mu = 110$. Equation (9.6), which defines the standard error of the mean, specifies the way the variability of means is related to n.

$$\sigma_{\bar{X}} = \frac{\sigma}{\sqrt{n}}. \tag{9.6}$$

Of course, the variability of individual scores in the population also affects the variability of means, and this, too, is specified in Equation (9.6) in the form of σ. For a given sample size (constant n), as the standard deviation σ increases, so does the standard error, $\sigma_{\bar{X}}$. For a given standard deviation (constant σ), as the sample size increases the standard error becomes smaller. In Figure 9.8, the standard deviation of individual scores is $\sigma = 10$. This is the variability illustrated in distribution A. Distribution B, illustrating the standard deviation of means from the same population when $n = 4$, has a standard error of

$$\sigma_{\bar{X}} = \frac{\sigma}{\sqrt{n}}.$$
$$= \frac{10}{\sqrt{4}}$$
$$= 5.$$

The standard error is still smaller in distribution C, where $n = 10$, so that

$$\sigma_{\bar{X}} = \frac{\sigma}{\sqrt{n}}$$
$$= \frac{10}{\sqrt{10}}$$
$$= 3.16.$$

THE NORMAL DISTRIBUTION OF SAMPLE MEANS Recall that a transformation to z scores maintains the form of the original distribution. Therefore, when a distribution of means is normally distributed, and then transformed to z scores, the result is a normal distribution; that is, the mean of the distribution is $\mu_z = 0$, and the standard error (which is the standard deviation of means) is $\sigma_{\bar{X}_z} = 1$.

Since the standard error of means is the standard deviation of a distribution of means, the standard error is used to transform means to z scores; that is, Equation (9.7a) is used to transform a mean to a z score.

$$z = \frac{(\bar{X} - \mu)}{\sigma_{\bar{X}}}, \tag{9.7a}$$

where $\sigma_{\bar{X}}$ is obtained through Equation (9.6).

Assuming a normal distribution, the Table of Probabilities Under the

Normal Curve (Table III in Appendix B) can be used to determine the probability of a particular mean. The raw-score mean is first transformed to a z score through Equation (9.7a), then a probability is located in the body of the table. When a desired z score can be specified (as for a specified critical value), but the equivalent raw-score mean is needed, Equation (9.7b) can be used.

$$\bar{X} = \mu + z\sigma_{\bar{x}} \qquad (9.7b)$$

The Central Limit Theorem This chapter is devoted to the normal distribution, so all the figures in this chapter have been drawn in the shape of the normal curve. But the conditions under which a normal distribution of outcomes can be assumed have not yet been discussed.

There are only a limited number of circumstances where individual events from a population of events are normally distributed. Biological traits, such as height, are often normally distributed, or at least approximately so. Some psychological traits, such as intelligence as measured by IQ tests, tend to be normally distributed.

In general, the issue of whether the individual events of a population are or are not normally distributed is an empirical issue. There is no logical basis for generating an expectation for normal distributions of individual events analogous to the development of an expectation of binomial distributions.

Fortunately, there is another basis for predicting the occurrence of normal distributions of outcomes. This is called the **central limit theorem**. It can be proven that the means of sufficiently large samples are normally distributed, or at least approximately so. Instead of looking at the individual scores of a population with mean μ and standard deviation σ, we look at large samples from the population. From each sample, a mean of the sample, $\bar{X}$, can be computed. The central limit theorem says that an infinite number of such sampled values will form a normal distribution (given sufficiently large samples).

A distribution of sampled statistics is called a **sampling distribution**. In the following sections the sampling distributions of means are discussed. Given large enough sample sizes, even if the original distribution of individual scores is not normally distributed, the sampling distribution of means will be approximately normally distributed.

If the distribution of individual scores is only mildly different than the normal distribution, even the means of small samples will be approximately normally distributed. If the distortion from the normal distribution is great, however, then large sample sizes must be used before the sampling distribution of means can be assumed to be approximately normally distributed.

It is the central limit theorem which gives the normal distribution its central place in statistics. In empirical work, general knowledge is rarely sought from just an individual score. Samples containing many scores are almost always collected. For example, samples of measures of many subjects, both before and after a treatment, are collected; or, samples of an untreated group versus a treated group are collected. The question is always whether the treatment makes a difference. The answer is obtained by comparing the means of the different groups. The central limit theorem tells us that our sampled means form normally shaped sampling distributions. Therefore, the normal distribution can often be used to tell the probability of different outcomes.

The way in which a null hypothesis can be rejected from an assumed sampling distribution of means is illustrated below.

USING THE NORMAL DISTRIBUTION FOR STATISTICAL INFERENCE

In statistical inference, a pattern of chance events is identified in the form of some probability distribution. The distribution, then, serves as a model of chance to signal an unlikely event. When an unlikely event occurs, it is concluded that there has been some interference with chance. A critical value is first selected, which marks the beginning of an extreme segment on the X axis, at and beyond which the null hypothesis will be rejected. This segment of the X axis contains the unlikely (low probability) events. It is often referred to as the **region of rejection** or **the critical region**. Figure 9.9(a) pictures a normal distribution with the critical region unshaded, beginning at a critical value of $z = -1.64$. Figure 9.9(b) pictures the same distribution, again with the critical region unshaded, but this time beginning at a critical value of $z = +1.96$.

If the null hypothesis is true (and therefore should not be rejected), the

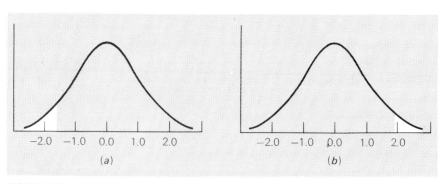

FIGURE 9.9
Normal distributions, with the critical value placed at $z = -1.64$ (a), and $z = +1.96$ (b). The critical regions are unshaded.

critical region of the distribution will still be reached some percent of the time. The percent of the time (the Type I error probability) depends on the critical value selected.

Suppose we decide to test a theory that students who are vegetarians suffer from protein deficiency, and so are not as smart as other students. A random sample of 64 vegetarian students at University State College are selected, and their IQ scores are obtained. The average IQ of this sample is found to be 112. This sample average is compared with the average IQ of the general population of students at University State College. The null hypothesis, as usual, is that the two groups are the same. The general college distribution of IQ scores forms the basis for the null hypothesis distribution.

Assume that the general college population at University State College has previously been tested and is found to have an average IQ of 115, with a standard deviation of 14. But the standard deviation of 14 refers to the variability of individual scores. We need a null hypothesis distribution against which the mean of 112 obtained from the sample of 64 vegetarian students can be tested; that is, the null hypothesis distribution has to be a sampling distribution of means. This is obtained by using the standard deviation to obtain a standard error for $n = 64$, with Equation (9.6).

$$\sigma_{\bar{x}} = \frac{\sigma}{\sqrt{n}}$$

$$= \frac{14}{\sqrt{64}}$$

$$= 1.75.$$

The value of $\sigma_{\bar{x}} = 1.75$ has been used in Figure 9.10 to construct a visual representation of a sampling distribution of means from the general student population at University State College. In Figure 9.10 the sampling distribution is presented in terms of both raw-score means (population mean = 115 and standard error = 1.75) and z score equivalents of the means (population mean = 0 and standard error = 1.00).

Figure 9.10 is a graphic presentation of the null hypothesis in the example. It presents the population mean $\mu = 115$ at the center. The X axis is marked off in standard error units, where $\sigma_{\bar{x}} = 1.75$. Thus, a raw score that is two standard errors above the mean is $\mu + 2\sigma_{\bar{x}} = 115 + 2(1.75) = 118.50$. Some points have been indicated on the X axis in terms of the standard error units (z score units). What is next required is an identification of a critical value in Figure 9.10. This is obtained by entering the normal probability tables and selecting a z score appropriate to the preselected Type I error probability. Assuming a Type I error probability of 5%, Table III yields

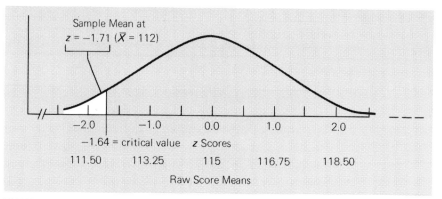

FIGURE 9.10
Sampling distribution of mean IQ scores, with a population mean of 115 and a standard error of 1.75. The unshaded area beginning at z = −1.64 represents the critical region. The slanted line at z = −1.71 (equivalent to $\bar{X}$ = 112) represents the sampled mean in the vegetarian example, which is within the critical region.

a critical value of 1.64; that is, a z score of 1.64 or greater will occur by chance 5% of the time.

It has been implicit in this discussion that any differences that are found will be at the left-hand tail, since only the possibility of vegetarians having a *lower* IQ has been considered. Thus, the critical value is set at −1.64. A z score of −1.64 or *less* will occur 5% of the time by chance. (Setting a critical value at only one tail of the distribution is called a **one-tailed test of significance.** This procedure will be reassessed below and compared with a **two-tailed test of significance.**)

Now the question is, does the sampled mean of 112 (from the sample of vegetarian students) reach (or surpass) the critical value of −1.64? In order to answer this question, we convert the raw score sample mean of 112 to a z score. This is done with Equation (9.7a):

$$z = \frac{\bar{X} - \mu}{\sigma_{\bar{X}}}$$

$$= \frac{112 - 115}{1.75}$$

$$= -1.71.$$

The sample mean of 112 is equivalent to a z score of −1.71. As seen in Figure 9.10, a z score of −1.71 is more extreme than the critical value of z = −1.64, and therefore surpasses the critical value. The null hypothesis, which states that the vegetarian students have the same IQ scores as the general college population, is therefore rejected. Consequently, it is concluded that the vegetarian students have a lower average IQ score than the general population of students at University State College.

Now suppose that another theory has been proposed, different than the theory of protein deficiency. Suppose that a researcher hypothesizes that a vegetarian diet keeps a child more alert because of the lower consumption of animal fat. This suggests a prediction of higher intelligence for vegetarians. The researcher may then establish a critical value of +1.64 rather than −1.64, shifting the interest to outcomes in the other tail of the distribution. Suppose that the 64 vegetarian students had, in fact, produced an average IQ of $\bar{X} = 118$ (in the opposite tail from, but just as extreme as, 112). The z score equivalent of 118 in this null hypothesis distribution is +1.71, which surpasses a critical value of +1.64. The researcher will then conclude that the vegetarian diets are associated with higher IQ scores among students at University State College.

In the logic used up to this point, there is a problem concerning the estimate of the Type I error probability. The probability of a Type I error was defined as the probability of a class of events occurring that lie at or beyond some preselected critical value. That is a correct definition of a Type I error probability. But from the above example it may seem that researchers are required to predict the direction in which an effect will occur. If this is required, two researchers jointly doing the same research may have opposite predictions. The study can then be statistically significant, with potentially opposite conclusions, given a finding in the critical region at either tail of the distribution. But if both tails of the distribution could lead to rejection of the null hypothesis, and each critical region covers 5% of chance happenings, then there is actually a 10% chance of significance when the null hypothesis is true; that is, if the null hypothesis is true, samples of the population will reach or surpass values of either +1.64 or −1.64 a total of 10% of the time.

This suggests that if statistical significance can be declared at either tail of the distribution, what appears to be a Type I error probability of 5% is actually a Type I error probability of 10%. What is required is a statement of Type I error probability that takes into account the probability of outcomes at both tails, or else a prior commitment to ignore extreme events in one of the tails.

DIRECTIONAL VERSUS NONDIRECTIONAL HYPOTHESES

Just as we decide, before we do our research, what our Type I error probability will be (and therefore what our critical value will be), we also decide before an experiment whether we will be looking for unlikely events at just one tail or both tails of the distribution.

Some statisticians believe that we should rarely, if ever, confine our Type I error calculations to just one tail of the distribution. Others feel that we should maximize our use of one-tailed tests of significance.

Assume the possibility is recognized that a particular alternative distribution can be either higher or lower than the null hypothesis distribution. For example, suppose that we want to know if vegetarian diets make a difference in IQ among the college population at University State College. Suppose it is not known whether the potential alternative distribution will lie to the right or the left of the null hypothesis distribution. In that case, critical values have to be defined at both tails of the null hypothesis distribution; that is, two critical values, which are usually symmetrically positioned at the two tails of the null hypothesis distribution, are needed. Whatever the Type I error probability that we wish to risk, we have to divide that probability between the two tails of the distribution.

If we wish to maintain a Type I error probability of 5% two tailed, then we set our critical values so that they are reached or surpassed only 2.5% of the time at each tail (assuming a true null hypothesis). Stated another way, if our critical value presents a cutoff for 2.5% of the area of the curve at each tail, then 5% of the distribution defines unlikely events, giving us our Type I error probability. The phrase "Type I error probability of .05 two tailed" implies two critical values, each with a probability of .025 of being reached or exceeded under a true null hypothesis. The phrase "Type I error probability of .10 two tailed" implies two critical values, each with a probability of .05 of being reached or exceeded under a true null hypothesis. On the other hand, the phrase, "Type I error probability of .05 one tailed" implies just one critical value, which is at only one tail of the distribution. That critical value has a probability of being reached or exceeded which is equal to the Type I error probability of .05 under a true null hypothesis.

When looking for the proportion in a tail of the distribution, we look at column 4 of Table III. For a Type I error probability of .05 two tailed we look in column 4 for a decimal value close to .0250, the proportion of the curve defined as the critical region of each tail. The z score associated with .0250 is 1.96. Thus, for a Type I error probability of .05 two-tailed we use **critical z score** values of ± 1.96. In the vegetarian example, the raw scores equivalent to $z = +1.96$ and $z = -1.96$ are obtained through Equation (9.7b).

$$\bar{X} = \mu + z\sigma_{\bar{x}} \qquad\qquad \bar{X} = \mu + z\sigma_{\bar{x}}$$
$$= 115 + (+1.96)(1.75) \qquad = 115 + (-1.96)(1.75)$$
$$= 115 + 3.43 \qquad\qquad = 115 - 3.43$$
$$= 118.43 \qquad\qquad\qquad = 111.57$$

Figure 9.11 illustrates the critical region for the example, with a two-tailed test.

The issue of whether to use one-tailed or two-tailed tests, or where each should be used, is still being debated. The issue is important because

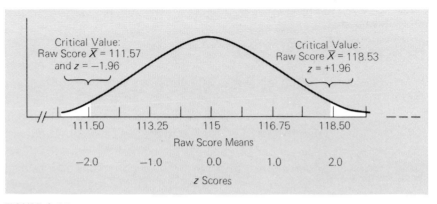

FIGURE 9.11
Sampling distribution of IQ scores with critical values at $z = +1.96$ and -1.96 (equivalent to $\bar{X} = 118.43$ and 111.57) for a two-tailed test with a Type I error probability of .05.

Type II error probabilities are greater with two-tailed than with one-tailed tests of significance. This point can be better understood with a graphic presentation of Type II error probabilities.

Graphic Presentation of Type II Error Probabilities

If the results of an experiment exceed the critical value, we reject the null hypothesis. Given a false null hypothesis, we will want to reject it. But the only way we can conclude that a null hypothesis is not true is to reach or surpass the critical value. A particular null hypothesis may be false, yet because of random sampling variability, the sampled mean may not reach or surpass the critical value. This will constitute a Type II error.

Figure 9.12 presents a graphic illustration of a **null hypothesis sampling distribution** which has been assumed in some experiment, and an **alternative sampling distribution** which is, in fact, correct in the situation.

It will be useful to be more specific about the two distributions in Figure 9.12. In the example concerning the IQ scores at University State College, the null hypothesis distribution is the sampling distribution of means of the general college population. This distribution was previously presented as Figure 9.10. The alternative distribution is the sampling distribution of means of IQ scores of vegetarian students at University State College. We will assume that the actual average of the IQ scores for the population of vegetarian students is $\mu = 113$. This population mean would not be known to the experimenter, who will only have a sample mean from that population.

The discussion of an alternative distribution is purely theoretical. We never know the exact location of the alternative distribution on the X axis.

But here, as in the preceding chapter, we pretend to know the location of the alternative distribution in order to make the theoretical discussion clearer.

The critical region is depicted in Figure 9.12 as a crosshatched area at the left tail of the null hypothesis distribution, starting at a critical value of −1.64. In any experiment <u>the critical value can only be located on the null hypothesis distribution,</u> since this is the only distribution about which we can be specific. The null hypothesis is that the vegetarian students are just like the general college population. We have the IQ scores for the general population of students at the school, so this offers a single specific distribution as our model (of the null hypothesis). The sampled mean of vegetarian student IQ scores can be compared with what is expected from this model, to see if the null hypothesis should be rejected; that is, the sample mean may or may not be beyond the critical value of the null hypothesis distribution.

Restating the facts of the example, the average IQ of the general college population is 115, with a standard deviation of 14. If 64 students are sampled at a time, the standard error will be $\sigma_{\bar{x}} = 14/\sqrt{64} = 1.75$. We pretend to know that the population mean of vegetarian students is different than that of the average college population, and is specifically 113. Assuming the same standard error for both distributions, the two distributions will

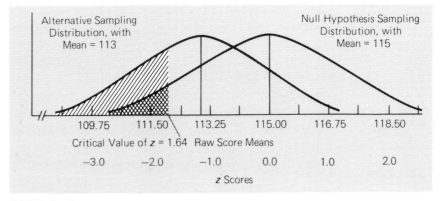

FIGURE 9.12
Null hypothesis sampling distribution with mean = 115, and true alternative sampling distribution with mean = 113. Standard error of the mean for both distributions is 1.75. One-tailed test of significance with a critical value at $z = -1.64$ (raw score mean of 112.13) is illustrated. Diagonally striped area of the alternative sampling distribution is equivalent to the percent of samples from the alternative distribution that would be detected as coming from an alternative distribution. In this example, with a one-tailed test, only 30.85 percent of the sample means will be detected as coming from an alternative distribution. Thus the Type II error probability is $1 - .3085 = .6915$.

be drawn as in Figure 9.12. The two distributions clearly overlap in Figure 9.12.

An important point to be appreciated with these overlapping distributions concerns the proportion of the alternative distribution that is *not* beyond the critical value of −1.64 (that is, the proportion of the alternative distribution to the right of −1.64). The proportion of the alternative distribution *not* beyond the critical value is the proportion of the samples of means from the alternative distribution that will *not* lead to rejection of the null hypothesis. Thus, the proportion of the alternative distribution that does not surpass the critical value is equivalent to the probability of a Type II error. This probability is presented as the unstriped area to the right of −1.64 in the alternative distribution.

In this instance, it is assumed that the alternative distribution is the correct distribution, and so is the only distribution being sampled. Since the alternative distribution is the correct one, it is desirable for the sample mean to lead to the rejection of the null hypothesis. Any sample that does not lead to rejection of the null hypothesis in this situation is an instance of a Type II error.

Type II Errors Compared in One- and Two-tailed Tests of Significance In Figure 9.12 a critical value is presented at only one tail of the null hypothesis distribution. This represents a one-tailed test of significance. What will happen to the probability of a Type II error if a two-tailed test is used?

It was previously indicated that going from a one- to a two-tailed test means reducing the probability of a Type I error at each tail by half, and then summing the two for the overall Type I error probability. In going to a two-tailed test, a more extreme critical value is required for rejection of the null hypothesis, but the value can occur at either tail to imply statistical significance. In the vegetarian example, in comparing Figures 9.10 and 9.11, we see that the critical value goes from −1.64 in a one-tailed test to ±1.96 in a two-tailed test, given a decision to accept a Type I error probability of .05. Thus, a larger absolute value (|1.96| rather than |1.64|) is necessary for significance in a two-tailed test. This means that the critical value is moved farther out on the tail. To appreciate what this will do to the probability of a Type II error, Figure 9.12 has been redrawn as Figure 9.13, with the critical value moved appropriately for a two-tailed significance test at the .05 level.

We can see in comparing Figures 9.12 and 9.13 that for a two-tailed test a larger proportion of samples from the alternative distribution will fail to reach the critical value. Therefore, the probability of a Type II error is larger with two-tailed tests of significance. In Figure 9.12, 69.15% of the true alternative distribution (the unstriped area) is outside the critical region. In Figure 9.13, which depicts a two-tailed test, 79.39% of the true alternative

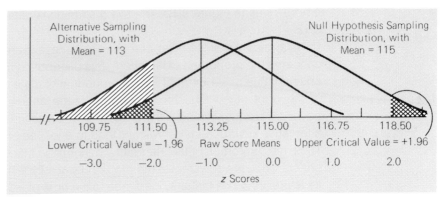

FIGURE 9.13

Null hypothesis sampling distribution with mean = 115, and true alternative sampling distribution with mean = 113. Standard error of the mean for both distributions is 1.75. Two-tailed test of significance with critical values at −1.96 and +1.96 (at raw score means of 111.57 and 118.43). Diagonally striped area of the alternative sampling distribution is equivalent to the percentage of samples from the alternative distribution that are detected as coming from an alternative distribution. In this example, with a two-tailed test, only 20.61% of the sample means will be detected as coming from an alternative distribution. Thus, the Type II error probability is 1 − .2061 = .7939.

distribution is outside the critical region. Therefore, in this example a one-tailed test of significance has a Type II error probability of .6915, while a two-tailed test of significance has a Type II error probability of .7939.

Conditions for Using a One-Tailed Test of Significance   In order to use a one-tailed test of significance, we must have some expectation of the direction in which a result will be found, if and when the results turn out to be statistically significant.

This is sometimes a matter of personal intuition, sometimes a matter of previous research, and sometimes a matter of socially shared assumptions. Many years ago we could have conceived of a psychologist testing for a difference in the intelligence of men and women, using a one-tailed test of significance. The assumption would have been that either men and women are the same, or men are more intelligent. A contemporary psychologist is not likely to treat the issue as a one-tailed test. He or she is just as likely to predict feminine as male superiority, given a prediction of a difference. The conclusion with a one-tailed test can only be that the sex predicted to be found superior is more intelligent, or that there is no difference. It is not possible to conclude that the non-predicted sex is more intelligent. With a one-tailed test, outcomes in the non-predicted tail are ignored, no matter how extreme the results in the non-predicted direction. You draw conclusions of differences between populations only if the results occur in the predicted direction.

Doubt About the Use of One-Tailed Tests of Significance The scientific enterprise is best appreciated as a series of operations designed to remove personal prejudice and personal preferences from conclusions. For example, proper experimental procedure requires that the person measuring the results in the experimental and control groups is not aware of which is the experimental group and which is the control group. When possible, the person collecting the data is not aware of the experimental hypothesis. Every effort is made to keep the results free of personal preferences or expectations as to outcomes. Tests are refined so that maximal agreement will be achieved in the scoring. All of these techniques are used to ensure that different people looking at the same data will emerge with the same conclusions. In these ways the scientific community uses scientific techniques to establish a body of data about which there will be universal agreement. If one-tailed tests are used, reliance is placed on the individual scientist's prior beliefs to determine the conclusions from the data. This conflicts with the philosophy aiming towards universal agreement about the results of experiments. One-tailed tests suggest that if a result occurs that is unlikely to be a chance happening, but in the non-predicted direction, the scientific community is to ignore it because the experimenter did not expect the result. Science has often played the role of destroyer of fondly held beliefs. This role would be harder to fulfill if the scientist's prior beliefs determined the acceptability of a conclusion.

A further problem is the assumption that the individual scientist can ignore results in the non-predicted tail, even given extreme findings in the non-predicted direction. The question is, can the person making a one-tailed prediction look at only one tail of a distribution? Let us look at a specific example.

Assume the testing of a drug which is predicted to be able to save lives in some frequently fatal illness. An experimenter testing the drug therefore decides to use a one-tailed test of significance. A significant increase in survivors will constitute a confirmation of the drug's curative powers. A lack of a significant increase or a decrease in survivors will *both* be treated only as a lack of evidence of the drug's effectiveness.

Assume that the experiment is run and, in fact, instead of more survivors, there are actually less survivors with than without the drug. Further, there is such a decrease in survivors (that is, so many more deaths in the drug group) that had there been a two-tailed test of significance the conclusion would have been that the drug is associated with an increase in deaths among people with the disease.

Will the scientist close her or his eyes to the unpredicted results, and proceed as though the only thing that has happened is that the drug has been shown not to be effective in increasing survival? If the same scientist then does a second study with the drug, will the scientist be unconcerned about the possibilities of greater risk for patients who volunteer to take the drug for purposes of the study?

It is suggested here that results that are unlikely under the null hypothesis distribution will cast doubt on the validity of that distribution, whether or not the unlikely events occur in the predicted tail of the distribution. If this is true, then both tails are always being used.

We must be able to ignore unlikely outcomes in one tail of the distribution, in order to use one-tailed tests. There is a question of whether this can be done.

Defense of One-Tailed Tests Those who believe in the use of one-tailed tests claim that we do, in fact, use cumulated implications of prior research, prior experience, and prior beliefs in drawing conclusions. When we are convinced in advance about a result, we are more ready to accept weaker evidence in its favor. When we are convinced that something is not true, we are more skeptical of data contrary to our belief. Many statisticians believe that this is desirable, and so insist on the use of personal expectation in drawing conclusions. Other statisticians believe that, desirable or not, we do incorporate prior expectations in drawing conclusions from new evidence. This suggests that there will be times when we will effectively ignore one tail of the distribution of possible outcomes and only be willing to draw conclusions from the other tail (of expected outcomes). If we use only one tail, we can invest all our Type I error probability in that one tail. This will reduce the critical value (as in our example, from 1.96 to 1.64). This will, in turn, reduce the probabilities of Type II errors. Type II errors are a major problem in psychological research.* The use of one-tailed tests reduces the extent of the problem.

The arguments in favor of one-tailed tests suggest that the scientist's expectations should be a part of the fabric of theory in the profession. The expectations exist, and have subtle influence, so why not make them part of the statistical theory? There is an approach to statistics which overtly incorporates the personal expectations of the scientist into statistical decisions. This is called Bayesian statistics, and a number of textbooks providing that approach have been published. Understandably, if you believe something to be true, you may be willing to accept less evidence (for example, use a less extreme critical value) as confirmation of your belief. A

*Cohen, J. The statistical power of abnormal–social psychological research: A review. *Journal of Abnormal and Social Psychology*, 1962, 65, 145–153.

finding that people with more education earn more money would probably require only a modest amount of evidence to be convincing. But if a study showed that the more educated the person the less they earned, it might be greeted with skepticism unless the evidence was overwhelming. You do not draw conclusions in a vacuum. You believe new things in the context of prior information and prior beliefs. If new facts violate your old assumptions, you may want the new evidence to be exceptionally strong before you believe the new facts. If you really are sure that the results can only occur in one direction, you may simply not believe results in the other direction, no matter how extreme. For example, suppose there is a study that shows that women are taller than men. You will probably conclude that there is a Type I error, or a confused scientist.

Summary of the Issues in One- versus Two-Tailed Tests of Significance There are basically two arguments *in favor of* the use of one-tailed tests:

1. One-tailed tests reduce the probability of Type II errors.
2. The use of one-tailed tests is congenial with a philosophy which says that prior experience should be used in drawing conclusions from new findings. A related but less extreme position is that this is how we draw conclusions, so let us do it overtly and get the advantage of less Type II errors.

There are basically two arguments *against* the use of one tailed tests:

1. One-tailed tests require that the scientist ignore unlikely outcomes in the non-predicted tail of the distribution. There is a question of whether this should be done, and whether this can be done.
2. A major purpose of scientific method is to circumvent the effects of personal bias in drawing conclusions from data collection. One-tailed tests interfere in that process. It is true that the findings from all studies should, and will, contribute to conclusions in an area of inquiry. But the scientist is freer to look at the overall pattern of findings if the conclusions from any one study are independent of all other studies.

These two points of view are clearly contradictory. Both are ably defended by highly respected statisticians. There are many additional arguments besides the philosophical and psychological arguments stressed here. There are also additional positions on the issue. For example, some respected statisticians believe that, given a two-tailed test of significance, the scientist does not have the right to draw conclusions about the direction of the effect, only that there is an effect. However, it is common practice to draw directional conclusions from the observed direction of difference with a significant two-tailed test.

Despite many articles on the topic, there is still no general agreement about the use of one-tailed tests. Up to this point in the text, one-tailed tests of significance have generally been used, since they simplify the introduction to statistical significance. From this point on in the text, two-tailed tests of significance are used.

SENTENCE
COMPLETIONS

The following incomplete sentences are taken from the underlined sentences in this chapter. Fill in the missing words and phrases, then correct them from the answers which follow.

1. The normal distribution is a _____distribution.
2. In a normal distribution, the individual points on the X axis each have probabilities that approach _____ .
3. In the normal distribution, when we know the area of a segment under the curve we also know the _____of an outcome defined as any event within that segment.
4. To use the table of probabilities under the normal curve, we first transform our raw scores to _____ _____.
5. Because the normal distribution is a _____distribution, corresponding intervals on both sides of the mean have the same probabilities.
6. A z score of 0 represents the _____ of the distribution.
7. The law of large numbers says that, as sample size is increased,

   _____

   _____ .

8. The standard deviation of a sampling distribution of means is called

   _____ .

   It is symbolized by _____ .
9. For a given sample size, as the standard deviation increases, the standard error _____ .

10. For a given standard deviation, as the sample size increases, the standard error _____ .

11. When a mean is converted to a z score, the denominator in the transforming equation is not the standard deviation, but rather the _____

_____.

12. The central limit theorem tells us that the means of sufficiently large samples are _____ distributed.

13. Given _____, even if the original distribution of individual scores is not normally distributed, the sampling distribution of means will be.

14. If the distribution of individual scores is only slightly different than the normal distribution, even the means of _____ samples will be approximately normally distributed.

15. We decide _____ an experiment whether we will be looking for unlikely events at just one tail or both tails of the distribution.

16. We decide _____ an experiment what our Type I error probability will be.

17. If we wish to maintain a Type I error probability of .05 two tailed, we set our critical values so that they can be reached or surpassed _____% of the time at each tail.

18. With a _____-tailed test, it is possible to find statistical significance with a less extreme critical value than with a _____ -tailed test.

19. With a one-tailed test, the probability of a Type II error is _____ than with a two-tailed test.

20. In order to use one-tailed tests of significance, we must be able to ignore unlikely outcomes in _____ _____ of the distribution.

21. In statistical inference, a pattern of chance events is identified in the form of some _____.

22. A _____ value is selected, which marks the beginning of a region on the distribution, at and beyond which the null hypothesis would be _____. This region contains _____ events. It is called the _____ region. It is also called the region of _____ .

23. The proportion of the time that the critical value is reached or surpassed when the null hypothesis is true is called the Type _____ error probability.

24. When the null hypothesis is not true we want to reject it. But the only way we can conclude that the null hypothesis is not true is to _____

_____.

25. In any experiment, the critical value can only be located on the _____ _____ distribution.

26. The proportion of the alternative distribution that does not surpass the critical value is equivalent to the probability of a Type _____error.

Answers 1. continuous 2. zero 3. probability 4. z scores (standard scores) 5. symmetric 6. mean 7. the means of samples are expected to be grouped more closely around the population mean. 8. the standard error of the mean; $\sigma_{\bar{x}}$ 9. increases 10. decreases 11. standard error of the mean 12. normally 13. large enough sample sizes 14. small 15. before 16. before 17. 2½ 18. one; two 19. smaller (less) 20. one tail 21. probability distribution (null hypothesis distribution) 22. critical; rejected; unlikely (low probability); critical; rejection 23. I 24. reach or surpass the critical value 25. null hypothesis 26. II

PROBLEMS

Problems 1–8 are a test of whether you know how to use Table III in Appendix B. If you have difficulty with these problems, reread the section titled *Using the Table of Probabilities Under the Normal Curve* (pp. 171–176).

1. Assume a normal distribution. What percentages of the scores are
   (a) above a z score of 1.8?   _____
   (b) below a z score of −1.9?   _____
   (c) above a z score of −1.9?   _____
   (d) between $z = 1.8$ and 1.9?   _____
   (e) between $z = 1.8$ and −1.8?   _____

2. Assume a normal distribution with a mean of 65 and a standard deviation of 5. Give the percentage of the scores contained within the following raw score intervals
   (a) between 70 and 71.25.   _____
   (b) between 58.5 and 55.   _____
   (c) between 71 and 62.5.   _____
   (d) above 78.5   _____
   (e) below 69.5   _____

3. An instructor assumes that only 5% of his class should receive an A, and only 10% a B. He believes that 20% of the students will not be able to pass his class, and expects to therefore give a failing grade of F to the lowest 20%. He will give a D to the next higher 15%, and a C to the remaining 50%. The grades will all be based on the final examination. The highest possible score on the final exam is 100. The mean of the final exam was 70, and the standard deviation was 10. What grades were associated with which scores?

   F _0_ –_____, D _____–_____, C _____–_____,
   B _____–_____, A _____– _100_.

4. The students in a class obtain an average grade of 86, with a standard deviation of 6. The scores are normally distributed. What percentage of the class had a grade above 95?

5. The students in a class obtain an average grade of 86, with a standard deviation of 6. The scores are normally distributed. What percentage of the class had grades between 80 and 90?

6. The students in a class obtain an average grade of 86, with a standard deviation of 6. The scores are normally distributed. What is the lowest score that a student in the class could have obtained, and still have done better than at least 33% of the class?

7. The average IQ at a liberal arts college is 115, with a standard deviation of 10. The scores are normally distributed. A student entering the school is reported to have an IQ of 130. What percentage of the students at the school does he surpass, in terms of his IQ score?

8. The average IQ at a liberal arts college is 115, with a standard deviation of 10. The scores are normally distributed. A student is reported to have an IQ of 110. What percentage of the students in the school does he surpass?

9. The city of Old York has a city-wide test each year for High School graduates. It is a competency test, used to be certain that the students in the high schools have learned a certain minimum in the course of their education. The ninth school district is considered a problem district, from which many students normally fail the exam. In past years the average score from that district has been 400, with a standard deviation of 72. (The rest of the city has an average of 500.) The average of 400 and the standard deviation of 72 have been so consistent in the ninth district that, to all intents and purposes, $\mu = 400$ and $\sigma = 72$ can be considered to be population parameters of the ninth district population.

A new school superintendent has developed a new program which she hopes will change the poor performance of this district. After a year under this new program, the superintendent looks over the latest competency test scores to see if there has been any change with the new program. Her question is, "Is the average in the ninth district any different this year than it normally is, allowing for some difference that is simply random variation?"

She observes that the mean this year, for the 576 graduating seniors from the ninth district, is 421. To test if this mean of 421 reflects some effect of the new program, she intends to employ a statistical test. Her first step is to state a null hypothesis.

(a) What is her null hypothesis?

(b) The superintendent decides to use a two-tailed test, with a .05 probability of a Type I error. What is her critical value?

(c) Having her critical value, what will she need to do to check her empirical mean of 421 against the tabled critical value?

(d) Compute the z score for her.

(e) What will she now conclude?

THE t DISTRIBUTION

In Chapter 9, it was indicated that, given sufficiently large samples, a distribution of sample means would tend to follow the normal distribution (the central limit theorem). Therefore, it will often be reasonable to assume a normal distribution of means as part of the null hypothesis.

If a normal distribution of means is transformed to z scores with Equation (9.7a),

$$z = \frac{\bar{X} - \mu}{\sigma_{\bar{X}}}$$

then the distribution of transformed means will constitute a normal distribution with a population mean of 0 and a standard error of 1. The probability of any mean being sampled can then be determined from the Table for Probabilities Under the Normal Curve (Table III in Appendix B). The mean in question is converted to a z score using Equation (9.7a). The probability of that z score is found in the body of Table III in Appendix B.

Unfortunately, a problem often exists in trying to use this procedure. Equation (9.7a) for z requires the standard error of the mean, $\sigma_{\bar{X}}$, which is computed through Equation (9.6),

$$\sigma_{\bar{X}} = \frac{\sigma}{\sqrt{n}} .$$

But Equation (9.6) requires the population standard deviation, σ, which is an actual population value, not an estimate. Yet many populations are infinitely large. Even if a population is not infinite, measuring everyone in a large population can be time consuming and costly. Therefore, given a question about differences between two groups of people on some measurable trait, we often cannot expect to have the actual population standard deviation, σ, for each group. The best that we can usually expect is an estimate of the population standard deviation, s, obtained from only a sample of the whole population of potential measurements.

In Chapter 5 the estimate of the standard deviation was given in Equation (5.7),

$$s = \sqrt{\frac{\Sigma(X - \bar{X})^2}{n-1}} .$$

The computational version of the estimate of the standard deviation was given in Equation (5.13),

$$s = \sqrt{\frac{\Sigma X^2 - (\Sigma X)^2/n}{n-1}} .$$

Table 10.1 presents a hypothetical sample of data from a hypothetical population. This table illustrates the computation of the sample mean $\bar{X}$ and

TABLE 10.1

Computation of sample statistics from a sample of a larger set of hypothetical data

X	X^2	Estimated Standard Deviation	Estimated Standard Error
2	4	$s = \sqrt{\dfrac{\Sigma X^2 - (\Sigma X)^2/n}{n-1}}$	$s_{\bar{x}} = \dfrac{s}{\sqrt{n}}$
4	16		
3	9	$= \sqrt{\dfrac{159 - (25)^2/5}{4}}$	$= \dfrac{2.92}{\sqrt{5}}$
9	81		
7	49		
$\Sigma X = 25$	$159 = \Sigma X^2$	$= \sqrt{8.5}$	$= 1.30$
		$= 2.92$	

$\bar{X} = \dfrac{\Sigma X}{n} = \dfrac{25}{5} = 5 =$ estimated (sample) mean.

the standard deviation s, which serve as *estimates* of the population mean and the population standard deviation, respectively. Such sample estimates of standard deviations are used to obtain estimates of standard errors; that is, instead of the population standard error, $\sigma_{\bar{x}}$, being computed as

$$\sigma_{\bar{x}} = \frac{\sigma}{\sqrt{n}},$$

the sample estimate of the standard error $s_{\bar{x}}$, is obtained with Equation (10.1).

$$s_{\bar{x}} = \frac{s}{\sqrt{n}}. \tag{10.1}$$

Table 10.1 illustrates the computation of the estimated standard error with Equation (10.1).

When an estimated standard deviation is used to obtain an **estimated standard error of the mean,** a distribution other than the normal distribution results. This new distribution is called the *t* **distribution,** and the scores that form this distribution are called *t* scores instead of *z* scores. The *t* and *z* distributions are similar, but there is an important difference between them.

The transformation to *t* scores inflates the standard error of the mean. Whereas means transformed to *z* scores result in a standard error of the mean equal to 1, the *t* transformation results in a standard error of the mean that is greater than 1.

The reason for this difference between the *t* and *z* distributions can be appreciated after comparing their respective equations. The equation for transforming means to *t* scores is given in Equation (10.2).

$$z = \frac{\bar{X} - \mu}{\sigma_{\bar{X}}} \qquad [9.7a]$$

$$= \frac{\bar{X} - \mu}{\sigma/\sqrt{n}}$$

$$t = \frac{\bar{X} - \mu}{s_{\bar{X}}} \qquad (10.2)$$

$$= \frac{\bar{X} - \mu}{s/\sqrt{n}}.$$

The only difference between Equation (10.2) for t and Equation (9.7a) for z is in the denominator, where, for t, the estimated standard deviation, s, is used in the estimate of the standard error.

The effect of this difference between the two transforming equations is that the use of an estimated standard deviation adds variability to the transformation. In the case of the z transformation, the only source of variability from sample to sample is in the means computed from each sample. This is the same single source of variability as in the distribution of raw-score means. No additional variability is added in the transformation to z scores, because all of the other terms in the formula for z (μ, σ, and n) are constants. But in the t transformation, the standard deviation, s, is a second (additional) source of sample-to-sample variability. The variability from sample estimates of the standard deviation adds to the sample-to-sample variability otherwise expected when sampling means. This additional source of variability increases the expected variability in a distribution of t scores. Thus, means transformed to t scores have more variability than would be present in a sampling distribution of the raw-score means. This results in a visually more spread out distribution, reflecting the enhanced variability of the scores. This is not the case with z scores, which maintain the shape of the distribution of raw-score means. An example should help to clarify this important difference between the z and t distributions.

Because of the wide use of IQ testing, distributions of IQ scores are one of the few types of distributions where it is common to have the population parameters (specifically, the population standard deviation along with the population mean). This will be contrasted below with a case where the population standard deviation is not available, and has to be estimated.

Assume a large subpopulation of children whose mothers all took a particular drug during pregnancy. There is a question of whether the drug had some effect on the intellectual development of these children.

The children, of course, all have potential IQ scores, if only there was sufficient time to test all of them. But assume that the subpopulation is very large, and it is impractical to test all the children. Instead, a sample of nine of these children is tested. (Larger samples would normally be used for such questions, but for expository purposes the number here is kept small.)

Assume that the average IQ score for the more general population of children on this test is 100, with a standard deviation of 15; that is, for children in general on this test, $\mu = 100$ and $\sigma = 15$.

The plan is to compare the mean of the sample of nine children from the drug-exposed subpopulation with the general population of children. Therefore, the variability within the general population should be re-expressed in terms of the population standard deviation of *means,* where n = 9; that is, the population standard error is needed. Using Equation (9.6)

$$\sigma_{\bar{x}} = \frac{\sigma}{\sqrt{n}}$$

$$= \frac{15}{\sqrt{9}}$$

$$= 5.$$

A distribution can be drawn that will illustrate the expected distribution of samples if nine simultaneously drawn IQ scores are repeatedly sampled, at random, from the general population. This is illustrated in Figure 10.1. If the drug group subpopulation is no different than the general population, the sample of nine children from the drug-exposed subpopulation should produce a mean that is likely under the distribution in Figure 10.1. That is, this figure offers a good null hypothesis sampling distribution for answering the question: "Are the children in the subpopulation intellectually equivalent to the general population of children?" The null hypothesis is that the sampling distribution of means from the general population will also accurately describe a distribution of sample means from the drug-exposed subpopulation. In Figure 10.1, the X axis identifies potentially sampled raw-score means, along with equivalent z scores.

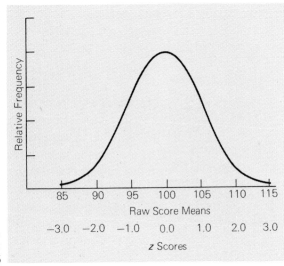

FIGURE 10.1

Distribution of mean scores of hypothetical IQ test with $n = 9$, $\mu = 100$, and $\sigma_{\bar{x}} = 5$

Now contrast this situation with one in which the population standard deviation is not available. Picture a laboratory where all of the work is done by some duty-bound research assistant, while the planning is done by an administrator who is frequently out of the laboratory, flying to Washington to obtain more grant money.

The research assistant was told to test the IQs of nine children, randomly selecting them from among the children whose mothers took the drug during pregnancy. The research assistant was then instructed to compare this subgroup with the general population to see if the drug had an effect on their intellectual development. The administrator told the research assistant the mean IQ of the general population on that IQ test, but neglected to state the population standard deviation.

That evening, after giving the assistant the instructions, the administrator flies to Washington. Unbeknownst to the research assistant, the plane is blown off course, lost in the Bermuda Triangle, and is never heard from again. Meanwhile, back at the lab, the research assistant, not having the population standard deviation, estimates the standard deviation from the sample of nine children and then computes a *t* score using Equation (10.2). When the administrator does not return when expected, the research assistant wonders what to do. He decides to repeat the study to show that he is diligent. When more time passes without the administrator returning, the research assistant keeps on repeating the study. He draws a pair of graphs, recording his sample means on one graph and his computed *t* scores on the other. In this way, there will be a clear record of what he has been doing. Also, the research assistant has always drawn inferences about distributions of means from individual sample means, but has never seen more than one sample mean from a given population. He will now have an empirical distribution of raw-score means, and of *t* scores computed from these means.

After several months of this activity, he has two graphs. He expects that

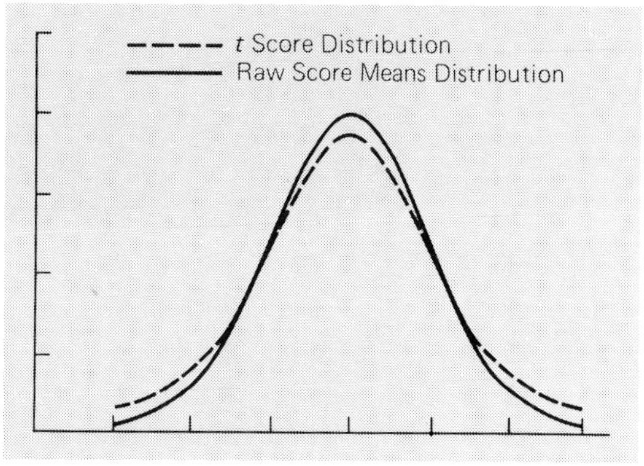

FIGURE 10.2
Hypothetical distribution of raw-score means, and the distribution formed when the raw-score means are converted to *t* scores

they will be identical, because one is composed of just the transformed t scores of the other. However, he thinks that he detects a slight difference. He draws the two curves on the same piece of graph paper, as in Figure 10.2.

If the researcher had been able to use z scores, the z-score and the raw-score distributions would have been identical. But, as previously indicated, t transformations introduce additional variability, causing the observed difference.

The problem causing the increased variability in the t distribution is the variable estimates of s. But that means that if the estimates of s were more reliable, the difference between the t distribution and a distribution of z scores would decrease. This is, in fact, what happens. The estimate of the standard deviation can be made more reliable by increasing the sample size; that is, larger sample sizes yield more dependable estimates of the population standard deviation. Therefore, with large sample sizes, the sample-to-sample values of t are affected less by variations in $s_{\bar{x}}$ (which is directly dependent on s). The result is that as the sample size increases, the distinction between the original raw-score distribution and the same distribution transformed to t scores decreases. If the original distribution is a normal distribution and the sample size is large, then the t distribution is very close to a normal distribution. The transformed t distribution will have a mean of 0 and a standard deviation approximating 1, just like a normal distribution of z scores. Any given value of t will have the same probability as an identical value of z. However, when small samples are used, the increased variability implies that larger values of t are more common. Whereas z scores maintain the original shape of the distribution, t transformations with small samples introduce distortions. Specifically, large values of t have a higher probability of occurring than large values of normally distributed z scores. For example, given a sample size of $n = 9$, a t value of 1.86 or greater has a probability of .10, but a z value of 1.86 or greater has a probability of .03.

For different sample sizes, different tables are needed for the probability of various t values. When the sample sizes get large enough, the table of probabilities under the normal curve can be entered with t scores, just as with z scores. But for most psychological research the sample sizes are sufficiently small that the special *t* **table**, described below, must be used.

The following three statements summarize the differences between the t distribution and the normal distribution.

The t distribution has greater expected variability than is found in the normal distribution.

Greater variability implies that the t distribution is a little flatter in the center and higher at the tails than the normal distribution.

As the sample size is increased, the differences between the two distributions decrease. This implies that there are different t distributions for different sample sizes.

USING THE t DISTRIBUTION FOR STATISTICAL INFERENCE In the example of the hard-working research assistant, a pair of distributions were constructed through repeated sampling. This is not a usual task for any researcher. The usual task involves inferences from much more limited sampling.

In the above example, the task would normally be to obtain a single sample mean, compare it to the known general population mean IQ of $\mu = 100$, and then divide this difference between $\bar{X}$ and μ by a measure of variability. This operation is described by Equation (9.7a) for z and Equation (10.2) for t; that is,

$$z = \frac{\bar{X} - \mu}{\sigma_{\bar{x}}}$$

and

$$t = \frac{\bar{X} - \mu}{s_{\bar{x}}}$$

Since the researcher in the example did not have the population standard error, $\sigma_{\bar{x}}$, he had to use a sample estimated standard error, $s_{\bar{x}}$, which resulted in a t score.

Assume that the data in Table 10.2 is the data that the researcher collected in a single sample. The computations for t are detailed in Table 10.2. The results indicate a t value of

$$t = \frac{\bar{X} - \mu}{s_{\bar{x}}}$$

$$= \frac{98 - 100}{1.90}$$

$$= -1.05.$$

TABLE 10.2
The computation of a t test, with a null hypothesis mean of 100

X	X^2	Estimated Standard Deviation:	Estimated Standard Error:
100	10,000		
105	11,025	$s = \sqrt{\dfrac{\Sigma X^2 - (\Sigma X)^2/n}{n-1}}$	$s_{\bar{x}} = \dfrac{s}{\sqrt{n}}$
90	8,100		
101	10,201		
90	8,100	$= \sqrt{\dfrac{86696 - (882)^2/9}{8}}$	$= \dfrac{5.70}{\sqrt{9}}$
95	9,025		
102	10,404		
95	9,025	$= 5.70$	$= 1.90$
104	10,816		
$\Sigma X = 882$	$86{,}696 = \Sigma X^2$	t Test	

$\bar{X} = \dfrac{\Sigma X}{n}$

$= \dfrac{882}{9}$

$= 98$

$t = \dfrac{\bar{X} - \mu}{s_{\bar{x}}}$

$= \dfrac{98 - 100}{1.90}$

$= -1.05$

Having obtained his t value, what would the assistant do next? As with a z score, the computed t score is compared with some preselected critical value of t to see if statistical significance has been obtained.

There is a table that offers critical values for t scores, the use of which is discussed immediately below.

The Table for the t Distribution A full description of the t distribution would require a different table for each value of n, each with the form of the table of normal probabilities. A simpler, less complete table has been devised which combines the important values from many tables into just one. The t table is generally entered in order to seek out critical t values associated with certain commonly used Type I error probabilities, such as .10, .05, .01, etc. Therefore, all that is needed is the set of critical values for the commonly used levels of Type I error. But different critical values are needed, depending on sample size. The t table lists critical values for common Type I error probabilities, showing different critical values for different sample sizes. The table for the critical values of t appears in Appendix B as Table IV.

Rather than differentiating critical values according to n, degrees of freedom are used. Degrees of freedom are closely related to sample size. In Chapter 5, where degrees of freedom were first discussed, it was indicated that degrees of freedom refer to the number of independent scores that are used to compute a statistic. Just as the estimated standard deviation has $n-1$ degrees of freedom, so does the statistic which incorporates an estimate of the standard deviation. Equation (10.2) uses one estimate of the standard deviation, so Equation (10.2) for t has $n-1$ degrees of freedom. Later in this chapter another equation for t is introduced that incorporates two estimates of the standard deviation, and which has $(n-1) + (n-1)$ degrees of freedom. There are additional formulas for t with still different degrees of freedom. For this reason, the table for t is expressed in terms of degrees of freedom, rather than n, making it useful for different formulas for t.

When using Equation (10.2), Table IV is entered at the row where the degrees of freedom are equal to $n-1$. We use the Type I error probability of our choice to select a column. The intersection of the row and column, in the body of the table, yields the critical value which must be reached or surpassed for statistical significance. There are two different column headings in the table. One is for one-tailed and the other is for two-tailed tests, as indicated in the table.

As an example of the use of the table, assume that we are operating with a Type I error probability of .01, and have a sample of 20 subjects. Our critical value is found in the 19th row ($n-1 = 19$) of Table IV. Assuming a two-tailed test, the critical value is ±2.861. If we use a one-tailed test, the critical value for 19 degrees of freedom is either $+2.539$, or -2.539, depending on the predicted direction of difference from the null. If we choose to operate with a 5% probability of a Type I error, two-tailed, the critical value (for 19 degrees of freedom) is ±2.093. If we assume a one-tailed test at 5% probability of a Type I error, the critical value is either $+1.729$ or -1.729.

Assume that there are 38 subjects, and the degrees of freedom are $n-1 = 37$. The table does not list 37 degrees of freedom. When the needed degrees of freedom are not listed, we go to the closest smaller valued row. Needing 37 degrees of freedom, we go to the row for 30 degrees of freedom. There, the table lists the value 2.042. Thus, given 37 degrees of freedom, the critical value for a two-tailed test at the .05 level is ±2.042.

As an illustration of the use of the *t* table, recall the lonely research assistant who was told to test nine children to see if their intellects had been affected by their mothers having taken a drug during pregnancy. In his laboratory, the usual Type I error probability was .05 two tailed. Since his $n = 9$, his *t* score was computed with $n - 1 = 8$ degrees of freedom. He would have looked up Table IV and gone to the row for 8 degrees of freedom. He would have selected the column headed .05 two tailed, and gone down the column until it intersected the row for 8 degrees of freedom. There he would have seen the value 2.306, the critical value that his computed *t* score would have had to have reached or surpassed for statistical significance. His computed *t* value was -1.05, so he did not have statistical significance.

It was indicated that the key to the use of the *t* distribution is the possession of a hypothesized population mean, but no direct knowledge of the population standard deviation. There are two classes of situations where this occurs. They represent the two most common uses of *t* tests. These two uses of *t* distributions are presented in the next two sections.

MATCHED-PAIR *t* TESTS

The matched-pair *t* test always involves a test of a set of observed *differences*, against a null hypothesis that assumes that the average of the differences is zero. The explication of this *t* test begins with an example.

Some years ago there appeared to be evidence that large doses of glucose (a form of sugar) could improve the intelligence of retarded youngsters. (Further investigation showed that this was not true.) Suppose you had been the person responsible for testing this new possibility, and that 12 randomly selected retarded youngsters were available to you.

There are many IQ tests for children, and several of these have a number of different forms. The different forms of the same test are expected to produce approximately the same estimates of intelligence for a particular child. Using a different form for each testing session, the test can be given more than once to the same child, without the repeated testing making a difference in the score.

A reasonable way, then, for you to test the effect of glucose on IQ is to test the sample of children twice. Each child is tested prior to any ingestion of glucose, and tested again after the ingestion of large doses of glucose. Assume that this was the procedure followed, and that the results are those in Table 10.3.

In the table, the first column signifies each subject; it is followed by two data and two computation columns. The two data columns are the IQ scores of the children before and after the ingestion of glucose. The column

TABLE 10.3

Computation of a matched-pair t test, with hypothetical data

Child	IQ Before (Without Glucose)	IQ After (With Glucose)	D Difference	D^2 (Difference)^2
1	45	48	−3	9
2	65	67	−2	4
3	69	67	+2	4
4	51	48	+3	9
5	60	65	−5	25
6	58	60	−2	4
7	54	53	+1	1
8	52	58	−6	36
9	50	48	+2	4
10	60	65	−5	25
11	68	69	−1	1
12	68	70	−2	4
			$\Sigma D = -18$	$\Sigma D^2 = 126$

t with Equation (10.4):

$$t = \frac{\Sigma D}{\sqrt{\dfrac{n \Sigma D^2 - (\Sigma D)^2}{n-1}}}$$

$$= \frac{-18}{\sqrt{\dfrac{(12)126 - (-18)^2}{11}}}$$

$$= \frac{-18}{10.39}$$

$$= -1.73$$

$$\bar{D} = \frac{\Sigma D}{n}$$

$$= \frac{-18}{12}$$

$$= -1.5$$

t with Equation (10.3):

$$t = \frac{\bar{D}}{s_{\bar{D}}}$$

$$= \frac{-1.5}{.87}$$

$$= -1.73$$

Standard deviation:

$$s_D = \sqrt{\frac{\Sigma D^2 - (\Sigma D)^2/n}{n-1}}$$

$$= \sqrt{\frac{126 - (-18)^2/12}{11}}$$

$$= \sqrt{9}$$

$$= 3$$

Standard error:

$$s_{\bar{D}} = \frac{s}{\sqrt{n}}$$

$$= \frac{3}{\sqrt{12}}$$

$$= .87$$

headed "Difference" is the difference between the "IQ Before" and "IQ After" scores.

In the use of the matched-pair t test, the focus is always on the column of difference scores. The importance of this column becomes clear if the null hypothesis is specified in this situation.

The null hypothesis, as usual, is a cynical hypothesis. The null hypothesis makes the assumption that the experimental variable, in this case glucose, is useless. Therefore, the null hypothesis is that the glucose should not make any difference in the children's IQ scores. What difference scores would be expected if the glucose were ineffective? Were we to live in the never-never land of perfect measurement, the null hypothesis would assume that in every case the difference score would be zero. But we know that there is always variability in measurement. Therefore, we would not be surprised to find some nonzero differences even if the null hypothesis were correct. What the null hypothesis realistically assumes is that the average of a very large number of these differences would be approximately zero; that is, sometimes the difference would be higher with glucose, sometimes lower, and sometimes there would be no difference. But the overall average of the differences would be expected to be zero if the null hypothesis is correct.

As suggested in the previous paragraph, the null hypothesis for the matched-pair t test usually includes a *theoretical* population mean of zero; that is, the null hypothesis specifies an expected average difference of zero. However, the theoretical speculations, or assumptions, would not include any basis for a theoretical standard deviation, just a theoretical population mean (of zero difference). When we have a null hypothesis population mean, but no population standard deviation, we are in a typical situation requiring a t test. We will have to estimate our standard deviation, computing s from our sample. Then we will use s to estimate the standard error, $s_{\bar{x}} = s/\sqrt{n}$, which is needed for the t test.

When working with difference scores, it is common to use D rather than X to symbolize the scores. The mean of the sampled differences is then symbolized as $\bar{D}$ rather than as $\bar{X}$. The estimate of the standard deviation is symbolized as s_D and the estimated standard error as $s_{\bar{D}}$.

The equation for the matched-pair t test follows the previous form of the t test given by Equation (10.2). With the new symbols, it is

$$t = \frac{\bar{D} - \mu}{s_{\bar{D}}}$$

However, when the matched-pair t test assumes a null hypothesis mean of $\mu = 0$, μ can be eliminated from the equation. The result is Equation (10.3).

$$
\begin{aligned}
t &= \frac{\bar{D}}{s_{\bar{D}}} \tag{10.3}\\[2mm]
&= \frac{\bar{D}}{s_D/\sqrt{n}}\\[2mm]
&= \frac{\bar{D}}{\sqrt{\dfrac{1}{n}\left[\dfrac{\Sigma D^2 - (\Sigma D)^2/n}{n-1}\right]}}
\end{aligned}
$$

The final form of Equation (10.3) can be algebraically simplified to the slightly more convenient computational version given in Equation (10.4).

$$t = \frac{\Sigma D}{\sqrt{\dfrac{n\Sigma D^2 - (\Sigma D)^2}{(n-1)}}} \qquad (10.4)$$

The important thing to remember in computations for matched-pair t tests is that you work only with the differences (in column 4 of Table 10.3), not the individual scores in the two groups. Also, in counting up sample size (n), the value of n is always the number of differences, and not the number of measurements. Consequently, degrees of freedom are computed using the number of difference scores as the value of n in $n-1$.

Table 10.3 offers the computations for the glucose example. The uses of both Equations (10.3) and (10.4) are illustrated, and both yield the same value of $t = -1.73$. The t Table (Table IV in Appendix B) indicates that for a two-tailed test of significance, at the .05 level, a t of ±2.201 is required (for 11 degrees of freedom). Thus, in this example, there is no statistical significance. There is no evidence that glucose increases IQ score.

Paired Scores from Different Subjects In the example of glucose and IQ there were repeated measures of the same subjects. This gave a natural basis for pairing the scores (each subject had two scores). It is also possible to match pairs of scores for extracting a difference score when the scores are not from the same subjects. What is required is that the subjects be matched on some additional variable which you know is related to the skill or trait being measured. That is, you match the subjects on something related to the dependent variable.

Suppose that you are doing a study to see which of two texts is better for a course. You have one half of a class reading one text, and the other half reading the other text. Thus, there are two groups, say A and B (with people randomly assigned to each group). You plan to use the final exam grades as the criterion of learning, to test the relative effectiveness of the two texts. Therefore, the final exam grades constitute your dependent variable.

If you pair each student in group A with another student in group B on the basis of prior overall grade-point average, you will be pairing the subjects on a trait (scholastic ability) that is related to the dependent variable (final exam score). Say a student in group A has a grade-point average of 3.1. You can pair that student with a student in group B who also has a grade-point average of 3.1. Grade-point average is related to each person's expected performance in the course in question. If in each pair the two people have the same grade-point average, we can more readily expect a difference score of zero, if the two texts are both of equal value. The null hypothesis will, as usual, assume that there is no difference between the two texts.

In summary, matched-pair *t* tests can be computed when the pairs of scores, one from each of two conditions, can be matched. The basis on which subjects are matched must be related to the dependent variable (the characteristic being measured for a difference).

As another example, assume an investigation of whether two diets, A and B, have a different effect on weight. One group is kept on diet A and the other on diet B. The criterion measure is a difference in weight between the two groups. But height is closely related to weight, so people in the two groups are matched according to their respective heights. A person of a particular height in group A is matched with a person of the same height in group B. This should help to make the resulting weights similar, if the diets are not differently effective. Additional matching can be done on the basis of bone structure, in conjunction with height matching, to make the pairings more similar. The use of the same subjects in both groups is just the most obvious and most complete basis for matching.

Just as careful matching is likely to make the null hypothesis look better if it is true, careful matching helps to make the null hypothesis look bad when it is false. The more completely that subjects are matched, the more sensitive that the statistical test will be to effective treatments; that is, incorrect null hypotheses will be more readily rejected (reducing Type II errors).

t TEST FOR THE DIFFERENCE BETWEEN TWO MEANS

A prior example used two groups of people: group A using one text, and group B using another. Their final exam scores constituted the dependent variable. Subjects were matched on grade-point average. The grade-point average could readily be made available for this purpose in many real-life circumstances. But suppose that this information was not available. Or suppose that it was desired, in this case, to use intelligence test scores as the matching variable. The subjects may never have been tested, and might not have had sufficient time available for being tested. There is actually a wide range of circumstances where no practical basis for matching subjects is available. Sometimes we do not know what kinds of variables are related to the dependent variable. For example, in comparing two forms of psychotherapy, we may want to use mental health, or degree of self-satisfaction, as dependent variables. But we may not know, at least with any degree of confidence, what other variables are related to such dependent variables.

In brief, there are often situations where it is not practical to match the subjects, and the same subjects cannot be used twice. These are, in fact, the more common situations. In these situations, a different form of *t* test is used.

When the scores of two groups are compared, and it is not possible to match the subjects in the two groups on a pair-wise basis, the two means of the two groups are compared. This is called the *t* **test for the difference between two means.**

The Null Hypothesis When Comparing Two Means The result of a study comparing two groups without pairing the subjects is two sampled means, which we symbolize as $\bar{X}_1$ and $\bar{X}_2$. The sampled difference between means, $\bar{X}_1 - \bar{X}_2$, is compared to the null hypothesis assumption of no difference between the means. The null hypothesis is that we have, in effect, sampled from the same population of dependent variable scores twice, and gotten two sample means from the same population. This implies that the null hypothesis is $\mu_1 - \mu_2 = 0$, where μ_1 and μ_2 are the population means for the dependent variable scores of the two groups.

Note that the two groups will have been clearly differentiated on an independent variable. The question is whether the controlled difference on the independent variable is related to the observed difference on the dependent variable. If $\mu_1 - \mu_2 \neq 0$, then the independent variable is related to the dependent variable.

Of course, even given a true null hypothesis of $\mu_1 - \mu_2 = 0$, we would not anticipate precisely zero as the *sample* difference between the means. Rather, we assume a probability distribution of differences $\bar{X}_1 - \bar{X}_2$, where the mean of the distribution of differences equals $\mu_1 - \mu_2$.

Think of endless pairs of means being theoretically sampled, with endless differences $\bar{X}_1 - \bar{X}_2$. If the null hypothesis is true, the long-run average of these differences is $\mu_1 - \mu_2 = 0$. In practice, a single sampled difference, $\bar{X}_1 - \bar{X}_2$, is examined to see just how far away it is from the null hypothesis expectation of zero. The difference between the sampled value, $\bar{X}_1 - \bar{X}_2$, and the null hypothesis value, $\mu_1 - \mu_2$, is not $\bar{X} - \mu$, but rather $(\bar{X}_1 - \bar{X}_2) - (\mu_1 - \mu_2)$. For this sampled difference to be evaluated, it must be converted to a *t* value. But this *t* value requires a standard error for the difference between means, symbolized as $s_{\bar{x}_1 - \bar{x}_2}$. The *t* test for the difference between two means can therefore be symbolized as

$$t = \frac{(\bar{X}_1 - \bar{X}_2) - (\mu_1 - \mu_2)}{s_{\bar{x}_1 - \bar{x}_2}} . \tag{10.5}$$

In practice, because the assumption is almost always made that $\mu_1 - \mu_2 = 0$, $(\mu_1 - \mu_2)$ can be dropped from Equation (10.5), yielding the frequently used symbolization of the formula for *t*,

$$t = \frac{\bar{X}_1 - \bar{X}_2}{s_{\bar{x}_1 - \bar{x}_2}} . \tag{10.6}$$

In this section, the standard error of the difference between two means [the denominator in Equation (10.6)] is examined.

The variability in $s_{\bar{X}_1-\bar{X}_2}$ is not determined by the standard error of only one sample, but by the combined variability brought about by two samples, that is, by variability in the sampling of both $\bar{X}_1$ and $\bar{X}_2$. This means that there is additional variability in $s_{\bar{X}_1-\bar{X}_2}$ when compared to $s_{\bar{X}}$.

When the sample sizes are the same in the two sampled groups, the increased standard error is obtained simply. The squares of the two standard error estimates, $s_{\bar{X}_1}^2$ and $s_{\bar{X}_2}^2$ are added together, and then the square root of the sum is taken. This is symbolized in Equation (10.7), which is the standard error of the difference between means when both groups have equal sample sizes.

TABLE 10.4

Computation of a t test for the difference between two means with equal n

Scores		Squares of Scores	
Group I	Group II	Group I	Group II
20	18	400	324
19	15	361	225
8	8	64	64
10	4	100	16
20	5	400	25
10	14	100	196
13	16	169	256
18	7	324	49
12	13	144	169
5	4	25	16
$\Sigma X_1 = 135$	$\Sigma X_2 = 104$	$\Sigma X_1^2 = 2087$	$\Sigma X_2^2 = 1340$

$$s_1^2 = \frac{\Sigma X_1^2 - (\Sigma X_1)^2/n}{n-1}$$

$$= \frac{2087 - (135)^2/10}{9}$$

$$= 29.39.$$

$$s_2^2 = \frac{\Sigma X_2^2 - (\Sigma X_2)^2/n}{n-1}$$

$$= \frac{1340 - (104)^2/10}{9}$$

$$= 28.71.$$

$$\bar{X}_1 = \frac{\Sigma X_1}{n} \qquad \bar{X}_2 = \frac{\Sigma X_2}{n}$$

$$= \frac{135}{10} \qquad = \frac{104}{10}$$

$$= 13.50 \qquad = 10.40.$$

$$t = \frac{\bar{X}_1 - \bar{X}_2}{s_{\bar{X}_1-\bar{X}_2}}$$

$$= \frac{13.50 - 10.40}{2.41}$$

$$= \frac{3.10}{2.41}$$

$$= 1.29.$$

$$s_{\bar{X}_1-\bar{X}_2} = \sqrt{\frac{s_1^2 + s_2^2}{n}}$$

$$= \sqrt{\frac{29.39 + 28.71}{10}}$$

$$= \sqrt{5.81}$$

$$= 2.41.$$

$$s_{\bar{X}_1 - \bar{X}_2} = \sqrt{s_{\bar{X}_1}{}^2 + s_{\bar{X}_2}{}^2} \qquad (10.7)$$

$$= \sqrt{\frac{s_1{}^2}{n} + \frac{s_2{}^2}{n}}$$

$$= \sqrt{\frac{s_1{}^2 + s_2{}^2}{n}}$$

The n in Equation (10.7) is the n in each group.

Table 10.4 offers a detailed computation of the t test for the difference between two means, with equal n in both groups.

Degrees of Freedom When Testing the Difference Between Means In the case of Equation (10.6) for t, where

$$t = \frac{\bar{X}_1 - \bar{X}_2}{s_{\bar{X}_1 - \bar{X}_2}}$$

there are two estimates of the variance [as seen in Equation (10.7)], along with two estimates of a mean. Each estimate of a mean, in each sample, reduces the freedom of the last (nth) score in a sample to vary in the estimate of the variance for that sample (as discussed in Chapter 5). Therefore, the degrees of freedom for t in Equation (10.6) are:

$$\begin{array}{l} \text{Degrees of freedom} \\ \qquad \text{for a } t \text{ test} \\ \text{between two means} \end{array} = (n_1 - 1) + (n_2 - 1) \qquad (10.8)$$

$$= n_1 + n_2 - 2.$$

In Table 10.4, where the n in each group is 10, the degrees of freedom equal $10 + 10 - 2 = 18$. Entering the table for t for a two-tailed test at the .05 level, a critical value of 2.101 is seen at 18 degrees of freedom. The computed t value in Table 10.4 is 1.29, so we do not have statistical significance.

Working with Different Sample Sizes Suppose that both sampled groups yield the same estimate of the variance, so that $s_1{}^2 = s_2{}^2$. Equation (10.7) can then be restated as

$$s_{\bar{X}_1 - \bar{X}_2} = \sqrt{\frac{s_1{}^2 + s_2{}^2}{n}}$$

$$= \sqrt{\frac{s^2 + s^2}{n}}$$

$$= \sqrt{s^2 \left(\frac{1}{n} + \frac{1}{n} \right)}, \qquad (10.9a)$$

when $s_1{}^2 = s_2{}^2$.

Some such common variance is needed when the sample sizes are not equal. If the sample sizes are not equal, then one estimate of the standard error, taken from one group, is based on a smaller sample than the other estimate of the standard error. Since estimates based on smaller samples are less reliable than those based on larger samples, we do not want the smaller sample to have as much weight as the larger sample in our estimate of $s_{\bar{x}_1 - \bar{x}_2}$. The two sampled variances are therefore each weighted by their respective sample sizes. Then a single weighted average of the two variances is used, instead of the two separate estimates. The equation is

$$s_{\bar{x}_1 - \bar{x}_2} = \sqrt{(\text{weighted average } s^2)\left(\frac{1}{n_1} + \frac{1}{n_2}\right)} \qquad (10.9b)$$

when the two groups have different sample sizes.

The weighted average s^2 in Equation (10.9b) has the form

$$\text{weighted average } s^2 = \frac{(n_1 - 1)s_1^2 + (n_2 - 1)s_2^2}{(n_1 - 1) + (n_2 - 1)} \qquad (10.9c)$$

$$= \frac{(n_1 - 1)s_1^2 + (n_2 - 1)s_2^2}{n_1 + n_2 - 2}.$$

Combining Equations (10.9b) and (10.9c) yields the general formula for the standard error of the difference between means, with unequal n:

$$s_{\bar{x}_1 - \bar{x}_2} = \sqrt{\frac{(n_1 - 1)s_1^2 + (n_2 - 1)s_2^2}{n_1 + n_2 - 2}\left(\frac{1}{n_1} + \frac{1}{n_2}\right)}. \qquad (10.10)$$

Equation (10.10) is used when you have previously computed the variances, s_1^2 and s_2^2, or will have some further need for them. A couple of steps can be saved if Equation (10.11) is used to compute the standard error of the difference between two means.

$$s_{\bar{x}_1 - \bar{x}_2} = \sqrt{\frac{\Sigma X_1^2 + \Sigma X_2^2 - (\Sigma X_1)^2/n_1 - (\Sigma X_2)^2/n_2}{n_1 + n_2 - 2}\left(\frac{1}{n_1} + \frac{1}{n_2}\right)} \qquad (10.11)$$

$$= \sqrt{\frac{\Sigma X_1^2 + \Sigma X_2^2 - (\Sigma X_1)^2/n_1 - (\Sigma X_2)^2/n_2}{n_1 + n_2 - 2}\left(\frac{n_1 + n_2}{n_1 \cdot n_2}\right)}.$$

Both equations (10.10) and (10.11) will yield the same answer. Either equation can be used in the denominator of Equation (10.6) for t,

$$t = \frac{\bar{X}_1 - \bar{X}_2}{s_{\bar{x}_1 - \bar{x}_2}},$$

when you have unequal n. They can also be used for equal n, since equations (10.10) and (10.11) both reduce to Equation (10.7) when $n_1 = n_2$. The complexity in Equation (10.11) sometimes causes students to forget to compute the numerator $(\bar{X}_1 - \bar{X}_2)$ when computing t with Equation (10.6). They then make the mistake of offering $s_{\bar{x}_1-\bar{x}_2}$ for t.

Equation (10.11) is not as complicated as it first appears. It merely requires that the two sets of scores are each summed, and the sums squared, yielding $(\Sigma X_1)^2$ and $(\Sigma X_2)^2$. The individual scores are squared, and then summed, yielding ΣX_1^2 and ΣX_2^2. The remaining values are all simply expressions involving the two sample sizes, n_1 and n_2.

Table 10.5 presents an example of the use of Equation (10.6) for t, with unequal n. In Table 10.5, Equation (10.11) is used to compute $s_{\bar{x}_1-\bar{x}_2}$.

TABLE 10.5
Computation of a t test for the difference between two means with unequal n

Group I	Group II		
X_1	X_2	X_1^2	X_2^2
8	10	64	100
7	8	49	64
7	9	49	81
8	6	64	36
$\Sigma X_1 = 30$	9	$\Sigma X_1^2 = 226$	81
	$\Sigma X_2 = 42$		$\Sigma X_2^2 = 362$

$$t = \frac{\bar{X}_1 - \bar{X}_2}{s_{\bar{x}_1-\bar{x}_2}}$$

degrees of freedom
$= n_1 + n_2 - 2$
$= 4 + 5 - 2$
$= 7.$

$$= \frac{7.50 - 8.40}{.81}$$

$$= \frac{-.90}{.81}$$

$$= -1.11.$$

$$s_{\bar{x}_1-\bar{x}_2} = \sqrt{\frac{\Sigma X_1^2 + \Sigma X_2^2 - (\Sigma X_1)^2/n_1 - (\Sigma X_2)^2/n_2}{n_1 + n_2 - 2} \left[\frac{n_1 + n_2}{n_1 \cdot n_2}\right]}$$

$$= \sqrt{\frac{226 + 362 - (30)^2/4 - (42)^2/5}{4 + 5 - 2} \left[\frac{4 + 5}{4 \cdot 5}\right]}$$

Critical value, at .05 two-tail, is 2.365.
Conclusion: not significant.

$$= \sqrt{\frac{10.2}{7} \cdot \frac{9}{20}}$$

$$= \sqrt{.66}$$

$$= \sqrt{.81}.$$

The matched-pair t test, and the t test for the difference between two means, both attempt to answer the question of whether the two variables are related. In every case, two groups are first distinguished on the independent variable, and then measured on the dependent variable. If the dependent variable scores are different depending on independent variable status, then the two variables are considered to be related.

THE POWER OF t TESTS Figure 10.3 is a graph of the null hypothesis distribution for a t test of the difference between two means. The location of the critical values are specified to visually express the Type I error probability. How would the Type II error probability be visually expressed? The Type II error can only be made when the null hypothesis is incorrect. Therefore, the Type II error can only be made when there is an alternative distribution, other than the null hypothesis distribution. An alternative distribution would have to be added to the figure to illustrate a Type II error probability. In order for a Type II error to be made, an alternative distribution would have to be the true distribution, but not recognized as such. A Type II error is made when the sample difference between means, $\bar{X}_1 - \bar{X}_2$, does not reach the critical value, despite the fact that the population difference, $\mu_1 - \mu_2$, is greater than 0.

In the case of a test of the difference between two means, the null hypothesis would be a distribution of differences between pairs of means, where the average difference would be zero $[(\mu_1 - \mu_2) = 0]$. The alternative distribution would be a distribution of differences between pairs of means, where the average of the differences would *not* be zero. An example of two such distributions of differences between sampled means is given in Figure 10.4, in which the null hypothesis distribution is on the left, with an average difference between two sampled means of zero. The alternative distribution of differences between two sampled means is on the right, where the average difference between two sampled means is $\mu_1 - \mu_2 = 1.4$; that is, with each sample $\bar{X}_1 - \bar{X}_2$ from the alternative distribution pictured in Figure 10.4, a sample is taken from a population of differences

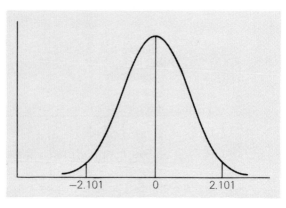

FIGURE 10.3
Graph of t distribution, 18 degrees of freedom. The values ±2.101 are the critical values of $\bar{X}_1 - \bar{X}_2$, sufficiently different from zero for statistical significance at the .05 level.

which is, on the average, 1.4. This is another way of saying that the two population means μ_1 and μ_2, from which $\bar{X}_1$ and $\bar{X}_2$ have been respectively sampled, are actually 1.4 standard errors apart. Of course, the sampled differences $\bar{X}_1 - \bar{X}_2$ will vary from sample to sample. Only the average of all these sampled differences will be 1.4. The question is, will the fact that there is a nonzero population difference be detected with the one sampled difference which will be examined in the t test? The probability of missing the difference between means is the Type II error probability. This is represented in the shaded area of the alternative distribution in Figure 10.4 (to the left of the critical value of +2.101). The Type II error probability is the percentage of the alternative distribution that is below the critical value of the null hypothesis distribution. In Figure 10.4 the probability of a Type II error is .75, since 75% of the alternative distribution is below the critical value.

It is useful to look at the other side of this issue. Instead of talking about the probability of a Type II error, the focus can be on the probability of recognizing that the two means come from different populations. The prob-ability that we will detect the fact that a null hypothesis is false is called **the power of the test**. The power of a test is equal to the proportion of the area of the alternative distribution that is beyond the critical value of the null hypothesis distribution.

$$\text{Power} = 1 - (\text{probability of a Type II error}).$$

In Figure 10.4, where the probability of a Type II error is .75,

$$\text{Power} = 1 - .75$$
$$= .25.$$

Power is represented in Figure 10.4 by the unshaded area in the alternative distribution.

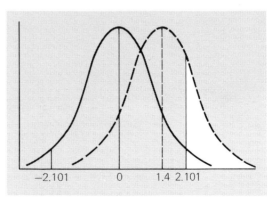

FIGURE 10.4
Graph of t distribution, 18 degrees of freedom. Null hypothesis distribution on the left, alternative on the right. The unshaded area corresponds to the power of the test.

−2.101   0   1.4 2.101

Because power and the Type II error are directly related, they are both affected by the same factors. The size of the difference between the null hypothesis mean and the mean of the true alternative distribution is a major factor in giving power to a statistical test. Simply put, large differences are easier to recognize. To state it another way, the greater the area of the alternative distribution that is beyond the critical value in the null hypothesis distribution, the more likely that the difference will be found to be significant, in a single sampling. If the difference $\mu_1 - \mu_2$, pictured as the mean of the alternative distribution of differences in Figure 10.4, was 3.4 rather than 1.4, much more of the alternative distribution would be beyond the critical value. A much larger proportion of sampled differences between means would be beyond the critical value. Almost any random sampling of two means would yield a significant difference. The incorrectness of the null hypothesis distribution would then be likely to be recognized. If the actual difference between the null and the alternative was much smaller, with the alternative having a mean difference of, say, $\mu_1 - \mu_2 = 0.3$, the null and alternative distributions would be closely overlapping. They would look like the pair of distributions pictured in Figure 10.5. It is unlikely that the alternative distribution would be recognized as correct. A sampled difference $\bar{X}_1 - \bar{X}_2$ would probably be below the critical value of 2.101. Therefore, the best prediction for any one sampling would be that the difference would not surpass the critical value. It would be a waste of time to do the research with such little power to recognize existing relationships between variables. Thus, the size of the difference between the null and alternative distributions is one of the **factors affecting the power of a test.**

A second factor affecting the power of a test is the size of the standard deviation. If the standard deviation is small, then even small differences in mean values will be detectable. The reason is that small standard devia-

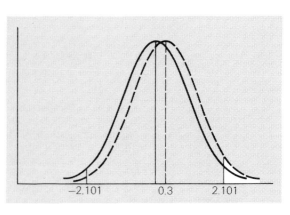

FIGURE 10.5
Graph of t distribution, 18 degrees of freedom. Null hypothesis on the left, alternative on the right. The unshaded area corresponds to the power of the test.

-2.101   0.3   2.101

tions yield small standard errors. This, in turn, means that the distributions become very narrow (given a constant scale on the X axis). Narrowing the distributions in Figure 10.4 would cause more of the alternative distribution to be beyond the null hypothesis distribution's critical value. Put another way, the same raw-score difference between population means would be more standard errors apart if the standard error were smaller.

Standard errors vary as a function of sample size and as a function of standard deviations. This can be clearly seen in Equations (10.1), (10.7), and (10.10). By increasing the sizes of the samples we use, we can reduce the standard errors. Smaller standard errors make it easier to detect differences from null hypotheses. In other words, the power of a statistical test is increased as the sample size is increased.

Sample Size and Power of a t Test In order to know the sample size required for a particular level of power, two things must be known:

1. the distance between the alternative distribution and the null hypothesis distribution; and
2. the size of the standard deviation.

If the distance between the two distributions is known, it means that an alternative distribution exists. If we already knew that, we would not have to do the research. When doing research, the distance between the null hypothesis and alternative distributions is not known.

However, it is possible to estimate the *usual* differences found in a particular research area when differences are, in fact, uncovered. This can be done by going through journal articles and seeing just what the distance is between treatment and control groups when statistical significance has been found. (Given an effective treatment, the difference between the control and treatment groups is an estimate of the difference between the null and alternative distributions.) This was done by Jacob Cohen, who went through a year of articles in the *Journal of Abnormal and Social Psychology*. He wrote an article summarizing his findings,* which was followed by a book† which presents useful tables for estimating power, along with helpful discussions of the topic.

One of the things that Cohen did was to trichotomize the degrees of difference that one can expect between population means in psychological research. He estimated that the most common difference between means is

*Cohen, J. The statistical power of abnormal-social psychological research: A review. *Journal of Abnormal and Social Psychology*, 1962, 65, 145–153.

†Cohen, J. *Statistical power analysis for the behavioral sciences*, Revised edition. (New York: Academic Press, 1977).

a difference of about half a standard deviation. He called this most common difference of $.5\sigma$ a medium difference. He defined a large difference as one involving a difference of $.8\sigma$ between population means. These larger (and less frequent) differences would be expected in areas with well-established paradigms that control (and thereby eliminate) a good deal of extraneous variance. He defined a small difference as a difference of $.2\sigma$. Small differences would be expected in exploratory research, field research, or any research which is poorly controlled (resulting in additional sources of extraneous variance).

Cohen's tables are not limited to small, medium, and large differences. But here the information has been abstracted from his tables for just small, medium, and large differences. The tables here are also limited to two levels of power, .80 and .50. It is rare to find power above .80 in the psychological literature, so .80 has been selected as a desirable but ambitious ideal of power. The .50 level of power has been selected as the minimal desirable level. Actually, .50 is a common level of power in research, according to Cohen's survey. But .50 power means that when your independent and dependent variables are related, there is only a .50 chance of recognizing that they are related. Given the time and trouble involved in most research, a .50 chance of recognizing a correct alternative hypothesis constitutes pretty poor odds. So it is not recommended that research be done at such a low level of power, and certainly not below that level.

The summary tables presented here, then, offer the required values of n for a less-than-desirable .50 power level, and an ideal level of .80 power. The sizes of samples in your research utilizing t tests should be somewhere between the values of n required for the two power levels. The closer your n is to the values that would yield .80 power, the better.

The sizes of samples needed for the two power levels are different depending on the difference between the population means. For example, for a small difference between the means of the null and alternative distributions ($.2\sigma$), 193 subjects would be needed in each group, in order for a t test for the difference between two means to have .50 power. Only 13 subjects per group would be needed for the case where the null and alternative distributions were $.8\sigma$ apart (a large difference). Therefore, the different sample sizes associated with a particular level of power are presented for small, medium, and large differences between population means. The level of control over extraneous variables, as described above, should indicate whether small, medium, or large differences are to be expected.

Table 10.6 offers suggested sizes of n for tests of the difference between two means. Table 10.7 offers suggested sizes of n for matched-pair tests.

The table does not reflect the fact that power increases as subjects are more closely matched on a relevant variable. Therefore the sizes of n suggested in Table 10.6 may be larger than needed, for the indicated power levels.

TABLE 10.6

Suggested number of measurements in each group (size of n in each group) for .50 and .80 power (Type I error probability .05 two-tailed). The power obtained is decreased as the n in the two groups becomes more dissimilar. Thus, if 64 are required in each group for .80 power, that would mean a total of 128 subjects. But if the 128 subjects were not evenly divided between the two groups, then power would be less than .80.

Difference between population means	Anticipated Power in t Test of a Difference Between Two Means	
	.50	.80
Large	13	26
Medium	32	64
Small	193	393

TABLE 10.7

Suggested number of differences (size of n) for .50 and .80 power (Type I error probability .05 two-tailed). Smaller n is required for closely matched subjects.

Difference between population means	Anticipated Power in Matched-Pair t Test	
	.50	.80
Large	7	14
Medium	17	33
Small	88	180

A NOTE ON ASSUMPTIONS It has generally been assumed that the t test is correctly computed when the populations of dependent variable scores are normally distributed, and the variances of both populations are equal. Because of the central limit theorem, the means of sufficiently large samples from a wide range of distribution shapes will be approximately normally distributed. This gives the t test its wide applicability. However, heavily skewed distributions do require very large sample sizes for accurate use of the *t* tables.

Besides the general issue of distribution shape, there are two more requirements that have to be considered. One is the range of the dependent variable values. A normal distribution assumes a continuous distribution. In practice, experimenters are often interested in distributions consisting of just a few possible outcomes. For example, "years of education" is a common dependent variable. Yet years of education generally range somewhere between 0 and 20 years, consisting of only 21 specific values for individual people. But the use of sample means results in the sampling of mean values between integers. Given large enough samples, the range of possible mean values can approach infinity. Thus, even though the original range of dependent variable scores is not continuous, the means can approach a continuous distribution. Therefore, *t* tests can be done with dependent variable scores that have a limited range. The smaller the set of the dependent variable scores, the larger the sample sizes should be.

A second assumption for *t* tests is generally identified as the need for **homogeneity of variance.** This means that there is an assumption that both samples are samples of populations with the same variance. In practice, this assumption can also be violated with minimal effects. As a rule of thumb, if the variance estimated from one sample is no more than twice the variance estimate obtained from the other sample, there is no cause for concern. But if one variance estimate is three times the other, or more, then the steps suggested below should be taken. Keeping sample sizes equal helps to minimize the distorting effects due to lack of homogeneity.

The **effect of violations of the assumptions** of the test is that the *t* table is less likely to be accurate in the indications of the probability of Type I errors associated with the critical values. Thus, if two variances are not equal, the Type I error probability shown in the table may be understated. A critical value ostensibly offering a Type I error probability of .05 may really offer a Type I error probability of .06 or, in extreme cases, .07. A combination of violations of assumptions (lack of homogeneity of variance *and* means that are not normally distributed) would be required for a tabled .05 error probability to actually be .08.

Since violations of assumptions affect the expected Type I error probability, one solution is to use a more conservative Type I error probability. If the assumptions seem heavily violated, use a Type I error probability of .02, rather than the usual .05. In this way, whatever the extent of the distortion, the Type I error probability level is still not likely to be greater than .05.

In summary, when in doubt about having met the assumptions of a normal distribution and homogeneity of variance, use large, equally-sized samples in each group. In case of a likelihood of extreme or multiple violations, use a conservative Type I error.

SENTENCE
COMPLETIONS
The following incomplete sentences are taken from the underlined sentences in this chapter. Fill in the missing words and phrases and then correct them from the answers which follow.

1. We often cannot expect to have the actual population standard deviation for each group. The best we can usually expect is an _____ of the population standard deviation, obtained from _____ _____ .

2. We use_____ _____ of the standard deviation to obtain an estimate of the standard error.

3. Means transformed to *t* scores have _____ _____ than would be present in a sampling distribution of the raw-score means.

4. The *t* distribution is a little _____ in the center and _____ at the tails than the normal distribution.

5. As we increase sample size, the difference between the normal and *t* distributions _____ .

6. The *t* table lists _____ _____ for common Type I error probabilities, showing different _____ _____ for different degrees of freedom.

7. In practically all applications of the matched-pair *t* test, the null hypothesis specifies an expected average difference of _____ .

8. The important thing to remember in computations for matched-pair *t* tests is that you work only with the _____ .

9. In the matched-pair *t* test, the value of *n* is always the number of _____ .

10. Matched-pair *t* tests can be computed when pairs of subjects, one from each of two conditions, can be matched. The basis on which subjects are matched must be related to the _____ _____ .

11. The more completely subjects are _____, the more sensitive the matched-pair t test will be to effective treatments.

12. When the means of two groups are compared and tested for significance, the test is called _____ _____.

13. If the dependent variable scores are different depending on the independent variable status, then the two variables are _____.

14. In the t test for the difference between two means, the null hypothesis is that we have sampled from the _____ population of dependent variable scores _____.

15. The greater the area of the alternative distribution that is beyond the critical value in the null hypothesis distribution, the _____ likely that the difference will be found to be significant.

16. When the size of the difference between the null hypothesis distribution and the true alternative distribution is larger, the power is _____.

17. The probability that we will detect the fact that a null hypothesis is _____ is called the power of the test.

18. The same raw score difference between population means will be _____ standard errors apart if the standard error is smaller.

19. By _____ the sizes of the samples that we use, we can reduce the standard errors.

20. The power of a statistical test increases as sample size is _____.

21. When our null hypothesis is false, and we do not reach or surpass our critical value, we call this a Type _____ error.

22. The effect of violations on the assumptions of the t test is that the t test is less likely to be accurate in the indications of _____ _____.

23. When in doubt about having met the assumptions of the t test of a _____ _____ and _____ of _____ , we use _____ samples. In case of a likelihood of extreme or multiple violations of assumptions, use a _____ Type I error level.

Answers 1. estimate; a sample of the population 2. sample estimates 3. more variability 4. flatter; higher 5. decreases 6. critical values; critical values 7. zero 8. differences 9. differences (pairs) 10. dependent variable 11. matched 12. the t test for the difference between two means 13. related 14. same; twice 15. more 16. greater (larger)(increased) 17. false 18. more 19. increasing 20. increased 21. II 22. the probability of Type I errors 23. normal distribution; homogeneity; variance; large; conservative (low probability) (smaller)

1. Obtain an estimate of the standard error of the mean for the population of scores from which the following scores have been sampled: 3, 4, 6, 3, 4.

2. There are two groups of children in an elementary school class. One group generally scores high on tests, receiving A grades in almost every subject. The other group generally receives D grades or fails the subject.

   The teacher wonders whether self-discipline and self-control are greater in the A than in the D group. She speculates that the self-control may be expressed as self-denial in a cookie availability situation. To test her theory, she has cookies available in an ambiguous situation and counts how many cookies each child takes. The results appear below.

   Is self-denial different in the two populations of A and D students, as represented in these two samples? Do the necessary statistical work, and reach a conclusion. Use a two-tailed significance level of .05.

   (a) Critical value in the table: _____

   (b) Computed t value: _____

   (c) Significant or not significant: _____

   (d) Verbalized conclusion: _____
   _____

   (e) Assume that the difference between the two groups was expected to be moderate in size. What would be the number of subjects needed in each group to have at least .50 power?

   Results: Cookies taken by A group: 1, 2, 1, 2, 2.
   Cookies taken by D group: 2, 1, 3, 4, 3.

3. One year, a graduate school takes all its students from large state universities. The next year they take all their students from small private colleges. A teacher in the graduate program wonders whether the two groups represent different intellectual populations, in terms of their ability to deal with the material in her course. Last year she had six students in her seminar, all from large state universities. This year she has four students from the private schools. She compares their final exam grades and does a statistical test to see if they appear to come from different populations. The final exam grades are given below. Do the computations that this teacher would have done. Use a two-tailed significance level of .05.

Large State Universities	Small Private Colleges
100	90
90	80
90	70
80	80
90	
80	

(a) Critical value in the table: _____

(b) Computed t value: _____

(c) Significant or not significant: _____

(d) Verbalized conclusion: _____
_____

4. During the Fall semester you had the first semester of each of four two-semester courses. Your first semester grades in these four courses were: Physics, D; Chemistry, C; Biology, B; and Psychology, C. The grade points for A, B, C, and D, are, respectively, 4, 3, 2, and 1. Therefore, the earned grade points for your four courses were Physics, 1; Chemistry, 2; Biology, 3; and Psychology, 2.

The second semester you used a different study technique. You wanted to see if that helped you in your classes. Since you took four classes in the same subject both semesters, you decided to test for the difference with a matched-pair t test. The second semester the four grades were Physics, B; Chemistry, B; Biology, A; and Psychology, A, with respective grade points of 3, 3, 4, and 4.

Do the matched-pair t test to see if you would conclude that the difference between your performance during the two semesters is anything other than a chance difference. Use a two-tailed significance level of .05.

(a) Critical value in the table: _____

(b) Computed t value: _____

(c) Significant or not significant: _____

(d) Verbalized conclusion: _____
_____

eleven

CORRELATION

Up to this point, the focus has been on whether one variable is related to another. For example, is diet related to intelligence? Is administration of a drug related to blood pressure?

The question of whether one variable is related to another can be answered by comparing two groups of measurements. For example, the IQ scores of people on some diet, A, can be compared with those on some diet, B. If the two sets of measurements are significantly different, we can conclude that the independent variable defining the groups (diet) is related to the dependent variable (IQ). The basic question, then, which was dealt with in previous chapters, is whether two variables are related to each other. The focus of this chapter is on the degree of relationship between two variables.

DEGREE OF RELATIONSHIP There are times when independent variables are easily dichotomized, readily identifying just two groups of measurements, as in the comparison of two different diets. Another example of a dichotomous independent variable is the comparison of a drug with a placebo. We could see if the presence or absence of the drug is related to some dependent measure, for example, blood pressure. Whereas the presence or absence of the drug offers a dichotomous variable, the dependent variable, blood pressure, is a continuous variable.

Suppose that instead of a dichotomous independent variable and a continuous dependent variable, we have two continuous variables. For example, suppose that the two variables are IQ and grade-point average (GPA). With two continuous variables we cannot simply identify two significantly different sets of IQs because we will not have dichotomized groups on GPA. Conversely, we cannot identify two significantly different sets of GPAs because we will not have dichotomized groups of IQs. We can, however, jointly list the paired scores (IQ and GPA) for each student, as in Table 11.1, and see if the paired scores tend to rise and fall together.

TABLE 11.1
IQs and grade-point averages for nine hypothetical students (perfect positive correlation)

Student	IQ	GPA
1	90	2.75
2	95	2.90
3	100	3.05
4	105	3.20
5	110	3.35
6	115	3.50
7	120	3.65
8	125	3.80
9	130	3.95

For example, we may find that people with higher IQs tend to have higher GPAs. This is another way of identifying two related variables. As will be seen below, this approach has the further advantage of indexing the degree of relationship.

In Table 11.1, the higher IQ scores are all paired with higher GPAs, and middle IQs with middle GPAs. The relationship pictured in Table 11.1 is a perfect one, with IQ and GPA rising and falling in perfect unison. Such a reliable relationship would be realistic if intelligence is the only thing that

CORRELATION as a Degree of Relationship:

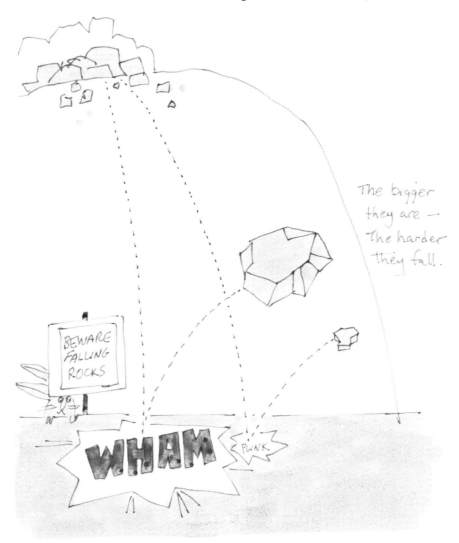

The bigger they are — The harder they fall.

affects grade-point averages. However, other things also affect grade-point averages. For example, students' interest in school, or other events in their lives, also affect their grades. Therefore, we expect something other than a perfect relationship between the two sets of scores. We may find that most higher-IQ people have high GPAs, with just a few high-IQ people having moderate or low GPAs. If *almost* all pairings of IQ and GPA are jointly high, moderate, or low, we can conclude that the relationship between IQ and GPA is a strong, though not a perfect, one. If there are many exceptions to paired scores being jointly high or low, we conclude that there is a weak relationship.

The new point being introduced here is that whereas unrelated variables by definition have no relationship, related variables can have different degrees of relationship. Thus, in addition to the question of whether variables are related, we will sometimes ask what is the degree of relationship. We will want to know the degree to which the paired scores co-relate. Therefore, we call a relationship between paired sets of scores a correlation. This chapter focuses on a discussion of a statistic which offers a numerical index of correlation.

LINEAR RELATIONSHIPS In the artificial (and unrealistic) data of Table 11.1, each subject's IQ score is related to that subject's GPA by the following equation:

$$Y = (.03)X + .05,$$

where Y is the GPA and X is the IQ. Of course, this is not obvious from mere inspection of the two columns of scores. But, in fact, this is the way in which the two columns of scores are related. For example, a subject with an IQ of 110 has a GPA of

$$Y = (.03)110 + .05$$

$$= 3.35$$

Whenever two sets of measurement X and Y are related according to an equation of the form

$$Y = bX + a, \tag{11.1}*$$

we have a linear relationship. We call it a linear relationship because when X and Y are related as in Equation (11.1), the graph of the relationship always forms a straight line. The data of Table 11.1 have been graphed in Figure 11.1.

Each dot in Figure 11.1 refers to a paired X and Y value. For example, the

---

*In this chapter, an asterisk has been placed next to those formulas that are of special importance.

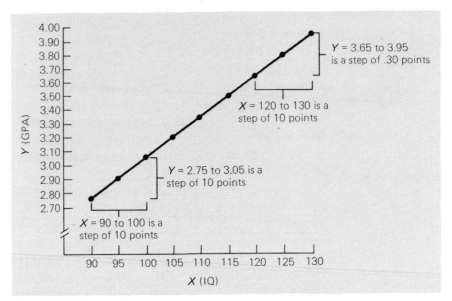

FIGURE 11.1
Graph of the hypothetical data in Table 11.1 (perfect correlation)

first dot in the bottom left-hand part of the graph is for subject 1 in Table 11.1, where $X = 90$ and $Y = 2.75$. A line has been drawn through all the dots for all the students, and it is a straight line. The curve drawn through any points (X,Y) is always a straight line if X is related to Y by Equation (11.1); that is, when X is related to Y by the linear equation $Y = bX + a$.

When two sets of scores are related, and the relationship can be graphed by a straight line, we call the relationship a **linear correlation**. Correlation between sets of paired scores means that there is a relationship between the sets of scores. But *linear* correlation specifies a particular form for that relationship. In linear correlation, there is a constant slope defining the relationship, which is b in Equation (11.1). For the hypothetical data graphed in Figure 11.1, $b = .03$. A *straight* sloping line means that for any constant change in X there is a constant change in Y. For example, if X is increased by 10 points, Y is increased by

$$Increase = (.03)X$$

$$= (.03)10$$

$$= .30,$$

no matter where the 10 point increase occurs along the X axis. The constant relationship between X and Y keeps the line straight in Figure 11.1. We only call the correlation a linear correlation when we can identify a best-fitting *straight* line in the graph.

Correlation does not have to be linear. For example, two sets of scores can be related by $Y = X^2$, or $Y = X^3$, etc. When the relationship between X and Y involves raising X to some power (other than 0 or 1) a straight line is not an accurate representation of the relationship. The subject of nonlinear correlation is an advanced topic with more limited applications in the social and behavioral sciences. Therefore, in this introductory text, the discussion is limited to linear correlation.

Correlation and Slope
As long as the coefficient b in Equation (11.1)

$$Y = bX + a$$

is nonzero, the line following the equation has a slope. In Figure 11.1 the line indicating the relationship between the two sets of scores is a straight *sloping* line ($b = .03$). A sloping line indicates changes in Y for changes in X. If the line of relationship is a straight *horizontal* line, then it implies that the same Y score exists for every different X score. For example, if people with different IQs (the X axis in Figure 11.1) all had the same GPA (the Y axis in Figure 11.1), then it would not be reasonable to speak of a relationship between IQ and GPA. It is the sloping line that suggests that there is a relationship. In Figure 11.1, the higher the IQ, the higher the GPA.

The absence of a sloping line implies no relationship. But the degree of slope is not so informative. Whether the sloping line has a steep or shallow slope does not indicate how closely the two sets of scores are related.

The difference in the scales of measurement for the two variables makes a difference in the slope, along with how closely values are positioned on the axes of the graph. Thus, the degree of slope is not informative when working with raw scores for two variables. But, if there is a relationship between the two sets of scores, then *some* nonzero *sloping* line exists for aiding in the prediction of Y from X.

If the two variables are standardized, and identical scales are used on the axes, slopes are informative. This situation is discussed in a later section of this chapter. But when working with raw scores, the significance of slope is limited to the fact that a zero slope ($b = 0$) means that no linear correlation exists.

Table 11.2 and Figure 11.2 offer an example of a correlation that is less than perfect. Once again, the data are hypothetical data of the association between IQ and GPA.

The graph in Figure 11.2 indicates less than perfect correlation by showing some (X, Y) points where the Y values are off the best-fitting straight line. The straight line in Figure 11.2 is drawn according to Equation (11.1), where, once again, $a = .05$ and $b = .03$ in

$$Y' = (.03)X + .05.$$

TABLE 11.2

IQ and grade-point averages for nine hypothetical students (less than perfect positive correlation)

Student	IQ	GPA
1	90	2.75
2	95	2.75
3	100	3.20
4	105	3.20
5	110	3.35
6	115	3.65
7	120	3.50
8	125	3.95
9	130	3.80

The predicted value is symbolized as Y' rather than as Y, since the predicted value of Y' is not always identical to the actual value of Y. As can be seen by the placement of points in Figure 11.2, six of the points are off the line of predicted (Y') values.

Strong correlation is reflected in relatively little variation of actual Y from predicted Y' scores. Weak correlation is reflected in a wide scattering of the dots off the prediction line.

Looking over the graph of Figure 11.2, you can see that there is a tendency for higher IQ scores to be associated with higher GPAs. But from

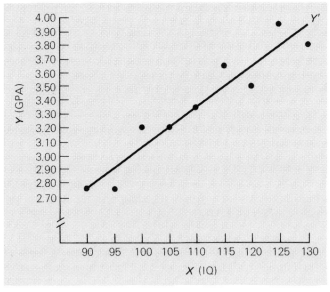

FIGURE 11.2

Graph of the hypothetical data in Table 11.2 (less than perfect correlation)

the occurrence of points off the prediction line, it is clear that the relationship is a loose one; that is, there is a correlation between the two sets of scores in Table 11.2, but it is not a perfect correlation.

In the real world, we rarely find paired sets of scores that obediently follow Equation (11.1) for every point placement. Rather, two sets of correlated scores are likely to only be imperfectly correlated. With imperfect correlation we can still find some best-fitting straight line which goes through the middle of the set of points, with some points off the line, as in Figure 11.2. But the line is only a compromise, placed to pass between some of the points when it can not touch all of them and remain straight. (A means of constructing this line, and finding values for a and b, is presented later in this chapter.)

It was previously stated that, given a best-fitting straight line with no slope (that is, where the coefficient $b = 0$), the correlation is zero. This zero correlation reflects the fact that knowing the value of X is not informative about the value of Y. But any arrangement of X,Y points such that X offers no information about Y should also yield a correlation of zero. Often, the pattern of X,Y points for no correlation is circular. When the points form a circular pattern, any centrally placed sloping line with an arbitrary slope fits as well as any other and is equally uninformative. An example of a circular pattern in shown in Figure 11.3.

In Figure 11.3, there is no better predictor of Y than the mean of the Y scores. The use of the mean of Y to predict each unknown Y is a way to

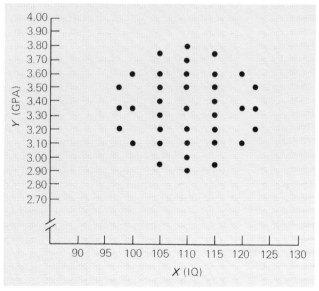

FIGURE 11.3
Graph of uncorrelated scores (hypothetical data)

minimize errors in prediction, when there is no correlation. This is an important generalization. When there is no correlation between two sets of scores X and Y, the best predictor for the set of Y scores is the mean of the Y scores. If a horizontal line were drawn through Figure 11.3 at the mean of the Y scores, it would represent a non-sloping prediction line. For each X score, the same Y score (the mean of the Y values) would be predicted.

Whenever there is a relationship between X and Y, predictions of Y scores are better, on the average, using X and a sloping prediction line, than they are if the mean of the Y scores is used as a constant prediction. The greater the improvement of prediction when using X and the sloping line, the higher the degree of correlation.

Note that although prediction is discussed as possible with correlated scores, correlation is *not* prediction. Correlation simply indicates how good an attempt at prediction *would* be. The better the *potential* prediction of Y from X, the closer the relationship between X and Y. The closer the relationship between X and Y, the higher the correlation between X and Y. It is in this sense that correlation means degree of relationship.

In Table 11.1 and 11.2 no X value is repeated. With actual tests and other sets of measurements there are generally many instances of repetitions of X values. For example, there could be several people with the same IQ score, but each having different GPAs. This is implied in Figure 11.3, and is seen again in Figure 11.4. In this figure, the many different Y scores associated with each X score form a vertical column of dots over each X score.

A pattern of linear relationship can be identified in Figure 11.4. For any X value, the Y scores, though varied, tend to group within a particular range

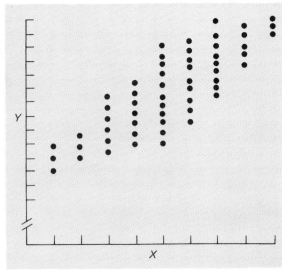

FIGURE 11.4
Correlated X and Y scores, with multiple occurrences of the same X scores

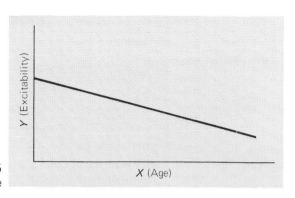

FIGURE 11.5
Graph with a negative slope

on the Y axis. The range is different for different X values. The higher the X value in Figure 11.4, the higher the midpoint of the range within which the Y scores are clustered. The pattern of dots suggests a correlation.

Negative Correlation Only the case of correlation with upward-sloping prediction lines has been examined. Upward-sloping graphs are called lines with **positive slope.** Correlation can also be just as helpful, and just as meaningful, with a downward-sloping prediction line. For example, suppose that we have a test of excitability (tendency to lose one's temper, tendency to become enthused quickly, etc.) We are interested in the correlation of excitability (Y) with age (X). We may find that the greater the age, the *less* the excitability; that is, a graph of the relationship of X and Y may look like Figure 11.5, which offers an example of a negatively sloping graph. If the prediction line for two sets of scores has a **negative slope,** we speak of a **negative correlation.** When it has a positive slope, we speak of a **positive correlation.** When there is no slope, we speak of zero correlation.

Correlation, then, will reflect a negative relationship when high scores on one measure are associated with low scores on another; a positive relationship when high scores on one measure are associated with high scores on another, and similar correspondence for low scores; and no relationship when there is no pattern of relationship between scores on the two measures.

THE CORRELATION COEFFICIENT AND ITS VALUES It is convenient to have some numbers that specify the degree of correlation. Further, it is helpful to have these numbers reflect whether the correlation is positive or negative.

The formulas for correlation have been algebraically manipulated so that a **perfect positive correlation** yields a correlation of +1; a **perfect nega-**

tive correlation yields a correlation of −1; and a complete absence of correlation yields a correlation of 0. Values between 0 and +1 reflect varying degrees of positive correlation. Values between 0 and −1 reflect varying degrees of negative correlation.

The formula used in this chapter to compute the index of correlation between two sets of scores X and Y yields a number called the **product moment correlation coefficient.** It is sometimes called Pearson's product moment correlation coefficient, after Karl Pearson, who developed the statistic.

When referring to the correlation coefficient in a population of paired scores X and Y, Pearson's correlation coefficient is symbolized as ρ_{XY}, using the Greek letter rho, appropriate to a population parameter. Since most psychological data employ samples, Pearson's correlation coefficient is more often estimated from samples. When Pearson's correlation coefficient is estimated from a sample of paired scores X and Y, it is symbolized as r_{XY}. In fact, Pearson's product moment correlation coefficient is most often simply referred to as **Pearson's r.**

The formula for Pearson's r is the same, regardless of whether the data are sample data or data of a complete population. The difference is in the interpretation of the correlation coefficient. It will be convenient to discuss the formula initially as if the data of the complete population are always available, introducing the cautionary notes for interpretation of sample data later in the discussion.

Pearson's product moment correlation coefficient consists of three components. Two should be familiar to you and one unfamiliar. The familiar components are the standard deviations for each set of scores, σ_X and σ_Y. Subscripts have been added to σ to differentiate the standard deviations of the two sets of scores, X and Y. Pearson's r is a ratio, where the denominator is the product of the two standard deviations, as in Equation (11.2).

$$\rho_{XY} = \frac{\sigma_{XY}}{\sigma_X \sigma_Y} . \qquad\qquad (11.2)^*$$

The respective standard deviations in the denominator of Pearson's r are conveniently computed with the computational formulas originally presented in Chapter 5, that is,

$$\sigma_X = \sqrt{\frac{\Sigma X^2 - (\Sigma X)^2/n}{n}}$$

and

$$\sigma_Y = \sqrt{\frac{\Sigma Y^2 - (\Sigma Y)^2/n}{n}}$$

The numerator of Pearson's r, σ_{XY}, is the unfamiliar part of the ratio. It is called the **covariance.**

Cross Products and the Covariance The covariance is the average cross product. A **cross product** is the product of associated deviations from means, $(X_i - \mu_X)(Y_i - \mu_Y)$; where μ_X is the mean of the X scores in the population of paired X and Y scores, and μ_Y is the mean of the Y scores in the population of paired X and Y scores. X_i is the score of the ith subject on variable X, and Y_i is the score of the ith subject on variable Y.

The cross products $(X_i - \mu_X)(Y_i - \mu_Y)$ can be summed over all n subjects in the population, yielding:

$$\text{Sum of cross products} = \sum_{i=1}^{n} (X_i - \mu_X)(Y_i - \mu_Y).$$

The average cross product is called the covariance. The defining formula for the covariance is

$$\sigma_{XY} = \frac{\sum_{i=1}^{n} (X_i - \mu_X)(Y_i - \mu_Y)}{n} \qquad (11.3)$$

where n is the number of paired X and Y scores in the population.

Were Equation (11.3) actually used to compute the numerator of Equation (11.2), the mean for each set of scores μ_X and μ_Y would have to be computed and then subtracted from each score to obtain deviation scores. In the case of the variance and the standard deviation, it was shown in Chapter 5 that there are equivalent computational formulas that permit the computation of statistics without first requiring the computation of deviation scores. Using the same rules of summation and algebra that were used in Chapter 5, a computational formula for the covariance can be constructed. The computational formula for the covariance is

$$\sigma_{XY} = \frac{\Sigma XY - [(\Sigma X)(\Sigma Y)]/n}{n}. \qquad (11.4)$$

Recall that in Equation (11.2) Pearson's r was presented as

$$\rho_{XY} = \frac{\sigma_{XY}}{\sigma_X \sigma_Y}.$$

Substituting the computational formulas into Equation (11.2) yields Equation (11.5a).

$$\rho_{XY} = \frac{\dfrac{\Sigma XY - [(\Sigma X)(\Sigma Y)]/n}{n}}{\sqrt{\dfrac{\Sigma X^2 - (\Sigma X)^2/n}{n}} \sqrt{\dfrac{\Sigma Y^2 - (\Sigma Y)^2/n}{n}}}. \qquad (11.5a)$$

If using sample data, the formula is

$$r_{XY} = \frac{S_{XY}}{S_X S_Y} \tag{11.5b}$$

$$= \frac{\dfrac{\Sigma XY - [(\Sigma X)(\Sigma Y)]/n}{n-1}}{\sqrt{\dfrac{\Sigma X^2 - (\Sigma X)^2/n}{n-1}} \sqrt{\dfrac{\Sigma Y^2 - (\Sigma Y)^2/n}{n-1}}}.$$

But multiplying the numerator and denominator of Equation (11.5a) by n^2, and Equation (11.5b) by $n(n-1)$, reduces *both* formulas to the same computational form.

$$\rho_{XY} = \frac{n\Sigma XY - (\Sigma X)(\Sigma Y)}{\sqrt{[n\Sigma X^2 - (\Sigma X)^2][n\Sigma Y^2 - (\Sigma Y)^2]}}, \tag{11.6a}$$

$$r_{XY} = \frac{n\Sigma XY - (\Sigma X)(\Sigma Y)}{\sqrt{[n\Sigma X^2 - (\Sigma X)^2][n\Sigma Y^2 - (\Sigma Y)^2]}}. \tag{11.6b}*$$

There is one subtle difference between Equations (11.6a) and (11.6b). In Equation (11.6a) for ρ_{XY}, the X and Y values are *all* the paired X,Y values in the population, and n is the number of paired values in the population. In Equation (11.6b) for r_{XY}, the X and Y values are just a *sample* of the paired X,Y values in the population, and n is the number of paired values in the *sample*. Therefore, the use of the symbol r_{XY} implies computation with only a sample of scores, which in turn implies only a sample *estimate* of the population correlation.

In Table 11.3, an example of the computation of an estimate of the product moment correlation coefficient is presented, using Equation (11.6b).

TABLE 11.3
Computation of a product moment correlation coefficient, using Equation (11.6b). The use of the symbol r_{XY} implies that the eight paired scores are a sample from a larger population of scores.

Subject	X	Y	XY	X²	Y²
1	3	1	3	9	1
2	6	8	48	36	64
3	7	8	56	49	64
4	4	2	8	16	4
5	2	3	6	4	9
6	8	7	56	64	49
7	9	9	81	81	81
8	1	4	4	1	16
	$\Sigma X = 40$	$\Sigma Y = 42$	$\Sigma XY = 262$	$\Sigma X^2 = 260$	$\Sigma Y^2 = 288$

$$r_{XY} = \frac{n\Sigma XY - (\Sigma X)(\Sigma Y)}{\sqrt{[n\Sigma X^2 - (\Sigma X)^2][n\Sigma Y^2 - (\Sigma Y)^2]}}$$

$$= \frac{8(262) - (40)(42)}{\sqrt{[8(260) - (40)^2][8(288) - (42)^2]}}$$

$$= \frac{416}{\sqrt{259200}}$$

$$= .82.$$

CORRELATION WITH z SCORES If the X and Y scores have first been converted to z scores, the picture of correlation is somewhat simpler. If both sets of scores have been converted to z scores, there will be two sets of scores on the same scale, each with a mean of 0 and a standard deviation of 1. Perfect correlation means identical standard scores for any pair of scores z_{X_i}, z_{Y_i} for some ith subject. Correlation decreases as differences $z_{X_i} - z_{Y_i}$ increase.

Computations with z scores are simplified because the standard deviation of a set of z scores is always 1. Thus, whenever a standard deviation appears in a formula, the value can be assumed to be 1. For example, Equation (11.2),

$$\rho_{XY} = \frac{\sigma_{XY}}{\sigma_X \sigma_Y},$$

when expressed for z scores, is symbolized as in Equation (11.7).

$$\rho_{z_X z_Y} = \frac{\sigma_{z_X z_Y}}{\sigma_{z_X} \sigma_{z_Y}}. \tag{11.7}$$

The denominator in Equation (11.7) is simply 1×1, reducing the equality to Equation (11.8).

$$\rho_{z_X z_Y} = \sigma_{z_X z_Y}. \tag{11.8}$$

Equation (11.8) implies that when working with z scores the correlation is equal to the covariance.

In Equation (11.3) it was indicated that the definition of the covariance is the average cross product

$$\sigma_{XY} = \frac{\sum_{i=1}^{n} (X_i - \mu_x)(Y_i - \mu_y)}{n}.$$

When the X and Y scores are z scores, Equation (11.3) can be restated as Equation (11.9), where z_{μ_X} and z_{μ_Y} are the respective means of the two sets of z scores.

$$\sigma_{z_X z_Y} = \frac{\sum_{i=1}^{n} (z_{X_i} - z_{\mu_X})(z_{Y_i} - z_{\mu_y})}{n}. \tag{11.9}$$

But the mean of any set of z scores, z_{μ_X} or z_{μ_Y}, is zero, so that Equation (11.9) can be restated as

$$\sigma_{z_X z_Y} = \frac{\sum_{i=1}^{n} (z_{X_i})(z_{Y_i})}{n}.$$

But, as seen in Equation (11.8), with z scores the covariance $\sigma_{z_X z_Y}$ is the correlation coefficient. Thus, given z scores, the computational formula for the Pearson r is simply the average product of paired z scores, as expressed in Equation (11.10).

$$\rho_{z_X z_Y} = \frac{\sum_{i=1}^{n} (z_{X_i})(z_{Y_i})}{n}.$$ (11.10)

Normally, when computing correlations, we do not have the z scores. Thus, Equation (11.10) is primarily useful in theoretical discussions of correlation found in advanced texts.

Further, we rarely have the complete population of scores, so it is most common to work with sample data. Therefore, the most common formula for computation of the Pearson product moment correlation coefficient (the Pearson r) is the formula for the estimate of the correlation coefficient from a sample, Equation (11.6b):

$$r_{XY} = \frac{n\Sigma XY - (\Sigma X)(\Sigma Y)}{\sqrt{[n\Sigma X^2 - (\Sigma X)^2][n\Sigma Y^2 - (\Sigma Y)^2]}}.$$

AN INTERPRETATION OF CORRELATION

When there is no relationship between two sets of scores, X and Y, our best prediction of each Y score is simply the mean of the Y scores. When there is a relationship between two sets of scores, we can use the X scores to improve our prediction of the Y scores.

Looking back at Figure 11.2, we can see how the X scores aid in predicting Y when the two sets of scores are correlated. The prediction line slopes upward as X (IQ) increases, suggesting higher Y (GPA) values with higher X values. By contrast, if we only use the mean of the Y scores as the single predictor, we will have a horizontal line, placed at the mean of the Y scores.

The Pearson r (r_{XY} or ρ_{XY}) gives us an estimate or measure (respectively), of the degree of relationship between X and Y. But we will sometimes want a second measure, which gives us even more specific information about the relationship between X and Y.

Our second measure incorporates the variance of the Y scores. The defining formula for the variance of the Y scores, Equation (5.1), is therefore reintroduced here.

$$\sigma_Y^2 = \frac{\sum_{i=1}^{n} (Y_i - \mu_Y)^2}{n}.$$ [5.1]

The variance, as seen in Equation (5.1), is the average squared difference from the mean. If every score is equal to every other Y score, then every Y score is equal to the mean of Y, μ_Y, and this yields $\sigma_Y^2 = 0$. There is no variability in scores to predict. In this sense, the variance indicates the degree to which there is something to predict. For example, if every subject in Table 11.2 had a GPA of 3.35, then Figure 11.2 would present a horizontal row of dots at $Y = 3.35$. The more the Y scores vary, the more information we require from our X scores in order to predict the Y scores accurately.

In summary, the variance of Y indicates the total amount of variability to be predicted. In addition, since the variance increases as the scores vary from the mean, the variance offers an index of the degree to which the mean is a poor predictor. If the mean of the Y scores is used as the single prediction, the error in prediction is given by the variance,

$$\sigma_Y^2 = \frac{\Sigma(Y - \mu_Y)^2}{n}.$$

When a correlation is present, allowing for an improvement in prediction, the predictor will be a sloping line rather than the horizontal line offered by the mean of the Y scores. The error when using a prediction-aiding sloping line is given by Equation (11.11).

$$\sigma_e^2 = \frac{\Sigma(Y - Y')^2}{n} \tag{11.11}$$

Equation (11.11) is called the variance of the error of estimate. Each $(Y - Y')$ in $\Sigma(Y - Y')^2$ refers to an error in prediction. Figure 11.6 pictures one of the values that would be squared and summed in the numerator of Equation (11.11) for the variance of the error of estimate.

When the correlation is nonzero, then a sloping line offers better prediction than the mean. This is reflected in the fact that σ_e^2 will be less than σ_Y^2. Therefore, a ratio of σ_e^2/σ_Y^2 is smaller when the sloping line offers better prediction. The ratio σ_e^2/σ_Y^2 gets smaller as the absolute value of correlation gets larger. If there is perfect prediction with the sloping line, σ_e^2 will equal zero, since each $Y - Y'$ in the numerator of the variance of the error of

FIGURE 11.6
Illustration of one of the values $(Y_i - Y')$ that is squared and summed in the computation of $\sigma_e^2 = \Sigma_i(Y_i - Y')^2/n$.

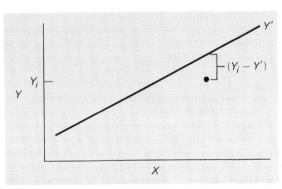

estimate will equal zero. Then σ_e^2/σ_Y^2 will equal zero. Any error in predic-tion of Y from X, using the sloping line of Y', means a value of σ_e^2/σ_Y^2 greater than zero.

σ_Y^2 is the amount of variability that needs to be predicted. σ_e^2 is the error in prediction—that is, the amount of variability that is not successfully predicted—when using the sloping line. The ratio σ_e^2/σ_Y^2 is the proportion of variance in Y *not* predictable from X. Its complement, $1 - (\sigma_e^2/\sigma_Y^2)$, is the proportion of variance in Y that *is* predictable from X (using the sloping line of Y').

$$\text{Proportion of variance in } Y \text{ predictable from } X = 1 - \frac{\sigma_e^2}{\sigma_Y^2}. \qquad (11.12)$$

Equation (11.12) offers a specific measure of relationship between X and Y. It is the proportion of variance in Y predictable from X. This can also be interpreted as the proportion of variance in Y associated with variance in X. Equation (11.12) can be contrasted with the Pearson r, which offers the vaguer index of the degree of relationship between X and Y. Equation (11.12) is clearly more specific. But the Pearson product moment correlaton coefficient has not been offered in such detail only to be discarded. The fact is that the Pearson r, *when squared*, also offers the proportion of variance in Y predictable from X; that is,

$$\rho_{XY}^2 = 1 - \frac{\sigma_e^2}{\sigma_Y^2} \qquad (11.13a)$$

$$= \text{proportion of variance in } Y \text{ predictable from } X.$$

Also,

$$r_{XY}^2 \approx 1 - \frac{\sigma_e^2}{\sigma_Y^2} \qquad (11.13b)*$$

$$= \text{proportion of variance in } Y \text{ predictable from } X,$$

where $\approx$ means approximately equals, since r_{XY} is only an estimate of ρ_{XY}. Thus, to measure (or estimate) the proportion of variance in Y predictable from X, simply compute the correlation coefficient ρ_{XY} (or its estimate, r_{XY}) and square it.

An important aspect of Equations (11.13a) and (11.13b) is that they offer a very specific interpretation of correlation. Statisticians working with the Pearson r almost always compute r_{XY}^2 to obtain an estimate of the proportion of variance in Y predictable from X.

As an example of the way in which correlaton can be interpreted, call height X and weight Y. In any large group of people the weight (Y values) vary from person to person. We would like to account for this variability by seeing to what degree the variability is related to other factors. For example, we may want a measure of the proportion of the variance in weight that is associated with variance in height.

A correlation between height and weight among some group of people, ρ_{XY}, can be computed using Equation (11.6a). The computed value of ρ_{XY} can then be squared. Assume that the correlation between height and weight is computed as $\rho_{XY} = .60$. Since $(.60)^2 = .36$, we can then say that 36% of the variance in weight is associated with variance in height, in that group of people; that is, 36% of the variance in weight is predictable from height, in that group of people.

Since the same value of $\rho_{XY} = .60$ will be found, regardless of which variable is called X and which is called Y, we can also say that 36% of the variance in height is predictable from weight, in that group of people.

If the group of people is a random sample from a larger population, $r_{XY}^2 = .36$ will represent the best estimate of the proportion of variance in weight associated with variance in height, in the population that contributed the sample.

Correlation and Causation   The squared Pearson correlation coefficient, ρ_{XY}^2, has been interpreted here as the proportion of variance in Y associated with variance in X, or the **proportion of variance in Y predictable from X.** Sometimes ρ_{XY}^2 is incorrectly interpreted as the proportion of variance in Y *accounted for* by X. This statement erroneously implies that we can assume a causal relationship between variables that are correlated. For example, if some proportion of the variance in weight is predictable from height, we may be tempted to say that the additional height is the reason for the additional weight. When we believe that we have accounted for a phenomenon, we believe that we know the reason for it, or that we have found its cause. But correlation does not automatically imply a cause and effect relationship between the two variables. Two variables can be correlated when they both share a relationship with a third variable. For example, we may find that greater damage at fires correlates with the number of firemen at the scene. But, finding such a correlation, we would not want to conclude that it is the firemen who are the cause of the increased damage. The larger the fire, or the more flammable the contents of the building, the more fire companies that are called out (giving rise to the term "four alarm fire"). Thus, the size of the fire, or the inflammability of the material, is the third variable that is associated with both the number of firemen present and the amount of damage.

Nonetheless, there is a real temptation to conclude that there are cause and effect relationships between correlated variables. This may be due to the fact that the reverse argument is a valid one; that is, we can infer statistical correlation from known cause and effect. If we know that in some town the firemen are underpaid and angry, and that they have decided to purposely cause additional damage with their axes and hoses, we will find a correlation between the number of firemen present and the amount of damage. Given known cause and effect, we will find a correlation, but given a correlation we cannot automatically infer cause and effect. Both variables can be covarying because of some third variable which is jointly affecting both of them.

In summary, correlation implies an association between paired sets of scores. The correlation coefficient ρ_{XY} indexes the degree of association between the two sets of scores. As ρ_{XY} varies from zero, it implies increasing covariability in the X and Y scores, with $+1$ or -1 implying perfect covariability. The square of the correlation coefficient, $\rho_{XY}{}^2$, reflects the proportion of the variability in the Y scores that are predictable from the X scores. The squared correlation coefficient then affords greater specificity to the notion of a degree of relationship between two variables. The more common symbol for Pearson's product moment correlation coefficient, however, is r_{XY}, because of the more common use of samples, rather than whole populations in psychological research. Therefore, statements of proportion of variability in Y associated with X are most often estimates obtained from $r_{XY}{}^2$.

THE POINT BISERIAL CORRELATION COEFFICIENT

The discussion of correlation was begun by noting that relationships between two variables can be conceptualized as concomitant rising and falling of the paired scores. This was best appreciated in those instances where both X and Y were continuously variable. The discussion went on to interpret the squared correlation coefficient, $\rho_{XY}{}^2$ (or its estimate, $r_{XY}{}^2$), as the proportion of variance in Y associated with the variance in X. When we interpret correlation as the proportion of variance in Y associated with variance in X, it becomes easier to think about correlation, even when one of the variables is dichotomized.

For example, what proportion of the variance in salaries is associated with a person's sex? There are many factors besides sex associated with salaries: type of job, education, ambition, intelligence, etc. But even for equally intelligent people on equivalent jobs, women tend to receive less pay. Thus, there is a relationship between sex and salary. Suppose that we wish to know what proportion of the variance in salaries is associated with sex? As previously indicated, we want to compute a correlation between sex and salary, and then square the result. A question such as this is generally answered with sample data, suggesting the use of Equation (11.6b) for r_{XY}.

But how do we compute the correlation between a dichotomous and a continous variable? Equation (11.6b) for r_{XY} requires some sampled paired numbers for X and Y values. We know what numbers are used for salaries, but what numbers do we use for sex?

The problem is easily handled by simply using a 1 for one sex, and a 0 for the other sex. The result will be two columns of numbers, where each person in some random sample has either a 0 or a 1 paired with their salary. Equation (11.6b) can then be used, and the computed value of r_{XY} will offer the correlation between the two variables. (Any other two numbers, besides 0 and 1, consistently used, will yield the same r_{XY} value.)

The need to compute the correlation between a dichotomous and a continous variable occurs fairly often. For this reason a simpler formula has been developed, made possible by the simplifying presence of only zeros and ones as one of the variables. The resulting formula is called the **point biserial correlation coefficient.** The formula for this point biserial correlation coefficient is given in Equation (11.14), where it is symbolized as r_{pb}.

$$r_{pb} = \frac{N\Sigma Y_{X_1} - n_{X_1}\Sigma Y}{\sqrt{n_{X_0} n_{X_1} [N\Sigma Y^2 - (\Sigma Y)^2]}} . \qquad (11.14)^*$$

Assume that in Equation (11.14) X is the dichotomous and Y is the continuous variable. ΣY, $(\Sigma Y)^2$, and ΣY^2 are interpreted as in previous sections. ΣY_{X_1} is the sum of those Y scores whose paired X scores are 1. For example, in Table 11.4, $\Sigma Y_{X_1} = 24$. The other new symbols in the formula all involve counting. There is n_{X_0}, which is the number of X scores that are zero; n_{X_1}, which is the number of X scores that are one; and N, the total number of paired scores (total number of people in the sample). Table 11.4 offers an example.

TABLE 11.4
Example of the computation of the point biserial correlation coefficient, with hypothetical data

Subject	X	Y	Y_{X_1}	Y^2
1	0	5		25
2	1	6	6	36
3	1	7	7	49
4	0	4		16
5	1	6	6	36
6	1	5	5	25
	$n_{X_1} = 4$	$\Sigma Y = 33$	$\Sigma Y_{X_1} = 24$	$\Sigma Y^2 = 187$
	$n_{X_0} = 2$			

$$r_{pb} = \frac{N\Sigma Y_{X_1} - n_{X_1}\Sigma Y}{\sqrt{n_{X_0} n_{X_1} [N\Sigma Y^2 - (\Sigma Y)^2]}}$$

n_{X_0} = number of pairs where ($X = 0$).
n_{X_1} = number of pairs where ($X = 1$).
N = total number of paired X,Y values in computation.

$$= \frac{6(24) - 4(33)}{\sqrt{2(4)[6(187) - (33)^2]}}$$

ΣY_{X_1} = sum of Y scores that are paired with ($X = 1$).

$$= .74.$$

A positive value of r_{pb} means that the Y_{X_1} values tend to be higher than the Y_{X_0} values. A negative correlation means that the Y_{X_0} values tend to be higher.

For simplicity in exposition, the numbers of paired scores in both Tables 11.3 and 11.4 have been kept unrealistically small. The issue of the number of scores for reliably estimating correlations is addressed in the following section.

STATISTICAL INFERENCE IN CORRELATION

Assume that we wish to know the degree of relationship between GPA and IQ. Assume further that we randomly select 100 students from the general population and compute the correlation between GPA and IQ. Assume that the computed value of the correlation coefficient is .60. We can use the computed value of r_{XY} as a rough *estimate* of the population correlation ρ_{XY}. But we cannot have much confidence in the accuracy of the estimate.

As is further specified in the next section, the sampled correlation of $r_{XY} = .60$ can be used to conclude that there is indeed a relationship between GPA and IQ in the general population. But the *degree* of the relationship in the general population is not likely to have been accurately gauged from a moderately sized sample of 100 subjects. The error in estimation can reasonably be expected to be as much as $\pm.15$ (that is, ρ_{XY} can reasonably be expected to be somewhere between .45 and .75). Estimation from smaller samples is even less informative about the true value of ρ_{XY}.

Assume now that instead of 100 subjects, that we use 5000 subjects. With this many subjects we can have reasonable confidence that r_{XY}, our estimate of ρ_{XY}, is accurate within $\pm.02$. When a sample is sufficiently large, it can function very much like the entire population in giving parameter values; that is, any values of r_{XY} that are obtained from a very large sample are likely to be close to the true population value. Therefore, given sufficiently large samples, it is possible to use sampled correlations as approximately accurate estimates of the population correlations. The required sample sizes vary with the amount of error you are willing to tolerate in your estimate, and the degree of confidence you wish to have in the accuracy of your estimate.

As a rough rule of thumb, if you wish to be within approximately .05 of the true population value ρ_{XY}, you should use at least 500–600 subjects. If you are willing to tolerate errors as large as $\pm.10$, you should use at least 200–300 subjects. Advanced texts give more specific values for specific degrees of confidence under the topic of confidence intervals for correlation coefficients.

Testing Sampled Correlations for Significance Assume that a question is raised as to whether or not GPA and IQ are related (rather than questioning the degree of relationship). But both GPA and IQ are continuous variables. We do not have a dichotomous independent variable with which to identify two groups for a t test.

We often face the question of whether or not X and Y are related, with both X and Y being continuous variables. What we do is simply compute a sample correlation and then test the sampled correlation for a significant difference from zero. The correlation of zero becomes a null hypothesis. We see if the sampled correlation is sufficiently different from zero to allow us to reject the idea of a zero correlation as the population correlation.

A rejection of a population correlation as being equal to zero implies that the variables are related (have a correlation greater than zero). Rejecting a null hypothesis to conclude that two variables are related sounds like a t test. In fact, a t test is used to reject the null hypothesis with a sample correlation coefficient. Instead of a t test between a hypothesized mean and a sampled mean of scores, a test is made between a hypothesized correlation (of zero) and a sampled correlation.

Assume that the relationship between two variables has just been tested in the above fashion, using a sample correlation, some r_{XY}. Further, assume that the variables are not, in fact, related; that is, the actual population correlation is $\rho_{XY} = 0$. If a sample had been taken with, say, 82 pairs of scores, any sample correlation value would be possible. The sample value

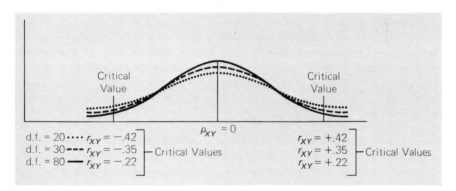

FIGURE 11.7

Pictures of distributions of sample correlations, when the population correlation is zero. The values of the sample correlations that lead to rejection of the population correlation of zero depend on the degrees of freedom. Larger degrees of freedom (and, therefore, larger sample sizes) allow smaller obtained sample correlations to be used to reject the null hypothesis of zero correlation. (Since $\rho_{XY} = 0$ in this distribution, rejection of $\rho_{XY} = 0$ is a Type I error. The critical values shown here are the critical values for making a Type I error with a probability of .05, two tailed.) The differences between the distributions have been exaggerated for visual clarity.

of r_{XY} may turn out to be $-.10$, $+.09$, or $-.007$, etc. However, given a population correlation of $\rho_{XY} = 0$, the most likely values will cluster around zero. Any value can occur, but larger values will have smaller probabilities.

The distribution of sample correlations, using 82 pairs of X,Y scores for each sample, will look like the solid line in Figure 11.7.

The test of whether or not the population correlation is zero will yield only one r_{XY} value, not a distribution. From that one sampled correlation, the researcher has to decide whether or not the population correlation is nonzero. This means having some predetermined critical correlation value, which, if reached or surpassed, will lead to the rejection of the null hypothesis of a zero correlation. Given 82 pairs of X,Y scores and a Type I error level of .05, a sampled correlation of $\pm.22$ will be the critical value leading to rejection of the null hypothesis of a population correlation equal to zero. (The method for obtaining the critical value is explained below.) If a smaller sample is used, a larger critical value will be required to reject the null hypothesis; that is, as smaller sample sizes are used, there is less confidence in the sample estimates, so a relatively large value of r_{XY} is required before it is taken as evidence that ρ_{XY} is greater than zero. For example, for 32 pairs of X,Y scores, the critical correlation value is $\pm.35$ at the two-tailed .05 Type I error level. For only 22 pairs of X,Y scores, the critical value is $\pm.42$.

Figure 11.7 pictures the three distributions for the three different sample sizes discussed above. The distribution is generally tabled in terms of degrees of freedom, which are directly related to, but not identical to, sample size. For testing sample correlations, the degrees of freedom are equal to $n-2$, where n is the number of paired scores in the sample. (Most often, n is also equal to the number of subjects, where each subject has two scores, paired by dint of being from the same subject.)

The distributions in Figure 11.7 change their shapes slightly with degrees of freedom. With smaller degrees of freedom, the standard deviation gets larger (extreme scores are more likely), so the distribution spreads out. This means that larger critical values are needed to constitute rare events. Thus, the critical values get larger with smaller degrees of freedom.

Given the degrees of freedom, rare events can be defined from a table of critical values for the t distribution, as in the familiar forms of the t test. Equation (11.15) is the formula for the t test using the sample correlation as a test of the null hypothesis.

$$t = r_{XY}\sqrt{\frac{n-2}{1-r_{XY}^2}} \tag{11.15}$$

The statistic t defined by Equation (11.15) has $n-2$ degrees of freedom. The value of t can be computed with Equation (11.15) using a sampled r_{XY}, and compared to the critical value of t in Table IV in Appendix B, at $n-2$ degrees of freedom.

Because of the frequent testing of correlations for significance with t tests, another table has been prepared which, in essence, has done the computations in Equation (11.15). In this text, this special table for testing correlations for significance is found in Appendix B as Table V. To use Table V, simply select a column for the desired Type I error level and find the row equal to $n-2$ degrees of freedom. Where the column and row intersect, the body of the table contains the correlation which yields statistical significance if inserted in Equation (11.15). Therefore, instead of computing t with Equation (11.15) and comparing the computed t to the tabled t, simply use Table V to find the critical correlation value and compare it to the sampled r_{XY}.

In practice, then, compute a sample correlation between two variables, and then consult Table V in Appendix B at $n-2$ degrees of freedom. If the sampled correlation equals or surpasses the tabled value, then statistical significance has been attained. This, in turn, leads to the conclusion that the population correlation is not zero; that is, if the critical correlation value has been reached or surpassed in the sample, the two variables that yield the sample correlation *are* considered related.

For example, Table 11.3 illustrated the computation of a product moment correlation, with $n = 8$. The resulting correlation was $r_{XY} = .82$. Assuming a two-tailed test of significance, with a Type I error probability of .05, we turn to Table V. At $n-2$ degrees of freedom we find .707 listed under the column for the desired Type I error probability. The sampled correlation of .82 exceeds the tabled value, so, if we are testing the possibilities of a relationship with the data in Table 11.3, we conclude that there is a relationship. The critical correlation value of .707 is the critical value for a two-tailed test at the .05 level. Therefore, the same conclusions would be drawn if the computed correlation were $-.82$.

Table V can also be used to test for a relationship from a sampled r_{pb}. The computation of a point biserial correlation was illustrated in Table 11.4. The data in Table 11.4 yielded $r_{pb} = .74$, with $n = 6$. Table V indicates a critical value of .811 at 4 degrees of freedom (two tailed at .05). The computed value does not reach the tabled value, so if Table 11.4 contains data from a test of a relationship between two variables, we conclude that there is no evidence to support a relationship.

Note that in both a point biserial correlation and a t test, one variable is dichotomized and the other is continuous. As just seen, the point biserial correlation, when incorporated in a t test, can be used to test whether or not a relationship exists between the dichotomous variable and the continuous variable. This is precisely what a direct t test would do. You may therefore recognize that computing a point biserial correlation and testing it for

TABLE 11.5
The same data tabled twice: Tabled for a point biserial correlation (from which a t test can be computed) and tabled for a direct t test for the difference between two means, $\bar{X}_0$ and $\bar{X}_1$. (Note that the degrees of freedom for the direct t test, $n_0 + n_1 - 2 = 4$, are numerically the same as the $n - 2 = 4$ when testing the point biserial for significance.)

Data for a Point Biserial			Data for a t Test		
Subject	X	Y	Group 0	Group 1	
1	0	5	5		
2	1	6		6	$t = \dfrac{\bar{X}_0 - \bar{X}_1}{s_{\bar{X}_0 - \bar{X}_1}}$
3	1	7		7	
4	0	4	4		Degrees of freedom $= n_0 + n_1 - 2$
5	1	6		6	$= 2 + 4 - 2$
6	1	5		5	$= 4$
			$\bar{X}_0 = 4.5$	$\bar{X}_1 = 6$	

significance should yield the same answer as a direct t test for a significant difference between means.

In Table 11.4, the two data columns consist of one column of zeros and ones (signifying status on the dichotomous variable) and another column of more variable numbers, which can be thought of as the dependent variable scores. If the t test is done directly, the two columns will contain only the dependent variable scores. The column in which each dependent variable score is placed will be equivalent to assignments of 0 or 1 (the independent variable dichotomy). Thus, Table 11.4 can be recast with the numbers associated with 0 restricted to one column, and the numbers associated with 1 restricted to the other column. Table 11.5 contrasts the two ways of tabling the data.

PREDICTION FROM REGRESSION LINES It is not uncommon for schools to want to predict grade-point averages using achievement examinations such as the SAT as the predictor variable. Industries also often wish to make predictions, perhaps of future absences from work or of supervisors' future on-the-job ratings. They may use scores on aptitude tests, given to all job applicants, as the predictor variable. When there are large numbers of subjects available (as there often are in large industries and schools), then such predictions can usefully be made.

Correlation indexes the degree of relationship between a set of predictor variables (X) and the scores being predicted (Y). The presence of correlation implies some potential predictability. The potential accuracy of such predictions was discussed in the sections introducing correlation. The computational details of making such predictions are discussed in this section.

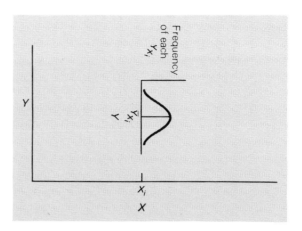

FIGURE 11.8
Illustration of a distribution of Y scores (symbolized Y_{x_i}), associated with some one X score (symbolized X_i). The mean of the Y scores associated with the one X score is symbolized as $\bar{Y}_{x_i}$.

In practice, a particular X score is selected (the score of a particular subject on the predictor variable). Then, using the information from the paired X and Y scores of previously observed subjects, some prediction is made about the most likely Y score for the new subject.

In previously observed pairings of X and Y scores, there may have been many occurrences of the same X score. It is further likely that all the subjects with the same X score did *not* have the same Y score. For any one X score, call it X_i, there is generally a frequency distribution of occurrences of varying Y_{x_i} scores, as illustrated in Figure 11.8.

What Y score would we want to predict, then, for future subjects with that X score? A simple way to proceed is to compute the mean of all the Y scores obtained by subjects with the particular X score. Then, this mean of all Y scores associated with the one X score will be the predicted Y score for this X score. The mean of the Y scores associated with a particular X score, say X_i, can be symbolized as $\bar{Y}_{x_i}$, as shown in Figure 11.8.

This is a reasonable and sometimes useful way to make predictions. But the method has some problems. For example, an infrequently occurring X score may not offer enough Y scores for a good estimate of $\bar{Y}_{x_i}$. Fortunately, there is another source of information for predicting Y scores from X scores that gives similar but more reliable results. It is often possible to identify some pattern in the relationships between the X and Y scores. The overall pattern of the relationship can then be used to suggest an expected Y score for each X score.

A linear pattern of relationship between X and Y scores was previously discussed when distinguishing linear from nonlinear correlation. As indicated in that discussion, a best-fitting straight (sloping) line often characterizes relationships between two variables. This best-fitting straight line can be used to predict one variable from the other. For example, in Figure

11.2, the line predicts a GPA of 3.65 for an IQ of 120 (although the data for the one subject with an IQ of 120 shows a GPA of 3.50, resulting in a data point that is off the line). The best-fitting straight line is called a **regression line**. When the relationship between X and Y can be summarized by a regression line, the relationship is identified as an instance of linear regression. Linear regression means that the relationship between X and Y can be summarized by Equation (11.1),

$$Y = bX + a,$$

which is the equation for a straight line. It is also possible to have nonlinear regression. This implies a regression curve rather than a straight regression line. Just as the discussion of correlation was restricted to linear correlation, this text similarly restricts the discussion of regression to linear regression.

The topic of linear regression concerns the prediction of scores (whose relationship can be summarized by a regression line). This should be distinguished from linear correlation, which indexes the accuracy of such a prediction in the form of a number indicating the degree of relationship between X and Y.

In order to make specific predictions about a particular Y from a particular X, the values of a and b in Equation (11.1) are needed. Different values are likely to be required for predictions between different sets of paired X and Y scores. Further, there will generally be different values of a and b, depending on whether we wish to predict the Y scores from the X scores, or the X scores from the Y scores.

When computing a correlation coefficient, the *degree of relationship* is symmetric. X is related to Y to the same degree that Y is related to X; that is, $r_{YX} = r_{XY}$. However, regression is generally not symmetric. Differences in the scale of the two variables generally result in different regression lines for predicting X from Y than from predicting Y from X. As will be seen with an example later (in Figures 11.9 and 11.10), the direction of prediction usually makes a difference in the slope of the regression line. This, in turn, makes a difference in the values of a and b in the prediction equation. Therefore, different values of a and b are usually required for predicting X from Y than Y from X.

Equation (11.1) for the two possible directions of prediction is now restated, with both a and b symbolically distinguished as to direction.

$$Y' = b_{YX} X + a_{YX}, \qquad (11.16)^*$$

$$X' = b_{XY} Y + a_{XY}. \qquad (11.17)^*$$

Equations (11.16) and (11.17) are called regression equations. Y' and X' in the regression equations are the predicted Y and X values, respectively, as distinguished from actually observed values Y and X. Thus, in Figure 11.2 the predicted Y value for $X = 120$ is $Y' = 3.65$, but $Y = 3.50$.

The coefficient b_{YX} in Equation (11.16) is the **slope of the regression line when predicting Y from X**. (It may be helpful to think of b_{YX} as $b_{Y\lfloor X}$.)

$$b_{YX} = \frac{n\Sigma XY - (\Sigma X)(\Sigma Y)}{n\Sigma X^2 - (\Sigma X)^2}.$$ (11.18)*

The coefficient b_{XY} in equation (11.17) is the **slope of the regression line when predicting X from Y**. (It may be helpful to think of b_{XY} as $b_{X\lfloor Y}$.)

$$b_{XY} = \frac{n\Sigma XY - (\Sigma X)(\Sigma Y)}{n\Sigma Y^2 - (\Sigma Y)^2}.$$ (11.19)*

The coefficients b_{YX} and b_{XY} are called **regression coefficients**.

The regression line can intercept the ordinate at different values when predicting Y from X versus predicting X from Y. The point on the ordinate where the regression line touches the ordinate is called the intercept. The coefficients a_{YX} and a_{XY} are the **intercepts for the regression lines** predicting Y from X and X from Y, respectively.

$$a_{YX} = \bar{Y} - b_{YX}\bar{X}$$ (11.20)*

$$a_{XY} = \bar{X} - b_{XY}\bar{Y}$$ (11.21)*

To simplify the computation and use of the terms in the equations for regression lines, Tables 11.6 and 11.7 are presented.

TABLE 11.6
Components in Equation (11.16) for predicting Y from X

Means		Formula
$\bar{X}$	$=$	$\dfrac{\Sigma X}{n}$
$\bar{Y}$	$=$	$\dfrac{\Sigma Y}{n}$
Slope		
b_{YX}	$=$	$\dfrac{n\Sigma XY - (\Sigma X)(\Sigma Y)}{n\Sigma X^2 - (\Sigma X)^2}$
Intercept		
a_{YX}	$=$	$\bar{Y} - b_{YX}\bar{X}$
Prediction		
Y'	$=$	$b_{YX}X + a_{YX}$

TABLE 11.7
Components in Equation (11.17) for predicting X from Y

Means		Formula
$\bar{X}$	$=$	$\dfrac{\Sigma X}{n}$
$\bar{Y}$	$=$	$\dfrac{\Sigma Y}{n}$
Slope		
b_{XY}	$=$	$\dfrac{n\Sigma XY - (\Sigma X)(\Sigma Y)}{n\Sigma Y^2 - (\Sigma Y)^2}$
Intercept		
a_{XY}	$=$	$\bar{X} - b_{XY}\bar{Y}$
Prediction		
X'	$=$	$b_{XY}Y + a_{XY}$

TABLE 11.8

Computations with hypothetical data, illustrating the use of Table 11.6 (predicting Y from X). $Y' = b_{YX}X + a_{YX}$.

Subject	Test X	Test Y	XY	X^2
1	1	2	2	1
2	2	4	8	4
3	3	6	18	9
4	6	12	72	36
5	8	15	120	64
6	10	15	150	100
	$\Sigma X = 30$	$\Sigma Y = 54$	$\Sigma XY = 370$	$\Sigma X^2 = 214$

$$\bar{X} = \frac{30}{6} \qquad \bar{Y} = \frac{54}{6}$$
$$= 5 \qquad\qquad = 9$$

$$b_{YX} = \frac{n\Sigma XY - (\Sigma Y)(\Sigma Y)}{n\Sigma X^2 - (\Sigma X)^2}$$

$$= \frac{6(370) - (30)(54)}{6(214) - (30)^2}$$

$$= 1.56$$

$$a_{YX} = \bar{Y} - b_{YX}\bar{X}$$
$$= 9 - (1.56)5$$
$$= 1.20$$

For any subject with the following X values,	we predict the following Y values,	where Y' $= b_{YX}X + a_{YX}$.
X	Y'	$= (1.56)X + 1.20$
1	2.76	$= (1.56)1 + 1.20$
2	4.32	$= (1.56)2 + 1.20$
3	5.88	.
4	7.44	.
5	9.00	.
6	10.56	
7	12.12	
8	13.68	
9	15.24	
10	16.80	$= (1.56)10 + 1.20$

Tables 11.8 and 11.9 illustrate the use of Tables 11.6 and 11.7. The data in Tables 11.8 and 11.9 are the same. The only difference is in the direction of prediction from X to Y or from Y to X. Figures 11.9 and 11.10 illustrate the resulting difference in regression lines when the direction of prediction is reversed.

Obtaining the Slope with ρ_{XY} Equations (11.18) and (11.19) offer formulas for computing the regression coefficients (b_{YX} and b_{XY}) when using raw data. If ρ_{XY}, σ_X, and σ_Y have previously been computed, there are simpler formulas for computing the regression coefficients, given below as Equations (11.22) and (11.23).

$$b_{YX} = \rho_{XY}\frac{\sigma_Y}{\sigma_X} \qquad\qquad (11.22)^*$$

TABLE 11.9
Computations with hypothetical data, illustrating the use of Table 11.7 (predicting X from Y). $X' = b_{XY}Y + a_{XY}$.

Subject	Test X	Test Y	XY	Y²
1	1	2	2	4
2	2	4	8	16
3	3	6	18	36
4	6	12	72	144
5	8	15	120	225
6	10	15	150	225

$$\Sigma X = 30 \qquad \Sigma Y = 54 \qquad \Sigma XY = 370 \qquad \Sigma Y^2 = 650$$

$$\bar{X} = \frac{30}{6} \qquad \bar{Y} = \frac{54}{6}$$

$$= 5 \qquad\qquad = 9$$

$$b_{XY} = \frac{n\Sigma XY - (\Sigma X)(\Sigma Y)}{n\Sigma Y^2 - (\Sigma Y)^2}$$

$$= \frac{6(370) - (30)(54)}{6(650) - (54)^2}$$

$$= .61$$

$$a_{XY} = \bar{X} - b_{XY}\bar{Y}$$

$$= 5 - (.61)9$$

$$= -.49$$

For any subject with the following Y values,	we predict the following X values,	where X' = $b_{XY}Y + a_{XY}$.
Y	X'	$= (.61)Y + (-.49)$
1	0.12	$= (.61)1 - .49$
2	0.73	$= (.61)2 - .49$
3	1.34	$= (.61)3 - .49$
4	1.95	.
5	2.56	.
6	3.17	.
.	.	.
.	.	.
.	.	.
14	8.05	$= (.61)14 - .49$
15	8.66	$= (.61)15 - .49$

$$b_{XY} = \rho_{XY}\frac{\sigma_X}{\sigma_Y}. \qquad\qquad (11.23)^*$$

The uses of Equations (11.22) and (11.23) are illustrated with the data in Tables 11.8 and 11.9. The required additional statistical values are

$$\rho_{XY} = .98,$$

$$\sigma_X = 3.58,$$

$$\sigma_Y = 5.73.$$

From Equation (11.22),

$$b_{YX} = .98\left(\frac{5.73}{3.58}\right)$$

$$= 1.57.$$

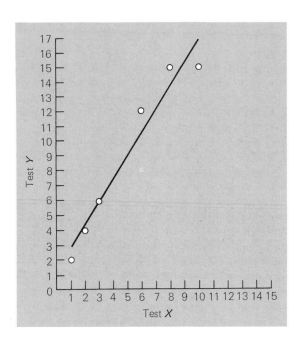

FIGURE 11.9
Graph of the data in Tables 11.8 and 11.9, showing the regression line for the prediction of scores on Test Y from scores on Test X. The open circles are the data points for the six subjects.

FIGURE 11.10
Graph of the data in Tables 11.8 and 11.9, showing the regression line for prediction of scores on Test X from scores on Test Y. The open circles are the data points for the six subjects.

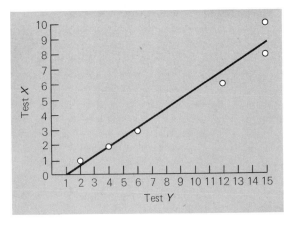

From Equation (11.23),

$$b_{XY} = .98 \left(\frac{3.58}{5.73}\right)$$

$$= .61.$$

We have just seen how the slope of a regression line can be computed as a function of the correlation between the variables. But we know that correlations are only expected to be accurate when computed from the entire population, or very large samples. Similarly, regression equations with sample data are only expected to be accurate when large bodies of data are used to estimate the coefficients. Therefore, the symbols used in this section are the symbols for population values (the parameters ρ_{XY}, σ_X, and σ_Y). The sample statistics r_{XY}, s_X, and s_Y can also be used, but unless the samples are very large, the predictions are likely to be inaccurate.

REGRESSION TOWARD THE MEAN When using z scores and predicting z_Y from z_X (or z_X from z_Y), the standard deviations in Equation (11.22) for the regression coefficient drop out (both being equal to one); that is, from Equation (11.22),

$$b_{YX} = \rho_{XY}\frac{\sigma_Y}{\sigma_X}$$

so

$$b_{z_Y z_X} = \rho_{z_X z_Y}\frac{\sigma_{z_Y}}{\sigma_{z_X}}$$

$$= \rho_{z_X z_Y}.$$

Therefore, when working with z scores, the slope is equal to the correlation. The equality of the correlation and the slope, in the case of z scores, gives correlation an interesting interpretation. Correlation is reflected in the slope. Given zero correlation, we will also have zero slope. The prediction would be the mean of the z scores. But the mean of any set of z scores is zero. Thus, with zero correlation between z scores, the regression line will not be distinguished from the X axis, which is a horizontal line at $z_Y = 0$.

Figure 11.11 presents an example of a very small correlation, where the scores and the X and Y axes are all expressed as z scores. Given higher correlations, a steeper slope appears, reaching a 45-degree slope when $b_{YX} = 1$, which is the point of perfect positive correlation, as in Figure 11.12; that is, when using z scores, if $b_{YX} = 1$, then $\rho_{XY} = 1$. Given perfect *negative* correlation with z scores, $b_{YX} = -1$ and $\rho_{XY} = -1$.

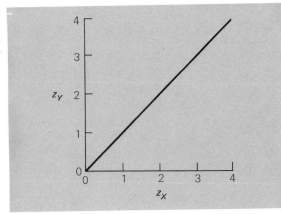

FIGURE 11.11
Small correlation between two sets of scores that have been converted to z scores.
$\rho_{z_X z_Y} = b_{z_Y z_X} = .06$.

In Figure 11.12, for any deviation from zero in z_X, we predict an equal deviation in z_Y. For $z_X = 2$, we predict $z_Y = 2$. This is why the slope (a ratio of changes in Y to changes in X) is equal to 1. When correlation is *between* 0 and 1, we do not predict equal changes in z_Y equivalent to those seen in z_X. Rather, for any change in z_X we predict some smaller change in z_Y. This can be seen in Figure 11.13, where the correlation is $\rho_{z_X z_Y} = .5$. What is seen in Figure 11.13 is a basic conservatism in prediction, because correlation is less than perfect. The smaller the correlation between X and Y, the less that we are willing to "go out on a limb" in predicting the same changes in Y that we see in X. Rather, we predict something closer to the mean of the Y scores (closer to zero, in the case of standard scores). Thus, in Figure 11.13, where $\rho_{z_X z_Y} = .5$, we predict $z_Y = 1$ for $z_X = 2$ ($b_{z_Y z_X} = z_Y / z_X = \frac{1}{2} = .5$). The lower the correlation, the lower the slope, and the more conservative we are in predicting differences from the mean of zero for Y.

FIGURE 11.12
Perfect positive correlation between two sets of scores that have been converted to z scores.
$\rho_{z_X z_Y} = b_{z_Y z_X} = 1$.

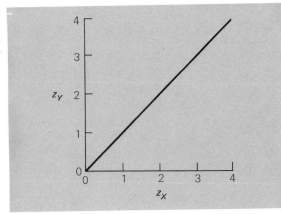

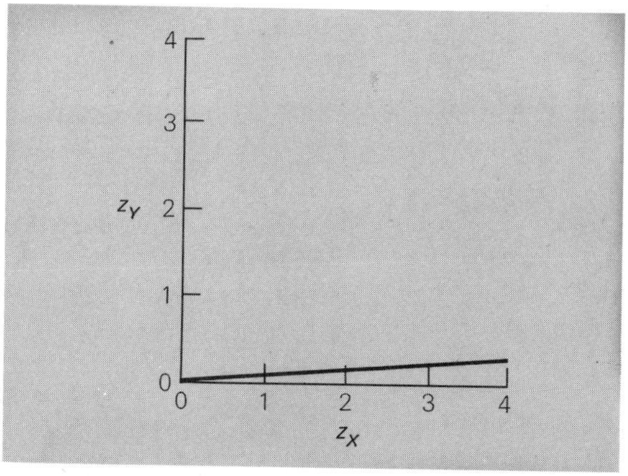

FIGURE 11.13
Less than perfect correlation between two sets of scores that have been converted to z scores.

$$\rho_{z_X z_Y} = b_{z_Y z_X} = .50.$$

conservative we are in predicting differences from the mean of zero for Y.

The phrase **regression toward the mean** is often used to describe the conservatism in prediction when correlation is less than perfect. The smaller the correlation, the closer we stick to the mean of the Y scores in our predictions. As correlation gets larger, we are more willing to make more drastic predictions about Y from information about X.

The regression toward the mean in prediction extends through all regression problems, not just those involving standard scores. The conversion to standard scores just makes regression to the mean easier to see, because both variables are on the same scale. The use of the term regression to describe the topic of prediction stems from the regression toward the mean in prediction.

A NOTE ABOUT ASSUMPTIONS It was originally assumed that the Pearson r is only correctly computed when both sets of scores are normally distributed continuous measures. Further, it was assumed that the set of scores in each subset of Y_{x_i} scores associated with each X_i score are normally distributed. (See Figure 11.8 for an illustration.) But these assumptions have been shown to be unnecessary. The Pearson r can offer informative descriptions of relationships between most sets of wide-ranging scores.

When correlations are tested for significance, then the assumptions have been considered more critical. Recent evidence, however, indicates that the assumptions are not really necessary, even for significance testing.* Thus we are not restricted to normally distributed measures for the Pearson r or point biserial.

*Havlicek, Larry L. & Peterson, Nancy L. Effect of the violation of assumptions upon significance levels of the Pearson r. *Psychological Bulletin*, 1977, *84*, 373–377.

SENTENCE COMPLETIONS

The following incomplete sentences are taken from the underlined sentences in this chapter. Fill in the missing words and phrases and then correct them from the answers which follow.

1. Whenever two sets of measurements X and Y are related according to an equation of the form $Y =$ _____, we have a linear relationship. We call it a linear relationship because when X and Y are related in this way, the graph of the relationship always forms a

   _____ _____ .

2. Correlation between sets of paired scores means that there is a _____ between the sets of scores.

3. In linear correlation, there is a constant slope defining the relationship, which is _____ in $Y = bX + a$.

4. When two sets of scores are unrelated, the best predictor of the set of Y scores is _____.

5. If there were some relationship between X and Y, prediction of Y scores would be better using _____ than the _____ of Y.

6. Good prediction is reflected in the _____ of the points on the graph to the _____.
   The better the prediction, the greater the degree to which the two sets of scores are _____ .

7. Linear correlation between sets of scores suggests that there is some

best-fitting straight line that _____, which could aid in predicting one set of scores from another.

8. The closer the relationship between X and Y, the _____ the correlation between them.

9. If the prediction line for two sets of scores slopes downward, we speak of _____ correlation. When it slopes upward, we speak of _____ correlation. When there is no slope, we have _____ correlation.

10. Correlation can reflect a negative relationship when high scores on one measure are associated with _____ scores on another measure. Correlation can reflect a positive relationship when high scores on one measure are associated with _____ scores on another measure.

11. A perfect positive correlation will yield a correlation of _____; a perfect negative correlation will yield a correlation of _____; and a complete absence of correlation will yield a correlation of _____. Values between _____ and _____ reflect varying degrees of positive correlation. Values between _____ and _____ reflect varying degrees of negative correlation.

12. The formula to compute the index of correlation between two sets of continuous scores X and Y yields a number called the _____ _____or, more simply, _____ _____. It is symbolized as _____ when computed from the complete population, and as _____ when computed from a sample.

13. To compute or estimate the correlation between a dichotomous and a continuous variable, a simpler formula has been developed. It is called the _____.

14. The average cross product is called the _____.

15. To obtain an estimate of the proportion of variance in Y that is _____ _____, compute r_{xy} and then square it.

16. The correlation coefficient r_{xy}, computed from _____ data, can be used as a rough _____ of the population correlation. The degree of relationship in the general population is not likely to have been accurately gauged from a _____ _____.

17. Given sufficiently _____ _____, it is possible to use sampled correlations as approximate estimates of population correlations.

18. To determine whether two variables are related, we can sometimes compute a sample correlation between two variables, and then consult a _____ at _____ degrees of freedom. If the sampled correlation has _____ or _____ the tabled value, then statistical significance has been attained.

19. When we test correlation for significance, we test whether a sampled correlation is significantly _____ from _____.
The correlation of _____ is our null hypothesis. We reject the null hypothesis if the sampled correlation is sufficiently different from _____ .

20. We call our best-fitting straight line a _____ _____.

21. The coefficient b_{YX} is the slope of the regression line when predicting _____ from _____. The coefficient b_{XY} is the slope of the regression line when predicting _____ from _____ .

22. For z scores, when $b_{YX} = .5$, $r_{XY} = $ _____. Given perfect negative correlation with z scores, $b_{YX} = $ _____and $r_{XY} = $ _____ .

23. The phrase _____is often used to describe the conservatism in prediction when the correlation is less than perfect. The smaller the correlation, the closer we stick to the _____of the Y scores in our predictions.

Answers 1. $bX + a$; straight line   2. relationship   3. b 4. the mean of the Y scores   5. X; mean   6. closeness; prediction line; correlated   7. slopes   8. higher   9. negative; positive; zero   10. low; high   11. $+1$; -1; 0; 0; $+1$; 0; -1 12. Pearson's product moment correlation coefficient; Pearson's r; ρ_{XY}; r_{XY} 13. point biserial correlation coefficient (point biserial)   14. covariance   15. associated with X (predictable from X)   16. sample; estimate; small sample   17. large samples   18. table; $n-2$; equaled; surpassed (exceeded)   19. different; zero; zero; zero   20. regression line   21. Y; X; X; Y 22. $.5$; -1; -1 23. regression toward the mean; mean

---

PROBLEMS

1. We want to estimate the relationship between a student's anxiety and the number of hours a day the student studies.

    The following students obtain the scores listed below on a test of anxiety. (A higher score means more anxiety.) The hours that each of the students studies each day is also listed.

    (a) Compute the appropriate measure for obtaining the desired estimate. (Note that the number of scores used here is far too small for a reliable estimate. We have kept the number of subjects small to keep the computations to a minimum.)

Student	Hours of Study	Anxiety Score
1	4	10
2	5	12
3	4	8
4	6	10
5	2	4
6	3	6

(b) Give an estimate of the proportion of variance in students' hours of study that is predictable from students' anxiety scores.

2. (a) In problem 1 you computed the correlation. Suppose that you also computed the two standard deviations and found that they were 1.29 for hours of study and 2.69 for anxiety scores. With this information, we can specify the regression equation for predicting a student's score on the anxiety test from the number of hours that she or he studies. Give this regression equation.

(b) Now give the regression equation for predicting the number of hours a student studies, given his or her anxiety score.

3. Suppose, for a particular population, there is a close relationship between IQ and income. An economist wishes to predict income from IQ in this population. The economist takes a very large sample and develops a regression equation. (Although anyone facing such a prediction problem will, in fact, use a huge sample, we will pretend that only five subjects were used, to keep computations simple in our example.) The hypothetical data follow.

Subject	IQ	Income (in thousands of dollars)
1	110	14
2	115	18
3	120	22
4	125	26
5	130	30

Compute the regression equation, using the five paired scores. Then use the regression equation to predict the income of someone from this population with an IQ of 123.

4. (a) Compute the correlation between IQ and income for the scores in problem 3.

(b) Assume that the correlation that you obtained in (a) is the true correlation for the entire population sampled by the five subjects. This correlation has implications for how good the predictions will be in problem 3. In one or two words, indicate how good these predictions will be.

5. We have obtained a correlation between hours of exercise and ability to lift weights, which is quite high. However, we only used four subjects in our study, so we want to be sure that the relationship between the two variables (amount of practice and weight lifting ability) is a real relationship, and not just a sampling accident. The correlation in the sample was .96.

(a) Using your sampling evidence, what is the procedure for checking whether or not there is a real correlation in the population?

(b) What would be the least value of the sample correlation that would have indicated that the positive correlation was not just a result of sampling variability? (Use .05 two tail.)

(c) Judging from the data of this study, are hours of exercise and weight lifting ability-related?

6. An experimenter obtained a correlation of .30 between amount of hours of sleep and the scores on an anxiety test (with 30 subjects). He needed an r of .36 for statistical significance. Check the appropriate conclusions below.

_ There is not sufficient evidence to indicate that hours of sleep and anxiety are related.

_ There is sufficient evidence to indicate that hours of sleep and anxiety are related.

_ The correlation of .30 is the true correlation in the population.

7. Suppose that the same experimenter in problem 6 had actually obtained a correlation of .40 in his study. Check the appropriate conclusions below.

_ There is not sufficient evidence to indicate that hours of sleep and anxiety are related.

_ There is enough evidence to indicate that hours of sleep and anxiety are related.

_ The correlation of .40 is the true correlation in the population.

8. It is commonly believed that the presence of a patrol car on the highway causes drivers to slow down. But the presence of patrol cars all along the highway would be very expensive.

A psychologist in the traffic safety department wants to try a less expensive method. Posters are devised that show huge pictures of patrol cars, ostensibly to advertise the helpfulness of the highway patrol. But the real purpose is to remind the drivers of the possible presence of patrol cars. For example, one poster says, "When you need help, he's always there." and shows the patrol car covering almost the entire poster.

To test the effectiveness of the sign idea, a hidden radar operation measures the speed of cars at a particular point on the highway, identified as point P. One of the patrol car signs is placed a short distance before point P. The speed of the cars is measured at point P both when the sign is present and when it is absent.

If this were a real experiment, hundreds or thousands of measurements of car speed would be taken. But for simplicity of computation, assume that the experiment was done and all the data are presented below.

With the sign, the speeds were: 50, 55, 50, and 60.
Without the sign, the speeds were: 50, 70, 65, 60, and 60.

Use the point biserial correlation formula to estimate the degree of relationship between presence of the sign and car speed. Then indicate the proportion of the variance in car speed that is estimated to be associated with the presence or the absence of the sign.

twelve

CORRELATION AND TESTS

Suppose someone is measured by an intelligence test and found to have an IQ of 117. If the subject is tested by a different person, will he or she obtain the same IQ score? If the subject is tested on a different day, will the score be the same? Will this person obtain a different score on another form of the same test? The answer to these questions is that it is reasonably likely that the individual's score will vary under different conditions and times.

Some intelligence tests are more consistent than others, but none is perfectly consistent. Yet intelligence tests are more consistent than most of the other commonly used psychological tests. This suggests that some inconsistency is to be anticipated with all psychological tests.

The technique of correlation is the major tool used to determine the degree to which tests are consistent in their measurements. The application of correlation to the question of consistency is discussed in the first section of this chapter, Reliability.

A second issue of importance in test construction and evaluation is the extent to which a test measures what it is supposed to measure. Even if a test is consistent, it can consistently measure the wrong thing. The technique of correlation is often used to determine whether tests measure what they are supposed to measure. This aspect of correlation is discussed in the second section of this chapter, Validity.

RELIABILITY

When a test is relatively consistent in its measurement, it is called a reliable test. However, **reliability** is really a matter of degree. The degree of reliability is expressed through a correlation coefficient called a **reliability coefficient**.

For example, suppose a large number of randomly selected people take a particular test and receive scores identified by the variable X. They then take the same test at another time, and all receive scores identified this time by the variable Y. A positive correlation between the two sets of scores, r_{XY}, will indicate the degree to which the two sets of scores are in agreement. The higher the correlation, the more similar the test scores on the two forms of the test. This correlation between paired scores of the same individuals, on two forms of the same test, is a measurement of the tests's reliability. The resulting correlation is a reliability coefficient. A computed correlation between two forms of the same test is just one of many different reliability coefficients, the most common of which are discussed below.

Values for Reliability Coefficients

A correlation coefficient usually varies between -1 and $+1$, where zero means no relationship. A negative correlation between two tests means that the higher people score on one test, the lower they are likely to score on the other. When measuring reliability, it is rare to encounter negative correla-

tions. The best bet is that responsible test construction will yield positive correlations between repeated test sessions. The issue is just how high the correlation will be. Correlations of .90 or higher are desirable for reliability coefficients, though .85 or higher is considered acceptable. When dealing with new tests, or informal measures, reliabilities as low as .80 are acceptable. For research purposes, reliabilities below .80 are tolerated. But reliability coefficients below .80 are too low for tests intended to aid in making decisions about individuals.

Sample Size in the Assessment of Reliability As indicated in the preceding chapter, correlation requires large samples for accuracy; that is, correlation coefficients are themselves unreliable when computed with small samples. For this reason, all reliability coefficients should be computed with sufficiently large samples, so that the resulting values will reflect population values rather than rough sample estimates of them. In the following discussions it is assumed that all measurements of reliability use hundreds of subjects in the samples.

Reliability and Number of Test Items

All other things being equal, reliability increases with the number of items in the test. The relationship between sample size and reliability is given by Equation (12.1).

$$r_{new} = \frac{kr_{old}}{1 + (k-1)r_{old}}.$$

(12.1)

The k in Equation (12.1) is the factor by which the size of a test is to be changed. Assume that a 15-item test is increased to a 45-item test. The test has been tripled in size, so $k = 3$.

Suppose that the 15-item test has a reliability coefficient of .70 (calculated with one of the reliability coefficients discussed below). Increasing the test to a 45-item test will yield an anticipated reliability coefficient of

$$r_{new} = \frac{kr_{old}}{1 + (k-1)r_{old}}$$

$$= \frac{3(.70)}{1 + 2(.70)}$$

$$= .88.$$

Test—Retest Reliability

An obvious definition of test–retest reliability is the correlation of the scores from the first administration of a test with the scores from the second administration of the same test. The resulting correlation is called the test–retest reliability coefficient.

The test–retest reliability coefficient is seldom computed because of the possible inflation of the correlation by the subjects' memories of their past answers, and because of possible practice effects. Yet, in measuring a test's reliability, the underlying purpose is to identify the degree of the test's consistency were it given repeatedly to the same person.

The same test given twice, but with practice effects and memory for past responses *excluded,* represents the ideal definition of reliability. The other reliability coefficients attempt to offer representations of what a test–retest reliability would look like for a test, with the problems of taking the same test twice removed.

The Alternate Test Form Reliability Coefficient

Two tests attempting to be duplicate measures of the same thing should have test items that come from some implicitly common pool of items. As an example, assume some test of abstract ability. The test constructor has some definition of abstraction and generates a set of items, all illustrating the same definition. In this sense, they will all be items from the same pool of items. The test items actually used in the test are those that the test constructor has been able to identify or create with the definition. Given more time, or other people working with the same definition, additional items consistent with that definition could probably be constructed. Thus, the items in the one version of the test could be thought of as a sample of those items from a potentially larger pool of items. The use of Equation (12.1) for projecting changing reliabilities given more items assumes that the additional items will all come from the same pool as the items in the shorter test.

Many tests have alternate forms which have been constructed with additional items from the same pool. Alternate forms of tests are needed for many purposes. A whole class of examples is provided by studies testing whether there is improvement when some therapeutic intervention is applied between the administrations of two forms of a test.

The correlation between two alternate forms offers the **alternate test form reliability coefficient.** It indicates how similar the information is when a person has scores from two forms of the same test. The alternate test form reliability coefficient indicates the extent to which we expect the two test scores to agree. It is the most realistic reliability coefficient. However, not all tests have alternate forms.

The Split-Half Reliability Coefficient How many items should there be in a test? Equation (12.1) suggests that the more items, the more reliable the test. However, other considerations, such as the time required to take the test and the availability of good items, must also be considered. The number of test items is arbitrary. A 40-item test could be conceived of as two separate 20-item forms of the same test, both forms being taken at the same sitting.

What is suggested here is that instead of taking two different forms of a test at two different times and correlating the scores, the same test can be split in half. This will yield two scores for each person. These paired scores can then be correlated.

The correlation between the two halves may, at first, appear to offer a reliability coefficient. However, as suggested by Equation (12.1), the correlation between two smaller tests (smaller by half in this case) should be less than the correlation between two alternate forms of the original test. The question is: What is the reliability of the original intact test, which is twice as large as either of the split-half tests? The correlation between the two split-half tests, therefore, has to be adjusted for projection to a test doubled in size.

Equation (12.1) suggests the required adjustment. The value of k in Equation (12.1) is set at 2, as in Equation (12.2), the equation for the split–half reliability coefficient, r_{sh}.

$$r_{sh} = \frac{2r_{12}}{1 + r_{12}}.$$ (12.2)

The subscripted r_{12} in Equation (12.2) refers to the correlation between the two halves of the test.

When obtaining the split-half reliability coefficient, the test can be split in half by a random procedure. However, the order of adjacent items in tests is often free of determining influences, and so at such times can be treated as a random order. Therefore, split-half reliabilities are commonly computed by first dividing the test into two halves: the odd-numbered items and the even-numbered items. Then two scores are computed, one from the even- and one from the odd-numbered items. Symbolize the even-numbered items as 2 and the odd-numbered items as 1. Then r_{12}, the correlation between these two subscores, is computed and placed into Equation (12.2). (The correlation r_{12} is identical to r_{xy}, the Pearson product moment correlation coefficient, with x and y representing the odd- and even-numbered test items, respectively.)

As an example, Table 12.1 presents the answers to a 10-question dichotomously answered test (true or false, yes or no), where the answers are symbolized by 0 and 1. A person's score on the whole test is the sum of responses to the 10 items. This is equivalent to the number of items answered with the response designated 1, since zeroes would not contribute to score totals. On a 10-item test, the scores can range from 0 to 10. For a split-half reliability, the test has two subtotals for each person, one from the odd- and one from the even-numbered items. The odd- and even-numbered items have been totaled separately in Table 12.1 as ΣX_1

TABLE 12.1
Split-half reliability of a 10-item hypothetical test, estimated with four hypothetical subjects. (In practice, hundreds of subjects are required for a reliable and useful estimate.)

Subjects	Test Items 1 2 3 4 5 6 7 8 9 10	X_1 Sum, Odd Items	X_2 Sum, Even Items	X_1X_2	$X_1{}^2$	$X_2{}^2$
1	1 1 1 0 1 1 0 1 1 1	4	4	16	16	16
2	0 1 1 0 1 1 1 0 1 1	4	3	12	16	9
3	0 1 1 0 1 1 0 0 0 1	2	3	6	4	9
4	0 1 1 0 0 0 0 0 1 1	2	2	4	4	4
		$\Sigma X_1 = 12$	$\Sigma X_2 = 12$	$\Sigma X_1X_2 = 38$	$\Sigma X_1{}^2 = 40$	$\Sigma X_2{}^2 = 38$

$$r_{sh} = \frac{2r_{12}}{1 + r_{12}} \qquad r_{12} = \frac{n\Sigma X_1X_2 - (\Sigma X_1)(\Sigma X_2)}{\sqrt{[n\Sigma X_1{}^2 - (\Sigma X_1)^2][n\Sigma X_2{}^2 - (\Sigma X_2)^2]}}$$

$$= \frac{2(.71)}{1 + .71} \qquad = \frac{4(38) - (12)(12)}{\sqrt{[4(40) - (12)^2][4(38) - (12)^2]}}$$

$$= .83 \qquad = .71$$

and ΣX_2. These two subtotals, along with $\Sigma X_1 X_2$, ΣX_1^2, and ΣX_2^2, are needed to compute r_{12}, the correlation between the two halves. Then r_{12} is incorporated into r_{sh}, as illustrated in the table.

In practice, a relibility coefficient computed with the data from four subjects is useless. But the same procedure is followed for 400 as for four subjects.

Coefficient Alpha The correlation between two samples of test items (from a larger pool of potential test items) is an index of the potential reliability of any test taken from that pool of items. This idea can be extended to the notion that the correlation between any two individual test items in that pool can be used as an index of the potential reliability of any test constructed from that pool of items. But given many items on a test, there are many potential correlations between paired items. A better representation of the correlation between any randomly selected pair of items can be obtained by computing all the correlations between all possible pairings, and then computing the average correlation. This average correlation between all pairs of items is symbolized here as $\bar{r}_{ij}$.

The average inter-item correlation, $\bar{r}_{ij}$, offers the correlation between two forms of the same test where each form consists of a single item. Suppose such an average inter-item correlation had been obtained from a k item test. The desired reliability coefficient is for a test form k times as large as that represented in the average inter-item correlation, $\bar{r}_{ij}$. Therefore, Equation (12.1), where k is the number of test items, offers the needed formula for going from the average inter-item correlation, $\bar{r}_{ij}$, to a coefficient of reliability for the k-item test. Restating Equation (12.1) with $\bar{r}_{ij}$ in place of r_{old} yields

$$r_{new} = \frac{k\bar{r}_{ij}}{1 + (k-1)\bar{r}_{ij}}$$

In practice, it would be tedious to compute the correlation between all possible pairs of test items to obtain $\bar{r}_{ij}$. For a 30-item test there are 435 such correlations. An equivalent computational formula has been developed which only uses variances. It uses the sum of the individual variances of all the test items, $\Sigma \sigma_i^2$, and the variance of the test score totals, σ_X^2. The formula is called **coefficient alpha**, and is given in Equation (12.3).

$$r_\alpha = \frac{k}{k-1}\left(1 - \frac{\Sigma \sigma_i^2}{\sigma_X^2}\right). \tag{12.3}$$

Without a computer, the computation of coefficient alpha can be time consuming because of the need to compute the variance of each item in the test. When test items are answered dichotomously, there is a simpler computational formula available, the **Kuder-Richardson version of coeffi-**

cient alpha. The variance of a dichotomous item is the product of the proportion answering with one alternative response (p) times the proportion answering with the other alternative response (q). The variance for the ith item is, therefore, p_iq_i. Equation (12.3) can be restated for dichotomously answered items as Equation (12.4).

$$r_\alpha = \frac{k}{k-1}\left(1 - \frac{\Sigma p_iq_i}{\sigma_x^2}\right). \tag{12.4}$$

In Equation (12.4), Σp_iq_i is the sum of the individual item variances, and σ_x^2 is the variance of the score totals of individual subjects.

Table 12.2 presents the same answers to a 10-question dichotomously answered test as Table 12.1. But in Table 12.2 coefficient alpha (Kuder-Richardson version), rather than the split-half reliability coefficient, is used to compute the reliability. The resulting reliability coefficients in the two tables are not the same. In practice they will not necessarily be identical but they are expected to be similar. The large discrepancy here is a result of the very small sample used as an illustration.

TABLE 12.2
Coefficient of reliability for a 10-item hypothetical test, estimated with four hypothetical subjects and computed with coefficient alpha, Kuder-Richardson version. (In practice, hundreds of subjects are required for a reliable estimate.) The proportion of subjects giving the response arbitrarily valued as 1, is p, and q is the proportion responding with the alternative response.

Subjects	Test Items										Test Totals	
	1	2	3	4	5	6	7	8	9	10	X	X²
1	1	1	1	0	1	1	0	1	1	1	8	64
2	0	1	1	0	1	1	1	0	1	1	7	49
3	0	1	1	0	1	1	0	0	0	1	5	25
4	0	1	1	0	0	0	0	0	1	1	4	16
Item p Values	.25	1	1	0	.75	.75	.25	.25	.75	1	$\Sigma X = 24$	$\Sigma X^2 = 154$
Item q Values	.75	0	0	1	.25	.25	.75	.75	.25	0		
p_iq_i	.1875	0	0	0	.1875	.1875	.1875	.1875	.1875	0	$\Sigma p_iq_i = 1.1250$	

$$\sigma_x^2 = \frac{\Sigma X^2 - (\Sigma X)^2/n}{n} \qquad r_\alpha = \frac{k}{k-1}\left(1 - \frac{\Sigma p_iq_i}{\sigma_x^2}\right)$$

$$= \frac{154 - (24)^2/4}{4} \qquad = \frac{10}{9}\left(1 - \frac{1.1250}{2.50}\right)$$

$$= 2.50 \qquad = .61$$

Comparisons of the Reliability Coefficients When developing a new test, the reliability of the test should always be determined. The best reliability coefficient when initially developing a test is coefficient alpha. When the test items are dichotomously answered, the Kuder-Richardson version of coefficient alpha [Equation (12.4)] is easily computed. When the individual items have larger score ranges, Equation (12.3) has to be used for coefficient alpha. A common substitute for coefficient alpha when no computer is available is the split-half reliability coefficient, using Equation (12.2).

With developed tests, which often have reliabilities computed from alternate forms, the alternate test form reliability coefficient offers the most realistic reliability coefficient.

When reading test manuals, the alternate form reliability is the critical value to look for, with coefficient alpha being a close second choice for information on test reliability. If neither of these is available, the split-half reliability coefficient is useful, and commonly indicated in test manuals.

VALIDITY The process of confirming that a test measures what it purports to measure is called **validating a test.** People give tests names that suggest what they are intended to measure. For example, a test may be called an "intelligence test," but does it measure intelligence? A test may be called a "test of mechanical ability," but does it really measure mechanical ability?

Suppose someone develops an intelligence test for fourth graders. It is a group intelligence test, to be given to an entire class at the same time. The teacher hands out the test forms to the students, gives them some general instructions ("Print your name. Read each question carefully. . ."), and then tells them to complete the test as quickly as possible. The test is timed. Each item on the test has some simple instructions appropriate to children reading at the fourth-grade level.

The group administration requires that the children be willing to cooperate and take the test seriously. Therefore, uncooperative and distracted children do poorly on the test. Children with reading problems spend too much time trying to understand the written instructions for each item. They may, in fact, misunderstand some of the questions. An intelligent child who is a slow reader may perform as an average child, or even worse. Children who read quickly may save some time. The result may be that the test is in large measure a test of reading level, rather than a test of intelligence. Given children who vary considerably in cooperative spirit, the test could possibly function as a test of cooperativeness. But all the test does is give each child a numerical score. How would one know whether the test score reflects reading level, willingness to cooperate with the teacher, or intelligence?

A large sample of children can be given both a previously validated, individually administered intelligence test, and the group intelligence test. The size of the correlation between the two tests will indicate the extent to which the group test is a valid measure of intelligence. Assuming the individually administered test is accepted as a measure of intelligence, it will serve as a reasonable criterion for validating the group test as an intelligence test.

Generally, a test validation procedure consists of the computation of a correlation between two sets of scores, one being test scores and the other some criterion of what the test should measure. The criterion can be a previously validated test or some behavioral measure. The resulting correlation is called a **validity coefficient.** Scholastic success was a frequently used behavioral criterion in the early development of intelligence tests. Correlations between test scores and school performance were used to obtain validity coefficients.

Examples of tests that may not measure what they purport to measure are sometimes seen in pencil-and-paper tests of abilities. For example, a paper-and-pencil test of mechanical ability was developed. It consisted of questions about the use of tools and mechanical processes. But, in fact, when tested against other criteria, it turned out that the test was actually a good test of mechanical *interest,* though a poor test of mechanical *ability.* The test seemed to reflect a person's vocabulary level in the area of

mechanics. Vocabulary development in a specialized area stems from the kinds of reading one does, and the things one tends to remember. This, in turn, can reflect the degree of interest in the topic. This is what the test did—it reflected interest in mechanics. But the test did not reflect a person's skills when actually working with tools. As in the case of the mechanical abilities test, a test may have little or no validity as a measure of one trait or ability, but it may be useful as a measure of some other trait or ability. Hopefully, the test measures what is suggested by the name of the test.

It is possible to think of a test as being invalid. This is a test with no correlation between the test and its criterion. But when a test is a valid measure of something, it is generally valid only to some degree. The size of the validity coefficient is taken as the degree of validity. It is rare to find coefficients of validity in excess of .60. Usually they are a good deal lower. Intelligence tests have tended to have the highest validity coefficients.

Testing Validity Through Tests of Significance A question in many validity studies is whether the test is in any way a valid measure of the trait. This can be answered through a test of whether there is a zero correlation between the test and its criterion. To answer that question, small samples can be used. The sample correlation is simply tested for significance using Table V in Appendix B, as discussed in the preceding chapter. Statistical significance implies that the correlation between the test and its criterion is greater than zero. This, in turn, implies that the test has some (unknown) degree of validity greater than zero.

RELIABILITY VERSUS VALIDITY A test can be reliable yet not valid for its intended use. It can consistently measure the wrong thing (from the point of view of its intended purpose). High reliability does not imply anything about validity. But high validity implies high reliability. In order for a test to be a valid measure of anything, it must have a reasonable reliability. If a test does not measure anything consistently, it cannot be a valid measure of anything. For this reason, low reliability suggests low validity.

IMPORTANT WORDS AND CONCEPTS Reliability (p. 271)
Reliability coefficient (p. 271)
Test–retest reliability coefficient (p. 273)
Alternate test form reliability coefficient (p. 274)
Split–half reliability coefficient (p. 274)
Coefficient alpha (p. 276)

Kuder–Richardson version of coefficient alpha (pp. 276–277)
Validating a test (p. 278)
Validity coefficient (p. 279)

SENTENCE COMPLETIONS The following incomplete sentences are taken from the underlined sentences in this chapter. Fill in the missing words and phrases and then correct them from the answers which follow.

1. The technique of correlation is the major tool used to determine the degree to which tests are _____.

2. When a test is relatively consistent in its measuremen, it is called a _____ test. This is actually a matter of degree, expressed through a correlation coefficient,· called a _____ _____ .

3. Correlations of _____ or higher are desirable for reliability coefficients, though _____ or higher is considered acceptable. Reliability coefficients below _____ are too low for tests intended to aid in making decisions about individuals.

4. All things being equal, reliability _____ with the number of items in the test.

5. The correlation of the scores from one administration of a test with the scores from another administration of the same test is called the _____ coefficient. This reliability coefficient is seldom computed, because of the possible inflation of the correlation by _____ _____ _____ .

6. The reliability coefficient derived from correlating two halves of the same test is called the _____.

7. There is a computational formula for a reliability coefficient which is derived from the average correlation between pairs of items and then boosted by a factor k, where k is the number of items. This reliability coefficient is called _____.

8. The correlation between two forms of the same test offers a particularly realistic _____ _____ .

9. The best reliability coefficient to use when developing a new test is _____. With developed tests, _____ is the most realistic index of the test's reliability.

10. The process of confirming that a test measures what it purports to measure is called _____.

11. Generally, a test validation procedure consists of the computation of a correlation between two sets of scores, one being test scores and the other some criterion of _____.
The criterion can be a _____;
or the criterion can be some _____ _____.
The resulting correlation is called a _____ _____.

12. It is possible to think of a test as being invalid. This is a test with _____ between the test and its criterion.

13. A question in many validity studies is whether the test is in any way a valid measure of the trait. In such studies, statistical significance implies that the correlation between the test and its criterion is _____ _____.

14. High _____ does not imply anything about _____.

15. Low _____ suggests low _____.

16. High _____ implies high _____.

Answers 1. consistent in their measurements 2. reliable; reliability coefficient 3. .90; .85; .80 4. increases 5. test–retest reliability; subjects' memory of their past answers, and because of possible practice effects 6. split-half reliability coefficient 7. coefficient alpha 8. reliability coefficient 9. coefficient alpha; the alternate test form reliability coefficient 10. validating a test 11. what the test should measure; previously validated test; behavioral measure; validity coefficient 12. no correlation 13. greater than zero 14. reliability; validity 15. reliability; validity 16. validity; reliability

---

PROBLEM

1. Pretend that the following data matrix represents the scores on individual items on an eight-item test, obtained by six subjects. The items have each been marked as correct or incorrect, represented by ones and zeros, respectively. Compute both coefficient alpha (using the Kuder-Richardson version) and the split-half reliability coefficient for this test. (Because of the small number of subjects the values of the two coefficients will be quite different.)

Subject	Item							
	1	2	3	4	5	6	7	8
1	1	1	1	1	0	1	1	1
2	0	1	1	1	1	1	0	1
3	0	0	0	0	1	0	0	0
4	0	1	0	0	0	1	0	0
5	1	0	1	0	0	1	1	0
6	0	0	0	1	0	0	0	1

ANALYSIS OF VARIANCE

thirteen

In the discussion of t tests, it was indicated that they are used to determine whether two variables are related. Two types of t tests were examined: The matched-pair t test and the t test for the difference between two means.

In the discussion of correlation, it was indicated that correlation can also be used to determine whether two variables are related. The sampled correlation has only to be subjected to a t test. Here again two types of statistics were discussed: The Pearson r and the point biserial.

All four statistical tests of a relationship between variables assume a continuous (or wide ranging) dependent variable. But to use the t tests or the point biserial, the independent variable must be dichotomized. If the independent variable, like the dependent variable, is continuous, then the Pearson r is used.* Some simplified examples which show when to use the different tests are presented below. All the examples use weight as the dependent variable.

Suppose the independent variable is sex, and someone wants to know if there is a relationship between weight and sex. A t test can be used, or the point biserial correlation can be estimated and then tested for significance with a t test. The data would be tabulated as in Table 13.1(a) and 13.1(b).

TABLE 13.1(a)
Table of data for a t test

Male	Female
140	110
150	120
.	.
.	.
.	.
$\bar{X}_1$	$\bar{X}_2$

TABLE 13.1(b)
Table of data for computing a point biserial
correlation coefficient

Sex Designation (X)	Weight (Y)
0	110
0	120
1	140
1	150
.	.
.	.
.	.

*In the chapter on correlation it was stated that the distributions do not really have to be continuous. Wide-ranging sets of discrete valued scores will also do in computing a Pearson r.

Note that for a direct t test, as in Table 13.1(a), the two groups identified in the dichotomy of the independent variable are represented by the means of the scores in each of the groups.

If our independent variable was the continuous variable of age, instead of the dichotomous variable of sex, we could use a Pearson r, which we would then test for significance to determine whether the variables are related. The data would be tabulated as in Table 13.2.

TABLE 13.2
Table of data for computing a Pearson correlation coefficient

Age (X)	Weight (Y)
18	110
40	120
16	140
25	150
.	.
.	.
.	.

But what if the independent variable is not dichotomously classifiable (like sex), not continuously measurable (like age), and not even wide ranging? For example, what if the independent variable consists of just three of four classifications? In this text, a variable which has been divided into a small number of different classes (say, from three to 10) is called a narrowly ranging variable.

An example of a narrowly ranging variable is socioeconomic class. Some researchers, using the dependent variable of weight, have shown that there is a relationship between socioeconomic class and weight. Socioeconomic class has been used quite frequently as an independent variable, and has been found to be related to many other variables.

When using socioeconomic class as an independent variable, different researchers have used different numbers of classifications. Sometimes socioeconomic class has been divided into lower, middle, and upper classes. Sometimes it has been divided into lower, lower-middle, upper-middle, and upper classes. Sometimes a lower-lower class is added, and sometimes an upper-upper class. Thus, the independent variable of socioeconomic class, in different studies, has ranged from three to six classes.

What statistic would be used when the independent variable is a narrowly ranging variable, and the dependent variable is continuous? The answer is an analysis of variance, which is the topic of this chapter. Table 13.3 illustrates the way that data might be tabled for an analysis of variance. Note that in analysis of variance, as in t tests, each of the groups is

TABLE 13.3
Table of data for computing an analysis of variance

Lower Class (G_1)	Middle Class (G_2)	Upper Class (G_3)
200	150	110
180	160	140
150	180	140
.	.	.
.	.	.
.	.	.
$\bar{X}_1$	$\bar{X}_2$	$\bar{X}_3$

represented by the mean of the scores in the group. In analysis of variance with more than two groups, this creates the problem of many potential comparisons. Later in the chapter it will be demonstrated how analysis of variance solves the problem of comparing many different means with a single test.

EXPERIMENTAL MANIPULATION VERSUS CLASSIFICATION

In the previous section, the words "classes" and "classifications" were used when referring to differences based on the independent variable. This choice of words was influenced by the example of the last section, which included the independent variable of socioeconomic class. More common designations for differences based on the independent variable are **treatments**, levels, groups, or some combination of these terms, such as "treatment groups" or "treatment levels."

The use of the word treatment stems from the fact that, historically, analysis of variance was used primarily as a statistic for testing the effectiveness of varied experimental manipulations. Different treatments were the basis for defining different groups. Early applications of analysis of variance were in agriculture, where different fertilizers or different amounts of water were applied to different sets of seeds. These different treatments constituted the independent variables when questioning whether different treatments made for differences in productivity. An example of different treatments in psychology would be a comparison of several different forms of psychotherapy, looking at their effects on reduction of symptoms. Different motivating circumstances might be compared to see if they have differential effects on the speed of task completion. An experimenter might test the effects of several drugs on blood pressure. In all these examples there would be **experimental manipulation** of the subjects. The subjects would be treated differently in the different groups. Thus, it would be appropriate to refer to distinctions on the independent variable as treatments or treatment groups.

Varied experimental manipulations are not the only basis for differentiating treatment groups. In the earlier example of a test of the relationship between socioeconomic class and weight, the different groups were differentiated by classification. **Classification** into different subpopulations is a frequent basis for independent variable classification. A common example is educational level. The distinctions could be: did not graduate from high school; graduated from high school; graduated from college; postgraduate degree. Personality characteristics have also been used frequently. A question might be something like: "Do authoritarian people differ from nonauthoritarian people in such and such?" Here the independent variable would merely be dichotomized. Diagnostic categories are also used. Endless studies have been done comparing "psychotics," "neurotics," and "normals."

The classifications always follow from already existing distinctions that can be made among the subjects. When classification is the basis for distinguishing groups, it might seem inappropriate to refer to the different groups as "treatment groups." But in the literature, groups are referred to as "treatments," regardless of whether distinctions are based on experimental manipulation or classification.

Another word that is used to refer to the distinctions on the independent variable is **levels.** The use of the phrase "different levels" to refer to the different treatments is particularly appropriate when the different groups can be ranked on the independent variable (different levels of education; different socioeconomic levels, etc.). The word level has, in fact, become a very commonly used designation for all differentiations on the independent variable, whether or not any ranking of the groups is implied. The literature uses the words "levels" and "treatments" interchangeably and synonymously.

SUMMARY OF WHEN TO USE ANALYSIS OF VARIANCE

Given a continuous dependent variable and a narrowly ranging independent variable, it is generally appropriate to use the analysis of variance to test for a relationship between the two variables. The differences on the independent variable can be based on experimental manipulation or simple classification into distinguishable subgroups. Both the differently treated and differently classified groups are referred to as the different treatments, treatment groups, levels, or treatment levels, all with the same meaning.

Control of the Independent Variable

In defining the independent variable through experimental manipulation, all subjects are randomly selected from the same population, randomly placed into different groups, and then treated differently in the different groups. Within a group all subjects are treated identically. The different groups are distinguished by different consistent treatments. When scientists speak of experimental control, this is one of its meanings. Careful application of differences permits clearer conclusions about the possible effects of differences.

In using classification as the basis for distinguishing groups on the independent variable, all subjects in all groups are treated identically. However, the subjects in each group are deliberately selected from different subpopulations. Thus, subpopulation membership is the only consistent difference between subjects in different groups. (To properly represent each subpopulation in the sample, selection of subjects from within each subpopulaton should be random.)

When classification defines the levels of the independent variable, the data are examined to see if scores on the dependent variable are related to the specific subpopulation memberships represented in the experiment. When experimental manipulation defines the levels of the independent variable, the data are examined to see if scores on the dependent variable are related to the specific treatments of the subjects in the experiment.

Conclusions About Cause and Effect Experimental manipulation of the independent variable allows the experimenter to conclude, from significant results, that the independent variable is an effective agent; that is, statistical significance permits the conclusion that the independent variable is at least one of the factors causing the observed differences in the dependent variable.

When classification is used to define the independent variable, it is impossible to draw conclusions about cause and effect. The reasons are the same as those given in Chapter 11 on the limitations of conclusions from observed correlations. Both variables could be jointly varying as a function of some third variable. Also, for many pairs of variables, which variable is the cause and which is the effect is not discernible. Therefore, conclusions with classified independent variables should be restricted to statements about the existence of relationships, avoiding conclusions about cause and effect. The restrictions on conclusions are so similar to the restrictions on conclusions from statistical correlation that analysis of variance with a classified independent variable is often called a correlational study, even though correlational statistics are not involved.

Let us use type of mental illness as an example of a classified independent variable. Assume that three groups of people, all diagnosed as possessing one or another of three types of mental illness, are all tested for IQ. Suppose that it is discovered that the three groups differ significantly in IQ, and further that all three groups differ significantly from a control group of people without any signs of mental illness.

Can we then conclude that the different forms of mental illness result in (cause) differences in intellectual functioning? or is it possible that people differing in intelligence are prone to different forms of mental illness? The direction of the effect, then, would not be discernible. It is also possible that there is some third factor jointly affecting both variables. For example, perhaps certain early experiences in life both affect intelligence and simultaneously predispose people to particular forms of mental illness. Then neither variable would qualify as a cause of the other. Rather, they would both simply vary together as a function of the third variable, early experience.

On the other hand, if there were some way to induce the different forms of mental illness in randomly selected groups of people, any significant differences observed in intelligence could more readily be attributed directly to the illness as a causative factor. Thus, experimental manipulation could permit some tentative conclusions about cause and effect. But there are obvious ethical problems with the use of experimental manipulation for answering such questions. That is why classification is often used to define independent variables, particularly when dealing with applied problems in psychology.

THE GROUP MEAN AS AN INDEX OF TREATMENT EFFECTS

In any single treatment group, all subjects are treated identically (or come from the same population if using a classified independent variable). There are several treatment groups, each receiving different types or amounts of some independent variable. If the independent variable is effective, it can be assumed to be adding or subtracting different amounts to the dependent variable values in different groups. For example, a particular level of increased motivation in one group might make the dependent variable of reaction time of subjects 20 milliseconds faster.

In Chapter 6 it was pointed out that adding or subtracting a constant from all the scores in a group changes the mean of the scores by the constant. Thus, the means can serve as an index of the differential effects of the various levels of the independent variable.

THE NULL HYPOTHESIS IN ANALYSIS OF VARIANCE

The null hypothesis in analysis of variance, as in t tests, is that the groups that have been sampled all come from the same population of dependent variable scores. Saying that groups have been sampled from the same population is another way of saying that the different treatments did not have different effects on the dependent variable scores. In other words, if the independent and dependent variables are not related, the different groups (of dependent variable scores) have, in effect, all been sampled from the same population. Since each group is represented by its mean, this reduces to the hypothesis that all groups have the same population mean.

From prior discussions in this text, you should remember that equal population means do not imply equal sample means. Suppose that the groups all come from the same population (implying a true null hypothesis). Some differences among sample means would be anticipated, simply due to sampling variability. The statistical technique of analysis of variance offers a way of distinguishing differences between several means that are due to sampling variability, from differences that are due to the sampling of different populations.

RANDOM VARIABILITY WITHIN A GROUP In this section, the assumption is again made that an independent variable, if effective, acts as a constant being added to the scores within a treatment group. The controlled independent variable is the only variable that can be considered as a constant within any one group. There are also other variables that are operating, but in an uncontrolled manner. For example, considering degree of distraction to be an uncontrolled variable, different subjects may experience momentary distractions. Considering alertness, fatigue, or amount of sleep as uncontrolled variables, different subjects could have had more or less sleep the previous night. The effects from one or more of these variables might impact on one subject in a group. Different uncontrolled variables might affect different subjects within a group. Thus, unpredictable variability might be seen within the scores of a group, caused by the effects of uncontrolled variables. Such variability will, in fact, always be present. There is an endless number of possible uncontrolled variables, each unpredictably affecting unpredictable subjects, all of this occurring in unpredictable patterns. The result is generally a distribution of scores that looks like a random distribution. Therefore, we call this unpredictable variability **random variability**.

Uncontrolled variables are not the only basis for random variability of scores. Subjects are randomly selected for each group. It is possible, for example, that a particular subject is a particularly high scorer on the dependent variable or is particularly anxious to please the experimenter. Variability among subjects on relevant but uncontrolled dimensions can also contribute to random variability among scores within a group. When the independent variable is a classified variable, the independent variable is one dimension on which all subjects within a group are identical. They are all members of some identical subpopulation. But the individuals in that subpopulation will vary on personal characteristics other than the controlled characteristic. If any of these are relevant to performance on the dependent variable, then subject variability will contribute to random variability of scores. It always does. Finally, there is the ever-present phenomenon of measurement error. Measurement error can also be expected to contribute to random variability of whatever is being measured.

In summary, there are many sources of variability within even a uniformly selected or treated group. The one source of variability that cannot contribute to the variance within a group is the influence of the independent variable. In Chapter 6 it was pointed out that adding a constant to every score in a group of scores does not change the variance of the scores within the group. (It only affects the mean of the group.) Therefore, it can be assumed that the independent variable, even if effective, would not contribute to score variability within a group. In other words, any variability found within the scores of any single group is considered random variability.

RANDOM VARIABILITY BETWEEN MEANS

All variability among individual scores within a group is random variability. Random variability implies unpredictable influences randomly adding or subtracting values from individual scores. This same random variability will affect means of groups. However, the influence of random variability on means is less than its influence on individual scores within a group.

Some scores will have been inflated and some deflated by random variability. Within a group, the random inflation and deflation of scores should have a tendency to cancel each other. To the extent that this cancelling process is present, the mean of each group will be less affected by random variability than the individual scores. Therefore, although means will vary from each other as a function of random variability, less random variabilty is expected between means than among individual scores within a group.

Another source of variability which will have an effect on means is effective treatments. Variability between means, then, can reflect both effective treatments *and* random variability.

USING VARIABILITY TO DETECT TREATMENT EFFECTS

In the preceding sections the following points were made.

1. Effective treatments *cannot* influence the variability *within* any treatment group.
2. The observed variability within a treatment group is exclusively random variability.
3. Effective treatments, when present, increase the variability between means.
4. In addition to treatment effects, the variability between means includes some random variability. If there are *no* treatment effects, then the variability between means is only random variability.

Thus, given a true null hypothesis, both the **variability within treatment groups** and between means is only random variability. Given a false null hypothesis, only the **variability between means** is inflated by treatment effects. The recognition of effective treatments would appear to require a comparison of variability between groups with variability within groups. An inflated between-groups variance would suggest effective treatments.

A problem in making this comparison is that when the treatments are not effective, within-groups variability is expected to be greater than the variability between means. Fortunately, there is a quantitative formula that specifies the relationship between the amount of the random variability expected within groups, and the amount of the random variability expected between means (when there are no treatment effects present). This permits use of the random variability observed within groups to specify the amount of random variability expected between means. When that expected random variability between means is convincingly exceeded, it is concluded that treatment effects are present.

TWO DIFFERENT VARIANCE ESTIMATES AS MEASURES OF VARIABILITY The relationship of variability among individual scores to variability between means, all sampled from the same population of scores, was specified in Chapter 9. This relationship was discussed in the context of the law of large numbers. The index of variability of interest in Chapter 9 was the standard deviation. The relationship of variability between means to variability among individual scores was given in Equation (9.6).

$$\sigma_{\bar{x}} = \frac{\sigma}{\sqrt{n}} . \qquad [9.6]$$

In equation (9.6), σ is the standard deviation of individual scores, and n is the number of scores used to compute each mean. The symbol $\sigma_{\bar{x}}$ is the standard deviation of the means of samples, which is commonly called the standard error of the mean.

It will be useful to square both sides of Equation (9.6),

$$\sigma_{\bar{x}}^2 = \frac{\sigma^2}{n},$$

and then multiply both sides of the equation by n:

$$n\sigma_{\bar{x}}^2 = \sigma^2. \qquad (13.1)$$

Equation (13.1) says that there are two ways to compute the variance of individual scores. The direct computation of the variance is σ^2, where

$$\sigma^2 = \frac{\Sigma(X - \mu)^2}{n_p},$$

and n_p is the total number of scores in the population. The second way to compute the variance of individual scores is to take all possible samples of size n, compute the mean for each such sample, and then compute the variance of all these means, which is $\sigma_{\bar{X}}^2$, the squared standard error of the mean. Then multiply $\sigma_{\bar{X}}^2$ by n, as required by Equation (13.1), to yield a value that will be equal to σ^2.

Thus, there is both a simple, direct way to compute σ^2 using individual scores, and an indirect way using the variance of sample means (the squared standard error of the mean), multiplied by n. Equation (13.1) indicates the quantitative relationship between the variance of means and the variance of individual scores.

But Equation (13.1) refers to population values. Analysis of variance is an inferential statistic, using limited randomly selected samples to draw conclusions about complete populations. Therefore, in practice, sample estimates of the variance, and of the squared standard error, are used in obtaining approximations to the terms in Equation (13.1).

The sample estimate of the variance of individual scores was presented in Chapter 5 in Equation (5.6) as

$$s^2 = \frac{\Sigma(X - \bar{X})^2}{n - 1},$$

where n is the number of scores in the sample.

In analysis of variance there will be two or more groups. Consequently, there will be two or more choices of groups to be used to compute s^2 for an estimate of σ^2; that is, each sample of scores within any one group offers one sample s^2 as an estimate of σ^2.

In analysis of variance all the groups are used. The estimate of the variance of individual scores from within each group, $s_1^2, s_2^2, \ldots,$ $s_j^2, \ldots$ are taken and then averaged. This average of variance estimates from within groups is called the **within-groups variance**, symbolized s_w^2. If there are g groups and the variance of any jth group is symbolized as s_j^2, the averaging process can be symbolized as

$$s_w^2 = \frac{\sum_{j=1}^{g} s_j^2}{g}$$

= within-groups variance.

The within-groups variance, s_w^2, is an estimate of σ^2 in Equation (13.1). The averaged estimate, s_w^2, is simply a better estimate of σ^2 than a single estimate s_j^2. Symbolically,

$$E[s_w^2] = \sigma^2, \tag{13.2}$$

where E stands for expectation. Verbally, Equation (13.2) says that the long-run average of sampled values of s_w^2 is expected to equal σ^2. Thus, the within-groups variance, s_w^2, will serve to estimate the right-hand side of Equation (13.1), σ^2, in

$$n\sigma_{\bar{x}}^2 = \sigma^2.$$

What can be used to estimate the left-hand side of Equation (13.1), $n\sigma_{\bar{x}}^2$?

Recall the discussions of the standard error of the mean in Chapter 10, which gave $s_{\bar{x}}$ as an estimate of $\sigma_{\bar{x}}$. Since $s_{\bar{x}}$, the estimate of the standard error of the mean, is the estimate of the standard deviation of means, a set of sampled means can be used to compute $s_{\bar{x}}$. This computed value is then squared and multiplied by n, the sample size, to yield $ns_{\bar{x}}^2$.

In an analysis of variance there will be several groups, each contributing a mean. The null hypothesis assumes that the sampled means have all been sampled from the same population, because the null hypothesis assumes that the independent variable has not been effective. Thus, the variance of the empirically obtained sample means, $s_{\bar{x}}^2$, can serve as an estimate of $\sigma_{\bar{x}}^2$ so that $ns_{\bar{x}}^2$ provides an estimate of $n\sigma_{\bar{x}}^2$.

Stated another way, assume an ineffective independent variable and several groups. A mean is computed for each group and a sample estimate of the variance of means, $s_{\bar{x}}^2$, is computed and multiplied by the sample size n. If this is done repeatedly with new sets of random samples of means from the same population, the long-run average of the resulting $ns_{\bar{x}}^2$ values will be expected to equal $n\sigma_{\bar{x}}^2$.

Symbolically,

$$E\left[ns_{\bar{x}}^2\right] = n\sigma_{\bar{x}}^2. \tag{13.3}$$

Recapitulating Equations (13.3), (13.1), and (13.2), in that order, we have

$$E\left[ns_{\bar{x}}^2\right] = n\sigma_{\bar{x}}^2,$$

$$n\sigma_{\bar{x}}^2 = \sigma^2,$$

and

$$\sigma^2 = E\left[s_w^2\right],$$

which imply that

$$E\left[ns_{\bar{x}}^2\right] = E\left[s_w^2\right].$$

Verbally, s_w^2 and $ns_{\bar{x}}^2$ have the same expectation. Of course, this is only true when the sample means used in computing $s_{\bar{x}}^2$ are all from the same population. Only a true null hypothesis yields means from the same population.

Perhaps you can now see the implicit logic of analysis of variance. Two sample estimates of variance are taken, s_w^2 and $ns_{\bar{x}}^2$. They have identical expectations when the null hypothesis is true. However, they have different expected values when the null hypothesis is false ($ns_{\bar{x}}^2$ being inflated by treatment effects). All that is needed is a comparison of s_w^2 and $ns_{\bar{x}}^2$ to see if they appear to be estimates of the same value. A sufficiently large discrepancy between the two sampled values would suggest that the null hypothesis is false.

The one additional requirement is some probability distribution for discrepancies between sampled values of $ns_{\bar{x}}^2$ and s_w^2; that is, some probability distribution is needed which specifies the probability of any possible discrepancy, *when the null hypothesis is true.* If an observed discrepancy between $ns_{\bar{x}}^2$ and s_w^2 is so large as to be unexpected in the probability distribution, it suggests that the null hypothesis is false. The distribution should offer probabilities for all possible discrepancies, given *no* treatment effects. If an observed discrepancy is large, and therefore has a low probability, the distribution (and the null hypothesis of no treatment effect) will be rejected. The distribution that gives the desired probability distribution for this purpose is called the **F distribution.**

THE F DISTRIBUTION The F distribution is not a distribution of expected *differences,* but rather a distribution of expected *ratios.* The F distribution is a distribution of ratios between two independent estimates of the variance from a single population.* In general, an F distribution is formed from randomly sampled ratios of the form

$$F = \frac{s_1^2}{s_2^2}$$

where s_1^2 and s_2^2 are two sample estimates of the same population variance. Using the two variance estimates discussed in this chapter, the **F ratio** consists of the ratio shown in Equation (13.4).

$$F = \frac{ns_{\bar{x}}^2}{s_w^2} . \tag{13.4}$$

It is expected that the two estimates of the variance in Equation (13.4) will form an F distribution which has a mean value close to 1; that is, sampled ratios, $ns_{\bar{x}}^2/s_w^2$, if endlessly sampled and computed, will form a distribution that has a mean value close to 1. But the expectation applies only when the null hypothesis is true; that is, when there are no treatment effects inflating the variability between means. When the null hypothesis is false, the numerator of the F ratio, $ns_{\bar{x}}^2$, should be inflated. This will result in an

---

*Although $ns_{\bar{x}}^2$ and s_w^2 are both obtained from the same body of data, it can be proved that they are each independent estimates of the variance.

enlarged *F* value which, if sufficiently greater than 1, would result in rejection of the null hypothesis.

Computational formulas are required for computing the *F* ratio from data. These formulas will be stated in terms of double subscript notation. Although the notation will initially appear cumbersome, the advantages of this notation should become apparent with use.

DOUBLE SUBSCRIPT NOTATION IN ANALYSIS OF VARIANCE Assume *g* treatment groups in an analysis of variance, with *n* subjects in each group. The score of the first subject in the first group is symbolized by X_{11}, that of the second subject by X_{21}, and that of the third subject by X_{31}. Speaking more generally, the score of the *i*th subject in the first group is symbolized by X_{i1}, and the score of the *i*th subject in the *j*th group by X_{ij}. The scores of *n* subjects in each of *g* groups are symbolized in Table 13.4.

The first subscript, *i*, ranging in values from 1 through *n*, refers to particular subjects. The second subscript, *j*, ranging in values from 1 through *g*, refers to the treatment groups (levels of the independent variable). For example, X_{23} symbolizes the score of the second subject in the third treatment group. To symbolize the mean of the *j*th group, $\bar{X}_{\cdot j}$ is used. The dot replaces the subscript for an individual subject. The mean of the sample of scores in the third group, for example, is symbolized as $\bar{X}_{\cdot 3}$.

TABLE 13.4
Analysis of variance data matrix (presented in symbolic form). Table entries represent scores on the dependent variable measure.

	Levels of Independent Variable							
	G_1	G_2	G_3	$\cdots$	G_j	$\cdots$	G_g	
	X_{11}	X_{12}	X_{13}	$\cdots$	X_{1j}	$\cdots$	X_{1g}	
	X_{21}	X_{22}	X_{23}	$\cdots$	X_{2j}	$\cdots$	X_{2g}	
	X_{31}	X_{32}	X_{33}	$\cdots$	X_{3j}	$\cdots$	X_{3g}	
	$\cdot$	$\cdot$	$\cdot$		$\cdot$		$\cdot$	
	$\cdot$	$\cdot$	$\cdot$		$\cdot$		$\cdot$	
	X_{i1}	X_{i2}	X_{i3}	$\cdots$	X_{ij}	$\cdots$	X_{ig}	
	$\cdot$	$\cdot$	$\cdot$		$\cdot$		$\cdot$	
	$\cdot$	$\cdot$	$\cdot$		$\cdot$		$\cdot$	
	X_{n1}	X_{n2}	X_{n3}	$\cdots$	X_{nj}	$\cdots$	X_{ng}	
Means of Treatment Groups	$\bar{X}_{\cdot 1}$	$\bar{X}_{\cdot 2}$	$\bar{X}_{\cdot 3}$	$\cdots$	$\bar{X}_{\cdot j}$	$\cdots$	$\bar{X}_{\cdot g}$	Grand Mean $= \bar{X}_{\cdot\cdot}$

$$\bar{X}_{\cdot j} = \frac{\sum_{i=1}^{n} X_{ij}}{n} \qquad \bar{X}_{\cdot\cdot} = \frac{\sum_{j=1}^{g}\sum_{i=1}^{n} X_{ij}}{gn}$$

Since there are n scores in each group, the mean of the jth group is computed as the sum of all the scores in the jth group divided by n. This is symbolized as

$$\bar{X}_{\cdot j} = \frac{\sum\limits_{i=1}^{n} X_{ij}}{n} \; .$$

The mean of all scores over all groups is sometimes referred to as the grand mean. To symbolize the grand mean, $\bar{X}_{\cdot\cdot}$ is used, the second dot replacing the subscript for a specific group. Since there are g groups and n scores in each group, there is a total of gn scores in the data matrix. The grand mean is computed as the sum of all the scores divided by gn. This is symbolized by

$$\bar{X}.. = \frac{\sum\limits_{j=1}^{g}\sum\limits_{i=1}^{n} X_{ij}}{gn}.$$

The grand mean $\bar{X}..$ is just a sample mean, the sample being the gn scores in the experiment. The actual (but generally unknown) population mean is symbolized as $\mu..$, while $\mu._j$ is used to symbolize the population mean for the jth treatment group.* An estimate of $\mu._j$ for the jth group is obtained in the form of a sampled mean $\bar{X}._j$, obtained from the scores sampled in the jth group.

THE WITHIN-GROUPS VARIANCE The double subscript notation introduced in the last section is used here to restate the equation for the variance. Earlier in this chapter, Equation (5.6) for the sample estimate of the variance was reintroduced. Repeating it again, we have

$$s^2 = \frac{\Sigma(X - \bar{X})^2}{(n-1)}, \qquad [5.6]$$

where $\bar{X}$ is the sample estimate of the mean, computed from n values of X. Equation (5.6) will now be restated in double subscript notation, with reference to the variance of the jth group. In double subscript notation, $\bar{X}$ is $\bar{X}._j$, the mean of the jth group. The X in

$$s^2 = \frac{\Sigma(X - \bar{X})^2}{n-1},$$

which stands for the very general ith score in the jth group, is symbolized as X_{ij}. Equation (5.6) can therefore be restated as in Equation (13.5).

$$s_j^2 = \frac{\sum\limits_{i=1}^{n}(X_{ij} - \bar{X}._j)^2}{n-1}. \qquad (13.5)$$

The j is used as a subscript in s_j^2 to indicate that the variance estimate is computed from some specific jth group with Equation (13.5).

---

*If the different levels were based on experimental manipulation, then the jth group's population mean, $\mu._j$ could, for example, refer to the mean of all the potential scores of everyone in the world were they exposed to treatment j and measured on the dependent variable; or it could refer to all adults so measured, if the population sampled was only adults. If the different levels were based on classification, $\mu._j$ would refer to the mean of all scores of all members of the jth subpopulation, were they measured on the dependent variable.

Table 13.5 gives some hypothetical data in an analysis of variance and demonstrates how Equation (13.5) is applied to the different groups.

TABLE 13.5
The defining equation for the variance estimated from a single group, as it applies in the case of some hypothetical data

	G_1	G_2	G_3	
	1	2	4	$s_j^2 = \dfrac{\sum\limits_{i=1}^{n} (X_{ij} - \bar{X}_{.j})^2}{n-1}$
	3	3	3	
	2	2	2	
	1	3	5	
	3	5	6	$s_1^2 = \dfrac{\sum\limits_{i=1}^{5}(X_{i1} - 2)^2}{5-1}$
$\sum\limits_{i=1}^{n} X_{ij} = 10$		15	20	
				$s_2^2 = \dfrac{\sum\limits_{i=1}^{5}(X_{i2} - 3)^2}{5-1}$
$\bar{X}_{.j} = \dfrac{\sum\limits_{i=1}^{n} X_{ij}}{n} = 2$		3	4	$s_3^2 = \dfrac{\sum\limits_{i=1}^{5}(X_{i3} - 4)^2}{5-1}$

(For s_1^2, the X_{ij} values are only those in the first column; for s_2^2, those in the second column, etc.)

Equation (13.5) is a defining formula which is not normally used for computations. A computational formula is offered in a later section. If the defining formula were used to estimate the variance in each group in Table 13.5, each X_{ij} value in the jth group would be subtracted from $\bar{X}_{.j}$, as suggested in Equation (13.5). For example, for the first group this would be

$$s_1^2 = \frac{\sum\limits_{i=1}^{5} (X_{i1} - 2)^2}{5-1},$$

where the X_{ij} values would be only those values in the first column of Table 13.5.

It was previously indicated that the average of the g variances, called the within-groups variance, offers the best estimate of the variance of individual scores. Thus, g estimates of s_j^2, each following the form of Equation (13.5),

$$s_j^2 = \frac{\sum\limits_{i=1}^{n} (X_{ij} - \bar{X}_{.j})^2}{n-1},$$

have to be averaged. Equation (13.6) summarizes the averaging operation, which is the defining formula for s_w^2.

$$s_w^2 = \frac{\sum\limits_{j=1}^{g} s_j^2}{g}$$

$$= \frac{\sum\limits_{j=1}^{g}\sum\limits_{i=1}^{n} (X_{ij} - \bar{X}_{.j})^2}{g(n-1)} \tag{13.6}$$

when there is an equal number of subjects in each group.

The Within-Groups Sum of Squares The numerator in Equation (13.6) can be recognized as a sum of squared differences within each group. This can be verbalized more briefly as a sum of squares, symbolized SS. It will be convenient to differentiate this sum of squares from other sums of squares by referring to the numerator of Equation (13.6) as the **within-groups sum of squares,** symbolized more specifically by SS_w.

$$SS_w = \sum\limits_{j=1}^{g}\sum\limits_{i=1}^{n} (X_{ij} - \bar{X}_{.j})^2.$$

The Within-Groups Degrees of Freedom In Chapter 5 the denominator term in the equation for the variance estimate,

$$s^2 = \frac{\sum(X - \bar{X})^2}{n-1},$$

was identified as the degrees of freedom; that is, each estimate of the variance, obtained from n scores, has $n-1$ degrees of freedom. The average of g such variance estimates has g times the degrees of freedom of one such estimate. Thus, $g(n-1)$, the denominator term in Equation (13.6), is the **within-groups degrees of freedom.** Equation (13.6), then, which is the defining formula for the within-groups variance, consists of the within-groups sum of squares, divided by the within-groups degrees of freedom. Symbolically,

$$s_w^2 = \frac{SS_w}{df_w}.$$

The degrees of freedom are almost equivalent to the number of squared differences, and equal the number of independent squared differences from the mean. This suggests an average or mean of squared differences. Consequently, the within-groups sum of squares, divided by the within-groups degrees of freedom, is called the **within-groups mean square,** symbolized MS_w. The relationship between terms is summarized in Equation (13.7).

$$s_w^2 = \frac{SS_w}{df_w}$$

$$= MS_w. \tag{13.7}$$

The Computational Formula for the Within-Groups Mean Square The computational formula for the within-groups mean square, MS_w, can be traced back to the variance estimates from within each treatment group. In Chapter 5, Equation (5.12) was presented as the computational formula for the variance estimate.

$$s^2 = \frac{\Sigma X^2 - (\Sigma X)^2/n}{n-1}. \tag{5.12}$$

In terms of double subscript notation, Equation (5.12), the computational formula for the variance estimate of some jth group is symbolized as in Equation (13.8).

$$s_j^2 = \frac{\sum_{i=1}^{n} X_{ij}^2 - \left(\sum_{i=1}^{n} X_{ij}\right)^2/n}{n-1}. \tag{13.8}$$

In Table 13.6, the computation of the variance estimate from each group is illustrated, using the same data as in Table 13.5.

To obtain the within-groups variance, the g individual variances (all the s_j^2 values) have to be averaged. Symbolically, this yields Equation (13.9), the computational formula for the within-groups mean square (the within-groups variance).

TABLE 13.6
Computation of the variance estimate from each group

	G_1	G_2	G_3		G_1^2	G_2^2	G_3^2	
	1	2	4		1	4	16	
	3	3	3		9	9	9	
	2	2	2		4	4	4	
	1	3	5		1	9	25	
	3	5	6		9	25	36	
$\sum_{i=1}^{n} X_{ij} = 10$		15	20	$\sum_{i=1}^{n} X_{ij}^2 = 24$		51	90	$s_j^2 = \dfrac{\sum_{i=1}^{n} X_{ij}^2 - \left(\sum_{i=1}^{n} X_{ij}\right)^2/n}{n-1}$

$$s_1^2 = \frac{24 - (10)^2/5}{5-1} \qquad s_2^2 = \frac{51 - (15)^2/5}{5-1} \qquad s_3^2 = \frac{90 - (20)^2/5}{5-1}$$

$$= 1.00 \qquad\qquad\qquad = 1.50 \qquad\qquad\qquad = 2.50$$

$$MS_w = \frac{\sum_{j=1}^{g} s_j^2}{g} \qquad (13.9)$$

$$= \frac{\sum_{j=1}^{g} \left[\sum_{i=1}^{n} X_{ij}^2 - \left(\sum_{i=1}^{n} X_{ij} \right)^2 \Big/ n \right]}{g(n-1)}$$

$$= \frac{\sum_{j=1}^{g} \sum_{i=1}^{n} X_{ij}^2 - \sum_{j=1}^{g} \left(\sum_{i=1}^{n} X_{ij} \right)^2 \Big/ n}{g(n-1)} .$$

The numerator in Equation (13.9),

$$SS_w = \sum_{j=1}^{g} \sum_{i=1}^{n} X_{ij}^2 - \sum_{j=1}^{g} \left(\sum_{i=1}^{n} X_{ij} \right)^2 \Big/ n, \qquad (13.10)$$

consisting of two terms, $\sum_{j=1}^{g} \sum_{i=1}^{n} X_{ij}^2$ and $\sum_{j=1}^{g} \left(\sum_{i=1}^{n} X_{ij} \right)^2 \Big/ n$, is the computational

formula for the within groups sum of squares. As seen previously, the denominator of Equation (13.9),

$$df_w = g(n-1), \qquad (13.11)$$

is the within-groups degrees of freedom.

Table 13.7 illustrates the use of Equation (13.9) in computing the within-groups mean square.

TABLE 13.7
Computing the within-groups mean square, MS_w

	G_1	G_2	G_3		G_1^2	G_2^2	G_3^2
	1	2	4		1	4	16
	3	3	3		9	9	9
	2	2	2		4	4	4
	1	3	5		1	9	25
	3	5	6		9	25	36
$\sum_{i=1}^{n} X_{ij} =$	10	15	20	$\sum_{i=1}^{n} X_{ij}^2 =$	24	51	90

$$\left(\sum_{i=1}^{n} X_{ij} \right)^2 = 100 \qquad 225 \qquad 400 \qquad \sum_{j=1}^{g} \sum_{i=1}^{n} X_{ij}^2 = 24 + 51 + 90 = 165$$

$$\frac{\sum_{j=1}^{g} \left(\sum_{i=1}^{n} X_{ij} \right)^2}{n} = \frac{(100 + 225 + 400)}{5} = 145$$

$$MS_w = \frac{SS_w}{df_w} = \frac{\sum_{j=1}^{g} \sum_{i=1}^{n} X_{ij}^2 - \sum_{j=1}^{g} \left(\sum_{i=1}^{n} X_{ij} \right)^2 \Big/ n}{g(n-1)} = \frac{165 - 145}{3(5-1)} = \frac{20}{12} = 1.67$$

Note the distinction between the two terms in SS_w [Equation (13.10)]:
$\sum_{j=1}^{g}\sum_{i=1}^{n}X_{ij}^2$ and $\sum_{j=1}^{g}\left(\sum_{i=1}^{n}X_{ij}\right)^2\Big/n$. The term $\sum_{j=1}^{g}\sum_{i=1}^{n}X_{ij}^2$ requires that every score be squared before the summing process begins. Thus it only uses the squared scores presented in the last three columns of Table 13.7. By contrast, in order to compute $\sum_{j=1}^{g}\left(\sum_{i=1}^{n}X_{ij}\right)^2\Big/n$, all the scores in each group must first be summed, as in the first three columns in Table 13.7. Then each group sum is squared, yielding a value $\left(\sum_{i=1}^{n}X_{ij}\right)^2$ for each group. These squared values are then summed, yielding $\sum_{j=1}^{g}\left(\sum_{i=1}^{n}X_{ij}\right)^2$. Finally, $\sum_{j=1}^{g}\left(\sum_{i=1}^{n}X_{ij}\right)^2$ is divided by n, yielding $\sum_{j=1}^{g}\left(\sum_{i=1}^{n}X_{ij}\right)^2\Big/n$.

THE BETWEEN-GROUPS VARIANCE

The variance estimate obtained with group means is called the **between-groups variance** to distinguish it from the within-groups variance. As indicated earlier, it is the variance estimate obtained with means, $s_{\bar{x}}^2$, multiplied by the sample size, n, yielding $ns_{\bar{x}}^2$.

A variance of means implies a sum of squared differences of group means from a grand mean divided by the degrees of freedom in the estimate, as in Equation (13.12).

$$s_{\bar{x}}^2 = \frac{\sum_{j=1}^{g}(\bar{X}._j - \bar{X}..)^2}{g-1}. \qquad (13.12)$$

In Equation (13.12), g is the number of group means, $\bar{X}._j$ is the mean of the jth group, and $\bar{X}..$ is the grand mean. To obtain $ns_{\bar{x}}^2$, both sides of Equation (13.12) must be multiplied by n. This yields Equation (13.13), the defining formula for the between-groups variance.

$$ns_{\bar{x}}^2 = \frac{n\sum_{j=1}^{g}(\bar{X}._j - \bar{X}..)^2}{g-1}. \qquad (13.13)$$

The Between-Groups Mean Square Equation (13.13) for the between-groups variance consists of a numerator sum of squares and a denominator which states the degrees of freedom. (There are g values of $\bar{X}._j$ in the estimate of the between-groups variance for g groups. The last $\bar{X}._j$ value is predetermined, given $\bar{X}..$, the sample grand mean. Thus, there are $g-1$ degrees of freedom in the estimate of the between-groups variance.)

The numerator of the between-groups variance is called the **between-groups sum of squares,**

$$SS_b = n\sum_{j=1}^{g}(\bar{X}_{.j} - \bar{X}_{..})^2,$$ (13.14)

and the denominator is called the **between-groups degrees of freedom,**

$$df_b = (g-1).$$ (13.15)

Recall that after similarly recognizing the within-groups variance as a ratio of a sum of squares and degrees of freedom, the within-groups variance was renamed the "within-groups mean square." Analogously, the between-groups variance can be renamed the **between-groups mean square.** This is summarized symbolically in Equation (13.16).

$$ns_{\bar{x}}^2 = \frac{SS_b}{df_b}$$ (13.16)

$$= MS_b.$$

The Computational Formula for the Between-Groups Mean Square Equation (13.14) for the between-groups sum of squares is a defining formula. A computational formula for SS_b will be needed. It is obtained from Equation (13.14) by the use of the rules of summation, some algebraic equivalences, and the application of double subscript notation. It is presented as Equation (13.17).

$$SS_b = \frac{\sum_{j=1}^{g}\left(\sum_{i=1}^{n}X_{ij}\right)^2}{n} - \frac{\left(\sum_{j=1}^{g}\sum_{i=1}^{n}X_{ij}\right)^2}{gn}.$$ (13.17)

The first term in Equation (13.17), $\sum_{j=1}^{g}\left(\sum_{i=1}^{n}X_{ij}\right)^2 \Big/ n$, is also found in SS_w, and its use was illustrated in Table 13.7. The other term, $\left(\sum_{j=1}^{g}\sum_{i=1}^{n}X_{ij}\right)^2 \Big/ gn$, is simply the sum of all scores, which is only squared *after* the summation of all scores in the data matrix, followed by division by the total number of scores (gn).

Combining Equations (13.15) to (13.17) yields the computational formula for the between-groups mean square, Equation (13.18).

$$MS_b = \frac{SS_b}{df_b}$$ (13.18)

$$= \frac{\sum_{j=1}^{g}\left(\sum_{i=1}^{n}X_{ij}\right)^2 \Big/ n - \left(\sum_{j=1}^{g}\sum_{i=1}^{n}X_{ij}\right)^2 \Big/ gn}{(g-1)}.$$

The between-groups mean square is an estimate of the variance, just as the within-groups mean square is an estimate of the variance. They are simply two different estimates of the variance. Equations (13.18) and (13.9) give the respective computational formulas for these two different estimates of the variance.

The multiple names for the same thing may be confusing. Although all the mean squares are variance estimates, the literature has come to use the designation "mean squares" in the context of analysis of variance. This is probably because in computation within analysis of variance, the focus is on the components of the variance (sum of squares and degrees of freedom) rather than on the intact variance.

THE F RATIO AND MEAN SQUARES
All the necessary components for computing the F ratio for a set of data have now been presented. Using the computational formulas, the F ratio can be restated in the following fashion.

$$F = \frac{MS_b}{MS_w} \qquad (13.19)$$

$$= \frac{SS_b/df_b}{SS_w/df_w}$$

$$= \frac{\left[\sum\limits_{j=1}^{g} \left(\sum\limits_{i=1}^{n} X_{ij} \right)^2 \bigg/ n - \left(\sum\limits_{j=1}^{g} \sum\limits_{i=1}^{n} X_{ij} \right)^2 \bigg/ gn \right] \bigg/ (g-1)}{\left[\sum\limits_{j=1}^{g} \sum\limits_{i=1}^{n} X_{ij}{}^2 - \sum\limits_{j=1}^{g} \left(\sum\limits_{i=1}^{n} X_{ij} \right)^2 \bigg/ n \right] \bigg/ g(n-1)}.$$

Table 13.8 presents the computation of the F ratio with Equation (13.19). The value for F obtained in Table 13.8 is

$$F = 2.99.$$

Recall that the value of F obtained from data is supposed to reflect the extent of the discrepancy between the two estimates of variance, the between-groups and within-groups estimates. The two estimates, renamed the between-groups mean square and the within-groups mean square, offer a ratio that is expected to be close to a value of 1, when there are no treatment effects.* The larger the ratio, the more likely that there are treatment effects inflating the numerator of the F ratio (the between-groups mean square). The critical value for concluding that treatment effects are present

---

*The precise expected value of F depends on df_w, being closer to 1 as df_w increases.

$$E[F] = \frac{g(n-1)}{g(n-1) - 2}.$$

TABLE 13.8
Computation of the F ratio with Equation (13.19). The three summation terms in the mean squares have been partially enclosed within the table.

	G_1	G_2	G_3		$G_1{}^2$	$G_2{}^2$	$G_3{}^2$
	1	2	4		1	4	16
	3	3	3		9	9	9
	2	2	2		4	4	4
	1	3	5		1	9	25
	3	5	6		9	25	36

$$\sum_{i=1}^{n} X_{ij} = \quad 10 \qquad 15 \qquad 20 \qquad\qquad \sum_{i=1}^{n} X_{ij}{}^2 = 24 \qquad 51 \qquad 90$$

$$\left(\sum_{i=1}^{n} X_{ij}\right)^2 = 100 \qquad 225 \qquad 400 \qquad\qquad \left| \sum_{j=1}^{g}\sum_{i=1}^{n} X_{ij}{}^2 = 24 + 51 + 90 = 165 \right|$$

$$\left| \frac{\sum_{j=1}^{g}\left(\sum_{i=1}^{n} X_{ij}\right)^2}{n} = \frac{(100 + 225 + 400)}{5} = 145 \right|$$

$$\sum_{j=1}^{g}\sum_{i=1}^{n} X_{ij} = 10 + 15 + 20 = 45$$

$$\left| \frac{\left(\sum_{j=1}^{g}\sum_{i=1}^{n} X_{ij}\right)^2}{gn} = \frac{(45)^2}{3 \cdot 5} = 135 \right|$$

$$MS_b = \frac{SS_b}{df_b} = \frac{\sum_{j=1}^{g}\left(\sum_{i=1}^{n} X_{ij}\right)^2 / n - \left(\sum_{j=1}^{g}\sum_{i=1}^{n} X_{ij}\right)^2 / gn}{g-1} = \frac{145 - 135}{3-1} = \frac{10}{2} = 5.00$$

$$MS_w = \frac{SS_w}{df_w} = \frac{\sum_{j=1}^{g}\sum_{i=1}^{n} X_{ij}{}^2 - \sum_{j=1}^{g}\left(\sum_{i=1}^{n} X_{ij}\right)^2 / n}{g(n-1)} = \frac{165 - 145}{3(5-1)} = \frac{20}{12} = 1.67$$

$$F = \frac{MS_b}{MS_w} = \frac{5}{1.67} = 2.99$$

depends on the degrees of freedom in both the numerator and denominator of the F ratio. For large degrees of freedom the critical value will be close to 2 or 3. For smaller degrees of freedom, the critical value will be close to 4 or 5. The precise critical values are listed in a Table for the F distribution. Its use is described in the following section.

The Table for Critical Values of F Three pieces of information are required for determining the critical value for an F ratio: the degrees of freedom in the numerator of the F ratio; the degrees of freedom in the F ratio denominator; and the Type I error probability.

In Appendix B, the table for critical values of the F distribution is Table VI. The body of the table has both light- and boldface-type entries. The light-face type gives the critical values for the .05 Type I error probability and the boldface the .01 Type I error probability.

The top of the table has numbers, each heading a column. These column headings refer to the degrees of freedom in the numerator of the F ratio. On the left-hand margin of the table are numbers placed adjacent to each row. These numbers refer to the degrees of freedom in the denominator of the F ratio.

In the last section, the computation of an F ratio was illustrated which had two degrees of freedom in the numerator and 12 in the denominator. The critical value for this pair of degrees of freedom is found in the second column and twelfth row of Table VI. Table VI indicates two values where column 2 meets row 12. For the .05 level the critical value is 3.88, and for the .01 level it is 6.93. The computed F value from the hypothetical data in the example is 2.99. Therefore, in this hypothetical example, statistical significance has not been reached. The preselected tabled value (either 3.88 or 6.93) has to be reached or surpassed for statistical significance. Since this has not happened, the conclusion is the equivocal one that there is no evidence of treatment effects, that is, no evidence that the independent variable is related to the dependent variable.

THE TOTAL SUM OF SQUARES AND TOTAL DEGREES OF FREEDOM   There is another variance estimate that has not been discussed. A variance estimate can be obtained from all the scores by summing the squared differences between individual scores and the grand mean, without regard to group membership. Specifically, this appears as in Equation (13.20), where the subscript t stands for total.

$$s_t{}^2 = \frac{\sum\limits_{j=1}^{g} \sum\limits_{i=1}^{n} (X_{ij} - \bar{X}_{..})^2}{gn - 1}. \tag{13.20}$$

As in the discussions of sum of squares and degrees of freedom for the within- and between-groups variances, a **total sum of squares,**

$$SS_t = \sum\limits_{j=1}^{g} \sum\limits_{i=1}^{n} (X_{ij} - \bar{X}_{..})^2, \tag{13.21}$$

and **total degrees of freedom,**

$$df_t = gn - 1, \tag{13.22}$$

can be recognized in Equation (13.20).

There will not be any need for the variance as estimated from the total scores (without regard to group membership), in the fashion of Equation (13.20). But the separate components, SS_t and df_t are useful.

The between-groups and within-groups sums of squares, for any single set of data, will always sum to the total sum of squares, that is,

$$SS_t = SS_w + SS_b. \tag{13.23}$$

Similarly, the within-groups and between-groups degrees of freedom will also sum to the total degrees of freedom. This can be proved as follows.

$$df_w + df_b = g(n-1) + (g-1) \quad \left[\text{Equations (13.11) and (13.15)}\right]$$
$$= gn - g + g - 1$$
$$= gn - 1$$
$$= df_t \quad \left[\text{Equation (13.22)}\right]. \tag{13.24}$$

To prove the equality of Equation (13.23), that is, that

$$SS_t = SS_w + SS_b,$$

we first convert Equation (13.21) for SS_t to a computational version. Using the rules of summation, algebra, and double subscript notation, the result is

$$SS_t = \sum_{j=1}^{g} \sum_{i=1}^{n} X_{ij}^2 - \left(\sum_{j=1}^{g} \sum_{i=1}^{n} X_{ij}\right)^2 \bigg/ gn. \tag{13.25}$$

The proof of Equation (13.23) then follows as indicated [first, from Equations (13.10) and (13.17)]:

$$SS_w + SS_b = \sum_{j=1}^{g} \sum_{i=1}^{n} X_{ij}^2 - \frac{\sum_{j=1}^{g}\left(\sum_{i=1}^{n} X_{ij}\right)^2}{n} + \frac{\sum_{j=1}^{g}\left(\sum_{i=1}^{n} X_{ij}\right)^2}{n} - \frac{\left(\sum_{j=1}^{g} \sum_{i=1}^{n} X_{ij}\right)^2}{gn}$$

$$= \sum_{j=1}^{g} \sum_{i=1}^{n} X_{ij}^2 - \frac{\left(\sum_{j=1}^{g} \sum_{i=1}^{n} X_{ij}\right)^2}{gn}$$

$$= SS_t \quad \left[\text{from Equation (13.25)}\right].$$

Equations (13.23) and (13.24) offer a check on part of the computations in analysis of variance.

A SUMMARY TABLE FOR ANALYSIS OF VARIANCE The computations of the F ratio in an analysis of variance are often presented in a summary table, having a form like Table 13.9. However, instead of the numbers normally found in the table, Table 13.9 presents the formulas used in computing the table entries.

TABLE 13.9

Abstract summary table of analysis of variance, showing formulas used in computing table entries

Sources of Variance	Sums of Squares	df	Mean Squares	F
Between groups	$\dfrac{\sum\limits_{j=1}^{g}\left(\sum\limits_{i=1}^{n}X_{ij}\right)^2}{n} - \dfrac{\left(\sum\limits_{j=1}^{g}\sum\limits_{i=1}^{n}X_{ij}\right)^2}{gn}$	$g-1$	$\dfrac{SS_b}{g-1}$	$\dfrac{MS_b}{MS_w}$
Within groups	$\sum\limits_{j=1}^{g}\sum\limits_{i=1}^{n}X_{ij}^{2} - \dfrac{\sum\limits_{j=1}^{g}\left(\sum\limits_{i=1}^{n}X_{ij}\right)^2}{n}$	$g(n-1)$	$\dfrac{SS_w}{g(n-1)}$	
Total	$\sum\limits_{j=1}^{g}\sum\limits_{i=1}^{n}X_{ij}^{2} - \dfrac{\left(\sum\limits_{j=1}^{g}\sum\limits_{i=1}^{n}X_{ij}\right)^2}{gn}$	$gn-1$		

Table 13.10 presents the standard numerical version of the summary table, using the data and computations of Table 13.8.

The F test computed in Table 13.8 and shown in Table 13.10 is nonsignificant. Table 13.11 contains data that yields statistical significance, and Table 13.12 summarizes the F test for the data in Table 13.11.

You should pause to compute the F ratio for the data in Table 13.11 and check the results against Table 13.12. Note the asterisk in Table 13.12, with the accompanying footnote at the bottom of the table. It is common to asterisk significant F ratios in the summary tables. An accompanying footnote then lists the probability of the largest tabled critical value which has been reached or surpassed. For example, the computed F of 5.69 surpasses the tabled critical value of 3.55, which is the critical value listed in Table VI (in Appendix B) for a Type I error probability of .05, given 2 and 18 degrees of freedom. But 5.69 does not surpass 6.01, which is the tabled critical value for a Type I error probability of .01 (at 2 and 18 degrees of freedom). Therefore, the footnote states, with reference to the computed F of 5.69: $p < .05$. This implicitly reads, "Given a true null hypothesis, the

TABLE 13.10

Summary table of analysis of variance (data and computations of Table 13.8)

SV	SS	df	MS	F
Between groups	10	2	5.00	2.99
Within groups	20	12	1.67	
Total	30	14		

TABLE 13.11

Hypothetical data for an analysis of variance. The sums of scores within groups and the sums of the squared scores within each group have been added to make it easier for you to practice computing an F ratio

	G_1	G_2	G_3		$G_1{}^2$	$G_2{}^2$	$G_3{}^2$
	1	2	4		1	4	16
	1	3	4		1	9	16
	2	3	6		4	9	36
	3	4	6		9	16	36
	3	4	7		9	16	49
	4	6	8		16	36	64
	6	8	9		36	64	81
$\sum_{i=1}^{n} X_{ij} =$	20	30	44	$\sum_{i=1}^{n} X_{ij}{}^2 =$	76	154	298

TABLE 13.12

Summary table of analysis of variance (data of Table 13.11)

SV	SS	df	MS	F
Between groups	41.53	2	20.77	5.69*
Within groups	65.71	18	3.65	
Total	107.24	20		

*$p < .05$

probability of having reached or surpassed an F ratio of 5.69 is less than .05." This same footnote would be used for any computed F between 3.55 and 6.00. If the computed value had equalled or surpassed 6.01, then the footnote would have read $p < .01$.

COMPUTATIONS WITH UNEQUAL n When there are different numbers of subjects in each treatment group, the symbol n as used in the degrees of freedom is no longer unambiguous. Instead of one n value, there is possibly a different n value for each treatment group. These multiple n values can be symbolized as n_1, n_2, etc, through n_g. A term such as $\sum_{j=1}^{g} \left(\sum_{i=1}^{n} X_{ij} \right)^2 \Big/ n$ would then be restated as $\sum_{j=1}^{g} \left[\left(\sum_{i=1}^{n_j} X_{ij} \right)^2 \Big/ n_j \right]$, suggesting that each component in the sum, each $\left(\sum_{i=1}^{n_j} X_{ij} \right)^2$, is divided by the number of subjects in that group, resulting in

$$\sum_{j=1}^{g}\left[\frac{\left(\sum_{i=1}^{n_j}X_{ij}\right)^2}{n_j}\right] = \frac{\left(\sum_{i=1}^{n_1}X_{i1}\right)^2}{n_1} + \frac{\left(\sum_{i=1}^{n_2}X_{i2}\right)^2}{n_2} + \cdots + \frac{\left(\sum_{i=1}^{n_j}X_{ij}\right)^2}{n_j} + \cdots + \frac{\left(\sum_{i=1}^{n_g}X_{ig}\right)^2}{n_g}.$$

Another term in the formulas is $\left(\sum_{j=1}^{g}\sum_{i=1}^{n}X_{ij}\right)^2\Big/gn$. The denominator, gn, only makes sense when there is one n value. Given several n values, what is really desired is

$$gn = n_1 + n_2 + \cdots + n_j + \cdots + n_g.$$

But this is the total number of scores in the matrix. It is then simpler to use the uppercase symbol N to symbolize the total number of scores in the matrix:

$$N = n_1 + n_2 + \cdots + n_j + \cdots + n_g.$$

This is also done in the case of degrees of freedom. For example,

$$g(n-1) = gn - g$$
$$= N - g,$$

when N replaces gn. For the unequal n situation, then, N is used in place of gn in the sum of squares and degrees of freedom formulas. The formulas for unequal n are summarized in Table 13.13.

TABLE 13.13
Abstract summary table of analysis of variance, showing formulas used in computing table entries when there are unequal n values

Sources of Variance	Sum of Squares	df	Mean Squares	F
Between groups	$\sum_{j=1}^{g}\left[\frac{\left(\sum_{i=1}^{n_j}X_{ij}\right)^2}{n_j}\right] - \frac{\left(\sum_{j=1}^{g}\sum_{i=1}^{n_j}X_{ij}\right)^2}{N}$	$g-1$	$\dfrac{SS_b}{g-1}$	$\dfrac{MS_b}{MS_w}$
Within groups	$\sum_{j=1}^{g}\sum_{i=1}^{n_j}X_{ij}^2 - \sum_{j=1}^{g}\left[\frac{\left(\sum_{i=1}^{n_j}X_{ij}\right)^2}{n_j}\right]$	$N-g$	$\dfrac{SS_w}{N-g}$	
Total	$\sum_{j=1}^{g}\sum_{i=1}^{n_j}X_{ij}^2 - \frac{\left(\sum_{j=1}^{g}\sum_{j=1}^{n_j}X_{ij}\right)^2}{N}$	$N-1$		

Table 13.14 offers some data and details the computation of the F ratio with unequal n. Table 13.15 offers the summary table for the analysis of variance of the data in Table 13.14. Note that the computed F surpasses the critical value at the .01 level for 3 and 12 degrees of freedom.

TABLE 13.14
Hypothetical data for an analysis of variance with unequal n, with computation of the F ratio. The three summation terms in the mean squares have been partially enclosed within the table.

G_1	G_2	G_3	G_4		$G_1{}^2$	$G_2{}^2$	$G_3{}^2$	$G_4{}^2$
1	1	1	5		1	1	1	25
2	2	2	7		4	4	4	49
4	4	3	8		16	16	9	64
	4	5	10			16	25	100
		5					25	

$$\sum_{i=1}^{n_j} X_{ij} = 7 \qquad 11 \qquad 16 \qquad 30$$

$$\sum_{i=1}^{n_j} X_{ij}{}^2 = 21 \qquad 37 \qquad 64 \qquad 238$$

$$\boxed{\sum_{j=1}^{g}\sum_{i=1}^{n_j} X_{ij}{}^2 = 21 + 37 + 64 + 238 = 360}$$

$$\frac{\left(\sum\limits_{i=1}^{n_j} X_{ij}\right)^2}{n_j} = \frac{7^2}{3} \qquad \frac{11^2}{4} \qquad \frac{16^2}{5} \qquad \frac{30^2}{4}$$

$$= 16.33 \quad = 30.25 \quad = 51.20 \quad = 225.00$$

$$\boxed{\sum_{j=1}^{g}\left[\frac{\left(\sum\limits_{i=1}^{n_j} X_{ij}\right)^2}{n_j}\right] = 16.33 + 30.25 + 51.20 + 225.00}$$

$$= 322.78$$

$$F = \frac{MS_b}{MS_w} = \frac{22.26}{3.10} = 7.18$$

$$\sum_{j=1}^{g}\sum_{i=1}^{n_j} X_{ij} = 7 + 11 + 16 + 30 = 64$$

$$\boxed{\frac{\left(\sum\limits_{j=1}^{g}\sum\limits_{i=1}^{n_j} X_{ij}\right)^2}{N} = \frac{64^2}{16} = 256}$$

$$MS_b = \frac{SS_b}{df_b} = \frac{\sum\limits_{j=1}^{g}\left[\left(\sum\limits_{i=1}^{n_j} X_{ij}\right)^2 / n_j\right] - \left(\sum\limits_{j=1}^{g}\sum\limits_{i=1}^{n_j} X_{ij}\right)^2 / N}{g-1} = \frac{322.78 - 256}{4-1} = \frac{66.78}{3} = 22.26$$

$$MS_w = \frac{SS_w}{df_w} = \frac{\sum\limits_{j=1}^{g}\sum\limits_{i=1}^{n_j} X_{ij}{}^2 - \sum\limits_{j=1}^{g}\left[\left(\sum\limits_{i=1}^{n_j} X_{ij}\right)^2 / n_j\right]}{N-g} = \frac{360 - 322.78}{16 - 4} = \frac{37.22}{12} = 3.10$$

TABLE 13.15

Summary table of analysis of variance (data and computations of Table 3.14)

SV	SS	df	MS	F
Between groups	66.78	3	22.26	7.18*
Within groups	37.22	12	3.10	
Total	104.00	15		

*$p < .01$

A NOTE ON ASSUMPTIONS

The basic assumptions for analysis of variance are the same as those for the *t* test. The remedies for violations of assumptions are also the same. At the end of Chapter 10 on *t* tests, there is a section titled A Note on Assumptions. The advice in the following section is essentially the same as that given in Chapter 10.

Summarizing the relevant material from Chapter 10, there should be homogeneity of variance and the scores should be normally distributed. In practice, however, the population of scores does not have to be normally distributed, providing the distribution is unimodal and not too skewed. As the distribution becomes more skewed, skewness can have some small effect on the Type I error probability, increasing it beyond the .05 or .01 levels assumed for the tabled critical values. Similarly, violations of homogeneity can alter the Type I error probability to some small degree. When both homogeneity of variance and normality of distribution are strongly violated, the effect on the Type I error probability can be strong enough to yield misleading results.

As in the case of the *t* tests, there are three remedies when the assumptions appear to be strongly violated: (1) Maximize the value of *n*; (2) Keep the value of *n* equal in all groups; (3) Set the Type I error levels at more conservative levels. For example, if the desired Type I error level is .05, use the critical value for the .01 level. Although the violations of assumptions may inflate the Type I error probability above .01, the inflated error probability will still be below .05.

A normal distribution of scores implies continuously distributed scores. However, this aspect of normality can also be violated with very little effect on the Type I error level, if sample size is not too small. Usually, wide-ranging scores are sufficient. In fact, given a very large value of *n,* narrowly ranging dependent variable scores can be used in analysis of variance.

One additional comment that does not apply to *t* tests concerns the number of levels of the independent variable examined in the study. From a statistical point of view, there is no real limitation to the number of levels of the independent variable in an analysis of variance. However, from a practical point of view, it is a matter of concern. The *F* test in analysis of variance is a test of whether the levels are different from each other; that is, the F test is a test of whether there are differences in the dependent variable among the populations represented by the sampled levels of the independent variable. As the number of populations represented (levels) increases, the F test requires larger sample differences between group means before they can be considered to be non-chance differences. Thus, the more levels of the independent variable appearing in the experiment, the less sensitive the F test will be to small differences in the dependent variable. In psychological research involving manipulated variables, the extent of differences usually found tend to be relatively small (in comparison to the size of variances). Thus, although there are no formal limitations on the number of levels of an independent variable used in an experiment, some thought should be given to keeping the number of levels small. You should hesitate to use more than five levels of a manipulated independent variable.

A NOTE ON THE IMPORTANCE OF THIS CHAPTER This chapter provides the basis for understanding Chapter 14, and both this chapter and Chapter 14 are necessary for understanding Chapter 15. Chapter 15, which contains a large amount of important material, can appear to be a difficult chapter to master. However, much of Chapter 15 consists of variations on the concepts discussed in 13 and 14. Chapter 15 is not particularly difficult if the earlier material is thoroughly understood.

IMPORTANT WORDS AND CONCEPTS Treatments (p. 287)
Experimental manipulation (p. 287)
Classification (p. 288)
Levels (p. 288)
Random variability (p. 291)
Variability within treatment groups (p. 293)
Variability between means (p. 293)
Within-groups variance (p. 294)
F distribution (p. 296)
F ratio (p. 296)
Within-groups sum of squares (p. 301)
Within-groups degrees of freedom (p. 301)
Within-groups mean square (p. 302)
Between-groups variance (p. 304)
Between-groups sum of squares (p. 305)
Between-groups degrees of freedom (p. 305)
Between-groups mean square (p. 305)
Total sum of squares (p. 308)
Total degrees of freedom (p. 308)

The following incomplete sentences are taken from the underlined sentences in this chapter. Fill in the missing words and phrases and then correct them from the answers which follow.

1. Given a continuous _____ variable and a narrowly ranging _____ variable, it is generally appropriate to use the analysis of variance to test for a relationship between the two variables.

2. The differences on the independent variable can be based on _____ or _____ into distinguishable subgroups.

3. The different groups, distinguished on the basis of the independent variable, are referred to as the different _____, or different _____.

4. In defining the independent variable through experimental manipulation, all subjects are randomly selected from the _____ _____ randomly placed into _____ _____ , and then treated _____ in the different groups.

5. In using classification as the basis for distinguishing groups on the independent variable, all subjects in all groups are treated _____. However, the subjects in each group are deliberately selected from _____ _____ .

6. The null hypothesis in analysis of variance, as in t tests, is that _____ _____

7. Given a true null hypothesis, both the variability within treatment groups and between means reflect only random variability. Given a false null hypothesis, only the variability _____ would be inflated by treatment effects.

8. The F distribution is not a distribution of expected differences, but rather a distribution of expected _____ .

9. The score of the ith subject in the jth group is symbolized as _____.

10. To symbolize the mean of the jth group, _____ is used.

11. The mean of all scores over all groups is sometimes referred to as _____. Its symbol is _____ .

12. The within-groups sum of squares, divided by the within-groups degrees of freedom, is called _____, symbolized _____ .

13. The value of F that is obtained from data is supposed to reflect the extent of the discrepancy between _____

14. The between-groups mean square and the within-groups mean square

offer a ratio that is expected to be close to a value of _____,
when there are _____.

15. The top of the F table has numbers, each heading a column. These
column headings each refer to the degrees of freedom in the
_____ of the F ratio. On the left-hand margin of the
table are numbers placed adjacent to each row. These numbers refer to
the degrees of freedom in the _____ of the F ratio.

16. The between-groups sum of squares and the within-groups sum of
squares, for any single set of data, will always sum to _____
_____. Similarly, the between-groups degrees of
freedom and the within-groups degrees of freedom will _____
_____.

17. The uppercase symbol N is used to symbolize _____
_____.

18. For the unequal n situation, N is used in place of_____ in the sum of
squares and degrees-of-freedom formulas.

19. When both _____and
_____ are strongly vio-
lated, the effects on the Type I error probability can be strong enough to
yield misleading results.

20. As in the case of t tests, there are three remedies when the assumptions
appear to be strongly violated:

a. _____

b. _____

c. _____

Answers 1. dependent; independent   2. experimental manipulation; classification   3. treatments; levels   4. same population; different groups; differently   5. identically; different subpopulations   6. the groups that have been sampled all come from the same population (all groups have the same population
mean)   7. between means   8. ratios   9. X_{ij} 10. $\bar{X}_{.j}$ 11. the grand mean; $\bar{X}_{..}$ 12.
the within-groups mean square; MS_w 13. the two estimates of variance   14. 1; no
treatment effects   15. numerator; denominator   16. the total sum of squares; sum to
the total degrees of freedom   17. the total number of scores   18. *gn*   19.
homogeneity of variance; normality of distribution   20. a. Maximize the value of
n.   b. Keep the value of n equal in all groups   c. Set the Type I error level at a more
conservative level.

PROBLEMS   1. Do an analysis of variance on the following data, taken from three
hypothetical groups. Set up and complete a summary table.

Group 1	Group 2	Group 3
1	2	3
2	2	4
1	4	2
4	5	6
3	5	7
1	3	8

2. Do an analysis of variance on the following data, taken from four hypothetical groups. Set up and complete a summary table.

Group 1	Group 2	Group 3	Group 4
6	2	3	0
8	4	1	2
6	5	2	4
4	3	2	
	2		
	2		

3. Find the critical F values for the following degrees of freedom and Type I error levels.

df_b	df_w	Type I Error Probability
5	20	.05
3	45	.05
4	80	.01
3	125	.01

f o u r t e e n

STATISTICS FOLLOWING SIGNIFICANCE

The previous chapter discussed the analysis of variance as a test of whether the independent and dependent variables are related. The focus was on the rationale for, and computation of, the F test.

Given a nonsignificant F test, the statistical analysis is considered finished. Given a significant F test, the statistical analysis generally continues. The additional questions asked and their associated statistical procedures are presented in this chapter.

In this first section the focus shifts from whether the variables are related, to the degree of the relationship. If the F test is significant, it implies that the variables are related. It is then reasonable to ask for some estimate of the degree of relationship.

DEGREE OF RELATIONSHIP IN ANALYSIS OF VARIANCE Degree of relationship was previously examined in the context of correlation coefficients. The meaning of correlation was most clearly specified in the square of the product moment correlation coefficient. The square of the product moment correlation coefficient offers a statement, or estimate, of the proportion of variance in one variable associated with the variance in the other variable. It is possible in analysis of variance to use this same definition of degree of relationship between two variables. The more the dependent variable varies in conjunction with the independent variable, the more closely the two are related. But in analysis of variance the variability is only measured in one variable, the dependent variable. How is variability to be defined in the independent variable? Variability in the independent variable is defined simply as membership in different treatment levels. The question of degree of relationship is then rephrased as: "What is the proportion of variance in the dependent variable that is associated with treatment level membership?"

The proportion of variance in the dependent variable scores associated with treatment level membership is obtained as a ratio. The *amount* of variance in the dependent variable scores associated with treatment level membership is in the numerator. The total variance in the dependent variable is in the denominator. The ratio then expresses the proportion of the total variance associated with treatment level membership. In equation form,

$$\begin{array}{c} \text{proportion of variance in} \\ \text{dependent variable scores} \\ \text{associated with treatment} \\ \text{level membership} \end{array} = \dfrac{\begin{array}{c} \text{amount of variance in dependent} \\ \text{variable scores associated with} \\ \text{treatment levels} \end{array}}{\begin{array}{c} \text{total amount of variance in} \\ \text{dependent variable scores} \end{array}} \cdot \qquad (14.1)$$

We need some specific definitions of both the variance associated with treatments and the total variance.

Sources of Variance in the Population of Dependent Variable Scores In the preceding chapter a summary table was presented for an analysis of variance. It included a column headed "sources of variance." This is a general term for between-groups and within-groups. It was pointed out in Chapter 13 that the specific source of variance for the within-groups mean square (MS_w) is random variance. For the between-groups mean square (MS_b) there are two specific sources of variance. Both random variance and treatment effects can affect MS_b. These more specific statements about the sources of variance are summarized in a new column, headed "Specific Sources of Variance," added to the abstract summary table which is presented as Table 14.1. An additional column, headed "Expected Values of Mean Squares," offers the symbolic expressions for the specific sources of variance. The following paragraphs explain the choice of the symbols.

Both MS_w and MS_b are estimates of population variances. MS_w is an estimate of random variance in the population of dependent variable scores. Random variance is most generally symbolized as σ_e^2. The subscripted e symbolizes the omnipresence of random variance as a source of error when attempting to estimate other parameters. In fact, random variance is frequently called **error variance.**

The specific sources of variance indicate that MS_b reflects both random variance and treatment effects. Amount of variance in the population of dependent variable scores associated with treatment levels is symbolized in this text as σ_{tr}^2. Equation 14.1 suggested the form to be taken by a computation of the proportion of variance associated with treatment levels. Looking back at Equation (14.1), the numerator can be seen to be σ_{tr}^2.

$$\sigma_{tr}^2 = \text{amount of variance in dependent variable scores associated with treatment levels.}$$

The denominator is "the total amount of variance in dependent variable scores." The only two variance components (in this analysis) are σ_e^2 and σ_{tr}^2. Therefore, the total variance can be defined as

$$\sigma_{tot}^2 = \sigma_{tr}^2 + \sigma_e^2.$$

TABLE 14.1
Abstract summary table of analysis of variance, showing specific sources of variance and expected values of mean squares

Sources of Variance	Sums of Squares	df	Mean Squares	Specific Sources of Variance	Expected Values of Mean Squares
Between groups	SS_b	$g-1$	$\dfrac{SS_b}{g-1}$	Treatment effects and random variance	$n\sigma_{tr}^2 + \sigma_e^2$
Within groups	SS_w	$N-g$	$\dfrac{SS_w}{N-g}$	Random variance	σ_e^2
Total	SS_{tot}	$N-1$			

Equation (14.2) symbolically restates Equation (14.1).

$$\rho_{\text{intraclass}} = \frac{\text{proportion of variance in dependent variable}}{\text{scores associated with treatment level membership}} \qquad (14.2)$$

$$= \frac{\sigma_{\text{tr}}^2}{\sigma_{\text{tot}}^2}$$

$$= \frac{\sigma_{\text{tr}}^2}{\sigma_{\text{tr}}^2 + \sigma_{\text{e}}^2} .$$

The proportion of variance in the dependent variable associated with treatment levels has been defined to offer a statement of degree of relationship between the variables. The degree of relationship as defined by Equation (14.2) is called the **intraclass correlation coefficient,** symbolized by $\rho_{\text{intraclass}}$. The Greek letter rho (ρ) is used because Equation (14.2) is expressed in terms of population variances. To be practical, the intraclass correlation coefficient has to be redefined in terms of sample values; that is, sample estimates of the population variances σ_{e}^2 and σ_{tr}^2 have to be used. MS_w offers the estimate of σ_{e}^2.

The population value of the variance being estimated by a mean square in a sample is the expected value of the mean square (the average expected value, given infinite sampling). Therefore,

$$E[MS_w] = \sigma_{\text{e}}^2,$$

so MS_w can be substituted for σ_{e}^2 in the estimated version of Equation (14.2). Unfortunately, MS_b does not simply estimate σ_{tr}^2. It reflects both σ_{tr}^2 and σ_{e}^2. A precise understanding of just how much of σ_{tr}^2 and σ_{e}^2 is estimated by MS_b requires some recollection of how MS_b is computed. Recall that in the computations of MS_b the variance obtained from means is multiplied by n:

$$MS_b = \frac{n \sum_{j}^{g} (\bar{X}_{\cdot j} - \bar{X}_{\cdot\cdot})^2}{g - 1} .$$

[Equations (13.13), (13.14), and (13.16) and their accompanying discussions illustrate this point.] The multiplication by n allows MS_b to act as another estimate of random variance, σ_{e}^2, when there are no treatment effects, since means vary less than individual scores precisely as a function of n. When treatment effects are present, **treatment variance** is added to σ_{e}^2. However, the use of n as a coefficient increases the estimate of any treatment variance by a factor of n, to $n\sigma_{\text{tr}}^2$. Therefore, the variance estimated by MS_b is

$$E[MS_b] = n\sigma_{\text{tr}}^2 + \sigma_{\text{e}}^2.$$

The expected values for the mean squares are summarized in the last column of Table 14.1. In order to obtain an estimate of treatment effects, σ_{tr}^2 has to be isolated from $n\sigma_{tr}^2 + \sigma_e^2$.

Estimating the Variance Due to Treatment Effects

This section illustrates the way that σ_{tr}^2 is isolated from

$$E[MS_b] = n\sigma_{tr}^2 + \sigma_e^2$$

and then estimated.

There is a mathematical theorem which states that "the expectation of a sum is the sum of the expectations." Recalling the expectations for MS_b and MS_w, this theorem leads to the following expectation.

$$E[MS_b - MS_w] = n\sigma_{tr}^2 + \sigma_e^2 - \sigma_e^2$$

$$= n\sigma_{tr}^2.$$

Dividing both sides of the preceding equality by n yields

$$\frac{E[MS_b - MS_w]}{n} = \sigma_{tr}^2.$$

In words, subtracting the computed value MS_w from the computed value MS_b and then dividing the difference by n yields an estimate of σ_{tr}^2.

An Estimate of the Intraclass Correlation Coefficient

The estimates of both σ_{tr}^2 and σ_e^2 can be substituted for the terms in Equation (14.2), offering an estimate of the **proportion of variance in dependent variable scores associated with treatment levels**. Equation (14.3), incorporating these substitutions, specifies that this estimated proportion is an estimate of the degree of relationship between the variables.

$$r_{intraclass} = \text{estimate of degree of relationship between the variables} \qquad (14.3)$$

$$= \text{estimate of proportion of variance in dependent variable scores associated with treatment levels}$$

$$= \frac{\text{estimate of } \sigma_{tr}^2}{\text{estimate of } \sigma_{tr}^2 + \text{estimate of } \sigma_e^2}$$

$$= \frac{\dfrac{(MS_b - MS_w)}{n}}{\dfrac{(MS_b - MS_w)}{n} + MS_w}.$$

Equation (14.3) can be computed following a significant F test in an analysis of variance. It offers a sample estimate of the intraclass correlation coefficient.

Computational Form for Estimating the Intraclass Correlation Coefficient Equation (14.3) can be simplified so that it is relatively easy to compute. The computational formula is presented as Equation (14.4).

$$r_{intraclass} = \frac{F - 1}{F - 1 + n}.$$

$$(14.4)$$

The F in Equation (14.4) is that computed in the course of the analysis of variance. The n is the number of subjects in each group. The formula assumes equal n across groups.

The computational formula looks very different from the defining formula, Equation (14.3). But the derivation of Equation (14.4) from (14.3) is surprisingly simple. The steps follow.

First, multiply both numerator and denominator of Equation (14.3) by n:

$$\frac{n[(MS_b - MS_w)/n]}{n[(MS_b - MS_w)/n + MS_w]} = \frac{MS_b - MS_w}{MS_b - MS_w + nMS_w}.$$

Then divide both numerator and denominator by MS_w:

$$\frac{(1/MS_w)(MS_b - MS_w)}{(1/MS_w)(MS_b - MS_w + nMS_w)} = \frac{MS_b/MS_w - MS_w/MS_w}{MS_b/MS_w - MS_w/MS_w + nMS_w/MS_w}$$

$$= \frac{MS_b/MS_w - 1}{MS_b/MS_w - 1 + n}$$

$$= \frac{F - 1}{F - 1 + n} \qquad \text{(recall that } F = MS_b/MS_w\text{)}.$$

Table 13.11 offered hypothetical data for an analysis of variance, and Table 13.12 summarized the computations for the analysis of variance. Entering the computed F of 5.69 from Table 13.12 into Equation (14.4) yields the estimate of the proportion of variance associated with treatment levels in the data of Table 13.11:

$$r_{intraclass} = \frac{F - 1}{F - 1 + n}$$

$$= \frac{5.69 - 1}{5.69 - 1 + 7}$$

$$= \frac{4.69}{11.69}$$

$$= .40.$$

The $n = 7$ is taken from the data in Table 13.11.

The value of .40 suggests that 40% of the variance in the dependent variable scores is associated with treatment level membership. Note that the intraclass correlation coefficient is not squared but directly offers the proportion of variance in one variable associated with another.

An equation estimating the degree of relationship between two variables [such as Equation (14.4)] should only be used after a significant F has been found. A significant F implies that there is a relationship between the variables. Only then does it make sense to obtain an estimate of the degree of relationship.

The estimate of the intraclass correlation coefficient is interpretable similarly to a squared Pearson r obtained with sample data. This means that unless the number of subjects is very large, the estimate of the proportion of variance associated with treatment levels will be a rough estimate.

Further, the estimate of the degree of relationship is often biased in some complex ways. Thus, the estimate of the proportion of variance associated with treatment effects is generally only a rough approximation. The greatest value of these estimates of degree of relationship is in indicating the *relative* importance of different independent variables. Computing an estimate of the proportion of variance associated with treatment levels can also point out the limited practical usefulness of relationships which, though statistically significant, sometimes account for very small proportions of the variance.

Omega-Squared In the preceding section, reference was made to bias in the computation of the proportion of variance associated with treatment levels. There are some corrections available for varied sources of potential bias.

The most common form of correction appears in a corrected version of Equation (14.4), usually called **omega-squared**. The correction in omega-squared merely requires that the term

$$\frac{MS_b - MS_w}{n}$$

in Equation (14.3) be multiplied by $(g-1)/g$. All other steps leading to Equation (14.4) are the same. A computational form of omega-squared is offered in Equation (14.5), again using the F ratio.

$$\omega^2 = \frac{(g-1)(F-1)}{(g-1)(F-1) + gn} \, . \tag{14.5}$$

If all groups do not have the same size n, then the total number of scores over all groups, N, replaces gn in Equation (14.5).

Once again using the data of Table 13.11 as summarized in Table 13.12, the value of omega-squared is:

$$\omega^2 = \frac{(g-1)(F-1)}{(g-1)(F-1)+gn}$$

$$= \frac{(3-1)(5.69-1)}{(3-1)(5.69-1)+3\cdot7}$$

$$= \frac{9.38}{30.28}$$

$$= .31.$$

The value of .31 is smaller than the value of .40 found with Equation (14.4).

The Conditions of Bias Requiring Omega-Squared The bias corrected for by omega-squared is present under a fairly common condition. This is the condition in which the levels of the independent variable used in the experiment are the only levels of interest. For example, assume a comparison of four different forms of psychotherapy. The question is whether these four different treatments are any different in their effectiveness. Any conclusions from the study would only be with reference to these four types of psychotherapy. In this case, omega-squared, Equation (14.5), would be the appropriate estimate of the proportion of variance associated with type of treatment.

Suppose instead that the independent variable were to be number of years of experience of the therapists (and only one form of therapy was being examined). The specific treatment levels used in the experiment (several different years of experience) were randomly selected from the much larger set of possible levels. The experimenter wished to draw conclusions about years of experience in general, though only selected years of experience were represented in the study. Under conditions such as these, in which the levels of the independent variable are random samples from a population of levels, the correction for bias in omega-squared is not needed. The estimate of the intraclass correlation, Equation (14.4), would be more appropriate. But when the levels used in the study are the only levels for which conclusions are to be drawn, then omega-squared is appropriate.

As another example, suppose that you want to compare the number of trials it takes for an animal to learn a particular response under different levels of an independent variable. The independent variable is period of food deprivation preceding the learning trials. Experimenters tend to use only a few standard periods of food deprivation: 24, 36, and, under special conditions, 48 hours. Assume that after an experiment the experimenter restricted the conclusions to these three periods of deprivation using the following verbalization: "Comparing 24, 36, and 48 hours of deprivation, the evidence showed that the number of trials to learn are not the same for the three periods of food deprivation." Or, the verbalization could have been, "The number of trials to learn differed as a function of which period of deprivation (24, 36, or 48 hours) was used." In both cases the conclusions are restricted to the three levels used in the study. This is therefore a situation in which omega-squared would be the appropriate estimate of degree of relationship. But suppose that, instead, the experimenter wanted to be able to say whether differences in length of food deprivation make a difference, without restricting the conclusions to the specific time periods used in the study. In this case, the experimenter would have to randomly select the time periods used from within the range of time periods to which the conclusions will apply. The correction used in omega-squared would not be needed, and the estimate of the intraclass correlation coefficient would be the appropriate choice for estimating the degree of relationship.

Since **random selection of levels** is only occasionally used, extrapolation of conclusions to nonrepresented levels is generally inappropriate. Therefore, more often that not, omega-squared is the appropriate choice for estimating the degree of relationship.

Omega-squared with t The analysis of variance with only two levels in the independent variable has the same form, and asks the same question, as a t test. Is the dichotomous independent variable related to the wide-ranging dependent variable? With more than two levels, only the analysis of variance can be used to answer the question of whether there is a relationship. But, with two levels, there is a choice. The experimenter can use either the analysis of variance or a t test. The same conclusions of significance or nonsignificance would be reached with either statistic. Specifically, the computed value of t, if squared, would equal the computed value of F. In keeping with this fact, the critical values of F which must be reached for significance are equal to t^2. The first column of the F table, which is a column of critical values given two levels in the independent variable (one degree of freedom), is, in every case, equal to the square of the corresponding value in the t table. As an example, for 10 degrees of freedom at the .05 level, Table IV in Appendix B for t lists a critical value of $t = 2.228$. Squaring 2.228 yields 4.96, which is the critical value found in Table VI for F at one and ten degrees of freedom, at the .05 level.

The identity of meaning and simple transformation between t and F with dichotomous independent variables permits the use of omega-squared with t tests. Given a significant t test for the difference between two means, the squared value of t can be placed into Equation (14.5) for omega-squared. This would yield an estimate of the proportion of variance in the dependent variable associated with the independent variable.

In summary, simply substitute t^2 for F in Equation (14.5) for omega-squared

$$\omega^2 = \frac{(g-1)(t^2-1)}{(g-1)(t^2-1) + gn} .$$

With two levels $(g-1) = (2-1) = 1$, so $(g-1)$ drops out of the formula. The value of gn is $2n$, where n is the number of subjects in each group. Thus, the formula for omega-squared with a t test of the difference between two means can be more simply stated as

$$\omega^2 = \frac{t^2 - 1}{t^2 - 1 + 2n} .$$

Given unequal n in the two groups, the formula can be restated as

$$\omega^2 = \frac{t^2 - 1}{t^2 - 1 + n_1 + n_2} .$$

MULTIPLE COMPARISONS The previous section discussed degree of relationship under the assumption that the two variables are found to be related. It offered another question following significance: "What is the degree of relationship between the variables?" Given significance, and given an independent variable with more than two levels, there is still another question to be asked: "Which levels of the independent variable differ from each other in their effects on the dependent variable?" An independent variable can be effective at some levels, and not at others. Some levels can have identical effects; other can differ.

In the previous chapter, analysis of variance was suggested for some research in which the experimental question was: "Is weight related to socioeconomic status?" Returning to this example, assume that there are four levels of socioeconomic status defining the independent variable: Lower class, lower-middle class, upper-middle class, and upper class. The dependent variable is simply weight.

The F test in an analysis of variance of this question would test whether socioeconomic class is related to weight. But, an additional potential question is: "Are upper-class people lighter than lower-class people?" Perhaps this is the only weight difference among the four classes, or perhaps the upper class is lighter than the upper middle class, and the lower-middle class is lighter than the lower class, but there is no difference between the two middle-class groups. There are many additional specific comparisons possible. Each such question involves a potential comparison of the mean weight of one group against another, or the average of the means of several groups combined and compared with another mean, or another combined mean, etc.

The above issue can be stated more generally. When there are more than two levels of an independent variable in an analysis of variance, the test of whether or not there is a relationship between the independent and dependent variables is really an oversimplification. There are actually several more specific questions implied in the question of relationship. There is the question of whether any one specific level is different from any other (in its effect on the dependent variable); and/or whether any one level is different from any combination of levels; and/or whether any one combination of levels is different from any other combination of levels.

As a consequence of the many implied additional questions, the F test in an analysis of variance (described in Chapter 13) is called an **omnibus F test.** A nonsignificant omnibus F test means that there is no evidence of any population differences between levels or combination of levels. A significant omnibus F test implies that there is evidence of a difference *somewhere* in the many different possible comparisons. It means that there is *at least one* significant difference somewhere among all possible comparisons. However, the omnibus F test does not specify the location of the population difference or differences.

Following a significant omnibus F test, in order to answer the question of where the implicit population difference or differences lie, additional statistical testing is required. Some of the apparent differences observed between groups means may be merely sampling differences reflecting random variability. Statistical tests are needed to determine just which of the differences between sampled means implies population differences.

The statistical tests of the many potential comparisons among means are called **multiple comparison tests.** When an omnibus F test is found statistically significant it is generally followed by multiple comparison tests. If the omnibus F test is not found statistically significant, multiple comparison tests are not done. This is because a nonsignificant omnibus F test implies that there is no evidence of anything other than random differences between means.

There are many different approaches to multiple comparison testing. All the different types of tests can be understood as different computational forms of the familiar t test for the difference between two means.* The t test will therefore be briefly reviewed, and then its application in multiple comparisons will be detailed.

---

*Games, Paul A. Inverse relation between the risks of Type I and Type II errors and suggestions for the unequal n case in multiple comparisons. *Psychological Bulletin,* 1971, 75, 97–102. The computations of the different multiple comparison tests can all be restated as t tests. However, the decision making processes for statistical significance are different for the different multiple comparison tests. The best known of these tests are the Duncan Range, Dunnett, Newman–Keuls, Scheffé, and Tukey tests.

Recall that a t test for the difference between two means is just a ratio containing a difference between two means in the numerator, $(\bar{X}_1 - \bar{X}_2)$, and a measure of variability, the standard error of the difference between two means, $s_{\bar{x}_1-\bar{x}_2}$, in the denominator. This was presented in Equation (10.6),

$$t = \frac{\bar{X}_1 - \bar{X}_2}{s_{\bar{x}_1-\bar{x}_2}},$$

where t is the value *computed* by the right-hand side of Equation (10.6). The computed value of t is compared with a *tabled critical* value of t, as the test of statistical significance. The t distribution is a distribution of expected values of t when $\bar{X}_1$ and $\bar{X}_2$ are both means that have been sampled from the same population.

In Equation (10.7), it was shown that the standard error of the difference between two means, $s_{\bar{x}_1-\bar{x}_2}$, is the square root of the two variance estimates, each divided by n, and summed:

$$s_{\bar{x}_1-\bar{x}_2} = \sqrt{\frac{s_1^2}{n} + \frac{s_2^2}{n}}.$$

In developing Equations (10.9a) and (10.9b) it was shown that, if an average variance estimate is computed, it can replace the two separate estimates, yielding

$$s_{\bar{x}_1-\bar{x}_2} = \sqrt{\frac{\text{average } s^2 + \text{average } s^2}{n}} \tag{14.6}$$

$$= \sqrt{\frac{2(\text{average } s^2)}{n}};$$

that is, if a single average variance can be computed, the standard error of the difference between two means is provided by the formula in Equation (14.6).

The purpose of this section is to show how the t test can be applied to comparing group means within the analysis of variance. Therefore, it would be helpful to replace the average s^2 in Equation (14.6) with an equivalent value computed in the course of the analysis of variance. In analysis of variance, the variances within groups are also averaged, yielding the within-groups mean square, MS_w. Therefore Equation (14.6) can be conveniently restated as Equation (14.7).

$$s_{\bar{x}_1-\bar{x}_2} = \sqrt{\frac{2MS_w}{n}}. \tag{14.7}$$

Equation (10.6),

$$t = \frac{\bar{X}_1 - \bar{X}_2}{s_{\bar{x}_1-\bar{x}_2}}.$$

can then be restated as

$$t = \frac{\bar{X}_1 - \bar{X}_2}{\sqrt{\dfrac{2MS_w}{n}}} \, . \tag{14.8}$$

If the computed t of Equation (14.8) exceeds a tabled critical t value, the two means being tested for a difference are assumed to come from two different populations. This would suggest that one source of the statistical significance in the omnibus F test (assuming a significant F) is the difference between the two levels that were tested with Equation (14.8).

It is convenient to symbolize the tabled critical value of t as t_{crit} to differentiate it from the computed value of t. It is also convenient to use the general subscript j, with and without a prime, to differentiate the different levels involved in any one comparison of means. Using double subscript notation, Equation (14.8) is restated as Equation (14.9).

$$t = \frac{\bar{X}_{.j} - \bar{X}_{.j'}}{\sqrt{\dfrac{2MS_w}{n}}} \, . \tag{14.9}$$

Then t is tested against the tabled critical value of t (t_{crit}), found in Table IV in Appendix B, to see if

$$\frac{\bar{X}_{.j} - \bar{X}_{.j'}}{\sqrt{\dfrac{2MS_w}{n}}} \geq t_{crit}.$$

If the left-hand side equals or exceeds the right-hand side, we have statistical significance. The denominator on the left-hand side has to be divided into each difference being examined. The computations are reduced if we restate the inequality as in Equation (14.10).

$$(\bar{X}_{.j} - \bar{X}_{.j'}) \geq t_{crit} \sqrt{\frac{2MS_w}{n}} \, . \tag{14.10}$$

Equation (14.10) implies that, once having multiplied t_{crit} by $\sqrt{2MS_w/n}$, the resulting value can be compared to the differences between any two means of interest. When the differences between any two such means exceeds the right-hand side of Equation (14.10), that comparison is considered statistically significant. This offers a convenient form for multiple comparisons, with equal n in all groups.

When n is not equal in the different groups, Equation (14.10) is restated as Equation (14.11).

$$(\bar{X}_{.j} - \bar{X}_{.j'}) \geq t_{crit} \sqrt{MS_w \left(\frac{1}{n_j} + \frac{1}{n_{j'}} \right)} \, , \tag{14.11}$$

where n_j and $n_{j'}$ are the two sample sizes of the two groups involved in any one comparison.

To illustrate the use of Equation (14.10), assume that the .05 level, two tailed, will be used in each comparison. All that is required then to determine the critical value of t are the degrees of freedom for entering the t table, Table IV in Appendix B. These are the degrees of freedom for the within-groups mean square, $g(n-1)$, or equivalently, $N-g$, when n is different for different groups. The use of Equation (14.10) for multiple comparisons is demonstrated in Table 14.2, using the data of Table 13.11 and the computations of Table 13.12.

Table 14.2 shows that only one of the comparisons, that between groups 1 and 3, is statistically significant. The evidence then suggests that the population of group 1 is different from group 3, but offers no evidence of a difference between 2 and 1 or 2 and 3. How can 1 and 3 be different, and 2 not be different from either of them?

This could appear to be the case if group 2 differs from the other groups by a smaller amount than 1 and 3 differ from each other. The less dramatic difference could then have been missed by a Type II error in each comparison involving group 2. An alternative explanation is that the one instance of statistical significance that was observed (group 1 versus group 3) was a Type I error, and in fact all groups come from the same population.

TABLE 14.2
Multiple comparisons of means for data in Table 13.11 and computations of Table 13.12

$$\bar{X}_{.j} = \frac{\Sigma X}{n}$$

$$\bar{X}_{.1} = \frac{20}{7}$$
$$= 2.86$$

$$\bar{X}_{.2} = \frac{30}{7}$$
$$= 4.29$$

$$\bar{X}_{.3} = \frac{44}{7}$$
$$= 6.29$$

$$\text{df}_w = g(n-1)$$
$$= 3(7-1)$$
$$= 18$$

$$t_{\text{crit}_{.05}} = 2.101 \qquad \text{MS}_w = 3.65$$

$$t_{\text{crit}_{.05}} \sqrt{\frac{2\text{MS}_w}{n}} = (2.101) \sqrt{\frac{2(3.65)}{7}}$$
$$= (2.101) \sqrt{1.04}$$
$$= 2.15$$

$$\bar{X}_{.j} - \bar{X}_{.j'} \geqslant t_{\text{crit}} \sqrt{\frac{2\text{MS}_w}{n}}$$

$$\bar{X}_{.2} - \bar{X}_{.1} = 4.29 - 2.86 = 1.43 \qquad 1.43 \not> 2.15$$
$$\bar{X}_{.3} - \bar{X}_{.2} = 6.29 - 4.29 = 2.00 \qquad 2.00 \not> 2.15$$
$$\bar{X}_{.3} - \bar{X}_{.1} = 6.29 - 2.86 = 3.43 \qquad 3.43 > 2.15$$

Each of the above comparisons was made with an individual probability of a Type I error of .05, using the *t* table to obtain the critical value. It is not common practice to use the .05 level in multiple comparisons, so the issue of selecting Type I error levels for multiple comparisons is discussed in the following section.

Adjusting the Type I Error Probability
There is one chance in 1000 of obtaining 10 heads in a row in 10 tosses of a fair coin. As discussed in Chapter 8, if you tossed a coin 10 times and then did this again and again, a total of 10,000 times, the probability of obtaining at least one instance of 10 heads in a row would no longer be so small. In fact, it is expected that there would be about 10 occurrences, of 10 heads in 10 tosses, among the 10,000 attempts. Looking at just a single instance of 10 tosses that produced 10 heads, we might be tempted to conclude that the unseen coin had two heads. Therefore, the 9999 other attempts should not be ignored in drawing conclusions about the coin.

Multiple comparisons suggest many *t* tests. Given a true null hypothesis, no rare events are expected in a single test of the hypothesis, yet some rare events are expected among large numbers of tests. What is required in multiple comparisons is some recognition of the number of comparisons being made. The probability of one or more comparisons being significant with a true null hypothesis is not the simple Type I error used in testing each comparison. The probability of at least one Type I error increases with the number of comparisons.

There is a formula which tells us the probability of one or more instances of spurious (false) statistical significance under these conditions. Assume that (unknown to the experimenter) all the group means involved in the comparisons have been sampled from the same population. Given C independent tests (comparisons) of differences between means, the probability of one or more instances of statistical significance is given by Equation (14.12).

$$\alpha_{ew} = 1 - (1 - \alpha_{pc})^C. \tag{14.12}$$

In Equation (14.12), α_{pc} is the **per-comparison, Type I error probability,** that is, the Type I error probability for each test of a difference between means. C is the number of comparisons (the number of tests of significance). α_{ew} is the probability of having *at least* one instance of statistical significance among the comparisons. The subscript ew stands for experimentwise. Multiple comparisons are always done within the context of a single experiment which calls for a number of individual comparisons. If any one conclusion of statistical significance is wrong (a Type I error), we have drawn an incorrect conclusion from the experiment. The probability of one or more incorrect conclusions of statistical significance is therefore considered the probability of an **experimentwise Type I error probability.** The probability α_{ew} is the overall probability of one or more unwarranted conclusions of statistical significance when each test of significance is made with a Type I error probability of α_{pc}.

For example, if we did five independent significance tests, each at the .05 level (so that $\alpha_{pc} = .05$) with all means sampled from the same population, there would be an experimentwise error probability of $\alpha_{ew} = .23$ of finding at least one statistically significant comparison; that is, Equation (14.12) indicates that

$$\alpha_{ew} = 1 - (1-\alpha_{pc})^C$$

$$= 1 - (1-.05)^5$$

$$= 1 - (.95)^5$$

$$= 1 - .77$$

$$= .23 .$$

On the other hand, if each of the comparisons was tested at the .01 level, the overall probability of one or more significant findings would be $\alpha_{ew} = .05$; that is,

$$\alpha_{ew} = 1 - (1-\alpha_{pc})^C$$

$$= 1 - (1-.01)^5$$

$$= 1 - (.99)^5$$

$$= 1 - .95$$

$$= .05 .$$

The probabilistic logic above has suggested a simple way to reduce the probability of reaching false conclusions in multiple comparisons. We merely lower the Type I error probability per comparison. The value of α_{pc} is set so that for the given number of multiple comparisons the experimentwise probability of finding one or more instances of spurious significance will be held to $\alpha_{ew} = .05$, or any other desired experimentwise error probability. For example, given five independent tests of significance, each one could be made at the per-comparison probability of $\alpha_{pc} = .01$. This would yield an experimentwise Type I error probability of $\alpha_{ew} = .05$.

The values of α_{pc}, given a desired value for α_{ew}, are closely approximated with Equation (14.13).

$$\alpha_{pc} = \frac{\alpha_{ew}}{C} . \tag{14.13}$$

Equation (14.13) suggests that we divide the desired experimentwise error probability into as many parts as there will be comparisons. For example, given 10 comparisons with a desired experimentwise error probability of $\alpha_{ew} = .05$, the value of α_{pc} would be

$$\alpha_{pc} = \frac{\alpha_{ew}}{C}$$

$$= \frac{.05}{10}$$

$$= .005.$$

The use of Equations (14.12) and (14.13) to establish reduced Type I error probabilities per comparison is just one approach to controlling the experimentwise error probability. The other methods are discussed in advanced texts on analysis of variance. When articles in the literature refer to the Scheffé, Tukey, or Newman–Keuls tests, or the Duncan range test, they are referring to these alternative approaches to controlling experimentwise error probabilities.

A problem in applying Equations (14.12) and (14.13) is that the t tables do not normally list the critical values for the odd, very small Type I error probabilities per comparison that are often needed. For example, suppose there were six comparisons, and it was desired to maintain an experimentwise error probability of .05. The necessary Type I error level per comparison would be .008; that is,

$$\alpha_{pc} = \frac{\alpha_{ew}}{C}$$

$$= \frac{.05}{6}$$

$$= .008$$

and

$$\alpha_{ew} = 1 - (1 - .\alpha_{pc})^{C}$$

$$= 1 - (1 - .008)^{6}$$

$$= .05.$$

But a t table would not give the critical values for a Type I error probability of .008. Only the Type I error probabilities that are commonly desired are listed. To deal with this problem a table has been developed by O. J. Dunn[*] which is presented in this text as Table VII in Appendix B. This table is used when you wish to maintain a specified *experimentwise* error probability.

[*]Dunn, O. J. Multiple comparisons among means. *Journal of the American Statistical Association*, 1961, *56*, 52–64.

Table VII offers the critical values for the experimentwise Type I error probabilities of .05 and .01, without requiring that you compute the per-comparison error probabilities.

The Dunn table (Table VII) has a different form than a t table. To use the Dunn table, three pieces of information are required. First, you must know the number of comparisons to be made. This tells you which row to select, using the column headed C in Table VII in Appendix B. Then the degrees of freedom for mean square within groups are located at the top of the table which indicates which column contains the critical value. Finally, where the column and row intersect, two values are found. As indicated in the column headed α_{ew}, one critical value is for $\alpha_{ew} = .05$ and the other is for $\alpha_{ew} = .01$.

As an example, assume an analysis of variance with four groups and five subjects in each group, yielding 20 degrees of freedom for MS_w. Assume six comparisons among the four groups with an experimentwise Type I error probability of .05. Table VII suggests that the critical value [the t_{crit} for Equation (14.10)] would be 2.93. Note that it is the number of comparisons (6) and not the number of groups that is used in entering Table VII. All the critical values in the Dunn table are for two-tailed tests of significance. When using the Dunn table, the signs of the differences being tested are ignored.

Table VII allows the experimenter to avoid computing Equation (14.13) for α_{pc}. All that the experimenter needs is the desired experimentwise error probability, α_{ew}; the number of comparisons, C; and the degrees of freedom for MS_w. The required critical value is then read from the body of the table and entered into Equation (14.10) or Equation (14.11) for multiple comparisons.

As an example, let us look at the results of an analysis of variance with five groups with varied ns, in which the omnibus F was significant. The means, respective values of n in each group, and MS_w are:

	$\bar{X}._1$	$\bar{X}._2$	$\bar{X}._3$	$\bar{X}._4$	$\bar{X}._5$
Means	2.50	2.75	1.25	4.00	6.00
n_j	10	15	15	20	10
$MS_w = 12$					

Three comparisons were carried out, with a decision to have a Type I error experimentwise of .05. The three comparisons were

$$\bar{X}._3 - \bar{X}._5 = 1.25 - 6.00 = -4.75,$$

$$\bar{X}._3 - \bar{X}._1 = 1.25 - 2.50 = -1.25,$$

$$\bar{X}._2 - \bar{X}._4 = 2.75 - 4.00 = -1.25.$$

Note that the resulting differences are all minus values but two-tailed tests are assumed so the signs of the differences are ignored. The different values of n_j require the use of Equation (14.11).

$$(\bar{X}._j - \bar{X}._{j'}) \geq t_{crit} \sqrt{MS_w\left(\frac{1}{n_j} + \frac{1}{n_{j'}}\right)}$$

Since an experimentwise Type I error probability is being maintained, the Dunn table is used, rather than the t table, to obtain the critical value. There are five groups with a total of 70 subjects, so that the df_w are $N - g = 65$. The Dunn table does not have a column for 65 degrees of freedom so, as is the case with all the other tables, we use the column with the closest smaller df, which in this case is 60. Three comparisons are planned, so the required critical value is located where $C = 3$ and 60 df intersect. It is 2.47 for the .05 level.

The first two comparisons involve the same values of $n_j = 15$ and $n_{j'} = 10$. The right-hand side of Equation (14.11) therefore takes the value

$$2.47 \sqrt{12\left(\frac{1}{15} + \frac{1}{10}\right)} = 2.47 \sqrt{12\left(\frac{1}{6}\right)}$$

$$= 3.49.$$

The absolute value of the first two comparisons must therefore reach or surpass 3.49. Only the comparison between groups 3 and 5 does. For the third comparison, between groups 2 and 4, the value to be reached or exceeded is

$$2.47 \sqrt{12\left(\frac{1}{15} + \frac{1}{20}\right)} = 2.47 \sqrt{12\left(\frac{7}{60}\right)}$$

$$= 2.92.$$

The difference between groups 2 and 4 does not reach or surpass 2.92, so the only significant comparison is between groups 3 and 5.

When to Use the Experimentwise Criterion for the Type I Error The Type I error level is a commitment to maintain a specified probability of making an incorrect decision about identical population means. The incorrect decision can be defined as a single decision involving a single comparison, or as reaching even one incorrect conclusion among many about the relationship between the independent and dependent variables. When defined in this second, broader way, we use the experimentwise criterion. We reduce the probability of the errors in individual comparisons to maintain some specified error probability for the complete set of conclusions about the relationship between the independent and dependent variable.

The literature has tended to follow the use of the experimentwise criterion. The exceptions have generally been when advance predictions have been made for theoretically important comparisons, called **a priori hypotheses.** Then the per-comparison criterion has often been set separately for each a priori hypothesis. Other comparisons in the analysis are treated together under an experimentwise criterion. Whether a priori hypotheses are separately treated with their own per-comparison Type I error levels varies among experimenters.

There has been little tendency to utilize the nature of the independent variable in deciding whether to use the experimentwise criterion. However, the nature of the differences among the levels of a variable can, at times, make the use of the experimentwise criterion appear to be unnecessary and overly conservative.

As an example, assume a study comparing several types of psychotherapy, resulting in a significant omnibus F test. There would then be a need to see which therapies were different from the others in effectiveness. The omnibus F test would have answered the question of whether form of therapy makes a difference among those compared. The Type I error probability for that decision was controlled with the critical value for the omnibus F. The question that remains is where the differences lie. This is really a set of several very different questions. The independent variable, type of psychotherapy, might involve grossly different forms of therapy. The fact that two specific therapies differ in effectiveness might have very little implication for the difference or lack of difference between two other specific forms of therapy. Each such comparison between two forms of therapy might deserve its own Type I error level. If all the multiple comparisons among different therapies were treated as one decision, then the Type I error probability would not be the probability of an incorrect decision about a single question. It would be the probability of one or more incorrect decisions among an arbitrary set of questions. The experimentwise criterion would appear to be inappropriate.

There is a second reason for sometimes preferring the exclusive use of the per-comparison criterion that is relevant when the levels of the independent variable *are* clearly related. For example, assume a study of the relationship between levels of social class and amount of sugar consumed. Comparing any two levels of social class for average grams of sugar consumed each day, the same implicit question could be recognized: "Is sugar consumption related to social class?" This same question would be implicit no matter which levels of social class were being examined. However, this question would have been previously answered affirmatively by a significant omnibus F, or no multiple comparisons would be done. Therefore, the one common question concerning the different levels of the independent variable would not need to be part of the multiple comparison tests. To be useful, the multiple comparisons would have to ask new questions specific to each comparison. For example, are upper-class people different than middle? Are middle different than lower? If worth asking, the questions should be asked separately, again suggesting the exclusive use of the per-comparison criterion.

It is suggested here that the nature of the levels of the independent variable, and the kinds of questions being asked, should determine which criteria to use. But you should be aware of the fact that the current most common practice is to use the experimentwise criterion for all comparisons concerning the same independent variable. The exception, at times, is for a priori comparisons.

The issue of when to use the experimentwise Type I error criterion will probably be reexamined over the coming years. In the meantime, a suggestion is made here for a middle course that might be congenial to differing points of view.

1. Do an omnibus *F* test first.
2. If the omninibus *F* test is significant, do multiple comparisons that would be theoretically meaningful if found significant. If the number of multiple comparisons is 7 or less, use the Dunn table to obtain the critical value maintaining a Type I error probability *experimentwise* of .05.
3. All comparisons not significant with the experimentwise criterion should be retested at the *per-comparison* Type I error probability of .05 .
4. If no additional instances of statistical significance are found with step 3, then simply interpret the results. If the liberalized Type I error levels of step 3 reveal additional instances of statistical significance, offer two sets of interpretations of the results. One would be Type I error conservative, and the other Type I error liberal.
5. If, following a significant omnibus *F* test, there are very many multiple comparison tests to be done, do them all at the per-comparison Type I error probability of .05. Then consider the study to be an exploratory study in regard to the multiple comparisons. All such comparisons found significant would have to be found significant in a second study to be taken seriously. In the second study the number of comparisons could be reduced by limiting the tests to the significant findings of the first study.

<table>
<tr><td>IMPORTANT
WORDS AND
CONCEPTS</td><td>Error variance (p. 322)
Intraclass correlation coefficient (p. 323)
Treatment variance (p. 323)
Proportion of variance in dependent variable scores associated with
   treatment levels (p. 324)
Omega-squared (p. 326)</td></tr>
</table>

Random selection of levels (p. 328)
Omnibus F test (p. 330)
Multiple-comparison tests (p. 330)
Per-comparison Type I error probability (p. 334)
Experimentwise Type I error probability (p. 335)
The Dunn table (p. 337)
A priori hypotheses (p. 339)

SENTENCE COMPLETIONS

The following incomplete sentences are taken from the underlined sentences in this chapter. Fill in the missing words and phrases and then correct them from the answers which follow.

1. The proportion of variance in the dependent variable scores that is associated with treatment level membership is obtained as a _____. The total variance in the dependent variable is in the _____.

2. _____ is an estimate of random variance in the population of dependent variable scores. Random variance is most generally symbolized as _____ .

3. _____ estimates both random variance and treatment variance. Treatment variance in this text is symbolized as _____.

4. The variance estimated by _____ is $n\sigma_{tr}^2 + \sigma_e^2$.

5. The total variance, symbolized as _____, can be defined as

_____ .

6. The numerator in the ratio for the proportion of variance associated with treatment levels is _____ .

7. Subtracting the computed value _____ from the computed value _____, and then dividing the difference by _____ yields an estimate of _____.

8. The estimate of the proportion of the variance associated with treatment levels is an estimate of the degree of _____
_____.

9. Given the conclusion that the two variables are related (a significant F test), the question is which _____ of the independent variable make a difference in the values of the _____ variable?

10. As a consequence of the many implied questions, the F test in an analysis of variance is called an _____ _____test.

11. A significant omnibus F test implies that there is _____
_____somewhere among all possible comparisons.

12. The statistical tests of the many potential _____
_____are called multiple comparisons.

13. All the different types of multiple comparisons can be understood as

different computational forms of the familiar _____
_____.

14. The _____ mean square is used in place of the average variance in the t test used for multiple comparisons.

15. The probability of at least one Type I error _____ with the number of comparisons.

16. α_{pc} is the _____.

17. α_{ew} is the _____.

18. The literature has tended to follow the use of α_{ew} whenever the comparisons all involve the same independent variable. The exceptions have been when _____, called _____, have been made for theoretically important comparisons.

Answers 1. ratio; denominator 2. MS_w; σ_e^2 3. MS_b; σ_{tr}^2 4. MS_b 5. σ_{tot}^2; $\sigma_{tr}^2 + \sigma_e^2$ 6. σ_{tr}^2 7. MS_w; MS_b; n; σ_{tr}^2 8. relationship between the variables 9. levels; dependent 10. omnibus F 11. at least one significant difference 12. comparisons among means (tests between means, etc.) 13. t test for the difference between means 14. within-groups 15. increases 16. Type I error probability per comparison 17. Type I error probability experimentwise 18. advance predictions; a priori hypotheses

_____
PROBLEMS
_____

1. Assume that an analysis of variance has been done on data containing five groups, with equal n, and with nine subjects per group. The omnibus F was found to be significant. The within-groups mean square was $MS_w = .85$.

   The means of the five groups were:

   $\bar{X}_{.1} = 2.00$
   $\bar{X}_{.2} = 3.22$
   $\bar{X}_{.3} = 5.56$
   $\bar{X}_{.4} = 6.33$
   $\bar{X}_{.5} = 7.56$

   Do the six multiple comparisons shown below, maintaining an experimentwise Type I error probability of .05. Indicate which comparisons are significant.

   $\bar{X}_{.2} - \bar{X}_{.1}$
   $\bar{X}_{.3} - \bar{X}_{.2}$
   $\bar{X}_{.4} - \bar{X}_{.3}$
   $\bar{X}_{.4} - \bar{X}_{.2}$
   $\bar{X}_{.4} - \bar{X}_{.1}$
   $\bar{X}_{.5} - \bar{X}_{.1}$

2. The following results are taken from Table 13.14 in the preceding chapter. The analysis of variance involved four groups with unequal ns. The computed MS_w was 3.10. The means and ns for each group are listed below. Do the suggested multiple comparisons, maintaining an experimentwise Type I error probability of .05. Indicate which comparisons are significant.

	$\bar{X}_{.1}$	$\bar{X}_{.2}$	$\bar{X}_{.3}$	$\bar{X}_{.4}$	Comparisons
Means	2.33	2.75	3.20	7.50	$\bar{X}_{.2} - \bar{X}_{.1}$
n_j	3	4	5	4	$\bar{X}_{.3} - \bar{X}_{.2}$
					$\bar{X}_{.4} - \bar{X}_{.3}$
					$\bar{X}_{.4} - \bar{X}_{.2}$

3. Assume an experiment involving 20 subjects in each of five groups. The computed value of F was 3.60. This is significant. What is the estimate of the proportion of the variance associated with treatment levels, if the five treatment levels are a random sample of an infinite number of possible levels of the independent variable?

4. If the experimenter in problem 3 planned to restrict her conclusions to the five levels of the independent variable used in the experiment, what would be an estimate of the proportion of the variance associated with treatment levels?

f.ifteen

TWO-FACTOR ANALYSIS OF VARIANCE

Three types of statistical techniques have been discussed in the previous chapters: correlation, t tests, and analysis of variance. The discussions all concerned the relationships between just two variables. In the discussions of t tests and analysis of variance a single independent variable was distinguished from a single dependent variable. In this chapter, some techniques for examining the relationships between two independent variables and a single dependent variable are introduced.

Independent variables are often called **factors**. The analysis of variance design previously discussed in Chapter 13 is therefore often called a one-factor design. This chapter presents formulas for a two-factor analysis of variance design.

A one-factor analysis of variance design is also called a **one-way analysis of variance,** and a two-factor design is called a **two-way analysis of variance.** Multifactor designs with three or four variables are also used. They are identical in principle to the two-factor design detailed in this chapter. As expected, a three-factor design is also called a three-way analysis of variance, and a four-factor design is called a four-way analysis of variance.

With a one-factor analysis of variance, double subscript notation (X_{ij}) is needed. For a two-factor analysis of variance, three subscripts (X_{ijk}), one for each independent variable plus one for subjects, are required. For a three-factor analysis of variance, four subscripts are needed.

SUBSCRIPT NOTATION IN MULTIFACTOR ANALYSIS OF VARIANCE Each independent variable in a multifactor analysis of variance will have its own number of levels in a particular experiment. There can be as few as two levels of an independent variable with no theoretical limit for the maximum allowable number of levels. In practice, from two to five levels are likely to be encountered in any one independent variable, and only rarely more than five levels.

Multifactor designs are always identified by the number of factors, and sometimes by the number of levels of each variable. Thus, a two-factor design containing two levels of one variable and three of another is often called a two-by-three design (symbolized 2×3). If there are three factors with two, three, and four levels of the respective factors, it can be called a $2 \times 3 \times 4$ design. The same design can be called a three-factor design or a three-way design, referring to the number of independent variables.

Where there are two or more independent variables, some symbol is required to identify each variable. With the one-factor analysis of variance design, G was used in this text to denote the single independent variable, and g to denote the number of levels of G. The letter g was used since g could stand for groups as in treatment groups. But there is a more common notation used when there are several independent variables in the experiment. The first letters of the alphabet are used to denote the different factors (different independent variables). For example, one factor would be symbolized by A containing a levels, a second factor symbolized by B with b levels, and a third factor by C with c levels.*

In a two-factor design, the sum of all scores is symbolized as:

$$\text{Sum of all scores in a two-factor design} = \sum_{i}^{n}\sum_{j}^{a}\sum_{k}^{b}X_{ijk}.$$

The sum of all scores in a three-factor design is symbolized as:

$$\text{Sum of all scores in a three-factor design} = \sum_{i}^{n}\sum_{j}^{a}\sum_{k}^{b}\sum_{m}^{c}X_{ijkm}.$$

Cells A two-factor design can be represented by a table such as Table 15.1. The matrix in the table represents a 3×4 design. In such a design, all subjects under, say, the second level of A and under the fourth level of B would all be under the same conditions. A set of uniform conditions is called a **cell**. This can be contrasted with a one-factor analysis of variance, where each *column* of scores (as in Tables 13.3–13.5) contains a uniform set of conditions; that is, in a one-factor design, all subjects at one level of the independent variable (represented by one column of scores) are in the same condition. In a two-factor design (as represented by the matrix in Table 15.1), the uniform conditions are defined by the levels of *both* independent variables. All subjects in the same *cell* are under the same conditions. In each of the cells in Table 15.1 there would be scores. Suppose there were five scores in each cell. Table 15.2 presents the abstract symbols for the

TABLE 15.1
A matrix for a two-factor, 3×4 design. The cell for the second level of A, fourth level of B, is shaded

*Often in the research literature, with several independent variables, the letters signifying the different variables follow from the names of the variables. If one factor is dependency, it might be represented by D. If another factor is anxiety, it might be represented by A.

346   Two-Factor Analysis of Variance

TABLE 15.2

Symbolic representation of five scores in cell A_2B_4 (the shaded cell) in Table 15.1

$$B_4$$

$$A_2 \quad \begin{array}{|c|} \hline X_{124} \\ X_{224} \\ X_{324} \\ X_{424} \\ X_{524} \\ \hline \end{array}$$

scores for the second level of A, fourth level of B (shaded in Table 15.1). The first subscript of X in Table 15.2 refers to subjects so it runs from 1 to 5. The second subscript refers to the level of A so it remains constant at 2. The third subscript is for the level of B so it is constant at 4.

In Chapter 13, when discussing one-factor designs, an unspecified score in an unspecified treatment group was referred to as the ith score in the jth group. In a two-factor design, an unspecified score in an unspecified cell is referred to as X_{ijk}, the ith score in the cell of the jth level of A, kth level of B.

A general matrix for a two-factor design is drawn up as in Table 15.3, in which there are a levels of A and b levels of B. (In Table 15.1, $a = 3$ and $b = 4$.) Assuming n scores in a cell, the cell in the jth row of the kth column of Table 15.3 would have its scores symbolized as $X_{1jk}, X_{2jk}, \cdots, X_{ijk}, \cdots, X_{njk}$.

Means of Cells, Columns, and Rows

The mean of a cell in a two-factor design is symbolized and computed as

$$\bar{X}_{.jk} = \frac{\sum\limits_{i}^{n} X_{ijk}}{n},$$

where n is the number of scores in a single *cell* of a data table (rather than the number of scores in a column or a row). The mean of cell A_2B_3 is

$$\bar{X}_{.23} = \frac{\sum\limits_{i}^{n} X_{i23}}{n}.$$

The number of scores in a single *level* of the B variable in a two-factor design is the number of scores in a single column, which is na, where a is the number of levels of A, each containing n scores. The mean of the third level of B is therefore symbolized as

$$\bar{X}_{..3} = \frac{\sum\limits_{i}^{n}\sum\limits_{j}^{a} X_{ij3}}{na}.$$

TABLE 15.3
General (symbolic) data matrix for a two-factor design

	B_1	B_2	$\cdots$	B_k	$\cdots$	B_b	
A_1	X_{111} X_{211} $\vdots$ X_{i11} $\vdots$ X_{n11}	X_{112} X_{212} $\vdots$ X_{i12} $\vdots$ X_{n12}	$\cdots$	X_{11k} X_{21k} $\vdots$ X_{i1k} $\vdots$ X_{n1k}	$\cdots$	X_{11b} X_{21b} $\vdots$ X_{i1b} $\vdots$ X_{n1b}	$\dfrac{\sum\limits_{i}^{n}\sum\limits_{k}^{b} X_{i1k}}{nb} = \bar{X}_{.1.}$
A_2	X_{121} X_{221} $\vdots$ X_{i21} $\vdots$ X_{n21}	X_{122} X_{222} $\vdots$ X_{i22} $\vdots$ X_{n22}	$\cdots$	X_{12k} X_{22k} $\vdots$ X_{i2k} $\vdots$ X_{n2k}	$\cdots$	X_{12b} X_{22b} $\vdots$ X_{i2b} $\vdots$ X_{n2b}	$\dfrac{\sum\limits_{i}^{n}\sum\limits_{k}^{b} X_{i2k}}{nb} = \bar{X}_{.2.}$
$\vdots$							
A_j	X_{1j1} X_{2j1} $\vdots$ X_{ij1} $\vdots$ X_{nj1}	X_{1j2} X_{2j2} $\vdots$ X_{ij2} $\vdots$ X_{nj2}	$\cdots$	X_{1jk} X_{2jk} $\vdots$ X_{ijk} $\vdots$ X_{njk}	$\cdots$	X_{1jb} X_{2jb} $\vdots$ X_{ijb} $\vdots$ X_{njb}	$\dfrac{\sum\limits_{i}^{n}\sum\limits_{k}^{b} X_{ijk}}{nb} = \bar{X}_{.j.}$
$\vdots$							
A_a	X_{1a1} X_{2a1} $\vdots$ X_{ia1} $\vdots$ X_{na1}	X_{1a2} X_{2a2} $\vdots$ X_{ia2} $\vdots$ X_{na2}	$\cdots$	X_{1ak} X_{2ak} $\vdots$ X_{iak} $\vdots$ X_{nak}	$\cdots$	X_{1ab} X_{2ab} $\vdots$ X_{iab} $\vdots$ X_{nab}	$\dfrac{\sum\limits_{i}^{n}\sum\limits_{k}^{b} X_{iak}}{nb} = \bar{X}_{.a.}$
	$\sum\limits_{i}^{n}\sum\limits_{j}^{a} X_{ij1}$	$\sum\limits_{i}^{n}\sum\limits_{j}^{a} X_{ij2}$		$\sum\limits_{i}^{n}\sum\limits_{j}^{a} X_{ijk}$		$\sum\limits_{i}^{n}\sum\limits_{j}^{a} X_{ijb}$	

$$\dfrac{\sum\limits_{i}^{n}\sum\limits_{j}^{a} X_{ijk}}{na} = \qquad \bar{X}_{..1} \qquad\qquad \bar{X}_{..2} \qquad\qquad\qquad \bar{X}_{..k} \qquad\qquad\qquad \bar{X}_{..b}$$

The number of scores in a single level of the A variable in a two-factor design is the number of scores in a single row, which is nb. The mean of the second level of A is therefore symbolized as

$$\bar{X}_{.2.} = \frac{\overset{n\ b}{\underset{i\ k}{\Sigma\Sigma}} X_{i2k}}{nb}.$$

The total number of scores in a two-factor matrix (with equal numbers of subjects in each cell) is nab. Therefore, the grand mean in a two-factor design is symbolized as

$$\bar{X}_{...} = \frac{\overset{n\ a\ b}{\underset{i\ j\ k}{\Sigma\Sigma\Sigma}} X_{ijk}}{nab}.$$

For a three-factor design, the grand mean is symbolized as

$$\bar{X}_{....} = \frac{\overset{n\ a\ b\ c}{\underset{i\ j\ k\ m}{\Sigma\Sigma\Sigma\Sigma}} X_{ijkm}}{nabc}.$$

MAIN EFFECTS A meaningful question in a two-factor design will often be whether the subjects in different levels of the A variable come from different populations; that is, is the A variable related to the dependent variable scores? For example, if the A variable were to be level of anxiety, and the dependent variable the ability to solve some problems (measured in terms of number of errors before solution), the question concerning variable A might be stated as: "Is level of anxiety related to the ability to solve the class of problems used in the experiment?" This would be tested by comparing the numbers of errors found at different levels of A. This comparison, involving just one of the variables, is called the testing of a **main effect**, specifically, the main effect of A. The mean score at each level of A would be compared with the mean score of every other level of A using an omnibus F test which is almost identical to the type of omnibus F test encountered previously in Chapter 13. Recall that the numerator of the F ratio, for a one-factor design, is a sum of squares for a treatment ($SS_{treatment}$) divided by its degrees of freedom. Specifically, for a one-factor design, the defining formula for $MS_{treatment}$ is

$$MS_{treatment} = \frac{SS_{treatment}}{df} \tag{15.1}$$

$$= \frac{n \overset{g}{\underset{j}{\Sigma}} (\bar{X}_{.j} - \bar{X}_{..})^2}{g-1},$$

where the left-most coefficient, n, is the number of scores in a treatment level, and g, in the denominator, is the number of levels. For a two-factor design, g is replaced by the number of levels in the variable of interest (such as a). Also, with more than one factor, n is no longer the number of scores in a level of the variable. For a level of variable A in a two-factor design the number of scores at each level is nb. Thus, Equation (15.1), when restated to constitute the defining formula for the mean square of A in a two-factor design, is

$$MS_A = \frac{SS_A}{df_A} \tag{15.2}$$

$$= \frac{nb \sum_{j}^{a}(\bar{X}_{.j.} - \bar{X}_{...})^2}{a - 1}.$$

The denominator of the F ratio consists of the average within-cell variance which is discussed in a later section of this chapter.

In a two-factor design there will be a B variable as well as an A variable. Continuing the example in which the A variable is level of anxiety, the B variable could be some controlled variation in the complexity of the problems. One of the questions might then be: "Is level of complexity related to the ability to solve the class of problems used in the experiment?" The test of significance for this variable would be a test of the main effect of B. The numerator of the F ratio for this test would be

$$MS_B = \frac{SS_B}{df_B} \tag{15.3}$$

$$= \frac{na \sum_{k}^{b}(\bar{X}_{..k} - \bar{X}_{...})^2}{b - 1}.$$

Thus there would be two possible tests for main effects in a two-factor experiment. In the example used, there would be a test of whether level of anxiety is related to number of errors, and a test of whether level of problem complexity is related to number of errors.

SIMPLE EFFECTS Level of anxiety (in the above example) might be related to number of errors, but only with very complex problems. Perhaps for simple problems the level of anxiety would not interfere with problem solution. Thus, given complex problems, the average number of errors in cells might increase for the cells in which subjects are more and more anxious, but for the simple problems level of anxiety might not make a difference. Such a possibility is illustrated in Table 15.4, where mean errors for complex problems are seen in one column and mean errors for simple problems in the other column.

TABLE 15.4

Hypothetical mean number of errors for subjects in different conditions (different cells). The data illustrates different simple effects of anxiety at the two different levels of complexity. It also illustrates varied simple effects of complexity at four different levels of anxiety.

		Simple Problems B_1	Complex Problems B_2
No anxiety	A_1	$\bar{X}_{.11} = 2$	$\bar{X}_{.12} = 4$
Mild anxiety	A_2	$\bar{X}_{.21} = 2$	$\bar{X}_{.22} = 6$
Moderate anxiety	A_3	$\bar{X}_{.31} = 2$	$\bar{X}_{.32} = 8$
Severe anxiety	A_4	$\bar{X}_{.41} = 2$	$\bar{X}_{.42} = 12$

Table 15.4 can also be looked at from the vantage point of different patterns depending on level of anxiety. There are four levels of anxiety in Table 15.4. The hypothetical data suggest that the increases in errors due to changes in complexity (changes within a single row) are further exaggerated by increasing levels of anxiety. For example, with no anxiety (top row) increased complexity is associated with doubling of errors. With severe anxiety (bottom row) there are six times as many errors in the complex problem condition.

What has been suggested is that different results can sometimes be obtained if the test of the effects of a variable is restricted to one or another level of a second variable. As implied in the above example, there are times when it is desirable to examine effects of a variable separately at each level of another variable. These tests are called tests of **simple effects,** in contrast to tests of main effects. Testing the effects of anxiety separately at each of the levels of complexity is a test of the simple effects of anxiety (there are two such tests possible.) Testing the effects of complexity separately at each of the levels of anxiety is a test of simple effects of complexity. (There are four such tests possible.)

The mean squares for each simple effect of A, each at a different level of B, are symbolized in this text as $MS_{A_{b_1}}$, $MS_{A_{b_2}}$, etc. For each simple effect of B, each at a different level of A, the symbols used in this text are $MS_{B_{a_1}}$, $MS_{B_{a_2}}$, etc.

The defining formula for the mean square for the simple effect of A at the first level of B is

$$MS_{A_{b_1}} = \frac{SS_{A_{b_1}}}{df_A}$$

$$= \frac{n\sum_{j}^{a}(\bar{X}_{\cdot j 1} - \bar{X}_{\cdot\cdot 1})^2}{a-1} .$$

The defining formula for the mean square for the simple effect of A at the second level of B is

$$MS_{A_{b_2}} = \frac{SS_{A_{b_2}}}{df_A}$$

$$= \frac{n\sum_{j}^{a}(\bar{X}_{\cdot j 2} - \bar{X}_{\cdot\cdot 2})^2}{a-1} .$$

Comparing the defining formula for simple effects to Equation (15.1) for the treatment effect in a one-factor design,

$$MS_{treatment} = \frac{SS_{treatment}}{df}$$

$$= \frac{n\sum_{j}^{g}(\bar{X}_{\cdot j} - \bar{X}_{\cdot\cdot})^2}{g-1} ,$$

it can be seen that the form for a simple effect is very much like that for the effect of the one independent treatment variable in a one-factor design. The test for a simple effect is done at one level of the second variable, ignoring (at each test) all the other levels of the second variable, as though there were no second variable.

INTERACTIONS When the simple effects of variable A are different, depending on the level of variable B at which they are tested, then it is said that an **interaction** is present. An interaction implies that the level of one variable makes a difference in the pattern of effects of the other variable.

If there is an interaction such that the level of *B* makes a difference in the pattern of effects across the levels of *A*, then the converse is also true; that is, the level of *A* will then make a difference in the pattern of effects associated with levels of *B*.

For example, if level of anxiety makes a difference in the kind of variations in means we find with different levels of complexity, then level of complexity will make a difference in the kind of variations in means we find with different levels of anxiety. This was suggested by the prior discussion of the hypothetical data in Table 15.4. The same data could be discussed as suggesting both varied simple effects of complexity and varied simple effects of anxiety.

As with other potential effects, interactions can appear to be present, yet only represent random variability. A test of a simple effect of a variable *A* might be done and found significant at one level of variable *B* but not significant at another. This could imply that at one level of *B*, differences on variable *A* have an effect on the dependent variable, but not at another level of variable *B*. If there were many levels of variable *B*, chance alone could account for apparent significance at one or another level and lack of significance at one or another level; that is, given enough levels of variable *B*, variable *A* might appear to have different effects on the dependent variable, on at least one or more levels of *B*. These apparent differences in effects could simply be due to chance variability expected in random sampling. Put another way, given enough rows (or columns), the means of cells, given only random variability, could give a visual impression of different patterns of means in different rows (or different columns) of a data matrix. Thus, before concluding that there are different patterns of means in different rows a statistical test must be done. The test is done to see if the differences are more than chance differences. The test used is the statistical test for an interaction.

The test for an interaction is a test of whether the patterns across rows (or columns) are more varied then would be expected given only random influences. Tests of simple effects are not done unless the test for an interaction is statistically significant; that is, given a *non*significant test of interaction, only main effects would be tested. Given a significant test of interaction, the tests of the simple effects would become more important than the tests of main effects. A significant interaction means that there *are* different patterns of relationships between one independent variable and the dependent variable, depending on the level of the second variable. The tests for simple effects are done to see in which rows (or columns) a relationship between one independent variable and the dependent variable exists.

The mean square for an interaction in a two-factor design is symbolized as $\overline{MS_{AB}}$. Its defining formula is

$$MS_{AB} = \frac{SS_{AB}}{df_{AB}}$$

$$= \frac{n\overset{a}{\underset{j}{\Sigma}}\overset{b}{\underset{k}{\Sigma}}(\bar{X}_{.jk} - \bar{X}_{.j.} - \bar{X}_{..k} + \bar{X}_{...})^2}{(a-1)(b-1)}.$$

The formula for MS_{AB} is complicated by its more complex meaning. Briefly, the MS_{AB} is the variance between cells after the variability due to row effects and column effects (separate effects of both independent variables) has been removed. What is left is the way the two variables interact (plus random variability).

Interpreting Interactions There are times when an interaction can eclipse a main effect. For example, the simple effects of variable B at two different levels of variable A could be opposite to each other. Table 15.5 shows a pattern of cell means that would result in no significant main effects for the B variable but would probably result in a significant test of the simple effects of B at each level of A. In Table 15.5 the two levels of A present opposite relationships between the B variable and the dependent variable. Such a difference in simple effects would probably result in a significant interaction (depending on the size of the within-cell variability which is not shown in the table). The significant interaction would signal the necessity of testing for the effects of the B variable separately at each level of A. Just looking at the main effect of B, it

TABLE 15.5
Pattern of an interaction that would eclipse a main effect for the B variable

	B_1	B_2	B_3	
A_1	$\bar{X}_{.11}$ $= 2$	$\bar{X}_{.12}$ $= 4$	$\bar{X}_{.13}$ $= 6$	$\bar{X}_{.1.} = 4$
A_2	$\bar{X}_{.21}$ $= 8$	$\bar{X}_{.22}$ $= 6$	$\bar{X}_{.23}$ $= 4$	$\bar{X}_{.2.} = 6$
	$\bar{X}_{..1} = 5$	$\bar{X}_{..2} = 5$	$\bar{X}_{..3} = 5$	

would appear as though variable B is not related to the dependent variable. This would give an erroneous impression of no relationship between the variables.

It is not always the case that interactions obscure main effects. For example, a significant interaction could result from differences across levels of B that are stronger at some levels of A than at others, but with all differences in the same direction. This is the case in Table 15.4 for the simple effects of problem complexity.

Conclusions from statistically significant interactions take the following general verbal form: "The pattern (or extent) of effects of variable B on the dependent variable differs, depending on the level of variable A."

In the anxiety and problem complexity example, a significant interaction would be verbalized as: "The pattern (or extent) of effects of problem complexity on errors in problem solutions differs depending on the level of anxiety within the subjects." Conversely: "The pattern (or extent) of effects of anxiety on errors in problem solutions differs depending on the level of problem complexity."

When people speak of humans as being very complex, they are speaking about, among other things, interaction effects. For example, you might be flattered by a compliment from a friend, but angered if the same compliment were to come from a salesperson trying to get you to buy something. The effects of a variable (e.g., how people speak to you, and how you then respond) often vary, depending on the status of other variables (such as your relationship to the person). What looks like unpredictable behavior can sometimes be recognized as predictable interactions. Thus, analysis of interactions is an important part of psychological research. Testing for interaction effects is consequently an important statistical technique.

In testing for an interaction effect, MS_{AB} is tested over MS_w in the form of the usual F ratio.

MS$_w$ IN THE TWO-FACTOR DESIGN In a one-factor design, the error term

$$MS_w = \frac{SS_w}{df_w}$$

$$= \frac{SS_w}{g(n-1)}$$

$$= s_w{}^2$$

is the average within-groups variance, where each group is a level of the single independent variable. The variance within a single level is a sample of random variance. MS_w is the average of the samples of random variance taken over all levels. So, for example, if there were three levels of the one independent variable in a one-factor design, there would be three variance estimates computed and averaged to obtain $s_w^2 = MS_w$. Each variance estimate would have $n-1$ degrees of freedom, so that the total degrees of freedom for MS_w in a one-factor design with three levels of the factor would be

$$df_w = g(n-1)$$

$$= 3(n-1).$$

In a two-factor design, the within-group variance estimates would again be averaged. But each variance estimate would be taken from within a *cell*, rather than within a level of one variable. Thus, if there were three levels of one variable and four levels of another, there would be $a \cdot b = 3 \cdot 4 = 12$ variance estimates computed within the 12 cells of the data matrix, each having $n-1$ degrees of freedom. The 12 variance estimates would be averaged, and the MS_w would have been computed with

$$df_w = ab(n-1)$$

$$= 12(n-1).$$

Remember the form of the variance estimate. For a single cell, say cell A_jB_k, the variance estimate is

$$s_{jk}^2 = \frac{\sum_{i}^{n} (X_{ijk} - \bar{X}_{\cdot jk})^2}{n-1}.$$

The average of all the variance estimates in a two-factor design yielding MS_w is

$$MS_w = \frac{1}{ab} \sum_{j}^{a} \sum_{k}^{b} \frac{\sum_{i}^{n} (X_{ijk} - \bar{X}_{\cdot jk})^2}{n-1} \tag{15.4}$$

$$= \frac{\sum_{i}^{n} \sum_{j}^{a} \sum_{k}^{b} (X_{ijk} - \bar{X}_{\cdot jk})^2}{ab(n-1)}.$$

Equation (15.4) is the defining formula for MS_w in a two-factor design. The numerator

$$SS_w = \sum_{i}^{n} \sum_{j}^{a} \sum_{k}^{b} (X_{ijk} - \bar{X}_{\cdot jk})^2$$

is the within-cells sum of squares, and the denominator

$$df_w = ab(n-1)$$

is the within-cells degrees of freedom.

F TESTS IN THE TWO-FACTOR DESIGN Given two independent variables in an analysis of variance design, you would do an F test for a main effect of A; an F test for a main effect of B; an F test for an interaction. If the test for an interaction were signifcant, you would then test for simple effects of either variable.

The degrees of freedom for the respective effects are:

$$df_A = a - 1,$$

$$df_B = b - 1,$$

$$df_{AB} = (a-1)(b-1).$$

The degrees of freedom for the mean square within cells, MS_w, is

$$df_w = ab(n-1).$$

Each effect is tested in an F ratio in which the mean square for the effect is in the numerator and MS_w is in the denominator.

$$F = \frac{MS_{effect}}{MS_w}.$$

Each resulting F ratio is compared with a tabled critical value using the degrees of freedom for the effect and the degrees of freedom within cells to find the critical value of F. For example, testing for the effect of variable A, an F ratio would be computed,

$$F = \frac{MS_A}{MS_w},$$

and tested against the value found in the F table at $(a-1)$ and $ab(n-1)$ degrees of freedom. For the test of interaction the F ratio would be

$$F = \frac{MS_{AB}}{MS_w},$$

with $(a-1)(b-1)$ and $ab(n-1)$ degrees of freedom. As discussed in Chapter 13, the critical value is usually selected so that the Type I error probability is .05.

For the simple effects the degrees of freedom are precisely the same as for the corresponding main effects. For example, the degrees of freedom for the simple effect of A at the first level of B are

$$df_{A_{b_1}} = df_A$$

$$= a - 1.$$

The same degrees of freedom, $a-1$, are used for testing the simple effects of A at each level of B. Similarly, for the simple effects of B

$$df_{B_{a_1}} = b - 1,$$

$$df_{B_{a_2}} = b - 1.$$

The F ratio for each simple effect is tested over the same value of MS_w with the same degrees of freedom as for the corresponding main effect.

COMPUTATION IN THE TWO-FACTOR DESIGN
Equations (15.2), (15.3), and (15.4) presented the respective defining formulas for MS_A, MS_B, and MS_w. In practice, these defining formulas would be replaced by equivalent computational formulas. In this section, the computational formulas for a two-factor design are presented.

Table 15.6 offers the general summary table for a two-factor analysis of variance, detailing the computational formulas for testing the main effects and interaction.

Table 15.7 offers some hypothetical data and Table 15.8 offers a useful way of re-expressing and summarizing the data. Table 15.9 presents the specific summary table with the mean squares and F ratios for the data of Tables 15.7 and 15.8.

You should pause and examine Tables 15.8 and 15.9, understanding the five basic sums at the bottom of Table 15.8. These five sums are the only components in the computational formulas used in Table 15.9.

The two main effects, A and B, are each tested against the tabled critical value of F, for 2 and 36 degrees of freedom (in Table VII in Appendix B).

TABLE 15.6
General summary table for a two-factor analysis of variance, showing formulas used in computing the table entries

Sources of Variance	Sums of Squares	Degrees of Freedom	Mean Squares	F
A	$\dfrac{\sum\limits_{j}^{a}\left(\sum\limits_{i}^{n}\sum\limits_{k}^{b}X_{ijk}\right)^2}{nb} - \dfrac{\left(\sum\limits_{i}^{n}\sum\limits_{j}^{a}\sum\limits_{k}^{b}X_{ijk}\right)^2}{nab}$	$a-1$	$\dfrac{SS_A}{a-1}$	$\dfrac{MS_A}{MS_w}$
B	$\dfrac{\sum\limits_{k}^{b}\left(\sum\limits_{i}^{n}\sum\limits_{j}^{a}X_{ijk}\right)^2}{na} - \dfrac{\left(\sum\limits_{i}^{n}\sum\limits_{j}^{a}\sum\limits_{k}^{b}X_{ijk}\right)^2}{nab}$	$b-1$	$\dfrac{SS_B}{b-1}$	$\dfrac{MS_B}{MS_w}$
AB interaction	$\dfrac{\sum\limits_{j}^{a}\sum\limits_{k}^{b}\left(\sum\limits_{i}^{n}X_{ijk}\right)^2}{n} - \dfrac{\sum\limits_{j}^{a}\left(\sum\limits_{i}^{n}\sum\limits_{k}^{b}X_{ijk}\right)^2}{nb}$ $-\dfrac{\sum\limits_{k}^{b}\left(\sum\limits_{i}^{n}\sum\limits_{j}^{a}X_{ijk}\right)^2}{na} + \dfrac{\left(\sum\limits_{i}^{n}\sum\limits_{j}^{a}\sum\limits_{k}^{b}X_{ijk}\right)^2}{nab}$	$(a-1)(b-1)$	$\dfrac{SS_{AB}}{(a-1)(b-1)}$	$\dfrac{MS_{AB}}{MS_w}$
Within cells	$\sum\limits_{i}^{n}\sum\limits_{j}^{a}\sum\limits_{k}^{b}X_{ijk}^2 - \dfrac{\sum\limits_{j}^{a}\sum\limits_{k}^{b}\left(\sum\limits_{i}^{n}X_{ijk}\right)^2}{n}$	$ab(n-1)$	$\dfrac{SS_w}{ab(n-1)}$	
Total	$\sum\limits_{i}^{n}\sum\limits_{j}^{a}\sum\limits_{k}^{b}X_{ijk}^2 - \dfrac{\left(\sum\limits_{i}^{n}\sum\limits_{j}^{a}\sum\limits_{k}^{b}X_{ijk}\right)^2}{nab}$	$abn-1$		

TABLE 15.7

Hypothetical data in a two-factor design

	B_1	B_2	B_3
A_1	1 3 5 3 3	0 1 0 3 1	7 4 5 5 4
A_2	0 1 1 1 2	1 1 0 0 3	3 1 3 1 2
A_3	2 4 2 1 1	2 2 4 4 3	5 6 7 6 6

Using a Type I error probability of .05, the critical value for both tests is 3.26. The degrees of freedom for interaction are 4. Looking at 4 and 36 degrees of freedom, the critical value for the interaction at the .05 level is found to be 2.63. The critical values for a .01 probability of a Type I error are 5.25 for the two main effects and 3.89 for the interaction.

The results, detailed in Table 15.9, show that the F for the A effect is 17.76, and the F for the B effect is 25.96, both significant at better than the .01 level. Thus, we can conclude that both independent variables are related to the dependent variable. But the interaction effect with an F of 4.79 is also significant. Consequently the simple effects become more important for drawing conclusions than the main effects.

The main effects indicate whether each independent variable, A and B, is related to the dependent variable. But a significant interaction can mean that there is a relationship between variable B and the dependent variable, but only at some levels of A; or else there is a relationship between B and the dependent variable at all levels of A, but the relationship is different at different levels of A. A test of simple effects for variable B, at each level of A, will indicate at which levels of A it is appropriate to conclude that there is a relationship between variable B and the dependent variable.

Table 15.10 presents the analysis of simple effects for the B variable for the data in Tables 15.7 and 15.8. The table indicates that there are significant simple effects at levels A_1 and A_3, but level A_2 does not reach significance. Therefore, we conclude that variable B is related to the dependent variable, but only at levels A_1 and A_3. There is no evidence of a relationship between variable B and the dependent variable at level A_2.

TABLE 15.8

Convenient form for listing and summarizing the hypothetical data in a two-factor design (preparatory to computing the mean squares). The data in this table are from Table 15.7.

	B_1	B_2	B_3	
	1	0	7	
	3	1	4	
	$5\ \bar{X}_{.11} = 3$	$0\ \bar{X}_{.12} = 1$	$5\ \bar{X}_{.13} = 5$	
	3	3	5	
	3	1	4	
	$\sum\limits_i^n X_{i11} = 15$	$\sum\limits_i^n X_{i12} = 5$	$\sum\limits_i^n X_{i13} = 25$	$\sum\limits_{i\ k}^{n\ b} X_{i1k} = 45$
	0	1	3	
	1	1	1	
	$1\ \bar{X}_{.21} = 1$	$0\ \bar{X}_{.22} = 1$	$3\ \bar{X}_{.23} = 2$	
	1	0	1	
	2	3	2	
	$\sum\limits_i^n X_{i21} = 5$	$\sum\limits_i^n X_{i22} = 5$	$\sum\limits_i^n X_{i23} = 10$	$\sum\limits_{i\ k}^{n\ b} X_{i2k} = 20$
	2	2	5	
	4	2	6	
	$2\ \bar{X}_{.31} = 2$	$4\ \bar{X}_{.32} = 3$	$7\ \bar{X}_{.33} = 6$	
	1	4	6	
	1	3	6	
	$\sum\limits_i^n X_{i31} = 10$	$\sum\limits_i^n X_{i32} = 15$	$\sum\limits_i^n X_{i33} = 30$	$\sum\limits_{i\ k}^{n\ b} X_{i3k} = 55$
	$\sum\limits_{i\ j}^{n\ a} X_{ij1} = 30$	$\sum\limits_{i\ j}^{n\ a} X_{ij2} = 25$	$\sum\limits_{i\ j}^{n\ a} X_{ij3} = 65$	$\sum\limits_{i\ j\ k}^{n\ a\ b} X_{ijk} = 120$
	$\bar{X}_{..1} = 2$	$\bar{X}_{..2} = 1.67$	$\bar{X}_{..3} = 4.33$	

Basic sums in the summary table formulas:

$$\left(\sum\limits_{i\ j\ k}^{n\ a\ b} X_{ijk}\right)^2 = (120)^2 = 14400$$

$$\sum\limits_j^a \left(\sum\limits_{i\ k}^{b\ n} X_{ijk}\right)^2 = (45)^2 + (20)^2 + (55)^2 = 5450$$

$$\sum\limits_k^b \left(\sum\limits_{i\ j}^{n\ a} X_{ijk}\right)^2 = (30)^2 + (25)^2 + (65)^2 = 5750$$

$$\sum\limits_{j\ k}^{a\ b} \left(\sum\limits_i^n X_{ijk}\right)^2 = (15)^2 + (5)^2 + \cdots + (30)^2 = 2250$$

$$\sum\limits_{i\ j\ k}^{n\ a\ b} X_{ijk}^2 = 1^2 + 3^2 + 5^2 + \cdots + 7^2 + 6^2 + 6^2 = 494$$

(Note that

$n = 5$

$a = 3$

$b = 3$)

TABLE 15.9
Summary table of the two-factor analysis of variance for the data in Tables 15.7 and 15.8. The formulas for this table appear in the general summary table, Table 15.6.

Sources of Variance	Sums of Squares	Degrees of Freedom	Mean Squares	F
A	$\dfrac{5450}{15} - \dfrac{14400}{45} = 43.33$	$(3-1) = 2$	$\dfrac{43.33}{2} = 21.67$	$\dfrac{21.67}{1.22} = 17.76^*$
B	$\dfrac{5750}{15} - \dfrac{14400}{45} = 63.33$	$(3-1) = 2$	$\dfrac{63.33}{2} = 31.67$	$\dfrac{31.67}{1.22} = 25.96^*$
AB interaction	$\dfrac{2250}{5} - \dfrac{5450}{15} - \dfrac{5750}{15} + \dfrac{14400}{45} = 23.34$	$(3-1)(3-1) = 4$	$\dfrac{23.34}{4} = 5.84$	$\dfrac{5.84}{1.22} = 4.79^*$
Within cells	$494 - \dfrac{2250}{5} = 44$	$3 \cdot 3(5-1) = 36$	$\dfrac{44}{36} = 1.22$	
Total	$494 - \dfrac{14400}{45} = 174$	$3 \cdot 3 \cdot 5 - 1 = 44$		

*$p > .01$.

TABLE 15.10
Summary table of tests of simple effects of variable B in a two-factor design. Data of Tables 15.7 and 15.8.

Level of Test of B	Sums of Squares	Degrees of Freedom	Mean Squares	F
B at A_1	$\dfrac{\sum\limits_{k}^{b}\left(\sum\limits_{i}^{n} X_{i1k}\right)^2}{n} - \dfrac{\left(\sum\limits_{i}^{n}\sum\limits_{k}^{b} X_{i1k}\right)^2}{nb}$	$b-1$	$\dfrac{SS_{B_{a_1}}}{b-1}$	$\dfrac{MS_{B_{a_1}}}{MS_w}$
	$\dfrac{(15)^2 + (5)^2 + (25)^2}{5} - \dfrac{(45)^2}{15} = 40$	2	20.00	16.39^*
B at A_2	$\dfrac{\sum\limits_{k}^{b}\left(\sum\limits_{i}^{n} X_{i2k}\right)^2}{n} - \dfrac{\left(\sum\limits_{i}^{n}\sum\limits_{k}^{b} X_{i2k}\right)^2}{nb}$	$b-1$	$\dfrac{SS_{B_{a_2}}}{b-1}$	$\dfrac{MS_{B_{a_2}}}{MS_w}$
	$\dfrac{(5)^2 + (5)^2 + (10)^2}{5} - \dfrac{(20)^2}{15} = 3.33$	2	1.67	1.37
B at A_3	$\dfrac{\sum\limits_{k}^{b}\left(\sum\limits_{i}^{n} X_{i3k}\right)^2}{n} - \dfrac{\left(\sum\limits_{i}^{n}\sum\limits_{k}^{b} X_{i3k}\right)^2}{nb}$	$b-1$	$\dfrac{SS_{B_{a_3}}}{b-1}$	$\dfrac{MS_{B_{a_3}}}{MS_w}$
	$\dfrac{(10)^2 + (15)^2 + (30)^2}{5} - \dfrac{(55)^2}{15} = 43.33$	2	21.67	17.76^*
Within cells	$\sum\limits_{i}^{a}\sum\limits_{j}^{b}\sum\limits_{k}^{n} X_{ijk}^2 - \dfrac{\sum\limits_{i}^{a}\sum\limits_{k}^{b}\left(\sum\limits_{i}^{n} X_{ijk}\right)^2}{n}$	$ab(n-1)$	$\dfrac{SS_w}{ab(n-1)}$	
	$494 - \dfrac{2250}{5} = 44$	36	1.22	

*$p < .01$.

DESIGNS WITH MORE THAN TWO FACTORS Three-factor designs are not uncommon. Occasionally we find a four-factor design. More than four factors in one analysis of variance design is unusual.

In multiple-factor designs we have as many main effects to test as there are variables, plus one or more interactions. In a three-factor design there are, in addition to the three main effects, three interactions between two factors ($AB, AC,$ and BC) and one three-factor interaction (ABC). Although three-factor interactions are interpretable, interactions involving more than three factors generally defy coherent interpretation.

As long as different subjects are used in each cell of the matrix, the testing of each effect and each interaction follows the general pattern suggested in this chapter, regardless of the number of factors. Each mean square for each effect, and each mean square for each interaction, is placed over the same within-cells mean square, and an F ratio is computed for each such ratio. The F ratios each have the form MS_{effect}/MS_w or $MS_{interaction}/MS_w$.

The value of MS_w is always obtained as the average within-cells variance. The number of cells depends on the number of factors and the number of levels for each factor. For a three-factor design there would be $a \cdot b \cdot c$ cells, each with $n-1$ degrees of freedom. The degrees of freedom for MS_w would thus be $abc(n-1)$. For a four-factor design, the degrees of freedom for MS_w would be $abcd(n-1)$. The degrees of freedom for variable A would always be $(a-1)$, regardless of the number of other factors, and $(b-1)$ for variable B, etc. The degrees of freedom for each interaction would have the form $(a-1)(b-1)$ for a two-factor interaction and $(a-1)(b-1)(c-1)$ for a three-factor interaction, regardless of the total number of factors in the design. Each main effect and each interaction would be tested against the tabled value of F found under the degrees of freedom for the main effect or interaction and the degrees of freedom within cells.

REPEATED MEASURES In this chapter, and the two previous chapters on analysis of variance, it was assumed that there were different subjects in every level of a variable; that is, each subject appeared in only one group, under one condition, and provided only one score for the analysis of variance. The subjects in different groups might have been exposed to, for example, different levels of anxiety while solving problems. The question might have been whether or not different levels of anxiety have different effects on the ability to solve problems. The one score from each subject could have been the number of errors in solving a set of problems.

But what if the question was whether experience with these kinds of problems makes them easier to solve? In that case, it would be useful and economical to use the same subjects throughout the experiment, giving the same subjects additional sets of problems. Each subject would be exposed to all levels of the independent variable. The first time they would be in the "zero previous experience" condition. The next time they would be in the "one previous experience" condition, and so on. This type of design is called a **repeated-measures design.** Whenever the same subjects are used at all levels of an independent variable the design is called a repeated-measures design. When different subjects are used in each level, the design is called a **completely randomized design** because a new random sample of subjects is selected for each level. Completely randomized designs are conceptually easier to work with. With repeated-measures designs, the F ratios involve varied denominator mean squares, not just the same MS$_w$ for all F tests. Repeated-measures designs are covered in more advanced texts.

STATISTICAL MODELS IN ANALYSIS OF VARIANCE In Chapter 14, when discussing a one-factor analysis of variance, two sources of variance were identified. One was random or error variance (symbolized as σ_e^2) and the other was treatment variance (symbolized as σ_{tr}^2). It was assumed that these are the only sources of variance contributing to score variability in the one-factor design. This assumption was possible only because error variance was assumed to include a wide variety of influences (subject variability, measurement error, and influences from uncontrolled variables).

It is common in advanced statistics texts to refer to models for various statistical designs. A **statistical model** is an equation which specifies the influences contributing to variability among the dependent variable values. It takes the form of an equation between a hypothetical individual score, some X value, and all the potential influences on the score. The most common models simply add all sources of variability to the average score in the population. The treatments, their interactions, and random variability (error variance), are some of the potential influences on the scores, supplying the reasons for any observed differences between the individual scores and the average score. In the case of the one-factor completely randomized design, the model is given by Equation (15.5).

$$X_{ij} = \text{average score} + \text{treatment effects} + \text{error.} \qquad (15.5)$$

For a two-factor completely randomized design, an appropriate model would be

$$X_{ijk} = \text{average score} + \text{treatment effects of } A + \text{treatment effects of } B$$
$$+ \text{interaction effects } AB + \text{error.} \qquad (15.6)$$

Models of statistics are in one sense somewhat arbitrary. As noted above, the error term could have been expanded and restated as several separate sources of variability, such as subject variability, measurement error, and influences from uncontrolled variables. Each of these separate sources of variability could be stated as an individual component in the model. For example, we could have as a model:

$$X_{ijk} = \text{average score} + \text{treatment effects of } A + \text{treatment effects of } B + \text{interaction effects } AB + \text{subject variability} + \text{measurement error} + \text{influences from uncontrolled variables.}$$

Each of the components specified in a model is a potential source of influence on score variability. These additional components are unspecified in completely randomized designs, because models are generally only useful when there is some way of estimating each of the separate components of the model. For example, MS_w is used to estimate the contribution due to error in the models for completely randomized designs expressed by Equations (15.5) and (15.6). It was also seen, in the preceding chapter, how the contribution of treatment variance could be isolated and estimated. But there is no way, in completely randomized designs, to estimate subject variability and measurement error as separate components. Conceptual isolation of a source of variance is generally not useful unless its size can be estimated.

In more advanced texts, designs with repeated measures on the same subjects are presented which allow for the separate estimation of the contributions due to subject variability. The models for these repeated-measures designs then include subject variability as separate components. For the completely randomized designs presented in this text, subject variability cannot be estimated, and so does not appear as a component in the models.

There is a number of advantages to being able to specify the components of a model, each of which can be estimated. One such advantage is the resulting possibility of estimating the proportion of variance associated with different variables; that is, the formulas for the estimate of the intraclass correlation coefficient, for omega-squared and other similar statistics, are derivable from the estimated components of the model.

Omega-Squared in the Two-Factor Design A model for the one-factor, completely randomized design was implicitly presented in Chapter 14 when discussing estimates of the degree of relationship. Although the word model was not used, the components of the model, σ_e^2 and σ_{tr}^2 were isolated in order to derive the desired formulas. In this way, the model was implicitly used for estimating degree of relationship. In deriving formulas for estimating the degree of relationship in multifactor analyses of variance, it would again be necessary to use the components in the specific models for the specific statistical designs.

The logic would be the same as the logic in the previous chapter, in which the one-factor design was discussed. Some estimate would be obtained for the variability contributed by a specific treatment effect, or interaction, and then this would be placed over the sum of all the estimates of variability from all contributing variance components. For example, in a two-factor completely randomized design, an estimate of the proportion of variance in the dependent variable associated with treatment variable A could take the form:

$$\text{Estimate of proportion of variance associated with variable } A = \frac{\sigma_{tr_a}^2}{\sigma_{tot}^2}$$

$$= \frac{\sigma_{tr_a}^2}{\sigma_{tr_a}^2 + \sigma_{tr_b}^2 + \sigma_{inter_{ab}}^2 + \sigma_{error}^2}.$$

The details of isolating components of variance and the discussions of corrections for bias would all follow the outline of the discussion found in Chapter 14. Bypassing the detail of these procedures, the results would offer the following equations for the relevant omega squares, given a two-factor, completely randomized design:

$$\omega_A^2 = \frac{(a-1)(F_A-1)}{(a-1)(F_A-1) + (b-1)(F_B-1) + (a-1)(b-1)(F_{AB}-1) + abn}, \tag{15.7}$$

$$\omega_B^2 = \frac{(b-1)(F_B-1)}{(a-1)(F_A-1) + (b-1)(F_B-1) + (a-1)(b-1)(F_{AB}-1) + abn}, \tag{15.8}$$

$$\omega_{AB}^2 = \frac{(a-1)(b-1)(F_{AB}-1)}{(a-1)(F_A-1) + (b-1)(F_B-1) + (a-1)(b-1)(F_{AB}-1) + abn}. \tag{15.9}$$

In a multifactor design the computation of all the omega-squares would permit a comparison among the significant factors to see which factors contributed more heavily to score variability. The omega-squared values would indicate which factors had stronger relationships with the dependent variable.

Omega-squared is an estimate of the proportion of variability in the dependent variable associated with a particular independent variable (or interaction). Consequently, omega-squared would not be computed for non-significant effects. Only significant sources of variance are sources for which the question of extent of relationship could make sense. For the analysis of variance summarized in Table 15.9, omega-squared would be computed for all the effects.

Looking at Table 15.9, the values would be found for using Equations (15.7), (15.8), and (15.9) to estimate the omega-squares:

$$\omega_A^2 = \frac{2(17.76 - 1)}{2(17.76 - 1) + 2(25.96 - 1) + 4(4.79 - 1) + 45}$$

$$= \frac{33.52}{143.60}$$

$$= .23,$$

$$\omega_B^2 = \frac{2(25.96 - 1)}{2(17.76 - 1) + 2(25.96 - 1) + 4(4.79 - 1) + 45}$$

$$= \frac{49.92}{143.60}$$

$$= .35,$$

$$\omega_{AB}^2 = \frac{4(4.79 - 1)}{2(17.76 - 1) + 2(25.96 - 1) + 4(4.79 - 1) + 45}$$

$$= \frac{15.16}{143.60}$$

$$= .11.$$

The computations offer an estimate of 23% of the variance in the dependent variable associated with differences in levels of variable A, and 35% of the variance in the dependent variable associated with differences in levels of variable B. The interaction between the two variables was estimated to account for 11% of the variance in dependent variable scores.

The F tests indicated that the interaction is significant and suggested the need for a simple effects analysis. But the omega-squared analysis indicates that the main effects are those associated with the greatest amount of variance. The main effects should therefore not be excluded from a discussion of the relationships between the variables in the study. The simple effects, though important, are part of an interaction which accounts for less of the variance than each of the main effects.

MULTIPLE COMPARISONS IN THE TWO-FACTOR DESIGN In the previous chapter, Equation (14.10) offered a general equation for making multiple comparisons:

$$(\bar{X}_{.j} - \bar{X}_{.j'}) \geq t_{crit} \sqrt{\frac{2MS_w}{nb}}. \qquad [14.10]$$

In a two-factor design for any arbitrary jth level of A, $\bar{X}_{.j}$ is the mean. For some other level of A, $\bar{X}_{.j'}$ is the mean. Thus, for multiple comparisons of the *A* factor in a two-factor, completely randomized design, Equation (14.10) would be restated as Equation (15.10).

$$(\bar{X}_{.j.} - \bar{X}_{.j'.}) \geq t_{\text{crit}} \sqrt{\frac{2MS_w}{nb}} .$$ (15.10)

Note that *nb* replaces *n* for the two-factor case, because each mean for a level of *A* in a two-factor design is computed from *nb* scores, where *b* is the number of levels of *B*, each containing *n* scores. For multiple comparisons of the *B* factor in a two-factor, completely randomized design, Equation (14.10) would be restated as in Equation (15.11).

$$(\bar{X}_{..k} - \bar{X}_{..k'}) \geq t_{\text{crit}} \sqrt{\frac{2MS_w}{na}} .$$ (15.11)

To illustrate the use of Equation (15.11), the data of Tables 15.8 and 15.9 will be used.

Illustration of Multiple Comparisons for a Main Effect
The means for the three levels of variable *B* can be found in Table 15.8.

$$\bar{X}_{..1} = 2.00,$$

$$\bar{X}_{..2} = 1.67,$$

$$\bar{X}_{..3} = 4.33.$$

Using a critical value of .05 two tailed, the critical value for equation (15.11) will be found in the *t* Table (Table IV in Appendix B). The degrees of freedom for entering the *t* Table are the degrees of freedom for MS_w, which in this example are $ab(n-1) = 36$. The critical value as given in Table IV is 2.042.

The differences between means for the levels of *B* are tested against Equation (15.11). For this example, Equation (15.11) yields the value

$$t_{\text{crit}} \sqrt{\frac{2MS_w}{na}} = 2.042 \sqrt{\frac{2(1.22)}{5 \cdot 3}}$$

$$= .82.$$

The differences between means contrasted with the value of Equation (15.11) take the following form:

$$\bar{X}_{..1} - \bar{X}_{..2} = 2.00 - 1.67 = 0.33, \qquad |0.33| \neq .82;$$

$$\bar{X}_{..1} - \bar{X}_{..3} = 2.00 - 4.33 = -2.33, \qquad |2.33| \geq .82;$$

$$\bar{X}_{..2} - \bar{X}_{..3} = 1.67 - 4.33 = -2.66, \qquad |2.66| \geq .82.$$

Thus, the significant multiple comparisons are B_1 versus B_3 and B_2 versus B_3.

If you wished to control the experimentwise error rate and use the Dunn table, the change would be in the value of t_{crit} in Equation (15.11). For 36 degrees of freedom with an experimentwise Type I error probability of .05, and three comparisons, the Dunn table lists, at 30 degrees of freedom (the closest smaller degrees of freedom listed), 2.54. The right-hand side of Equation (15.11) would then have the values

$$t_{crit}\sqrt{\frac{2MS_w}{na}} = 2.54\sqrt{\frac{2(1.22)}{5 \cdot 3}}$$

$$= 1.02.$$

The same differences that surpass .82 (2.33 and 2.66) also surpass 1.02; and the one difference that does not surpass 1.02 (.33) also does not surpass .82. In this instance, the conclusions would be the same with or without controlling the experimentwise error probability.

Illustration of Multiple Comparisons for Simple Effects Given a significant interaction and a discovery of some levels of variable A containing significant B effects, multiple comparisons should be done at those levels of A which show significant effects of B. Therefore, a proper analysis of the data in Table 15.7 would consist of **multiple comparisons of simple effects** of B at levels A_1 and A_3. That analysis follows.

When doing multiple comparisons with simple effects in a two-factor design, the only change in Equations (15.10) and (15.11) is that the denominator under the radical is simplified to n since there are only n scores used for each mean of one variable at a single level of another variable. Multiple comparisons for the A variable at the kth level of variable B would take the form of Equation (15.12).

$$(\bar{X}_{.jk} - \bar{X}_{.j'k}) \geq t_{crit}\sqrt{\frac{2MS_w}{n}}. \tag{15.12}$$

Similarly, multiple comparisons for the B variable at the jth level of variable A would take the form of Equation (15.13).

$$(\bar{X}_{.jk} - \bar{X}_{.jk'}) \geq t_{crit}\sqrt{\frac{2MS_w}{n}}. \tag{15.13}$$

The data of Table 15.8 again offer the needed values for means. For each cell within level A_1, the means are

$$\bar{X}_{.11} = 3,$$

$$\bar{X}_{.12} = 1,$$

$$\bar{X}_{.13} = 5.$$

Equation (15.13) for this example would have the values

$$t_{crit}\sqrt{\frac{2MS_w}{n}} = 2.042\sqrt{\frac{2(1.22)}{5}}$$

$$= 1.43.$$

368 Two-Factor Analysis of Variance

Note that the same mean square is used, which means that the same degrees of freedom are used to enter the t table. Thus, the comparison for simple effects is almost identical to that for main effects, with n replacing na as the only difference.

The comparisons at level A_1 are:

$$\bar{X}._{11} - \bar{X}._{12} = 3 - 1 = 2, \qquad |2| \geq 1.43;$$
$$\bar{X}._{11} - \bar{X}._{13} = 3 - 5 = -2, \qquad |-2| \geq 1.43,$$
$$\bar{X}._{12} - \bar{X}._{13} = 1 - 5 = -4, \qquad |-4| \geq 1.43.$$

Thus, all comparisons are significant at level A_1.

For level A_3 the means are:

$$\bar{X}._{31} = 2,$$
$$\bar{X}._{32} = 3,$$
$$\bar{X}._{33} = 6.$$

The comparisons at level A_3 are:

$$\bar{X}._{31} - \bar{X}._{32} = 2 - 3 = -1, \qquad |-1| \not\geq 1.43;$$
$$\bar{X}._{31} - \bar{X}._{33} = 2 - 6 = -4, \qquad |-4| \geq 1.43;$$
$$\bar{X}._{32} - \bar{X}._{33} = 3 - 6 = -3, \qquad |-3| \geq 1.43.$$

Thus, at level A_3, the significant differences among levels of B are between levels 1 and 3 and levels 2 and 3.

As with the test of the main effect, a more conservative test could be done using the more conservative critical value of 2.54 (from the Dunn table). This would result in a test for each multiple comparison against the value

$$t_{crit}\sqrt{\frac{2MS_w}{n}} = 2.54\sqrt{\frac{2(1.22)}{5}}$$
$$= 1.77.$$

As with the test of the main effects, the same pattern of results would be obtained with the more conservative value, in this example.

Basically, the analysis of multiple comparisons with simple effects showed that for the simple effects of B at level A_1 all paired comparisons are significant, but at level A_3 only two of the three comparisons are significant. The main effects analysis duplicates the pattern at level A_3.

The analysis of simple effects yields a richer analysis than the analysis of main effects. But an analysis of simple effects is only justified following a significant F test of the interaction.

SENTENCE COMPLETIONS

1. _____ variables are often called factors.

2. A one-factor analysis of variance design is also called a one-_____ analysis of variance.

3. A two-factor design containing two _____of one variable and three of another is often called a two-by-three design.

4. In a two-factor design, the sum of all scores would be symbolized as _____ (indicate all of the subscripts).

5. A set of uniform conditions is called a _____.

6. The i subscript in X_{ijk} refers to _____, the j refers to levels of variable _____, and the k refers to levels of variable _____ .

7. The mean of the second level of B in a two-factor design is symbolized as _____ $= \sum_{i}^{n}\sum_{j}^{a} X_{ij2} \Big/ na$.

8. The omnibus F test of the different levels of variable A in a two-factor design is called a test of the _____ _____of A.

9. For a level of variable A in a two-factor design, the number of scores at each level is _____ .

10. There are times when it is desirable to examine effects of a variable separately at each level of another variable. These tests are called tests of _____ _____ .

11. The mean squares for each _____effect of _____ , each at a different _____, are symbolized in this text as MS_{Ab_1}, MS_{Ab_2}, etc.

12. An interaction implies that the level of one variable _____ _____ _____ .

13. Tests of simple effects are not done unless _____ _____ .

14. The tests for _____ _____are the

tests done to determine in which rows (or columns) a relationship between one independent variable and the dependent variable exists.

15. The mean square for _____ is the variance between cells, after the variability due to row effects and column effects have been removed.

16. There are times when an interaction can eclipse a _____ _____.

17. Conclusions from statistically significant interactions take the following general verbal form. "The pattern (or extent) of effects of variable A on the dependent variable _____ depending on _____ _____."

18. In testing for an interaction effect, the MS_{AB} is tested over _____ in the F ratio.

19. The degrees of freedom for the respective effects (assuming a two-factor design) are: $df_A =$ _____ ; $df_B =$ _____; $df_{AB} =$ _____; $df_w =$ _____.

20. In a completely randomized design, each effect is tested in an F ratio in which the mean square for the effect is in the numerator and _____ is in the denominator.

21. In a two-factor design, the test for the effect of variable A compares the computed value of F against a tabled value of F found at _____ and _____ degrees of freedom. The test for the effect of the interaction would have its computed F compared with the tabled F at _____ and _____ degrees of freedom.

22. Comparing the degrees of freedom for tests of main effects with the degrees of freedom for tests of simple effects, we would find that ____ _____.

23. A significant interaction can mean that there is a relationship between variable B and the dependent variable, but only _____ _____, or else there is a relationship between B and the dependent variable at all levels of A, but the relationship is _____ _____ . A test of simple effects for variable B, at each level of A, will indicate at which levels of A it is appropriate to conclude that _____ _____.

24. The value of MS_w is always obtained as the average _____ _____ .

25. Whenever the same subjects are used at all levels of an independent variable the design is called a _____ _____ design. When different subjects are used in each level, the design is called a _____ _____ design.

26. A statistical model is an equation which indicates the _____ _____among the dependent variable values.

27. Given a significant interaction, examination of the multiple comparisons among the levels of variable B should take place at the levels of the A variable which were shown to have _____.

28. The comparison for simple effects is almost identical to the comparison for main effects, with _____ as the only difference in the formula.

Answers 1. Independent   2. way   3. levels   4. $\sum\limits_{i}^{n}\sum\limits_{j}^{a}\sum\limits_{k}^{b}X_{ijk}$ 5. cell   6. subjects; A;

B 7. $\bar{X}_{..2}$ 8. main effect   9. nb 10. simple effects   11. simple; A; level of B 12. makes a difference in the pattern of effects of the other variable   13. the test for interactions is statistically significant   14. simple effects   15. interactions   16. main effect   17. differs; the level of variable B 18. MS_w 19. $(a-1)$; $(b-1)$; $(a-1)(b-1)$; $ab(n-1)$ 20. MS_w 21. $(a-1)$; $ab(n-1)$; $(a-1)(b-1)$; $ab(n-1)$ 22. they are the same   23. at some levels of A; different at the different levels of A; there is a relationship between variable B and the dependent variable   24. within-cell variance   25. repeated measures; completely randomized   26. factors contributing to variability   27. significant B effects   28. n replacing na or nb

---

PROBLEMS   **1.** Assume the following matrix of data in a 3×4 analysis of variance with seven subjects in each cell.

Variable B

Variable A	B_1	B_2	B_3	B_4
	4	2	0	5
	3	2	0	6
	4	3	1	6
A_1	5	4	2	7
	4	5	3	8
	3	6	4	8
	5	6	4	9
	3	3	0	7
	4	4	0	7
	5	4	0	8
A_2	5	5	1	9
	5	6	2	10
	6	6	2	11
	7	7	2	11
	2	4	0	9
	4	5	1	10
	6	6	2	10
A_3	6	6	3	11
	6	6	4	12
	8	7	5	12
	10	8	6	13

(a) Do the analysis of variance, completing the usual summary table.
(b) Obtain the omega-squared values for the significant effects.
(c) Do the multiple comparisons on the main effects for A. Compare all the means for all levels of A with each other (there are three such comparisons). Use the critical value $\alpha_{pc} = .05$ (found in the t table) and repeat the multiple comparisons with $\alpha_{ew} = .05$ (found in the Dunn table).

2. Assume the following matrix of data in a 2×3 analysis of variance with 5 subjects in each cell.

Variable A	Variable B		
	B_1	B_2	B_3
	2	4	4
	3	4	5
A_1	4	5	6
	5	6	7
	6	6	8
	5	4	1
	5	4	2
A_2	6	6	3
	7	8	4
	7	8	5

(a) Do the analysis of variance, completing the usual summary table.
(b) In part (a), the interaction will be found to be significant. Therefore, test the simple effects of variable A at each of the three levels of variable B. Summarize your work in a table like Table 15.10 in the text. Note that your formulas should have $\overset{a}{\Sigma}$ in place of $\overset{b}{\Sigma}$, since Table 15.10 presents the analysis of variable B at the different levels of variable A.
(c) As an exercise, now test the simple effects for variable B at each of the two levels of A. Then do multiple comparisons within the one level of A at which B will be found significant in the test of simple effects for variable B.

CHI-SQUARE

sixteen

In the previous sections of this text, two statistics were presented for testing whether there is a relationship between two variables. These two statistics are *t* tests and analysis of variance. For both of these statistics the dependent variable is always a score. The dependent variable could be the time to respond in a reaction-time task, the number of errors in solving a problem, an individual's weight, annual income, or grade-point average, etc. Each subject either offers a scoreable response or is measured in terms of some characteristic or achievement, such as income or grade-point average, with the measured variable offering the subject's score. The average score in each group is then compared to see if group membership (the independent variable) is related to the scores (the dependent variable).

This chapter discusses an additional statistic, called chi-square. The chi-square statistic is used when the data are categories rather than scores. For example, suppose a political scientist, or a social psychologist, wants to test whether social class is related to satisfaction with the performance of the current President of the United States. The researcher could categorize each member of a random sample of people in the United States as coming from one of three different socioeconomic classes (lower, middle, upper class), and then ask: "Are you satisfied with the performance of the President of the United States?"

The subjects' responses would be classified into one of three categories: yes, no, or don't know (d.k.). If the data were tabled, as in Table 16.1, there would be no scores to compare in the different socioeconomic groups.

If there were no scores to compare in the different socioeconomic groups, there would be no group means to compare with each other. What, then, would constitute the criterion for whether social class is related to type of response? The criterion measure would be relative frequency of category use, comparing the patterns of category use among the different socioeconomic classes. Each subject is jointly classified on the two variables (socioeconomic class and response category). The experimenter constructs a table listing the numbers of people in each socioeconomic

TABLE 16.1
Hypothetical data in response to the question: "Are you satisfied with the performance of the President of the United States?"

Lower Class	Middle Class	Upper Class
no	no	yes
d.k.	yes	yes
no	yes	d.k.
yes	no	yes
etc.	etc.	etc.

class that use each category. A table indicating the frequencies of outcomes that are jointly classified on two variables is called a **contingency table**. The existence of a relationship between the two variables is recognized when the classifications on one variable are related to (contingent on) the classifications on the other variable. Table 16.2 presents a contingency table containing hypothetical data for the example. Note that each subject's joint classification by social class and response places that subject in one and only one cell within the table. The number in each cell is the number of people classified as indicated by the row and column of the cell.

Table 16.2 offers a 3 × 3 table, since there are three levels of each variable. If there were five socioeconomic classes identified in the study, the table would be a 3 × 5 table. Suppose that a researcher were interested in whether socioeconomic class is related to whether or not people ever enter psychotherapy. A chi-square statistic could be used to evaluate the collected data. People in different socioeconomic classes would be dichotomized as having experienced psychotherapy or not. This would yield a 2 × 3 table if there were three socioeconomic classes, or a 2 × 5 table if there were five socioeconomic classes identified in the study.

Most independent variables are classified variables. Therefore, whenever there is no wide-ranging set of measurements for a dependent variable, just a nominally classified variable, the chi-square statistic should be considered. That is, when both variables are classified variables, the chi-square statistic may be appropriate. Restrictions on the use of chi-square are discussed later in this chapter.

TABLE 16.2
Hypothetical data in the form of a contingency table

		Class		
		Lower class	Middle class	Upper class
	Yes	228	243	194
Response	No	120	251	161
	D.K.	82	90	60

THE CHI-SQUARE STATISTIC AND THE NULL HYPOTHESIS The underlying question in chi-square tests is the same question as in *t* tests and omnibus *F* tests in analysis of variance. The question is, are the two variables related? In *t* tests and analysis of variance the relationship is identified through differences between mean *scores* in different groups. But there are no mean scores in chi-square tables. There are just *frequencies* in different cells, where each cell is a joint classification on two variables. The chi-square statistic offers a criterion for deciding when the classifications on the two variables are related.

As in the case of t tests and analysis of variance, it is necessary to first identify a pattern of random events under a null hypothesis; that is, an appropriate distribution of random events must be identified. If the results are unusual under an assumed null hypothesis distribution, then the null hypothesis of no relationship is rejected. The chi-square statistic, as described below, has a known distribution when the variables are not related. This chi-square distribution is used to select critical values. These critical values are used in the same manner as the critical values in the t table.

The chi-square formula, presented later in this chapter, converts the pattern of cell frequencies into the needed chi-square statistic. It can be intuitively helpful to know what kinds of patterns of cell frequencies do and do not yield statistically significant chi-square values. An example will be introduced for this purpose.

Assume that a female experimenter solicits contributions from 40 men, asking them to contribute to NOW, the National Organization for Women. Half the time, the experimenter dresses in a traditionally or stereotypically feminine fashion (flowered pattern chiffon fabric, high-heeled shoes), and half the time in a traditionally or stereotypically masculine fashion (a tweed fabric tailored suit, low-heeled oxfords). She wishes to know if the men's willingness to contribute to NOW is related to her attire. If there is no relationship between her attire and the men's willingness to contribute, what would be the expected pattern of frequencies? Table 16.3 presents one table of hypothetical data that would be consistent with no relationship between the variables.

Note that Table 16.3 offers totals for each level of classification on each variable in the margins of the table. These marginally placed totals of frequencies in each column and each row are called **marginal frequencies**. For example, Table 16.3 indicates that 20 of the requests were made

TABLE 16.3

Hypothetical data showing no relationship between experimenter's attire and men's willingness to contribute

		Attire		
		Feminine	Masculine	
Contribution	Yes	10	10	20
	No	10	10	20
		20	20	$N = 40$

in feminine and 20 in masculine attire (bottom of the table). Twenty of the potential contributors did contribute and 20 did not, as seen in the marginals on the right-hand side of the table.

If there was no relationship between the variables, the pattern seen in the marginal frequencies for one variable should be repeated at each level of the other variable. For example, in Table 16.3 there are equal numbers of people contributing and not contributing (seen in the right-hand marginals). Therefore, if there is no relationship between the variables, approximately that same equality of contributors and non-contributors should be seen in each column. The pattern of frequencies in the two columns within the table is identical to the pattern of marginal frequencies on the right-hand side of the table.

Suppose the experimenter had actually found only 10 people contributing, and 30 not contributing, as seen in the marginal frequencies of Table 16.4. In this case, a pattern of no relationship would be one in which the same one-to-three ratio (10:30) seen in the marginals for the contributions variable was seen again at each level of the attire variable. In Table 16.4 this is the case. Whether confronted by feminine or masculine attire, the ratio of non-contributors to contributors is again 1:3.

If the marginals were unequal for the different levels within *both* variables, the expectations for each cell would follow the proportions from both sets of marginal frequencies. A formula incorporating both sets of marginal frequencies is used to specify **expected frequencies**. The formula is presented as Equation (16.1) in the next section.

In summary, when there is no relationship between the variables, the frequencies in the body of the table follow, at least approximately, the pattern of frequencies in the marginals.

When there is a relationship between the variables, the pattern of frequencies in the body of the table deviates from the pattern of marginal frequencies. Table 16.5 gives an extreme example, and Tables 16.6 and

TABLE 16.4
Hypothetical data showing no relationship between experimenter's attire and willingness to contribute (unequal marginals on one variable)

		Attire		
		Feminine	Masculine	
Contribution	Yes	5	5	10
	No	15	15	30
		20	20	N = 40

16.7 offer less extreme examples of hypothetical data that would suggest that the variables are related and therefore would result in rejection of the null hypothesis.

The principal characteristic that 2 × 2 contingency tables for related variables have in common is relatively large frequencies on one diagonal pair of cells, and relatively small frequencies on the other diagonal pair.

TABLE 16.5
Data suggesting that the variables are related (data leading to rejection of the null hypothesis)

		Attire		
		Feminine	Masculine	
Contribution	Yes	20	0	20
	No	0	20	20
		20	20	N = 40

TABLE 16.6
Data suggesting that the variables are related (data leading to rejection of the null hypothesis)

		Attire		
		Feminine	Masculine	
Contribution	Yes	15	5	20
	No	5	15	20
		20	20	N = 40

TABLE 16.7
Data suggesting that the variables are related (data leading to rejection of the null hypothesis)

		Attire		
		Feminine	Masculine	
Contribution	Yes	8	2	10
	No	5	25	30
		13	27	N = 40

It was indicated in the previous section that expected frequencies (for unrelated variables) are based on the pattern of marginal frequencies. The formula for the chi-square statistic uses the differences between the expected and observed cell frequencies to determine whether variables are related. This suggests that the expected frequencies are needed before the chi-square statistic can be computed. To illustrate the computation of expected frequencies, Table 16.7 is reproduced as Table 16.8, with the expected frequencies included. The expected frequencies are presented in the upper-left corner of each of the cells.

TABLE 16.8
Contingency table with expected and observed frequencies

		Attire		
		Feminine	Masculine	
Contribution	Yes	3.25 / 8	6.75 / 2	10
	No	9.75 / 5	20.25 / 25	30
		13	27	$N = 40$

The formula for obtaining expected frequencies is

$$E_{jk} = \frac{(rm_j)(cm_k)}{N},$$ (16.1)

where E_{jk} is the expected frequency for the cell in the jth row of the kth column. The marginal of the jth row is rm_j and the marginal of the kth column is cm_k. The letter N is the sum of all frequencies in the contingency table, that is, the total number of subjects, or total number of responses, in the experiment. The sum of the marginal frequencies of either variable (that is, either rows or columns) is the sum of observed frequencies, and equals N. The sum of all the expected frequencies in the table also equals N.

The expected frequency of the cell in the upper-left-hand corner of Table 16.8 is

$$E_{11} = \frac{(rm_j)(cm_k)}{N}$$

$$= \frac{(10)(13)}{40}$$

$$= 3.25.$$

For the cell in the first row, second column of Table 16.8, the expected frequency is

$$E_{12} = \frac{(10)(27)}{40}$$
$$= 6.75.$$

The expected frequencies are computed after the observed frequencies are entered in each cell. The observed frequencies are summed in each row and column to obtain the marginal frequencies. Given the marginal frequencies, each rm_j and each cm_k, and the total number of frequencies, N, Equation (16.1) yields the expected frequencies for each cell.

Computing the Chi-Square

The formula for the chi-square statistic is

$$\chi^2 = \Sigma_j \Sigma_k \left[\frac{(O_{jk} - E_{jk})^2}{E_{jk}} \right],\tag{16.2}$$

where O_{jk} is the observed frequency in the cell in the jth row of the kth column and E_{jk} is the expected frequency defined by Equation (16.1). The double summation in Equation (16.2) implies that the value

$$\frac{(O_{jk} - E_{jk})^2}{E_{jk}}$$

is to be computed for each cell and then totaled over all rows and all columns, that is, over all cells.

Table 16.8 offers the information needed to compute the chi-square with Equation (16.2).

$$\chi^2 = \Sigma_j \Sigma_k \left[\frac{(O_{jk} - E_{jk})^2}{E_{jk}} \right]$$

$$= \frac{(8 - 3.25)^2}{3.25} + \frac{(2 - 6.75)^2}{6.75} + \frac{(5 - 9.75)^2}{9.75} + \frac{(25 - 20.25)^2}{20.25}$$

$$= 6.94 + 3.34 + 2.31 + 1.11$$

$$= 13.70.$$

To summarize, to compute the chi-square statistic, the observed frequencies are simply entered into a table. Then the observed cell frequencies are subtotaled to obtain the marginal frequencies. The marginal frequencies are used to obtain the expected frequencies, with the aid of Equation (16.1). Finally, Equation (16.2) is used to compute chi-square.

TABLE 16.9

Hypothetical data for a 2 × 3 contingency table

		Variable A			
		I	II	III	
Variable B	I	20	5	15	40
	II	10	40	30	80
		30	45	45	$N = 120$

As another example, the chi-square statistic is computed for the hypothetical data in Table 16.9. First use Equation (16.1) to compute the expected values, as summarized in Table 16.10. Combining Tables 16.9 and 16.10, in the form of Table 16.11, yields a table summarizing everything that is needed to compute the chi-square statistic. Applying Equation (16.2) to the information in Table 16.11 yields the desired chi-square value.

TABLE 16.10

Expected frequencies for the data in Table 16.9

		Variable A		
		I	II	III
Variable B	I	$E_{11} = \dfrac{(40)(30)}{120} = 10$	$E_{12} = \dfrac{(40)(45)}{120} = 15$	$E_{13} = \dfrac{(40)(45)}{120} = 15$
	II	$E_{21} = \dfrac{(80)(30)}{120} = 20$	$E_{22} = \dfrac{(80)(45)}{120} = 30$	$E_{23} = \dfrac{(80)(45)}{120} = 30$

TABLE 16.11

Completed contingency table for computing the chi-square statistic, combining the observed frequencies from Table 16.9 with the expected frequencies from Table 16.10

		Variable A			
		I	II	III	
Variable B	I	10 / 20	15 / 5	15 / 15	40
	II	20 / 10	30 / 40	30 / 30	80
		30	45	45	$N = 120$

$$\chi^2 = \Sigma_j \Sigma_k \left[\frac{(O_{jk} - E_{jk})^2}{E_{jk}} \right]$$

$$= \frac{(20 - 10)^2}{10} + \frac{(5 - 15)^2}{15} + \frac{(15 - 15)^2}{15} + \frac{(10 - 20)^2}{20}$$

$$+ \frac{(40 - 30)^2}{30} + \frac{(30 - 30)^2}{30}$$

$$= 10.00 + 6.67 + 0 + 5.00 + 3.33 + 0$$

$$= 25.$$

The Chi-Square Distribution and Degrees of Freedom In the previous sections a method for computing the chi-square statistic was presented. The chi-square statistic is computed in order to have a numerical index of just how much the observed frequencies deviate from the expected frequencies in the cells of the contingency table. The expected frequencies in the contingency table are the expected frequencies only when the null hypothesis is true. The further apart the expected and observed frequencies, the larger the value of the computed chi-square. Given a large enough value of chi-square, the null hypothesis is rejected. A table has been constructed which lists the critical values for rejection of the null hypothesis. It is called the chi-square table.

The chi-square table is Table VIII in Appendix B. It contains the critical values for the most frequently used Type I error probabilities for the chi-square distribution. The chi-square distribution, like the t distribution, has a different shape with different degrees of freedom, so the critical values change with changing degrees of freedom. The chi-square table only requires one value for degrees of freedom to know which row of the table to enter. The formula for degrees of freedom for the chi-square test, when working with two variables, is

$$df = (r-1)(c-1), \tag{16.3}$$

where r is the number of rows and c is the number of columns in the matrix; that is, r and c are the number of levels of the two variables. For Table 16.11, the degrees of freedom are

$$df = (2-1)(3-1)$$

$$= 2.$$

Looking at Table VIII in Appendix B, the degrees of freedom are indicated in the left-hand margin of the table. Critical values for two degrees of freedom are found in the second row of the table. Critical values at the .05

level are found in the column headed .05. Where the row and column meet, the chi-square table lists 5.99. The data in Table 16.11 yield a computed chi-square value of 25. Since 25 surpasses 5.99, the results are significant. In fact, the computed chi-square of 25 surpasses the critical value for a .001 Type I error probability (listed in Table VIII as 13.82).

Chi-Square with a 2 × 2 Contingency Table

The chi-square statistic is often used with 2 × 2 contingency tables. This is because there are so many dichotomous variables and variables that are usefully reduced to dichotomies. Some examples are male/female, yes/no, comply/did not comply, error/no error, agree/disagree.

There is a shorter computational procedure for using chi-square with 2 × 2 tables which avoids the step of computing the expected frequencies. Equation (16.4) offers this faster single formula for computing the chi-square with a 2 × 2 table.*

$$\chi^2 = \frac{N(AD - BC)^2}{(A+B)(C+D)(A+C)(B+D)} . \tag{16.4}$$

The letters in Equation (16.4) are identified in Table 16.12, where the letters each refer to observed frequencies in the various cells. The larger the values in one diagonal (say A and D), as contrasted with the other diagonal, the larger the numerator in Equation (16.4). Thus, larger discrepancies in the frequencies of the two diagonals lead to larger values for the computed

TABLE 16.12
General 2 × 2 contingency table with observed frequencies expressed in symbols required for the use of equation (16.4). A, B, C, and D refer to the observed frequencies in the different cells.

		Variable X		
		I	II	
Variable Y	I	A	B	$rm_1 = (A+B)$
	II	C	D	$rm_2 = (C+D)$
		$cm_1 = (A+C)$	$cm_2 = (B+D)$	

*Journal articles incorporating the chi-square statistic with 2 × 2 contingency tables will usually mention the use of Yate's correction. Yate's correction results in a smaller value of chi-square. It had been assumed, until recently, that Yate's correction is required when using Equation (16.4). Recent evidence, however, shows that the correction is unnecessary and, in fact, can introduce a small amount of error in most psychological applications. The evidence is contained in the following article: Camilli, Gregory, & Hopkins, Kenneth D. Applicability of chi-square to 2 × 2 contingency tables with small expected cell frequencies. *Psychological Bulletin*, 1978, *85*, 163–167.

chi-square statistic. The denominator, which may look complicated, is simply the product of the four marginal frequencies.

The degrees of freedom for a 2 × 2 matrix, from Equation (16.3), equal

$$df = (r-1)(c-1)$$
$$= (2-1)(2-1)$$
$$= 1.$$

Table 16.13 offers an example for practicing computation with Equation (16.4). Applying Equation (16.4) to the data in Table 16.13 yields:

$$\chi^2 = \frac{N(AD - BC)^2}{(A+B)(C+D)(A+C)(B+D)}$$
$$= \frac{50(14 \cdot 19 - 6 \cdot 11)^2}{(20)(30)(25)(25)}$$
$$= 5.33.$$

The Table for the chi-square distribution, Table VIII in Appendix B, indicates that a value of 3.84 would be sufficient for significance at the .05 level, with one degree of freedom. The obtained value of 5.33 for the data in Table 16.13 is therefore statistically significant.

As another example, Table 16.8, previously computed the long way, can be computed with Equation (16.4). This yields

$$\chi^2 = \frac{40(8 \cdot 25 - 2 \cdot 5)^2}{(10)(30)(13)(27)}$$
$$= 13.71,$$

which, except for rounding error in the second decimal place, is the same answer as obtained with the longer method.

TABLE 16.13
Hypothetical data, where the two variables are sex of respondent and dichotomous response to some question (yes/no)

		Sex		
		Male	Female	
Response	Yes	14	6	20
	No	11	19	30
		25	25	

SINGLE-VARIABLE PROBLEMS (THE GOODNESS-OF-FIT TEST) There are times when only one variable is identified, and the question is whether the frequencies of occurrence are different at the different levels of the variable.

For example, people entering a large office building might face a choice of four different doors at the front entrance. An architect might wish to know whether there is any difference in the use made of the four doors. An observer would therefore simply watch a sample of people entering the building and note which door is used by each person when the people first enter the building in the morning. The data might look like the hypothetical data in Table 16.14.

Assume that a total of 80 people have been observed (the sum of the observed frequencies in the cells of the table). What would be the expected values for the cells? A null hypothesis of no difference in the use of the four doors would suggest that the 80 people should be expected to use the four doors equally. Thus the expected frequencies should be the same in each case: N divided by the number of cells, implying expected frequencies of 20 in each cell.

The procedure is identical to that in the two-variable case with contingency tables that are larger than 2×2; that is, Equation (16.2),

$$\chi^2 = \Sigma_j \Sigma_k \left[\frac{(O_{jk} - E_{jk})^2}{E_{jk}} \right],$$

is used to compute chi-square. However, for the single-variable chi-square, there is only one row. Therefore, summation over rows, Σ_j, is not needed. The equation in this form is applied to the data in Table 16.14.

$$\chi^2 = \Sigma_k \left[\frac{(O_k - E_k)^2}{E_k} \right]$$

$$= \frac{(10 - 20)^2}{20} + \frac{(20 - 20)^2}{20} + \frac{(30 - 20)^2}{20} + \frac{(20 - 20)^2}{20}$$

$$= 5 + 0 + 5 + 0$$

$$= 10.$$

TABLE 16.14
Hypothetical data and expected frequencies for a single-variable chi-square statistical test

	Door		
I	II	III	IV
20	20	20	20
10	20	30	20

$N = 80$

The degrees of freedom in the single-variable case are the number of cells minus one. In this example there are four cells, so there are three degrees of freedom. The chi-square table, Table VIII in Appendix B, indicates that the critical value for the .05 level, at three degrees of freedom, is 7.82. Consequently, the computed chi-square value of 10 is statistically significant. Some doors are used more than others.

The expected frequencies do not all have to be the same. For example, the admissions officer of a school might wish to know if socioeconomic class is a factor in applications to the school. Suppose that the applicants were divided into three socioeconomic classes. Answering the question of whether socioeconomic class is related to applications to the school would require first knowing the relative frequency of the three socioeconomic classes in the general population. The null hypothesis would be that the applications to the school are in the same proportions as the socioeconomic classes in the population. If all social classes were equally disposed to apply to the school, and middle-class students were more numerous in the general population, then many more applications would be expected from middle-class students. This would result in varied expected frequencies in the different cells. Table 16.15 illustrates what the expected values would be for 200 subjects if the proportions of lower-, middle-, and upper-socioeconomic classes were .25, .60, and .15, respectively.

It is not unusual for a psychological theory to predict a specific distribution of outcomes with different expected frequencies for different levels of a variable. The chi-square statistic offers a convenient test for such a theoretical prediction.

In summary, the one-variable chi-square test is a test of whether the observations fit some a priori expectations or theory. The expectations can simply be equal probabilities, or proportions matching some population proportions, or some more elaborate frequency distribution following from some theory. The single-variable chi-square test is therefore a test of whether the observed frequencies fit the predicted frequency distribution. What has been identified here as the single-variable chi-square test is more commonly called the **goodness-of-fit test.**

TABLE 16.15

Hypothetical expected frequencies for a single-variable chi-square test, with varied expected frequencies

Socioeconomic Class		
Lower	Middle	Upper
50	120	30

RESTRICTIONS ON THE USE OF CHI-SQUARE

1. Scores cannot be entered into a chi-square table. A subject does not add a numerical score to any cell, only a one (1) to the frequency in the appropriate cell. If the subjects have actual scores, a statistic other than chi-square should be considered.

2. Every contribution to the frequencies in the table must be independent of every other contribution from that population. Violations of the independence assumption often stem from the inclusion of observations from one subject more than once in the table. Assuming that the subjects are sampled from a larger population of subjects, each subject must contribute just one time to the frequencies in the table. Consider again the example where an architect wishes to see if different entrance doors are used more or less frequently. Assume that the count is taken of people entering the building throughout the day, summing frequencies of usage of each door. It is possible that the same people might occasionally be reentering the building. This would mean that some of the frequencies would come from repeated contributions of the same people, and some from varied individuals. Two observations from the same subject, in many instances, are more likely to be similar than observations from different subjects. This would violate the assumption of independent observations from the same population. For this reason, the door study was previously described as consisting of frequencies of door use when people *first* came in, in the morning.

When using chi-square with a sample of subjects, data from the same subject must never appear more than once in the table; that is, each subject adds a 1 to the frequency in just one cell.

3. All observations must be included in the table. No data can be omitted. This may seem like an unnecessary warning; however, this is a surprisingly easy mistake.

As an example, suppose that an organization wishes to solicit contributions by mail. Assume that they try four different forms of a letter, randomly mailing the four different types of solicitation. They wish to answer the

TABLE 16.16
Hypothetical data showing the distribution of contributions according to letter type. The numbers in the cells show the number of contributions received from people contacted with the particular type of letter.

Letter Type			
I	II	III	IV
40	72	29	60

question of whether the type of letter makes a difference in whether or not they receive a contribution. They hope that this will help them in decisions about future mailings.

Whenever a contribution is received, the treasurer makes a note of the type of letter that was used, tabling the data as shown in Table 16.16. Seeing the data in the form of Table 16.16 might help you understand how a person could be tempted to consider this to be a one-variable problem when treating the data with the chi-square statistic. But this would be incorrect. It would be a case of not using all the data. There are really two variables here: type of letter, and whether *or not* a person responds with a contribution. Whether or not a person responds is a dichotomous variable. The second level, "not responding," has to have its data included. Thus, the proper table, if this problem were treated with chi-square, would be Table 16.17.

When counting frequencies and assigning them to cells, all levels of both variables must be represented. The user of chi-square should reexamine any apparent single-variable problem to be certain that a second variable is not implicitly present.

This last example of type of letter and contributions could also be analyzed using the analysis of variance. This would be useful if there was reasonable variability in the amounts contributed. Chi-square would ignore possible differences in varying amounts of the contributions elicited by different letters. It would only indicate if the letters made a difference in the number of people contributing.

This example then offers an instance of a choice point and relevant considerations in selecting statistics. If the data are to be treated in terms of frequencies of contributions and no contributions, chi-square is the obvious choice. If the data are to be treated in terms of scores (in this case, amounts of contributions), then analysis of variance would be the correct choice. The

TABLE 16.17
The correct contingency table, if the chi-square statistic were used to analyze the data in the Type of Letter and Contribution question. The numbers in the body of the table are hypothetical frequencies.

		Letter Type			
		I	II	III	IV
Contribution	Yes	40	72	29	60
	No	460	428	471	440

brief chapter following this one summarizes the relevant considerations in choosing among all the statistics discussed in this text.

4. In past uses of chi-square, it has generally been assumed that there are minimal numbers required as expected frequencies. For example, it has been assumed that in a 2 × 2 contingency table, no cell should have an expected frequency of less than 5. For larger contingency tables, progressively smaller expected values were tolerated. It was assumed that having too few expected frequencies would lead to incorrect estimates of Type I error probabilities. However, recent research suggests that these minimal expected frequencies are not a necessary assumption for the use of chi-square.* (The only disadvantage with low expected frequencies is the possibility of low power.)

SINGLE SUBJECT CHI-SQUARE There are times when a single subject is being examined. In this case, the population of observations being sampled is the population of that one person's responses. The sample of observations can often be seen as independent observations of the events in that restricted population.† For example, an interviewer could be interviewing people on the street as part of a survey. The interviewer's supervisor wishes to know if there is a relationship between the interviewer's approaching people and how the passersby are dressed. The supervisor therefore observes the interviewer approaching people on the street. People passing are categorized (by the supervisor) as either well dressed, unexceptionally dressed, or poorly dressed. Only those people passing at a time when the interviewer is not busy interviewing are included in these observations by the supervisor. Each such person passing is then categorized according to dress and, further, according to whether or not he or she is approached by the interviewer. The data would appear in a 2 × 3 table categorized as in Table 16.18.

The same subject, that is, the one interviewer, would be used throughout. The passing people would not be subjects, but rather opportunities for the subject to make one of the two responses (approaching the passerby or not). (Each passerby would be similar to a trial in an experiment, where three different conditions, the three classes of dress, would be presented in

---

*Camilli, Gregory & Hopkins, Kenneth D. Applicability of chi-square to 2 × 2 contingency tables with small expected cell frequencies. *Psychological Bulletin,* 1978, *85,* 163–167. Bradley, Drake R., Bradley, T. D., McGrath, Steven G., & Cutcomb, Steven D. Type I error rate of the chi-square test of independence in $r \times c$ tables that have small expected frequencies. *Psychological Bulletin,* 1979, *86,* 1290–1297.

†A single subject can violate the independence assumption when there are sequential dependencies. When consecutive responses are more similar (or more different) than nonconsecutive responses, the observations are not independent.

TABLE 16.18

Form for a table relating the dress of passersby to an interviewer's propensity to approach them

		Dressed		
		Well	Unexceptionally	Poorly
Approached	Yes			
	No			

some random order.) The three different classes of dress would be three levels of an independent variable, and approaching or not approaching each passerby would be the dichotomous dependent variable. The experimental question would be whether a person's dress affects this interviewer's disposition to interview the person. The null hypothesis would be that dress is not a factor in this interviewer's selection of people to interview.

If we were interested in whether people in general are biased in whom they tend to interview, a random sample of people as interviewers would be required. Each such interviewer in the sample would contribute a single observation, such as his or her first choice of someone to interview.

In summary, when using chi-square, either every observation should be based on the response of a different subject, or every response should be based on the same subject (where there are no known sequential dependencies in the subject's responses). Having both multiple subjects and multiple contributions from each subject would violate the requirement that each observation be an independent observation from the same population, making the use of chi-square inappropriate.

DEGREE OF RELATIONSHIP IN CHI-SQUARE When the chi-square test has led to the conclusion that there is a relationship between two variables, a second question can be: "What is the degree of relationship?"

The computed value of chi-square can be converted to a measure of degree of relationship. For a two-by-two contingency table (two dichotomous variables), the measure of strength of relationship is called the **phi-coefficient**, symbolized by ϕ. Equation (16.5) gives the formula.

$$\phi = \sqrt{\frac{\chi^2}{N}} \tag{16.5}$$

The χ^2 in Equation (16.5) is simply the computed chi-square and N is the total number of frequencies in the table.

When dealing with a larger contingency table (say, a 2×3, 3×3, or 3×4), the formula is changed to Equation (16.6), called **Cramer's phi.**

$$\text{Cramer's } \phi = \sqrt{\frac{\chi^2}{N(s-1)}} . \qquad (16.6)$$

The s in Equation (16.6) is the smaller of r or c; that is, s is the number of rows or columns in the matrix, whichever is smaller (or they can both be equal). Equation (16.6) reduces to the regular phi-coefficient when dealing with a 2×2 table, since $(s-1)$ then equals 1 and therefore cannot affect the computed value.

The phi-coefficient for a 2×2 table is equivalent in meaning to Pearson's correlation coefficient. The squared phi-coefficient for a 2×2 table offers an estimate of the proportion of variance in one variable associated with the variance in the other variable.

On the other hand, Cramer's phi does not strictly correspond to the computation of a Pearson r, so should not be squared. Thus the measures of degree of relationship in contingency tables that are larger than 2×2 are less clearly interpretable. However, Cramer's phi does vary between zero and one as a function of degree of relationship, so it is loosely interpreted in a manner similar to Pearson's r.

Traditionally, another measure of degree of relationship has been used when the chi-square table has been larger than 2×2. This other measure is called the **contingency coefficient,** symbolized C. The formula for C is given in Equation (16.7).

$$C = \sqrt{\frac{\chi^2}{N + \chi^2}} . \qquad (16.7)$$

The contingency coefficient does not vary between 0 and 1, but rather has an upper limit less than 1. This limit depends on the size of the matrix, being as small as .71 when the smaller of r or c is equal to 2. This makes it difficult to interpret C similarly to r.

The contingency coefficient is commonly found in the older literature, but will probably give way to Cramer's phi.

Computing the Degree of Relationship   The data in Table 16.13 yield a chi-square of $\chi^2 = 5.33$. Treating this value with Equation (16.5) to obtain the phi-coefficient yields

$$\phi = \sqrt{\frac{\chi^2}{N}}$$

$$= \sqrt{\frac{5.33}{50}}$$

$$= \sqrt{.11}$$

$$= .33.$$

The square of the phi-coefficient $(.33)^2 = .11$, is an estimate of the proportion of the variance in responses (yes or no) associated with the sex of the respondent.

The data in Table 16.11 yields a chi-square of $x^2 = 25$. Transformation of x^2 to Cramer's phi would be appropriate to obtain an index of degree of relationship. Table 16.11 is a 2 × 3 table, so s, the smaller of 2 or 3, is equal to 2. Thus, using Equation (16.6) to calculate Cramer's phi, the chi-square of 25 is transformed to

$$\text{Cramer's } \phi = \sqrt{\frac{x^2}{N(s-1)}},$$

$$= \sqrt{\frac{25}{120}}$$

$$= \sqrt{.21}$$

$$= .46.$$

The value of .46 offers an indication of the degree of relationship, where the index could vary between 0 and 1. But it would not be proper to square the computed value, .46, to estimate proportion of variance in one variable associated with the other. You have to be satisified here with just a relative index of relationship.

IMPORTANT WORDS AND CONCEPTS

Contingency table (p. 376)
Marginal frequencies (p. 377)
Expected frequencies (p. 378)
Goodness-of-fit test (p. 387)
Phi-coefficient (p. 391)
Cramer's phi (p. 392)
Contingency coefficient (p. 392)

SENTENCE COMPLETIONS

The following incomplete sentences are taken from the underlined sentences in this chapter. Fill in the missing words and phrases and then correct them from the answers which follow.

1. The chi-square statistic is used when the data are _____.
2. A table indicating the frequencies of outcomes that are jointly classified on two variables is called a _____ _____.
3. The principal characteristic that 2 × 2 contingency tables for related

variables have in common is relatively _____
_____ on one diagonal, and relatively _____
_____ on the other diagonal pair of cells.

4. The sum of the marginal frequencies of either variable equals _____.

5. The sum of all the expected frequencies in the table equals _____.

6. The expected frequencies in the table are the expected frequencies only when _____.

7. The single variable chi-square test is called the _____ _____test. It is a test of whether the observed frequencies _____ the _____ frequency distribution.

8. The degrees of freedom in the single-variable chi-square test are _____ .

9. The chi-square statistic cannot use _____in the cells. Every contribution to the frequencies in the table must be _____ of every other. Given a sample of many subjects, no subject can contribute _____ to the frequencies in the table.

10. For a 2 × 2 contingency table, the measure of strength of relationship derived from the chi-square statistic is called the _____.

11. The squared phi-coefficient offers an estimate of _____
_____
_____ ,
but this is not true of _____.

Answers 1. categorized (classified) 2. contingency table 3. large frequencies; small frequencies 4. *N* 5. *N* 6. the null hypothesis is true (the variables are related) 7. goodness-of-fit; fit; predicted (expected or a priori) 8. number of cells minus one 9. scores; independent; more than one time 10. phi-coefficient 11. the proportion of variance in one variable associated with the variance in the other variable; Cramer's phi

---

PROBLEMS 1.

Variable A

	I	II	III	IV
I	5	15	5	5
Variable B **II**	0	10	10	10
III	25	5	5	5

For the above contingency table, answer the following questions.

(a) Obtain the expected frequencies.

(b) Compute the chi-square statistic.

(c) What are the degrees of freedom?

(d) What is the critical value for the chi-square test at the .05 level?

(e) Would you conclude that the variables are related?

(f) Compute Cramer's phi for this data.

2. Answer the following questions for the 2 × 2 contingency table shown below.

Variable A

	I	II
I	15	10
II	5	35

Variable B

(a) Compute chi-square, using Equation (16.4).

(b) What are the degrees of freedom?

(c) What is the critical value at the .05 level?

(d) Would you conclude that the variables are related?

(e) Compute the phi-coefficient.

3. Recompute the chi-square for the contingency table in problem 2, using Equation (16.2). You should obtain the same answer as with Equation (16.4) (allowing for rounding error).

4. The table below offers some hypothetical expected frequencies for the applications to a school in terms of social class.

Socioeconomic Class

Lower	Middle	Upper
50 / 10	120 / 130	30 / 60

Assume that the actual frequencies of applications are the values in the middle of each cell.

(a) Compute the chi-square for this problem.

(b) How might you express the Type I error probability level of the outcome?

(c) What would be an appropriate verbalization of the general conclusion from the collection of the data and the statistical analysis?

seventeen

POSTSCRIPT: CHOOSING A STATISTIC

In this text, four different types of statistics have been discussed in some detail:

1. The t test (difference between means and matched-pair t tests).
2. Correlation (Pearson r, point biserial, and test of significance of a correlation).
3. Analysis of variance (and related indices of degree of relationship: omega-squared and the intraclass correlation coefficient).
4. Chi-square (and related indices of degree of relationship: phi coefficient and Cramer's phi).

With the introduction of each statistic, an attempt was made to indicate when the statistic should be used. The focal point in these decisions was often whether the variables were dichotomous, narrowly ranging, or wide ranging.

For example, given a dichotomous independent variable and a continuous (or wide-ranging) dependent variable, a t test probably would be used to draw a conclusion about whether the variables are related, and a point biserial probably would be used for an index of the degree of relationship between the variables. If both variables were dichotomous variables, a chi-square probably would be used to draw a conclusion about whether the variables are related, and the computed chi-square value would be converted to a phi-coefficient for an index of degree of relationship.

There are actually three pertinent facts that are generally used in the selection of the appropriate statistic from among those studied in this text:

1. Do we wish to know whether the variables are related, or are we asking for an estimate of the degree of relationship?
2. Are the levels of the variables dichotomous, narrowly ranging, or widely ranging and possibly continuous? A related question is whether the variables are classified or measured. Classified variables tend to be either dichotomous or narrowly ranging.
3. If one variable is dichotomous, are the scores in the two groups paired (matched in some way, or involving the same subjects twice)?

Once these questions have been answered, then the appropriate statistic can usually be selected.

There are other caveats concerning assumptions that have been discussed in previous chapters. There are also other statistics available that have not been discussed in this introductory text. However, for a wide range of purposes, the statistics presented in this text will be appropriate.

Table 17.1 summarizes when to use the various statistics discussed in this text for two-variable experiments. The margins of the table are divided into dichotomous, narrowly ranging, or widely ranging, referring to the numbers of levels of the variables. A narrowly ranging variable is defined

TABLE 17.1

Selecting the correct statistic. Above and below the dotted lines in the table, two different questions are assumed asked:

Are the variables related?

What is the degree of relationship?

To estimate the proportion of variance in one variable associated with variance in the other variable, square the Pearson r, the point biserial, and the phi coefficient. Omega-squared directly estimates the proportion of associated variance.

		ONE VARIABLE		
		Dichotomous	Narrowly Ranging or Classified	Widely Ranging or Continuous
OTHER VARIABLE	Dichotomous	χ^2 ---------- ϕ coefficient	χ^2 ---------- Cramer's ϕ	t test[a] ---------- Point biserial[b]
	Narrowly Ranging or Classified		χ^2 ---------- Cramer's ϕ	Analysis of variance -------- ω^2
	Widely Ranging or Continuous			Test $r > 0$ -------- Pearson r [c]

[a]If the scores of the two groups are paired, use the matched-pair t test. If not, use the t test for the difference between two means.
[b]The scores of the two groups must *not* be paired.
[c]Only if the scores of the two variables are paired.

here as one with three to ten values or classes. Anything larger than that is considered widely ranging. Identifying the number of levels for each variable determines the appropriate cell in the table. In the case of the chi-square statistic as discussed in Chapter 16, nominal classification of both variables was used as a signal for consideration of the statistic. Any useful nominal classification is likely to be either dichotomous or narrowly ranging. The table indicates the way in which the range of each variable is used in choosing a statistic.

The upper statistic in each cell is the correct statistic when the question is whether the variables are related. The bottom statistic in each cell is the correct statistic when you want an estimate of the degree of relationship between the variables. The role of the pairing of scores in the choice of statistics is noted in the footnotes to the appropriate statistics.

The material summarized in Table 17.1 appeared primarily at the beginning of the chapters, when each new statistic was introduced. It is therefore likely that much of this material has been obscured by the later material of the chapters. It should be helpful to return to the appropriate sections of the earlier chapters to read the suggestions about when to use each statistic. These sections are listed below, with the page numbers in parentheses.

Chapter 11

First few pages, stopping at the section headed: Linear Relationships (pp. 231–233).
Section headed: Correlation and Causation (pp. 247–248).
Section headed: The Point Biserial Correlation Coefficient, to Equation 11.14. (pp. 248–249).

Chapter 13

The first few pages, stopping at the section headed: Experimental Manipulation versus Classification (pp. 285–287).
The paragraph on p. 288 adjacent to the heading, Summary of When to Use Analysis of Variance.

Chapter 14

First four paragraphs on p. 321.
The section headed: The Conditions of Bias Requiring Omega-Squared (pp. 327–328).

Chapter 15

Section headed: Simple Effects (pp. 350–352).
Section headed: Interactions (pp. 352–355).

Chapter 16

First two sections, up to section headed: Expected Frequencies in Chi-Square (pp. 375–379).
Section headed: Restrictions on the Use of Chi-Square, to end of chapter (pp. 388–393).

After reading the suggested sections, test your understanding by answering the following set of questions offering practice in the use of Table 17.1. In answering, distinguish between the *t* test for matched pairs and the *t* test for the difference between two means. Also distinguish between one- and two-factor analyses of variance. The table does not list two-factor analysis of variance, but the presence of a second independent variable, or a question of interaction, will suggest the use of two-factor analysis of variance. The correct answers are on p. 404.

1. Are men more dominant than women? A random sample of 100 men and 200 women is obtained, and they are all given a test for dominance

which simply classifies each person as either dominant or not dominant.

What statistic would answer the question, "Is dominance a sex-related characteristic?"

2. A cancer research organization has data on a large sample of the American population who have died over the past 20 years. They have information indicating the type of smoking done by each individual (pipe smoker, cigar smoker, cigarette smoker, or nonsmoker). They also have the age at death for each person in their sample.

The organization wants to see if their data supports the contention that smoking is related to age at death. Which statistic would they use?

3. The scientist directing the project in question 2 wants to add another variable to the study. The scientist believes that the differences in age at death that will be found when comparing the different groups would be affected by the extent of smog in the environment.

For this new extended study, the people in the sample are divided up into those who lived in areas with heavy smog and those who lived in areas that were relatively free from smog. Smoking habit remains the other independent variable, and the dependent variable remains age at death.

The new question of major interest to the scientist is whether the pattern of differences in age at death attributed to smoking habits would be influenced by whether people lived in smog-filled environments.

What is the appropriate statistic?

4. There is a notion that early discrimination training increases the IQ of children; that is, color discriminations (particularly subtle ones), discriminations among musical tones, etc., if fostered in children, are expected to increase IQ.

A group of identical twins is used in an experiment to test this theory. One member of each twin pair gets this early discrimination training, but the other does not. Then, at a later date, their respective IQ scores are obtained.

Which statistic would be used to test the hypothesis?

5. Assume that a new interpretation of the frustration aggression hypothesis says that it is not all people who become aggressive when frustrated, but only those who have been brought up in a home where physical punishment is used become aggressive when frustrated.

To test this hypothesis, two groups of children are found. One group is brought up in homes where physical punishment is used as a form of discipline. The other group consists of children whose parents chastise them verbally, or remove privileges, but do not actually hit them.

The children are all placed in a situation where they are frustrated in the course of play activity. The play situation includes a doll that the children have in their hands at the time of the frustration experience.

The experimenter intends to have judges classify the children as either physically aggressive or not physically aggressive toward the doll (at the time of frustration).

Which statistic would be used?

6. Assume now that in the situation in question 5, the experimenter has the raters give each child a numerical rating indicating just how physically aggressive the child is. Each child receives a score on a scale from 1 to 20, indicating extent of aggressiveness, rather than just being categorized as aggressive or not.

Which statistic should be used?

7. A teacher sees students straggling into her class at highly diverse times. She secretly records when each person comes into her class. Everyone in the class at the bell gets a score of zero. Then, as each late person comes in, the number of seconds after the bell that the person arrives is recorded. Number of seconds late, then, is each person's individual score. The scores ranged from 0 to 600 (for people who were 10 minutes late).

The teacher also has each person's exam average over the semester. She wants some estimate of the degree of relationship between a person's lateness and his or her exam scores in her class.

Which statistic should she use?

8. Now suppose the teacher in problem 7 has computed the necessary statistic for answering her question in problem 7. She would now like to know if arrival time and exam performance are, in general, related.

If her class could be considered to be a random sample, what statistical procedure would be appropriate?

9. Now suppose that the teacher in questions 7 and 8 is not really looking for an estimate of the degree of relationship between lateness and exam performance. Assume, instead, that she intends to simply divide her class into two groups: Those who are and those who are not late. She then wants to see if there is a relationship between being late to class and exam performance.

Which single statistic would then be appropriate?

10. There is a good test for measuring authoritarian personality. An experimenter decides to see if being an authoritarian person is related to success in a particular profession. To this end, the experimenter selects 100 members of the profession, and on the basis of the test categorizes each of them as authoritarian or nonauthoritarian. She then evaluates their individual professional histories, from which she categorizes each of them as being successful or unsuccessful in his or her profession.

What statistical test would be useful in answering the question of whether authoritarian personality is related to success in this profession?

11. Assume that in the study described in question 10 there are now not one, but rather three professions involved in the study.

The members of each of the three professions, rather than simply being categorized as authoritarian or nonauthoritarian, have their actual scores on the authoritarian test assigned to them. (The scores range from −45 to +65.) The question being asked is whether the different professions tended to have members that are different on the scale of authoritarianism.

Which statistic should be used?

12. Assume that in the year 2000 there are four different forms of psychotherapy available for curing phobias. An experimenter arranges for different phobic people to each receive one of the four psychotherapies. (A total of 100 people participate in the study.) At the end of the therapy, each patient is categorized as cured or not cured.

What statistic is appropriate for testing the question of whether the form of psychotherapy is related to success in curing phobias?

13. The study in question 12 is done, and no differences are found among the four therapies. In fact, each patient, in every treatment group, is cured. The experimenter then decides that a new question has to be asked.

Assuming that all the therapies are equally effective, are any of the therapies faster than any of the others? That is, is there less time required to obtain a cure for any one therapy than for any of the others?

The experimenter goes back to the data and for each patient records the number of sessions that were needed before the patient was considered cured. The patients' respective scores (required number of sessions) range from 10 to 70.

What statistic would be appropriate for testing the question of whether the form of psychotherapy is related to the number of sessions required to cure a phobia?

14. An experimenter wishes to know if strong doses of glucose can improve performance on an intelligence test. He gives an IQ test to a random sample of school children, twice to each child. One time, with each child, the test is taken after a large dose of glucose. The other time, with the same child, the test is taken without a prior dose of glucose. (The experimenter uses two equivalent forms of the same IQ test.)

Which statistic should he use?

15. An experimenter is interested in hyperactivity and diet. She believes that the greater the amounts of certain food dyes that are consumed, the more hyperactive a child will be. She looks at children considered hyperactive, and children not considered hyperactive, and then measures the amount of these food dyes that each child consumes in an average month. The amounts vary from 0 to 500 mg.

What statistic would enable her to determine if there is a relationship between hyperactivity and consumption of these food dyes?

16. The experimenter in question 15 has now developed a way of measuring degree of hyperactivity, on a scale from 1 to 30. She wishes to use the scale to obtain some estimate of the degree of relationship between amount of these food dyes that are consumed, and the extent of hyperactivity.

    Which statistic should she use?

17. People living near an airport claim that the jets have hurt their hearing. An audiologist decides to see if their claim is justified. No tests of hearing were made before they moved to the airport vicinity, so he has to use different people for comparisons. He selects people who live in the same town, sufficiently far from the airport so that they cannot hear the planes taking off and landing. He wants to compare the hearing of the two groups to test the claim of the people who live near the airport. Both groups are given hearing tests which yield a score of hearing loss relative to some norms. The test scores range from 0 to 40.

    Which statistic should be used?

18. Assume, now, that the audiologist in question 17 wants to take special care in his study, and for each person living near the airport he wants his control sample (those people not living near the airport) to include one person of the same age and sex. (He assumes that age and sex are both related to hearing loss.)

    Assuming that he sets up his samples in this particularly careful way, maintaining this special similarity between the two groups, which statistic would be most appropriate to answer the question of whether living near the airport has a negative effect on hearing?

19. It is generally recognized that a large proportion of men are interested in football, and that this is less often true for women. It is a simple matter to categorize people as interested or not interested in football. What is wanted is some estimate of the degree of relationship between gender and whether or not a person is interested in football. Two steps answer the question of how to proceed statistically. What are they?

20. People are classified as depressed, in part, by the presence of self-deprecation, comments about their unworthiness, guilt, etc. A psychologist wants some estimate of the degree of relationship between the number of negative comments made by a person about him or herself and whether or not he or she is classified as clinically depressed. A group of depressed people, and a group of non-depressed people, are engaged in a conversation, which is recorded. The recorded conversations are then audited by trained observers who count the number of self-deprecating statements made by each person. (They range in this sample from 0 to 40.)

What statistic would give an estimate of the degree of relationship?

21. In question 20, it is now desired to obtain some estimate of the proportion of variance in negative self-statements that are associated with whether or not a person is depressed.

    What would be the next step, then, assuming that a correct statistic was computed for question 20?

22. Given a very simple repetitive task, high-IQ people tend to do poorly. An industrial psychologist wants to get an estimate of the proportion of variance in poor performance at a simple repetitive task that is associated with IQ. Poor performance is measured by number of errors (which ranged from 4 to 40 in the sample).

    Which statistic should be computed? What second step is needed to answer the specific question being asked?

23. You want to know whether working women consume different amounts of liquor than full-time housewives (measured in ounces per week). You wish to examine the data for possible differences, comparing women in urban, suburban, and rural areas.

    Which statistic should you use?

24. You have done the statistical work called for in question 23. You have obtained statistical significance in answer to the question of whether housewives consume different amounts of alcohol than working women. You have also found that there are different amounts of liquor consumed by women living in rural, urban, and suburban areas. You wish to estimate the proportion of variance in liquor consumption associated with whether a woman works, as well as the proportion of variance associated with where the women live. (You want to see which factor appears to have the stronger association with liquor consumption.)

    Which statistic should you use?

Answers: 1. Chi-square   2. One-factor analysis of variance   3. Two-factor analysis of variance   4. *t* test, matched pairs   5. Chi-square   6. *t* test, difference between two means   7. Correlation (Pearson *r*)   8. Test the correlation for significance   9. *t* test, difference between two means   10. Chi-square   11. One-factor analysis of variance   12. Chi-square   13. One-factor analysis of variance   14. *t* test, matched pairs   15. *t* test, difference between two means   16. Correlation (Pearson *r*)   17. *t* test, difference between two means   18. *t* test, matched pairs   19. Chi-square, transformed to a phi coefficient   20. Point biserial correlation   21. Square the point biserial   22. Pearson *r*, squared   23. Two-factor analysis of variance   24. Omega-squared

appendix a

SOME USEFUL PRINCIPLES OF ELEMENTARY ALGEBRA

In order to master this text, you need a working knowledge of arithmetic and elementary algebra. If you think your knowledge of these areas might be a bit rusty, you should review the basic principles presented in this section and then do the practice algebra exercises at the end. This brief refresher course can help you avoid the common mistakes that sometimes trip up students in introductory statistics.

REDUCING FRACTIONS We often encounter fractions that can be reduced. Reducing a fraction does not change its numerical value. For example, consider the fraction

$$\frac{30}{50}.$$

The first step is to think of numbers that can be divided into both 30 and 50. The numbers 2, 5, and 10 may come to mind. We choose 10 because it is the largest common value and will therefore give us the most reduced fraction.

$$\frac{30}{50} = \frac{\frac{30}{10}}{\frac{50}{10}}$$

$$\frac{30}{50} = \frac{3}{5}$$

This equality says that 30/50 and 3/5 are equivalent. Had we chosen 5 as the common value instead of 10, we would have gotten the same answer—with a little more work:

$$\frac{30}{50} = \frac{\frac{30}{5}}{\frac{50}{5}}$$

$$= \frac{6}{10}$$

The fraction can be reduced further if we divide numerator and denominator by 2:

$$\frac{6}{10} = \frac{\frac{6}{2}}{\frac{10}{2}}$$

$$= \frac{3}{5}$$

As another example,

$$\frac{24}{42} = \frac{\dfrac{24}{6}}{\dfrac{42}{6}}$$

$$= \frac{4}{7}.$$

As long as it is the same number that is divided into both the numerator and denominator, the value of the fraction is unaffected. Expressed in general symbolic form,

$$\frac{a}{e} = \frac{\dfrac{a}{b}}{\dfrac{e}{b}}.$$

In other words, if a/e equals some value X, then $\dfrac{a/b}{e/b}$ also equals that same value X. If

$$X = \frac{a}{e},$$

then it is also true that

$$X = \frac{\dfrac{a}{b}}{\dfrac{e}{b}}.$$

Multiplying both the numerator and denominator by the same number also maintains the value of the fraction. If the multiplier is larger than 1, this is the reverse of reducing the fraction. For example, consider the fraction

$$\frac{6}{12}.$$

Multiplying both numerator and denominator by 3 gives

$$\frac{(3)6}{(3)12}$$

$$= \frac{18}{36}.$$

Thus,

$$\frac{6}{12} = \frac{18}{36}.$$

The original fraction, 6/12, could have been reduced to 1/2.

$$\frac{\frac{6}{6}}{\frac{12}{6}} = \frac{1}{2}$$

Since 6/12 = 1/2, and 6/12 = 18/36, then 18/36 must also equal 1/2. Let's reduce 18/36 to see if this is true:

$$\frac{18}{36} = \frac{\frac{18}{18}}{\frac{36}{18}}$$

$$= \frac{1}{2}$$

Adding equal numbers to both the numerator and denominator does *not* maintain the equality. For example,

$$\frac{6+5}{12+5} \neq \frac{6}{12}.$$

Similarly, *subtracting* equal numbers from both the numerator and denominator of a fraction does not maintain the equality.

ADDING AND SUBTRACTING FRACTIONS Adding and subtracting fractions becomes possible if we follow the rule that fractions can only be added (or subtracted) if they have (or are given) common denominators. The common denominator is maintained while the numerators are added. For example,

$$\frac{1}{4} + \frac{2}{4} = \frac{3}{4}.$$

If the fractions do not have a common denominator, they are given a common denominator. For example,

$$\frac{1}{10} + \frac{1}{20} = \frac{(2)1}{(2)10} + \frac{1}{20}$$

$$= \frac{2}{20} + \frac{1}{20}$$

$$= \frac{3}{20}.$$

As another example,

$$\frac{5}{10} - \frac{6}{20} = \frac{(2)5}{(2)10} - \frac{6}{20}$$

$$= \frac{10}{20} - \frac{6}{20}$$

$$= \frac{4}{20}.$$

This fraction can be reduced. Dividing both numerator and denominator by 4 yields

$$\frac{4}{20} = \frac{1}{5}.$$

The problem of subtracting 6/20 from 5/10 could also have been solved by recognizing that 6/20 can be reduced to 3/10. Dividing numerator and denominator of 6/20 by 2 gives 3/10. The problem is restated as follows

$$\frac{5}{10} - \frac{6}{20} = \frac{5}{10} - \frac{3}{10}$$

$$= \frac{2}{10}$$

$$= \frac{1}{5}.$$

In many instances, including the examples just given, we can achieve a common denominator by changing just one fraction. In other instances, both fractions need to be changed to achieve a common denominator. This is accomplished by multiplying both the numerator and denominator of the first fraction by the denominator of the second fraction, and also multiplying both numerator and denominator of the second fraction by the denominator of the first fraction. This sentence becomes easier to understand when illustrated:

$$\frac{a}{x} + \frac{b}{y} = \frac{(y)(a)}{(y)(x)} + \frac{(x)(b)}{(x)(y)}$$

$$= \frac{ya}{yx} + \frac{xb}{xy}$$

$$= \frac{ya + xb}{yx}.$$

(Note that yx = xy.)

Now let's consider a specific example:

$$\frac{3}{8} + \frac{4}{9} = \frac{(9)3}{(9)8} + \frac{(8)4}{(8)9}$$

$$= \frac{27}{72} + \frac{32}{72}$$

$$= \frac{59}{72}.$$

Finally, all of the above rules for adding and subtracting fractions apply no matter how many fractions we are adding or subtracting.

MULTIPLYING AND DIVIDING FRACTIONS Multiplying fractions is quite simple. Just multiply the two numerators to get the product numerator and multiply the two denominators to get the product denominator. For example,

$$\frac{3}{4} \cdot \frac{5}{7} = \frac{(3)(5)}{(4)(7)}$$

$$= \frac{15}{28}.$$

Dividing one fraction by another is simplified by following the rule that the divisor (the fraction on the bottom) is inverted ("flipped over") and then multiplied by the other fraction. To illustrate:

$$\frac{\frac{3}{4}}{\frac{5}{7}} = \frac{3}{4} \cdot \frac{7}{5}$$

$$= \frac{21}{20}.$$

SOLVING FOR AN UNKNOWN The fourth set of principles involves solving for an unknown in an algebraic equation. Most equalities that are observed in statistics involve some unknown value, often symbolized by X or Y. For example, the equality could look like

$$2X = 10,$$

with the question being "What is the value of X?" We solve for X by isolating X on one side of the equation. But in isolating the unknown it is critical that the equality of the two sides of the equation be maintained. This is accomplished by always treating both sides of the equation identically. If a

411   Solving for an Unknown

number is subtracted from (or added to) one side, then the same number must be subtracted from (or added to) the other side of the equation. Similarly, dividing (or multiplying) one side of the equation by a number requires dividing (or multiplying) the other side by the same number, to maintain the equality. Consider again the equation

$$2X = 10.$$

In order to isolate X on one side of the equation, we must divide 2X by 2. To maintain the equality, we must also divide the other side of the equation by 2:

$$\frac{2X}{2} = \frac{10}{2}$$

$$\frac{\cancel{2}X}{\cancel{2}} = 5$$

$$X = 5.$$

As another example consider the equality

$$X + 6 = 18.$$

Subtracting 6 from both sides of the equation will allow us to isolate X:

$$X + 6 - 6 = 18 - 6$$

$$X = 12.$$

In general, any mathematical operation that is done to one side of an equation can be done to the other, and the equality will be maintained. We can multiply, divide, add, subtract, and even square both sides, or take the positive square roots of both sides. For example, if

$$X = \sqrt{3 + Y}, \tag{1}$$

by squaring both sides we can also represent this equality as

$$X^2 = 3 + Y. \tag{2}$$

Specifically, if $Y = 22$, then Equation (1) can be restated as

$$X = \sqrt{3 + 22}$$

$$X = \sqrt{25}$$

$$X = 5,$$

and Equation (2) can be restated as

$$X^2 = 3 + 22$$

$$X^2 = 25$$

$$X = 5.$$

We get the same answer, X = 5, whether we use Equation (1) or Equation (2) because squaring both sides of the equation does not change the relationship between the two sides of the equation.

INEQUALITIES Sometimes it is necessary to express an inequality. An example is

$$15 < 17,$$

which reads "15 is less than 17" (inequalities are usually read from left to right). There are four signs of inequality.

> *Greater than.*   X > Y reads: *X is greater than Y.*

≥ *Greater than or equal to.*   X ≥ Y reads: *X is greater than or equal to Y.*

< *Less than.*   X < Y reads: *X is less than Y.*

≤ *Less than or equal to.*   X ≤ Y reads: *X is less than or equal to Y.*

Most inequalities will include an unknown value, with a set of solutions to the unknown. As with equalities, the procedure for isolating the unknown involves performing identical operations on both sides of the inequality. For example, the inequality

$$X + 7 < 17$$

is solved by subtracting 7 from both sides of the equation:

$$X + 7 - 7 < 17 - 7$$

$$X < 10.$$

Thus X is equal to any number less than 10.

If the original inequality had been

$$X + 7 \leq 17,$$

then

$$X + 7 - 7 \leq 17 - 7$$

$$X \leq 10,$$

and the solution set would have included 10. As another example,

$$2X + 30 \leq 40$$

$$2X + 30 - 30 \leq 40 - 30$$

$$2X \leq 10$$

$$\frac{2X}{2} \leq \frac{10}{2}$$

$$X \leq 5$$

Inequalities are also like equalities in that we can perform any mathematical operation on an inequality so long as that operation is done to both sides of the inequality. However, when solving for an unknown in an inequality we must remember to change the direction of the sign when the inequality is multiplied or divided by a negative number. For example, when the inequality

$$15 < 17$$

is multiplied by -2 we must change the "less than" sign to a "greater than" sign:

$$-30 > -34.$$

To solve the inequality

$$-\frac{X}{3} < 5,$$

we multiply each side by -3 (and remember to reverse the direction of the sign) to get

$$-\frac{X}{3}(-3) > 5(-3)$$

$$X > -15$$

THE CORRECT SEQUENCE IN ADDITION AND SUBTRACTION The last principle is a very simple one, but it involves mistakes that are made often. When adding and subtracting several numbers, such as ($18 + 12 - 8 - 6$), the operations of addition and subtraction must be carried out one at a time and from left to right. Note the stages in this example:

$$(18 + 12 - 8 - 6) = (30 - 8 - 6)$$

$$= (22 - 6)$$

$$= 16$$

It is sometimes *erroneously* done from right to left:

$$(18 + 12 - 8 - 6) \neq (18 + 12 - 2).$$

If you wished to sum the negative numbers first, there is a principle to help you avoid errors:

$$-X - Y = -(X + Y).$$

That is, placing a sum in parentheses and putting a minus on the outside reverses the signs within the parentheses. Thus, negative numbers in a sum can be collected by *adding* them and then subtracting this subtotal. For example,

$$[18 + 12 - 8 - 6] = [18 + 12 - (8 + 6)]$$
$$= [18 + 12 - 14]$$
$$= 30 - 14$$
$$= 16.$$

SOME PRACTICE ALGEBRA EXERCISES

Reduce the following fractions:

1. $\dfrac{12}{36}$

2. $\dfrac{14}{28}$

3. $\dfrac{64}{72}$

Add the following fractions:

4. $\dfrac{1}{6} + \dfrac{1}{7} =$

5. $\dfrac{3}{4} + \dfrac{2}{3} =$

6. $\dfrac{5}{6} + \dfrac{6}{7} =$

7. $\dfrac{14}{28} + \dfrac{1}{2} =$

8. $\dfrac{3}{4} + \dfrac{8}{32} =$

9. $\dfrac{3}{4} + \dfrac{3}{16} =$

10. $\dfrac{5}{8} - \dfrac{4}{6} =$

Find the value of X:

11. $\dfrac{2}{3} X = 4$

12. $5X + 12 = 52$

13. $\dfrac{5}{6} X - 3 = 7$

Isolate Y on one side of the following inequality:

14. $4Y - 2X < 20$

Obtain the following sums:

15. $35 + 7 + 20 - 8 - 3 - 1 =$

16. $30 - 16 - 6 + 2 + 4 =$

Answers:

1. $\dfrac{1}{3}$

2. $\dfrac{1}{2}$

3. $\dfrac{8}{9}$

4. $\dfrac{7 + 6}{42} = \dfrac{13}{42}$

5. $\dfrac{9 + 8}{12} = \dfrac{17}{12}$

6. $\dfrac{71}{42}$

7. $\dfrac{1}{2} + \dfrac{1}{2} = 1$

8. $\dfrac{3}{4} + \dfrac{1}{4} = 1$

9. $\dfrac{12}{16} + \dfrac{3}{16} = \dfrac{15}{16}$

10. $\dfrac{5}{8} - \dfrac{2}{3} = \dfrac{15 - 16}{24}$ or $\dfrac{5}{8} - \dfrac{4}{6} = \dfrac{30 - 32}{48} = \dfrac{-2}{48} = -\dfrac{1}{24}$

11. $2X = 12$
    $X = 6$

12. $5X = 40$
    $X = 8$

13. $\dfrac{5}{6}X = 10$
    $5X = 60$
    $X = 12$

14. $4Y < 20 + 2X$
    $Y < 5 + \dfrac{1}{2}X$

15. 50

16. 14

appendix b

TABLES

TABLE I

Squares, Square Roots, and Reciprocals of Integers from 1 to 1000

n	n^2	$\sqrt{n}$	$\dfrac{1}{n}$	$\dfrac{1}{\sqrt{n}}$
1	1	1.0000	1.000000	1.0000
2	4	1.4142	.500000	.7071
3	9	1.7321	.333333	.5774
4	16	2.0000	.250000	.5000
5	25	2.2361	.200000	.4472
6	36	2.4495	.166667	.4082
7	49	2.6458	.142857	.3780
8	64	2.8284	.125000	.3536
9	81	3.0000	.111111	.3333
10	100	3.1623	.100000	.3162
11	121	3.3166	.090909	.3015
12	144	3.4641	.083333	.2887
13	169	3.6056	.076923	.2774
14	196	3.7417	.071429	.2673
15	225	3.8730	.066667	.2582
16	256	4.0000	.062500	.2500
17	289	4.1231	.058824	.2425
18	324	4.2426	.055556	.2357
19	361	4.3589	.052632	.2294
20	400	4.4721	.050000	.2236
21	441	4.5826	.047619	.2182
22	484	4.6904	.045455	.2132
23	529	4.7958	.043478	.2085
24	576	4.8990	.041667	.2041
25	625	5.0000	.040000	.2000
26	676	5.0990	.038462	.1961
27	729	5.1962	.037037	.1925
28	784	5.2915	.035714	.1890
29	841	5.3852	.034483	.1857
30	900	5.4772	.033333	.1826
31	961	5.5678	.032258	.1796
32	1024	5.6569	.031250	.1768
33	1089	5.7446	.030303	.1741
34	1156	5.8310	.029412	.1715
35	1225	5.9161	.028571	.1690
36	1296	6.0000	.027778	.1667
37	1369	6.0828	.027027	.1644
38	1444	6.1644	.026316	.1622
39	1521	6.2450	.025641	.1601
40	1600	6.3246	.025000	.1581

(continued)

From Peatman, J. G.: *Descriptive and Sampling Statistics*. Copyright © 1947 by Harper & Row, Publishers, Inc. Reprinted by permission of Harper & Row, Publishers, Inc.

TABLE I *(continued)*

n	n^2	$\sqrt{n}$	$\dfrac{1}{n}$	$\dfrac{1}{\sqrt{n}}$
41	1681	6.4031	.024390	.1562
42	1764	6.4807	.023810	.1543
43	1849	6.5574	.023256	.1525
44	1936	6.6332	.022727	.1508
45	2025	6.7082	.022222	.1491
46	2116	6.7823	.021739	.1474
47	2209	6.8557	.021277	.1459
48	2304	6.9282	.020833	.1443
49	2401	7.0000	.020408	.1429
50	2500	7.0711	.020000	.1414
51	2601	7.1414	.019608	.1400
52	2704	7.2111	.019231	.1387
53	2809	7.2801	.018868	.1374
54	2916	7.3485	.018519	.1361
55	3025	7.4162	.018182	.1348
56	3136	7.4833	.017857	.1336
57	3249	7.5498	.017544	.1325
58	3364	7.6158	.017241	.1313
59	3481	7.6811	.016949	.1302
60	3600	7.7460	.016667	.1291
61	3721	7.8102	.016393	.1280
62	3844	7.8740	.016129	.1270
63	3969	7.9373	.015873	.1260
64	4096	8.0000	.015625	.1250
65	4225	8.0623	.015385	.1240
66	4356	8.1240	.015152	.1231
67	4489	8.1854	.014925	.1222
68	4624	8.2462	.014706	.1213
69	4761	8.3066	.014493	.1204
70	4900	8.3666	.014286	.1195
71	5041	8.4261	.014085	.1187
72	5184	8.4853	.013889	.1179
73	5329	8.5440	.013699	.1170
74	5476	8.6023	.013514	.1162
75	5625	8.6603	.013333	.1155
76	5776	8.7178	.013158	.1147
77	5929	8.7750	.012987	.1140
78	6084	8.8318	.012821	.1132
79	6241	8.8882	.012658	.1125
80	6400	8.9443	.012500	.1118

TABLE I *(continued)*

n	n^2	$\sqrt{n}$	$\dfrac{1}{n}$	$\dfrac{1}{\sqrt{n}}$
81	6561	9.0000	.012346	.1111
82	6724	9.0554	.012195	.1104
83	6889	9.1104	.012048	.1098
84	7056	9.1652	.011905	.1091
85	7225	9.2195	.011765	.1085
86	7396	9.2736	.011628	.1078
87	7569	9.3274	.011494	.1072
88	7744	9.3808	.011364	.1066
89	7921	9.4340	.011236	.1060
90	8100	9.4868	.011111	.1054
91	8281	9.5394	.010989	.1048
92	8464	9.5917	.010870	.1043
93	8649	9.6437	.010753	.1037
94	8836	9.6954	.010638	.1031
95	9025	9.7468	.010526	.1026
96	9216	9.7980	.010417	.1021
97	9409	9.8489	.010309	.1015
98	9604	9.8995	.010204	.1010
99	9801	9.9499	.010101	.1005
100	10000	10.0000	.010000	.1000
101	10201	10.0499	.009901	.0995
102	10404	10.0995	.009804	.0990
103	10609	10.1489	.009709	.0985
104	10816	10.1980	.009615	.0981
105	11025	10.2470	.009524	.0976
106	11236	10.2956	.009434	.0971
107	11449	10.3441	.009346	.0967
108	11664	10.3923	.009259	.0962
109	11881	10.4403	.009174	.0958
110	12100	10.4881	.009091	.0953
111	12321	10.5357	.009009	.0949
112	12544	10.5830	.008929	.0945
113	12769	10.6301	.008850	.0941
114	12996	10.6771	.008772	.0937
115	13225	10.7238	.008696	.0933
116	13456	10.7703	.008621	.0928
117	13689	10.8167	.008547	.0925
118	13924	10.8628	.008475	.0921
119	14161	10.9087	.008403	.0917
120	14400	10.9545	.008333	.0913

(continued)

TABLE I *(continued)*

n	n²	$\sqrt{n}$	$\dfrac{1}{n}$	$\dfrac{1}{\sqrt{n}}$
121	14641	11.0000	.008264	.0909
122	14884	11.0454	.008197	.0905
123	15129	11.0905	.008130	.0902
124	15376	11.1355	.008065	.0898
125	15625	11.1803	.008000	.0894
126	15876	11.2250	.007937	.0891
127	16129	11.2694	.007874	.0887
128	16384	11.3137	.007813	.0884
129	16641	11.3578	.007752	.0880
130	16900	11.4018	.007692	.0877
131	17161	11.4455	.007634	.0874
132	17424	11.4891	.007576	.0870
133	17689	11.5326	.007519	.0867
134	17956	11.5758	.007463	.0864
135	18225	11.6190	.007407	.0861
136	18496	11.6619	.007353	.0857
137	18769	11.7047	.007299	.0854
138	19044	11.7473	.007246	.0851
139	19321	11.7898	.007194	.0848
140	19600	11.8322	.007143	.0845
141	19881	11.8743	.007092	.0842
142	20164	11.9164	.007042	.0839
143	20449	11.9583	.006993	.0836
144	20736	12.0000	.006944	.0833
145	21025	12.0416	.006897	.0830
146	21316	12.0830	.006849	.0828
147	21609	12.1244	.006803	.0825
148	21904	12.1655	.006757	.0822
149	22201	12.2066	.006711	.0819
150	22500	12.2474	.006667	.0816
151	22801	12.2882	.006623	.0814
152	23104	12.3288	.006579	.0811
153	23409	12.3693	.006536	.0808
154	23716	12.4097	.006494	.0806
155	24025	12.4499	.006452	.0803
156	24336	12.4900	.006410	.0801
157	24649	12.5300	.006369	.0798
158	24964	12.5698	.006329	.0796
159	25281	12.6095	.006289	.0793
160	25600	12.6491	.006250	.0791

TABLE I *(continued)*

n	n^2	$\sqrt{n}$	$\dfrac{1}{n}$	$\dfrac{1}{\sqrt{n}}$
161	25921	12.6886	.006211	.0788
162	26244	12.7279	.006173	.0786
163	26569	12.7671	.006135	.0783
164	26896	12.8062	.006098	.0781
165	27225	12.8452	.006061	.0778
166	27556	12.8841	.006024	.0776
167	27889	12.9228	.005988	.0774
168	28224	12.9615	.005952	.0772
169	28561	13.0000	.005917	.0769
170	28900	13.0384	.005882	.0767
171	29241	13.0767	.005848	.0765
172	29584	13.1149	.005814	.0762
173	29929	13.1529	.005780	.0760
174	30276	13.1909	.005747	.0758
175	30625	13.2288	.005714	.0756
176	30976	13.2665	.005682	.0754
177	31329	13.3041	.005650	.0752
178	31684	13.3417	.005618	.0750
179	32041	13.3791	.005587	.0747
180	32400	13.4164	.005556	.0745
181	32761	13.4536	.005525	.0743
182	33124	13.4907	.005495	.0741
183	33489	13.5277	.005464	.0739
184	33856	13.5647	.005435	.0737
185	34225	13.6015	.005405	.0735
186	34596	13.6382	.005376	.0733
187	34969	13.6748	.005348	.0731
188	35344	13.7113	.005319	.0729
189	35721	13.7477	.005291	.0727
190	36100	13.7840	.005263	.0725
191	36481	13.8203	.005236	.0724
192	36864	13.8564	.005208	.0722
193	37249	13.8924	.005181	.0720
194	37636	13.9284	.005155	.0718
195	38025	13.9642	.005128	.0716
196	38416	14.0000	.005102	.0714
197	38809	14.0357	.005076	.0712
198	39204	14.0712	.005051	.0711
199	39601	14.1067	.005025	.0709
200	40000	14.1421	.005000	.0707

(continued)

TABLE I *(continued)*

n	n^2	$\sqrt{n}$	$\dfrac{1}{n}$	$\dfrac{1}{\sqrt{n}}$
201	40401	14.1774	.004975	.0705
202	40804	14.2127	.004950	.0704
203	41209	14.2478	.004926	.0702
204	41616	14.2829	.004902	.0700
205	42025	14.3178	.004878	.0698
206	42436	14.3527	.004854	.0697
207	42849	14.3875	.004831	.0695
208	43264	14.4222	.004808	.0693
209	43681	14.4568	.004785	.0692
210	44100	14.4914	.004762	.0690
211	44521	14.5258	.004739	.0688
212	44944	14.5602	.004717	.0687
213	45369	14.5945	.004695	.0685
214	45796	14.6287	.004673	.0684
215	46225	14.6629	.004651	.0682
216	46656	14.6969	.004630	.0680
217	47089	14.7309	.004608	.0679
218	47524	14.7648	.004587	.0677
219	47961	14.7986	.004566	.0676
220	48400	14.8324	.004545	.0674
221	48841	14.8661	.004525	.0673
222	49284	14.8997	.004505	.0671
223	49729	14.9332	.004484	.0670
224	50176	14.9666	.004464	.0668
225	50625	15.0000	.004444	.0667
226	51076	15.0333	.004425	.0665
227	51529	15.0665	.004405	.0664
228	51984	15.0997	.004386	.0662
229	52441	15.1327	.004367	.0661
230	52900	15.1658	.004348	.0659
231	53361	15.1987	.004329	.0658
232	53824	15.2315	.004310	.0657
233	54289	15.2643	.004292	.0655
234	54756	15.2971	.004274	.0654
235	55225	15.3297	.004255	.0652
236	55696	15.3623	.004237	.0651
237	56169	15.3948	.004219	.0650
238	56644	15.4272	.004202	.0648
239	57121	15.4596	.004184	.0647
240	57600	15.4919	.004167	.0645

TABLE I *(continued)*

n	n^2	$\sqrt{n}$	$\dfrac{1}{n}$	$\dfrac{1}{\sqrt{n}}$
241	58081	15.5242	.004149	.0644
242	58564	15.5563	.004132	.0643
243	59049	15.5885	.004115	.0642
244	59536	15.6205	.004098	.0640
245	60025	15.6525	.004082	.0639
246	60516	15.6844	.004065	.0638
247	61009	15.7162	.004049	.0636
248	61504	15.7480	.004032	.0635
249	62001	15.7797	.004016	.0634
250	62500	15.8114	.004000	.0632
251	63001	15.8430	.003984	.0631
252	63504	15.8745	.003968	.0630
253	64009	15.9060	.003953	.0629
254	64516	15.9374	.003937	.0627
255	65025	15.9687	.003922	.0626
256	65536	16.0000	.003906	.0625
257	66049	16.0312	.003891	.0624
258	66564	16.0624	.003876	.0623
259	67081	16.0935	.003861	.0621
260	67600	16.1245	.003846	.0620
261	68121	16.1555	.003831	.0619
262	68644	16.1864	.003817	.0618
263	69169	16.2173	.003802	.0617
264	69696	16.2481	.003788	.0615
265	70225	16.2788	.003774	.0614
266	70756	16.3095	.003759	.0613
267	71289	16.3401	.003745	.0612
268	71824	16.3707	.003731	.0611
269	72361	16.4012	.003717	.0610
270	72900	16.4317	.003704	.0609
271	73441	16.4621	.003690	.0607
272	73984	16.4924	.003676	.0606
273	74529	16.5227	.003663	.0605
274	75076	16.5529	.003650	.0604
275	75625	16.5831	.003636	.0603
276	76176	16.6132	.003623	.0602
277	76729	16.6433	.003610	.0601
278	77284	16.6733	.003597	.0600
279	77841	16.7033	.003584	.0599
280	78400	16.7332	.003571	.0598

(continued)

TABLE I *(continued)*

n	n^2	$\sqrt{n}$	$\dfrac{1}{n}$	$\dfrac{1}{\sqrt{n}}$
281	78961	16.7631	.003559	.0597
282	79524	16.7929	.003546	.0595
283	80089	16.8226	.003534	.0594
284	80656	16.8523	.003521	.0593
285	81225	16.8819	.003509	.0592
286	81796	16.9115	.003497	.0591
287	82369	16.9411	.003484	.0590
288	82944	16.9706	.003472	.0589
289	83521	17.0000	.003460	.0588
290	84100	17.0294	.003448	.0587
291	84681	17.0587	.003436	.0586
292	85264	17.0880	.003425	.0585
293	85849	17.1172	.003413	.0584
294	86436	17.1464	.003401	.0583
295	87025	17.1756	.003390	.0582
296	87616	17.2047	.003378	.0581
297	88209	17.2337	.003367	.0580
298	88804	17.2627	.003356	.0579
299	89401	17.2916	.003344	.0578
300	90000	17.3205	.003333	.0577
301	90601	17.3494	.003322	.0576
302	91204	17.3781	.003311	.0575
303	91809	17.4069	.003300	.0574
304	92416	17.4356	.003289	.0574
305	93025	17.4642	.003279	.0573
306	93636	17.4929	.003268	.0572
307	94249	17.5214	.003257	.0571
308	94864	17.5499	.003247	.0570
309	95481	17.5784	.003236	.0569
310	96100	17.6068	.003226	.0568
311	96721	17.6352	.003215	.0567
312	97344	17.6635	.003205	.0566
313	97969	17.6918	.003195	.0565
314	98596	17.7200	.003185	.0564
315	99225	17.7482	.003175	.0563
316	99856	17.7764	.003165	.0563
317	100489	17.8045	.003155	.0562
318	101124	17.8326	.003145	.0561
319	101761	17.8606	.003135	.0560
320	102400	17.8885	.003125	.0559

TABLE I *(continued)*

n	n^2	$\sqrt{n}$	$\dfrac{1}{n}$	$\dfrac{1}{\sqrt{n}}$
321	103041	17.9165	.003115	.0558
322	103684	17.9444	.003106	.0557
323	104329	17.9722	.003096	.0556
324	104976	18.0000	.003086	.0556
325	105625	18.0278	.003077	.0555
326	106276	18.0555	.003067	.0554
327	106929	18.0831	.003058	.0553
328	107584	18.1108	.003049	.0552
329	108241	18.1384	.003040	.0551
330	108900	18.1659	.003030	.0550
331	109561	18.1934	.003021	.0550
332	110224	18.2209	.003012	.0549
333	110889	18.2483	.003003	.0548
334	111556	18.2757	.002994	.0547
335	112225	18.3030	.002985	.0546
336	112896	18.3303	.002976	.0546
337	113569	18.3576	.002967	.0545
338	114244	18.3848	.002959	.0544
339	114921	18.4120	.002950	.0543
340	115600	18.4391	.002941	.0542
341	116281	18.4662	.002933	.0542
342	116964	18.4932	.002924	.0541
343	117649	18.5203	.002915	.0540
344	118336	18.5472	.002907	.0539
345	119025	18.5742	.002899	.0538
346	119716	18.6011	.002890	.0538
347	120409	18.6279	.002882	.0537
348	121104	18.6548	.002874	.0536
349	121801	18.6815	.002865	.0535
350	122500	18.7083	.002857	.0535
351	123201	18.7350	.002849	.0534
352	123904	18.7617	.002841	.0533
353	124609	18.7883	.002833	.0532
354	125316	18.8149	.002825	.0531
355	126025	18.8414	.002817	.0531
356	126736	18.8680	.002809	.0530
357	127449	18.8944	.002801	.0529
358	128164	18.9209	.002793	.0529
359	128881	18.9473	.002786	.0528
360	129600	18.9737	.002778	.0527

(continued)

TABLE I *(continued)*

n	n^2	$\sqrt{n}$	$\dfrac{1}{n}$	$\dfrac{1}{\sqrt{n}}$
361	130321	19.0000	.002770	.0526
362	131044	19.0263	.002762	.0526
363	131769	19.0526	.002755	.0525
364	132496	19.0788	.002747	.0524
365	133225	19.1050	.002740	.0523
366	133956	19.1311	.002732	.0523
367	134689	19.1572	.002725	.0522
368	135424	19.1833	.002717	.0521
369	136161	19.2094	.002710	.0521
370	136900	19.2354	.002703	.0520
371	137641	19.2614	.002695	.0519
372	138384	19.2873	.002688	.0518
373	139129	19.3132	.002681	.0518
374	139876	19.3391	.002674	.0517
375	140625	19.3649	.002667	.0516
376	141376	19.3907	.002660	.0516
377	142129	19.4165	.002653	.0515
378	142884	19.4422	.002646	.0514
379	143641	19.4679	.002639	.0514
380	144400	19.4936	.002632	.0513
381	145161	19.5192	.002625	.0512
382	145924	19.5448	.002618	.0512
383	146689	19.5704	.002611	.0511
384	147456	19.5959	.002604	.0510
385	148225	19.6214	.002597	.0510
386	148996	19.6469	.002591	.0509
387	149769	19.6723	.002584	.0508
388	150544	19.6977	.002577	.0508
389	151321	19.7231	.002571	.0507
390	152100	19.7484	.002564	.0506
391	152881	19.7737	.002558	.0506
392	153664	19.7990	.002551	.0505
393	154449	19.8242	.002545	.0504
394	155236	19.8494	.002538	.0504
395	156025	19.8746	.002532	.0503
396	156816	19.8997	.002525	.0503
397	157609	19.9249	.002519	.0502
398	158404	19.9499	.002513	.0501
399	159201	19.9750	.002506	.0501
400	160000	20.0000	.002500	.0500

TABLE I *(continued)*

n	n^2	$\sqrt{n}$	$\dfrac{1}{n}$	$\dfrac{1}{\sqrt{n}}$
401	160801	20.0250	.002494	.0499
402	161604	20.0499	.002488	.0499
403	162409	20.0749	.002481	.0498
404	163216	20.0998	.002475	.0498
405	164025	20.1246	.002469	.0497
406	164836	20.1494	.002463	.0496
407	165649	20.1742	.002457	.0496
408	166464	20.1990	.002451	.0495
409	167281	20.2237	.002445	.0494
410	168100	20.2485	.002439	.0494
411	168921	20.2731	.002433	.0493
412	169744	20.2978	.002427	.0493
413	170569	20.3224	.002421	.0492
414	171396	20.3470	.002415	.0491
415	172225	20.3715	.002410	.0491
416	173056	20.3961	.002404	.0490
417	173889	20.4206	.002398	.0490
418	174724	20.4450	.002392	.0489
419	175561	20.4695	.002387	.0489
420	176400	20.4939	.002381	.0488
421	177241	20.5183	.002375	.0487
422	178084	20.5426	.002370	.0487
423	178929	20.5670	.002364	.0486
424	179776	20.5913	.002358	.0486
425	180625	20.6155	.002353	.0485
426	181476	20.6398	.002347	.0485
427	182329	20.6640	.002342	.0484
428	183184	20.6882	.002336	.0483
429	184041	20.7123	.002331	.0483
430	184900	20.7364	.002326	.0482
431	185761	20.7605	.002320	.0482
432	186624	20.7846	.002315	.0481
433	187489	20.8087	.002309	.0481
434	188356	20.8327	.002304	.0480
435	189225	20.8567	.002299	.0479
436	190096	20.8806	.002294	.0479
437	190969	20.9045	.002288	.0478
438	191844	20.9284	.002283	.0478
439	192721	20.9523	.002278	.0477
440	193600	20.9762	.002273	.0477

(continued)

TABLE I *(continued)*

n	n^2	$\sqrt{n}$	$\dfrac{1}{n}$	$\dfrac{1}{\sqrt{n}}$
441	194481	21.0000	.002268	.0476
442	195364	21.0238	.002262	.0476
443	196249	21.0476	.002257	.0475
444	197136	21.0713	.002252	.0475
445	198025	21.0950	.002247	.0474
446	198916	21.1187	.002242	.0474
447	199809	21.1424	.002237	.0473
448	200704	21.1660	.002232	.0472
449	201601	21.1896	.002227	.0472
450	202500	21.2132	.002222	.0471
451	203401	21.2368	.002217	.0471
452	204304	21.2603	.002212	.0470
453	205209	21.2838	.002208	.0470
454	206116	21.3073	.002203	.0469
455	207025	21.3307	.002198	.0469
456	207936	21.3542	.002193	.0468
457	208849	21.3776	.002188	.0468
458	209764	21.4009	.002183	.0467
459	210681	21.4243	.002179	.0467
460	211600	21.4476	.002174	.0466
461	212521	21.4709	.002169	.0466
462	213444	21.4942	.002165	.0465
463	214369	21.5174	.002160	.0465
464	215296	21.5407	.002155	.0464
465	216225	21.5639	.002151	.0464
466	217156	21.5870	.002146	.0463
467	218089	21.6102	.002141	.0463
468	219024	21.6333	.002137	.0462
469	219961	21.6564	.002132	.0462
470	220900	21.6795	.002128	.0461
471	221841	21.7025	.002123	.0461
472	222784	21.7256	.002119	.0460
473	223729	21.7486	.002114	.0460
474	224676	21.7715	.002110	.0459
475	225625	21.7945	.002105	.0459
476	226576	21.8174	.002101	.0458
477	227529	21.8403	.002096	.0458
478	228484	21.8632	.002092	.0457
479	229441	21.8861	.002088	.0457
480	230400	21.9089	.002083	.0456

TABLE I *(continued)*

n	n^2	$\sqrt{n}$	$\dfrac{1}{n}$	$\dfrac{1}{\sqrt{n}}$
481	231361	21.9317	.002079	.0456
482	232324	21.9545	.002075	.0455
483	233289	21.9773	.002070	.0455
484	234256	22.0000	.002066	.0455
485	235225	22.0227	.002062	.0454
486	236196	22.0454	.002058	.0454
487	237169	22.0681	.002053	.0453
488	238144	22.0907	.002049	.0453
489	239121	22.1133	.002045	.0452
490	240100	22.1359	.002041	.0452
491	241081	22.1585	.002037	.0451
492	242064	22.1811	.002033	.0451
493	243049	22.2036	.002028	.0450
494	244036	22.2261	.002024	.0450
495	245025	22.2486	.002020	.0449
496	246016	22.2711	.002016	.0448
497	247009	22.2935	.002012	.0449
498	248004	22.3159	.002008	.0449
499	249001	22.3383	.002004	.0448
500	250000	22.3607	.002000	.0447
501	251001	22.3830	.001996	.0447
502	252004	22.4054	.001992	.0446
503	253009	22.4277	.001988	.0446
504	254016	22.4499	.001984	.0445
505	255025	22.4722	.001980	.0445
506	256036	22.4944	.001976	.0445
507	257049	22.5167	.001972	.0444
508	258064	22.5389	.001969	.0444
509	259081	22.5610	.001965	.0443
510	260100	22.5832	.001961	.0443
511	261121	22.6053	.001957	.0442
512	262144	22.6274	.001953	.0442
513	263169	22.6495	.001949	.0442
514	264196	22.6716	.001946	.0441
515	265225	22.6936	.001942	.0441
516	266256	22.7156	.001938	.0440
517	267289	22.7376	.001934	.0440
518	268324	22.7596	.001931	.0439
519	269361	22.7816	.001927	.0439
520	270400	22.8035	.001923	.0439

(continued)

TABLE I *(continued)*

n	n^2	$\sqrt{n}$	$\dfrac{1}{n}$	$\dfrac{1}{\sqrt{n}}$
521	271441	22.8254	.001919	.0438
522	272484	22.8473	.001916	.0438
523	273529	22.8692	.001912	.0437
524	274576	22.8910	.001908	.0437
525	275625	22.9129	.001905	.0436
526	276676	22.9347	.001901	.0436
527	277729	22.9565	.001898	.0436
528	278784	22.9783	.001894	.0435
529	279841	23.0000	.001890	.0435
530	280900	23.0217	.001887	.0434
531	281961	23.0434	.001883	.0434
532	283024	23.0651	.001880	.0434
533	284089	23.0868	.001876	.0433
534	285156	23.1084	.001873	.0433
535	286225	23.1301	.001869	.0432
536	287296	23.1517	.001866	.0432
537	288369	23.1733	.001862	.0432
538	289444	23.1948	.001859	.0431
539	290521	23.2164	.001855	.0431
540	291600	23.2379	.001852	.0430
541	292681	23.2594	.001848	.0430
542	293764	23.2809	.001845	.0430
543	294849	23.3024	.001842	.0429
544	295936	23.3238	.001838	.0429
545	297025	23.3452	.001835	.0428
546	298116	23.3666	.001832	.0428
547	299209	23.3880	.001828	.0428
548	300304	23.4094	.001825	.0427
549	301401	23.4307	.001821	.0427
550	302500	23.4521	.001818	.0426
551	303601	23.4734	.001815	.0426
552	304704	23.4947	.001812	.0426
553	305809	23.5160	.001808	.0425
554	306916	23.5372	.001805	.0425
555	308025	23.5584	.001802	.0424
556	309136	23.5797	.001799	.0424
557	310249	23.6008	.001795	.0424
558	311364	23.6220	.001792	.0423
559	312481	23.6432	.001789	.0423
560	313600	23.6643	.001786	.0423

TABLE I *(continued)*

n	n^2	$\sqrt{n}$	$\dfrac{1}{n}$	$\dfrac{1}{\sqrt{n}}$
561	314721	23.6854	.001783	.0422
562	315844	23.7065	.001779	.0422
563	316969	23.7276	.001776	.0421
564	318096	23.7487	.001773	.0421
565	319225	23.7697	.001770	.0421
566	320356	23.7908	.001767	.0420
567	321489	23.8118	.001764	.0420
568	322624	23.8328	.001761	.0420
569	323761	23.8537	.001757	.0419
570	324900	23.8747	.001754	.0419
571	326041	23.8956	.001751	.0418
572	327184	23.9165	.001748	.0418
573	328329	23.9374	.001745	.0418
574	329476	23.9583	.001742	.0417
575	330625	23.9792	.001739	.0417
576	331776	24.0000	.001736	.0417
577	332929	24.0208	.001733	.0416
578	334084	24.0416	.001730	.0416
579	335241	24.0624	.001727	.0416
580	336400	24.0832	.001724	.0415
581	337561	24.1039	.001721	.0415
582	338724	24.1247	.001718	.0415
583	339889	24.1454	.001715	.0414
584	341056	24.1661	.001712	.0414
585	342225	24.1868	.001709	.0413
586	343396	24.2074	.001706	.0413
587	344569	24.2281	.001704	.0413
588	345744	24.2487	.001701	.0412
589	346921	24.2693	.001698	.0412
590	348100	24.2899	.001695	.0412
591	349281	24.3105	.001692	.0411
592	350464	24.3311	.001689	.0411
593	351649	24.3516	.001686	.0411
594	352836	24.3721	.001684	.0410
595	354025	24.3926	.001681	.0410
596	355216	24.4131	.001678	.0410
597	356409	24.4336	.001675	.0409
598	357604	24.4540	.001672	.0409
599	358801	24.4745	.001669	.0409
600	360000	24.4949	.001667	.0408

(continued)

TABLE I *(continued)*

n	n^2	$\sqrt{n}$	$\dfrac{1}{n}$	$\dfrac{1}{\sqrt{n}}$
601	361201	24.5153	.001664	.0408
602	362404	24.5357	.001661	.0408
603	363609	24.5561	.001658	.0407
604	364816	24.5764	.001656	.0407
605	366025	24.5967	.001653	.0407
606	367236	24.6171	.001650	.0406
607	368449	24.6374	.001647	.0406
608	369664	24.6577	.001645	.0406
609	370881	24.6779	.001642	.0405
610	372100	24.6982	.001639	.0405
611	373321	24.7184	.001637	.0405
612	374544	24.7386	.001634	.0404
613	375769	24.7588	.001631	.0404
614	376996	24.7790	.001629	.0404
615	378225	24.7992	.001626	.0403
616	379456	24.8193	.001623	.0403
617	380689	24.8395	.001621	.0403
618	381924	24.8596	.001618	.0402
619	383161	24.8797	.001616	.0402
620	384400	24.8998	.001613	.0402
621	385641	24.9199	.001610	.0401
622	386884	24.9399	.001608	.0401
623	388129	24.9600	.001605	.0401
624	389376	24.9800	.001603	.0400
625	390625	25.0000	.001600	.0400
626	391876	25.0200	.001597	.0400
627	393129	25.0400	.001595	.0399
628	394384	25.0599	.001592	.0399
629	395641	25.0799	.001590	.0399
630	396900	25.0998	.001587	.0398
631	398161	25.1197	.001585	.0398
632	399424	25.1396	.001582	.0398
633	400689	25.1595	.001580	.0397
634	401956	25.1794	.001577	.0397
635	403225	25.1992	.001575	.0397
636	404496	25.2190	.001572	.0397
637	405769	25.2389	.001570	.0396
638	407044	25.2587	.001567	.0396
639	408321	25.2784	.001565	.0396
640	409600	25.2982	.001563	.0395

TABLE I *(continued)*

n	n^2	$\sqrt{n}$	$\dfrac{1}{n}$	$\dfrac{1}{\sqrt{n}}$
641	410881	25.3180	.001560	.0395
642	412164	25.3377	.001558	.0395
643	413449	25.3574	.001555	.0394
644	414736	25.3772	.001553	.0394
645	416025	25.3969	.001550	.0394
646	417316	25.4165	.001548	.0393
647	418609	25.4362	.001546	.0393
648	419904	25.4558	.001543	.0393
649	421201	25.4755	.001541	.0393
650	422500	25.4951	.001538	.0392
651	423801	25.5147	.001536	.0392
652	425104	25.5343	.001534	.0392
653	426409	25.5539	.001531	.0391
654	427716	25.5734	.001529	.0391
655	429025	25.5930	.001527	.0391
656	430336	25.6125	.001524	.0390
657	431649	25.6320	.001522	.0390
658	432964	25.6515	.001520	.0390
659	434281	25.6710	.001517	.0390
660	435600	25.6905	.001515	.0389
661	436921	25.7099	.001513	.0389
662	438244	25.7294	.001511	.0389
663	439569	25.7488	.001508	.0388
664	440896	25.7682	.001506	.0388
665	442225	25.7876	.001504	.0388
666	443556	25.8070	.001502	.0387
667	444889	25.8263	.001499	.0387
668	446224	25.8457	.001497	.0387
669	447561	25.8650	.001495	.0387
670	448900	25.8844	.001493	.0386
671	450241	25.9037	.001490	.0386
672	451584	25.9230	.001488	.0386
673	452929	25.9422	.001486	.0385
674	454276	25.9615	.001484	.0385
675	455625	25.9808	.001481	.0385
676	456976	26.0000	.001479	.0385
677	458329	26.0192	.001477	.0384
678	459684	26.0384	.001475	.0384
679	461041	26.0576	.001473	.0384
680	462400	26.0768	.001471	.0383

(continued)

TABLE I *(continued)*

n	n^2	$\sqrt{n}$	$\dfrac{1}{n}$	$\dfrac{1}{\sqrt{n}}$
681	463761	26.0960	.001468	.0383
682	465124	26.1151	.001466	.0383
683	466489	26.1343	.001464	.0383
684	467856	26.1534	.001462	.0382
685	469225	26.1725	.001460	.0382
686	470596	26.1916	.001458	.0382
687	471969	26.2107	.001456	.0382
688	473344	26.2298	.001453	.0381
689	474721	26.2488	.001451	.0381
690	476100	26.2679	.001449	.0381
691	477481	26.2869	.001447	.0380
692	478864	26.3059	.001445	.0380
693	480249	26.3249	.001443	.0380
694	481636	26.3439	.001441	.0380
695	483025	26.3629	.001439	.0379
696	484416	26.3818	.001437	.0379
697	485809	26.4008	.001435	.0379
698	487204	26.4197	.001433	.0379
699	488601	26.4386	.001431	.0378
700	490000	26.4575	.001429	.0378
701	491401	26.4764	.001427	.0378
702	492804	26.4953	.001425	.0377
703	494209	26.5141	.001422	.0377
704	495616	26.5330	.001420	.0377
705	497025	26.5518	.001418	.0377
706	498436	26.5707	.001416	.0376
707	499849	26.5895	.001414	.0376
708	501264	26.6083	.001412	.0376
709	502681	26.6271	.001410	.0376
710	504100	26.6458	.001408	.0375
711	505521	26.6646	.001406	.0375
712	506944	26.6833	.001404	.0375
713	508369	26.7021	.001403	.0375
714	509796	26.7208	.001401	.0374
715	511225	26.7395	.001399	.0374
716	512656	26.7582	.001397	.0374
717	514089	26.7769	.001395	.0373
718	515524	26.7955	.001393	.0373
719	516961	26.8142	.001391	.0373
720	518400	26.8328	.001389	.0373

TABLE I *(continued)*

n	n^2	$\sqrt{n}$	$\dfrac{1}{n}$	$\dfrac{1}{\sqrt{n}}$
721	519841	26.8514	.001387	.0372
722	521284	26.8701	.001385	.0372
723	522729	26.8887	.001383	.0372
724	524176	26.9072	.001381	.0372
725	525625	26.9258	.001379	.0371
726	527076	26.9444	.001377	.0371
727	528529	26.9629	.001376	.0371
728	529984	26.9815	.001374	.0371
729	531441	27.0000	.001372	.0370
730	532900	27.0185	.001370	.0370
731	534361	27.0370	.001368	.0370
732	535824	27.0555	.001366	.0370
733	537289	27.0740	.001364	.0369
734	538756	27.0924	.001362	.0369
735	540225	27.1109	.001361	.0369
736	541696	27.1293	.001359	.0369
737	543169	27.1477	.001357	.0368
738	544644	27.1662	.001355	.0368
739	546121	27.1846	.001353	.0368
740	547600	27.2029	.001351	.0368
741	549081	27.2213	.001350	.0367
742	550564	27.2397	.001348	.0367
743	552049	27.2580	.001346	.0367
744	553536	27.2764	.001344	.0367
745	555025	27.2947	.001342	.0366
746	556516	27.3130	.001340	.0366
747	558009	27.3313	.001339	.0366
748	559504	27.3496	.001337	.0366
749	561001	27.3679	.001335	.0365
750	562500	27.3861	.001333	.0365
751	564001	27.4044	.001332	.0365
752	565504	27.4226	.001330	.0365
753	567009	27.4408	.001328	.0364
754	568516	27.4591	.001326	.0364
755	570025	27.4773	.001325	.0364
756	571536	27.4955	.001323	.0364
757	573049	27.5136	.001321	.0363
758	574564	27.5318	.001319	.0363
759	576081	27.5500	.001318	.0363
760	577600	27.5681	.001316	.0363

(continued)

TABLE I *(continued)*

n	n^2	$\sqrt{n}$	$\dfrac{1}{n}$	$\dfrac{1}{\sqrt{n}}$
761	579121	27.5862	.001314	.0363
762	580644	27.6043	.001312	.0362
763	582169	27.6225	.001311	.0362
764	583696	27.6405	.001309	.0362
765	585225	27.6586	.001307	.0362
766	586756	27.6767	.001305	.0361
767	588289	27.6948	.001304	.0361
768	589824	27.7128	.001302	.0361
769	591361	27.7308	.001300	.0361
770	592900	27.7489	.001299	.0360
771	594441	27.7669	.001297	.0360
772	595984	27.7849	.001295	.0360
773	597529	27.8029	.001294	.0360
774	599076	27.8209	.001292	.0359
775	600625	27.8388	.001290	.0359
776	602176	27.8568	.001289	.0359
777	603729	27.8747	.001287	.0359
778	605284	27.8927	.001285	.0359
779	606841	27.9106	.001284	.0358
780	608400	27.9285	.001282	.0358
781	609961	27.9464	.001280	.0358
782	611524	27.9643	.001279	.0358
783	613089	27.9821	.001277	.0357
784	614656	28.0000	.001276	.0357
785	616225	28.0179	.001274	.0357
786	617796	28.0357	.001272	.0357
787	619369	28.0535	.001271	.0356
788	620944	28.0713	.001269	.0356
789	622521	28.0891	.001267	.0356
790	624100	28.1069	.001266	.0356
791	625681	28.1247	.001264	.0356
792	627264	28.1425	.001263	.0355
793	628849	28.1603	.001261	.0355
794	630436	28.1780	.001259	.0355
795	632025	28.1957	.001258	.0355
796	633616	28.2135	.001256	.0354
797	635209	28.2312	.001255	.0354
798	636804	28.2489	.001253	.0354
799	638401	28.2666	.001252	.0354
800	640000	28.2843	.001250	.0354

TABLE I *(continued)*

n	n^2	$\sqrt{n}$	$\dfrac{1}{n}$	$\dfrac{1}{\sqrt{n}}$
801	641601	28.3019	.001248	.0353
802	643204	28.3196	.001247	.0353
803	644809	28.3373	.001245	.0353
804	646416	28.3549	.001244	.0353
805	648025	28.3725	.001242	.0352
806	649636	28.3901	.001241	.0352
807	651249	28.4077	.001239	.0352
808	652864	28.4253	.001238	.0352
809	654481	28.4429	.001236	.0352
810	656100	28.4605	.001235	.0351
811	657721	28.4781	.001233	.0351
812	659344	28.4956	.001232	.0351
813	660969	28.5132	.001230	.0351
814	662596	28.5307	.001229	.0351
815	664225	28.5482	.001227	.0350
816	665856	28.5657	.001225	.0350
817	667489	28.5832	.001224	.0350
818	669124	28.6007	.001222	.0350
819	670761	28.6182	.001221	.0349
820	672400	28.6356	.001220	.0349
821	674041	28.6531	.001218	.0349
822	675684	28.6705	.001217	.0349
823	677329	28.6880	.001215	.0349
824	678976	28.7054	.001214	.0348
825	680625	28.7228	.001212	.0348
826	682276	28.7402	.001211	.0348
827	683929	28.7576	.001209	.0348
828	685584	28.7750	.001208	.0348
829	687241	28.7924	.001206	.0347
830	688900	28.8097	.001205	.0347
831	690561	28.8271	.001203	.0347
832	692224	28.8444	.001202	.0347
833	693889	28.8617	.001200	.0346
834	695556	28.8791	.001199	.0346
835	697225	28.8964	.001198	.0346
836	698896	28.9137	.001196	.0346
837	700569	28.9310	.001195	.0346
838	702244	28.9482	.001193	.0345
839	703921	28.9655	.001192	.0345
840	705600	28.9828	.001190	.0345

(continued)

TABLE I *(continued)*

n	n^2	$\sqrt{n}$	$\dfrac{1}{n}$	$\dfrac{1}{\sqrt{n}}$
841	707281	29.0000	.001189	.0345
842	708964	29.0172	.001188	.0345
843	710649	29.0345	.001186	.0344
844	712336	29.0517	.001185	.0344
845	714025	29.0689	.001183	.0344
846	715716	29.0861	.001182	.0344
847	717409	29.1033	.001181	.0344
848	719104	29.1204	.001179	.0343
849	720801	29.1376	.001178	.0343
850	722500	29.1548	.001176	.0343
851	724201	29.1719	.001175	.0343
852	725904	29.1890	.001174	.0343
853	727609	29.2062	.001172	.0342
854	729316	29.2233	.001171	.0342
855	731025	29.2404	.001170	.0342
856	732736	29.2575	.001168	.0342
857	734449	29.2746	.001167	.0342
858	736164	29.2916	.001166	.0341
859	737881	29.3087	.001164	.0341
860	739600	29.3258	.001163	.0341
861	741321	29.3428	.001161	.0341
862	743044	29.3598	.001160	.0341
863	744769	29.3769	.001159	.0340
864	746496	29.3939	.001157	.0340
865	748225	29.4109	.001156	.0340
866	749956	29.4279	.001155	.0340
867	751689	29.4449	.001153	.0340
868	753424	29.4618	.001152	.0339
869	755161	29.4788	.001151	.0339
870	756900	29.4958	.001149	.0339
871	758641	29.5127	.001148	.0339
872	760384	29.5296	.001147	.0339
873	762129	29.5466	.001145	.0338
874	763876	29.5635	.001144	.0338
875	765625	29.5804	.001143	.0338
876	767376	29.5973	.001142	.0338
877	769129	29.6142	.001140	.0338
878	770884	29.6311	.001139	.0337
879	772641	29.6479	.001138	.0337
880	774400	29.6648	.001136	.0337

TABLE I *(continued)*

n	n^2	$\sqrt{n}$	$\dfrac{1}{n}$	$\dfrac{1}{\sqrt{n}}$
881	776161	29.6816	.001135	.0337
882	777924	29.6985	.001134	.0337
883	779689	29.7153	.001133	.0337
884	781456	29.7321	.001131	.0336
885	783225	29.7489	.001130	.0336
886	784996	29.7658	.001129	.0336
887	786769	29.7825	.001127	.0336
888	788544	29.7993	.001126	.0336
889	790321	29.8161	.001125	.0335
890	792100	29.8329	.001124	.0335
891	793881	29.8496	.001122	.0335
892	795664	29.8664	.001121	.0335
893	797449	29.8831	.001120	.0335
894	799236	29.8998	.001119	.0334
895	801025	29.9166	.001117	.0334
896	802816	29.9333	.001116	.0334
897	804609	29.9500	.001115	.0334
898	806404	29.9666	.001114	.0334
899	808201	29.9833	.001112	.0334
900	810000	30.0000	.001111	.0333
901	811801	30.0167	.001110	.0333
902	813604	30.0333	.001109	.0333
903	815409	30.0500	.001107	.0333
904	817216	30.0666	.001106	.0333
905	819025	30.0832	.001105	.0332
906	820836	30.0998	.001104	.0332
907	822649	30.1164	.001103	.0332
908	824464	30.1330	.001101	.0332
909	826281	30.1496	.001100	.0332
910	828100	30.1662	.001099	.0331
911	829921	30.1828	.001098	.0331
912	831744	30.1993	.001096	.0331
913	833569	30.2159	.001095	.0331
914	835396	30.2324	.001094	.0331
915	837225	30.2490	.001093	.0331
916	839056	30.2655	.001092	.0330
917	840889	30.2820	.001091	.0330
918	842724	30.2985	.001089	.0330
919	844561	30.3150	.001088	.0330
920	846400	30.3315	.001087	.0330

(continued)

TABLE I *(continued)*

n	n^2	$\sqrt{n}$	$\dfrac{1}{n}$	$\dfrac{1}{\sqrt{n}}$
921	848241	30.3480	.001086	.0330
922	850084	30.3645	.001085	.0329
923	851929	30.3809	.001083	.0329
924	853776	30.3974	.001082	.0329
925	855625	30.4138	.001081	.0329
926	857476	30.4302	.001080	.0329
927	859329	30.4467	.001079	.0328
928	861184	30.4631	.001078	.0328
929	863041	30.4795	.001076	.0328
930	864900	30.4959	.001075	.0328
931	866761	30.5123	.001074	.0328
932	868624	30.5287	.001073	.0328
933	870489	30.5450	.001072	.0327
934	872356	30.5614	.001071	.0327
935	874225	30.5778	.001070	.0327
936	876096	30.5941	.001068	.0327
937	877969	30.6105	.001067	.0327
938	879844	30.6268	.001066	.0327
939	881721	30.6431	.001065	.0326
940	883600	30.6594	.001064	.0326
941	885481	30.6757	.001063	.0326
942	887364	30.6920	.001062	.0326
943	889249	30.7083	.001060	.0326
944	891136	30.7246	.001059	.0325
945	893025	30.7409	.001058	.0325
946	894916	30.7571	.001057	.0325
947	896809	30.7734	.001056	.0325
948	898704	30.7896	.001055	.0325
949	900601	30.8058	.001054	.0325
950	902500	30.8221	.001053	.0324
951	904401	30.8383	.001052	.0324
952	906304	30.8545	.001050	.0324
953	908209	30.8707	.001049	.0324
954	910116	30.8869	.001048	.0324
955	912025	30.9031	.001047	.0324
956	913936	30.9192	.001046	.0323
957	915849	30.9354	.001045	.0323
958	917764	30.9516	.001044	.0323
959	919681	30.9677	.001043	.0323
960	921600	30.9839	.001042	.0323

TABLE I *(concluded)*

n	n^2	$\sqrt{n}$	$\dfrac{1}{n}$	$\dfrac{1}{\sqrt{n}}$
961	923521	31.0000	.001041	.0323
962	925444	31.0161	.001040	.0322
963	927369	31.0322	.001038	.0322
964	929296	31.0483	.001037	.0322
965	931225	31.0644	.001036	.0322
966	933156	31.0805	.001035	.0322
967	935089	31.0966	.001034	.0322
968	937024	31.1127	.001033	.0321
969	938961	31.1288	.001032	.0321
970	940900	31.1448	.001031	.0321
971	942841	31.1609	.001030	.0321
972	944784	31.1769	.001029	.0321
973	946729	31.1929	.001028	.0321
974	948676	31.2090	.001027	.0320
975	950625	31.2250	.001026	.0320
976	952576	31.2410	.001025	.0320
977	954529	31.2570	.001024	.0320
978	956484	31.2730	.001022	.0320
979	958441	31.2890	.001021	.0320
980	960400	31.3050	.001020	.0319
981	962361	31.3209	.001019	.0319
982	964324	31.3369	.001018	.0319
983	966289	31.3528	.001017	.0319
984	968256	31.3688	.001016	.0319
985	970225	31.3847	.001015	.0319
986	972196	31.4006	.001014	.0318
987	974169	31.4166	.001013	.0318
988	976144	31.4325	.001012	.0318
989	978121	31.4484	.001011	.0318
990	980100	31.4643	.001010	.0318
991	982081	31.4802	.001009	.0318
992	984064	31.4960	.001008	.0318
993	986049	31.5119	.001007	.0317
994	988036	31.5278	.001006	.0317
995	990025	31.5436	.001005	.0317
996	992016	31.5595	.001004	.0317
997	994009	31.5753	.001003	.0317
998	996004	31.5911	.001002	.0317
999	998001	31.6070	.001001	.0316
1000	1000000	31.6228	.001000	.0316

TABLE II
Random Numbers

80583	93944	52456	73766	06830	53656	95043	52628
18453	24065	08458	95366	53473	07541	45547	70808
60814	37777	10057	42332	63335	20483	31732	57254
07236	12152	05088	65825	64169	49022	86995	90328
71396	89215	30722	22102	39542	07772	35841	85721
26849	84547	14663	56346	70774	35439	46850	52341
60352	33049	53633	70863	95596	20094	69248	93446
92087	96294	43514	37481	38649	06343	14013	31711
15701	08337	98588	09495	92176	72535	56303	87352
85275	36898	71569	75673	81007	47749	81304	48557
26857	73156	46758	70472	66067	42792	70284	24320
14633	84924	73750	85788	54244	91030	90415	93615
15694	48297	57256	61342	30945	75789	39904	02192
80613	19019	93119	56077	69170	37403	88152	00077
45688	32486	40744	56974	08345	88975	45134	63538
75545	35247	18619	13674	86864	29901	14908	08830
81122	11724	74627	73707	69979	20288	87342	78818
38904	13141	32392	19763	93278	81757	52548	54091
13902	63742	78464	22501	68107	23621	71586	73417
08972	11598	62095	36787	63535	24170	64756	03324
24152	00023	12302	80783	93584	72869	60096	21551
39024	00867	76378	41605	11303	22970	07855	39269
49458	74284	05041	49807	44035	52166	21282	21296
20158	34243	46978	35482	17395	96131	35947	67807
37051	93029	47665	64382	87648	85261	04986	83666
86015	46874	32444	48277	58303	29822	93174	93994
23108	88222	88570	74015	73515	90400	71148	43674
54880	87873	95160	59221	61222	60561	62326	18462
29748	12102	80580	41867	85496	57560	81604	18811
07944	05600	60478	03343	45875	21069	85644	47217

From Downie, N. M., & Starry, A. R.: *Descriptive and Inferential Statistics*. Copyright © 1977 by N. M. Downie and Allan R. Starry. Reprinted by permission of Harper & Row, Publishers, Inc.

TABLE II (continued)

30389	87374	64278	58044	14924	39650	95294	00583
26870	76150	68476	64659	70312	05682	66986	34091
35124	67018	41361	82760	90850	64618	80620	51727
21375	05871	93823	43178	24781	89683	55411	85695
17714	53295	07706	17813	40902	05069	99083	06720
84618	97553	31223	08420	72682	07385	90726	57104
09604	60475	94119	01840	21443	41808	68984	83632
20466	68795	77762	20791	01176	28838	36421	16428
52781	76514	83483	47055	80582	71944	92638	40355
78494	72306	94541	37408	13177	55292	21036	82848
93692	25527	21785	41101	91178	10174	43708	66354
66146	63210	47458	64809	98189	81851	46062	27647
28992	63165	40405	68032	96717	54244	71171	15102
46182	49126	71209	92061	39448	93136	42175	88350
47269	15747	85561	29671	58137	17820	54358	64578
14738	86667	28825	35793	28976	66252	19715	94082
19056	13939	12843	82590	09815	93146	38793	85774
75814	85986	83824	52692	54130	55160	54196	34108
62448	46385	63011	98901	14974	40344	60014	07201
80395	81114	88325	80851	43667	70883	16315	53969
35075	33949	27767	43584	85301	88977	60365	94653
56623	34442	13025	14338	54066	15243	83799	42402
36409	83232	80217	26392	98525	24335	32960	07405
57620	52606	10875	62004	90391	61105	19322	53845
07399	37408	54127	57326	26629	19087	11220	94747
68980	05339	60311	42824	37301	42678	31751	57260
14454	04504	49739	71484	92003	98086	88492	99382
07481	83828	78626	51594	16453	94614	30934	47744
27499	98748	66692	13986	99837	00582	22888	48893
35902	91386	44071	28091	97362	97703	78212	16993

(continued)

TABLE II *(concluded)*

96207	44156	32825	29527	04220	86304	03061	18072
59175	20695	51981	50654	94938	81997	07954	19814
05128	09719	47677	26269	62290	64464	06958	92983
13499	06319	20971	87749	90429	12272	99599	10507
64421	80814	66281	31003	00682	27398	43622	63147
74910	64345	78542	42785	13661	58873	34677	58300
61318	31855	81333	10591	40510	07893	45305	07521
76503	34513	81594	13628	51215	90290	59747	68277
11654	99892	61613	62269	50263	90212	16520	69676
92852	55866	00397	58391	12609	17646	68652	27376
01158	63267	41290	67312	71857	15957	79375	95220
55823	47641	05870	01119	92784	26340	33521	26665
66821	41576	82444	99005	04921	73701	59589	49067
96277	48257	20247	81759	45197	25332	20554	91409
43947	51680	48460	85558	15191	18782	59404	72059
01918	28316	60833	25983	01291	41349	42614	29297
70071	14736	43529	06318	38384	74761	34994	41374
11133	07586	88722	56736	66164	49431	99385	41600
78138	66559	94813	31900	54155	83436	66497	68646
27482	45476	74457	90561	72848	11834	48509	23929
88651	22596	25163	01889	70014	15021	15470	48355
74843	93413	65251	07629	37239	33295	20094	98977
28597	20405	36815	43625	18637	37509	73788	06533
74022	84617	64397	11692	05327	82162	60530	45128
65741	14014	04515	25624	95096	67946	44372	15486
58838	73859	83761	60873	43253	84145	36066	94850
52623	07992	14387	06345	80854	09279	74384	89342
07759	51777	51321	92246	60000	77074	38992	22815
27493	70939	72472	00008	40890	18002	36151	99073
11161	78576	05466	55306	93128	18464	57178	65762

TABLE III
Table of Probabilities Under the Normal Curve

1	2	3	4	1	2	3	4
z	Area from Mean to z	Area from −∞ to z	Area from z to +∞	z	Area from Mean to z	Area from −∞ to z	Area from z to +∞
0.00	.0000	.5000	.5000	0.35	.1368	.6368	.3632
0.01	.0040	.5040	.4960	0.36	.1406	.6406	.3594
0.02	.0080	.5080	.4920	0.37	.1443	.6443	.3557
0.03	.0120	.5120	.4880	0.38	.1480	.6480	.3520
0.04	.0160	.5160	.4840	0.39	.1517	.6517	.3483
0.05	.0199	.5199	.4801	0.40	.1554	.6554	.3446
0.06	.0239	.5239	.4761	0.41	.1591	.6591	.3409
0.07	.0279	.5279	.4721	0.42	.1628	.6628	.3372
0.08	.0319	.5319	.4681	0.43	.1664	.6664	.3336
0.09	.0359	.5359	.4641	0.44	.1700	.6700	.3300
0.10	.0398	.5398	.4602	0.45	.1736	.6736	.3264
0.11	.0438	.5438	.4562	0.46	.1772	.6772	.3228
0.12	.0478	.5478	.4522	0.47	.1808	.6808	.3192
0.13	.0517	.5517	.4483	0.48	.1844	.6844	.3156
0.14	.0557	.5557	.4443	0.49	.1879	.6879	.3121
0.15	.0596	.5596	.4404	0.50	.1915	.6915	.3085
0.16	.0636	.5636	.4364	0.51	.1950	.6950	.3050
0.17	.0675	.5675	.4325	0.52	.1985	.6985	.3015
0.18	.0714	.5714	.4286	0.53	.2019	.7019	.2981
0.19	.0753	.5753	.4247	0.54	.2054	.7054	.2946
0.20	.0793	.5793	.4207	0.55	.2088	.7088	.2912
0.21	.0832	.5832	.4168	0.56	.2123	.7123	.2877
0.22	.0871	.5871	.4129	0.57	.2157	.7157	.2843
0.23	.0910	.5910	.4090	0.58	.2190	.7190	.2810
0.24	.0948	.5948	.4052	0.59	.2224	.7224	.2776
0.25	.0987	.5987	.4013	0.60	.2257	.7257	.2743
0.26	.1026	.6026	.3974	0.61	.2291	.7291	.2709
0.27	.1064	.6064	.3936	0.62	.2324	.7324	.2676
0.28	.1103	.6103	.3897	0.63	.2357	.7357	.2643
0.29	.1141	.6141	.3859	0.64	.2389	.7389	.2611
0.30	.1179	.6179	.3821	0.65	.2422	.7422	.2578
0.31	.1217	.6217	.3783	0.66	.2454	.7454	.2546
0.32	.1255	.6255	.3745	0.67	.2486	.7486	.2514
0.33	.1293	.6293	.3707	0.68	.2517	.7517	.2483
0.34	.1331	.6331	.3669	0.69	.2549	.7549	.2451

(continued)

Adapted from Edwards, A. L.: *Statistical Methods, 3rd ed.* Copyright © 1973, 1967 by Allen L. Edwards. First edition copyright 1954 by Allen L. Edwards under the title *Statistical Methods for the Behavioral Sciences.* Reprinted by permission of Holt, Rinehart and Winston.

TABLE III (continued)

1 z	2 Area from Mean to z	3 Area from $-\infty$ to z	4 Area from z to $+\infty$	1 z	2 Area from Mean to z	3 Area from $-\infty$ to z	4 Area from z to $+\infty$
0.70	.2580	.7580	.2420	1.05	.3531	.8531	.1469
0.71	.2611	.7611	.2389	1.06	.3554	.8554	.1446
0.72	.2642	.7642	.2358	1.07	.3577	.8577	.1423
0.73	.2673	.7673	.2327	1.08	.3599	.8599	.1401
0.74	.2704	.7704	.2296	1.09	.3621	.8621	.1379
0.75	.2734	.7734	.2266	1.10	.3643	.8643	.1357
0.76	.2764	.7764	.2236	1.11	.3665	.8665	.1335
0.77	.2794	.7794	.2206	1.12	.3686	.8686	.1314
0.78	.2823	.7823	.2177	1.13	.3708	.8708	.1292
0.79	.2852	.7852	.2148	1.14	.3729	.8729	.1271
0.80	.2881	.7881	.2119	1.15	.3749	.8749	.1251
0.81	.2910	.7910	.2090	1.16	.3770	.8770	.1230
0.82	.2939	.7939	.2061	1.17	.3790	.8790	.1210
0.83	.2967	.7967	.2033	1.18	.3810	.8810	.1190
0.84	.2995	.7995	.2005	1.19	.3830	.8830	.1170
0.85	.3023	.8023	.1977	1.20	.3849	.8849	.1151
0.86	.3051	.8051	.1949	1.21	.3869	.8869	.1131
0.87	.3078	.8078	.1922	1.22	.3888	.8888	.1112
0.88	.3106	.8106	.1894	1.23	.3907	.8907	.1093
0.89	.3133	.8133	.1867	1.24	.3925	.8925	.1075
0.90	.3159	.8159	.1841	1.25	.3944	.8944	.1056
0.91	.3186	.8186	.1814	1.26	.3962	.8962	.1038
0.92	.3212	.8212	.1788	1.27	.3980	.8980	.1020
0.93	.3238	.8238	.1762	1.28	.3997	.8997	.1003
0.94	.3264	.8264	.1736	1.29	.4015	.9015	.0985
0.95	.3289	.8289	.1711	1.30	.4032	.9032	.0968
0.96	.3315	.8315	.1685	1.31	.4049	.9049	.0951
0.97	.3340	.8340	.1660	1.32	.4066	.9066	.0934
0.98	.3365	.8365	.1635	1.33	.4082	.9082	.0918
0.99	.3389	.8389	.1611	1.34	.4099	.9099	.0901
1.00	.3413	.8413	.1587	1.35	.4115	.9115	.0885
1.01	.3438	.8438	.1562	1.36	.4131	.9131	.0869
1.02	.3461	.8461	.1539	1.37	.4147	.9147	.0853
1.03	.3485	.8485	.1515	1.38	.4162	.9162	.0838
1.04	.3508	.8508	.1492	1.39	.4177	.9177	.0823

TABLE III (continued)

1 z	2 Area from Mean to z	3 Area from −∞ to z	4 Area from z to +∞	1 z	2 Area from Mean to z	3 Area from −∞ to z	4 Area from z to +∞
1.40	.4192	.9192	.0808	1.75	.4599	.9599	.0401
1.41	.4207	.9207	.0793	1.76	.4608	.9608	.0392
1.42	.4222	.9222	.0778	1.77	.4616	.9616	.0384
1.43	.4236	.9236	.0764	1.78	.4625	.9625	.0375
1.44	.4251	.9251	.0749	1.79	.4633	.9633	.0367
1.45	.4265	.9265	.0735	1.80	.4641	.9641	.0359
1.46	.4279	.9279	.0721	1.81	.4649	.9649	.0351
1.47	.4292	.9292	.0708	1.82	.4656	.9656	.0344
1.48	.4306	.9306	.0694	1.83	.4664	.9664	.0336
1.49	.4319	.9319	.0681	1.84	.4671	.9671	.0329
1.50	.4332	.9332	.0668	1.85	.4678	.9678	.0322
1.51	.4345	.9345	.0655	1.86	.4686	.9686	.0314
1.52	.4357	.9357	.0643	1.87	.4693	.9693	.0307
1.53	.4370	.9370	.0630	1.88	.4699	.9699	.0301
1.54	.4382	.9382	.0618	1.89	.4706	.9706	.0294
1.55	.4394	.9394	.0606	1.90	.4713	.9713	.0287
1.56	.4406	.9406	.0594	1.91	.4719	.9719	.0281
1.57	.4418	.9418	.0582	1.92	.4726	.9726	.0274
1.58	.4429	.9429	.0571	1.93	.4732	.9732	.0268
1.59	.4441	.9441	.0559	1.94	.4738	.9738	.0262
1.60	.4452	.9452	.0548	1.95	.4744	.9744	.0256
1.61	.4463	.9463	.0537	1.96	.4750	.9750	.0250
1.62	.4474	.9474	.0526	1.97	.4756	.9756	.0244
1.63	.4484	.9484	.0516	1.98	.4761	.9761	.0239
1.64	.4495	.9495	.0505	1.99	.4767	.9767	.0233
1.65	.4505	.9505	.0495	2.00	.4772	.9772	.0228
1.66	.4515	.9515	.0485	2.01	.4778	.9778	.0222
1.67	.4525	.9525	.0475	2.02	.4783	.9783	.0217
1.68	.4535	.9535	.0465	2.03	.4788	.9788	.0212
1.69	.4545	.9545	.0455	2.04	.4793	.9793	.0207
1.70	.4554	.9554	.0446	2.05	.4798	.9798	.0202
1.71	.4564	.9564	.0436	2.06	.4803	.9803	.0197
1.72	.4573	.9573	.0427	2.07	.4808	.9808	.0192
1.73	.4582	.9582	.0418	2.08	.4812	.9812	.0188
1.74	.4591	.9591	.0409	2.09	.4817	.9817	.0813

(continued)

TABLE III *(continued)*

1	2	3	4	1	2	3	4
z	Area from Mean to z	Area from −∞ to z	Area from z to +∞	z	Area from Mean to z	Area from −∞ to z	Area from z to +∞
2.10	.4821	.9821	.0179	2.45	.4929	.9929	.0071
2.11	.4826	.9826	.0174	2.46	.4931	.9931	.0069
2.12	.4830	.9830	.0170	2.47	.4932	.9932	.0068
2.13	.4834	.9834	.0166	2.48	.4934	.9934	.0066
2.14	.4838	.9838	.0162	2.49	.4936	.9936	.0064
2.15	.4842	.9842	.0158	2.50	.4938	.9938	.0062
2.16	.4846	.9846	.0154	2.51	.4940	.9940	.0060
2.17	.4850	.9850	.0150	2.52	.4941	.9941	.0059
2.18	.4854	.9854	.0146	2.53	.4943	.9943	.0057
2.19	.4857	.9857	.0143	2.54	.4945	.9945	.0055
2.20	.4861	.9861	.0139	2.55	.4946	.9946	.0054
2.21	.4864	.9864	.0136	2.56	.4948	.9948	.0052
2.22	.4868	.9868	.0132	2.57	.4949	.9949	.0051
2.23	.4871	.9871	.0129	2.58	.4951	.9951	.0049
2.24	.4875	.9875	.0125	2.59	.4952	.9952	.0048
2.25	.4878	.9878	.0122	2.60	.4953	.9953	.0047
2.26	.4881	.9881	.0119	2.61	.4955	.9955	.0045
2.27	.4884	.9884	.0116	2.62	.4956	.9956	.0044
2.28	.4887	.9887	.0113	2.63	.4957	.9957	.0043
2.29	.4890	.9890	.0110	2.64	.4959	.9959	.0041
2.30	.4893	.9893	.0107	2.65	.4960	.9960	.0040
2.31	.4896	.9896	.0104	2.66	.4961	.9961	.0039
2.32	.4898	.9898	.0102	2.67	.4962	.9962	.0038
2.33	.4901	.9901	.0099	2.68	.4963	.9963	.0037
2.34	.4904	.9904	.0096	2.69	.4964	.9964	.0036
2.35	.4906	.9906	.0094	2.70	.4965	.9965	.0035
2.36	.4909	.9909	.0091	2.71	.4966	.9966	.0034
2.37	.4911	.9911	.0089	2.72	.4967	.9967	.0033
2.38	.4913	.9913	.0087	2.73	.4968	.9968	.0032
2.39	.4916	.9916	.0084	2.74	.4969	.9969	.0031
2.40	.4918	.9918	.0082	2.75	.4970	.9970	.0030
2.41	.4920	.9920	.0080	2.76	.4971	.9971	.0029
2.42	.4922	.9922	.0078	2.77	.4972	.9972	.0028
2.43	.4925	.9925	.0075	2.78	.4973	.9973	.0027
2.44	.4927	.9927	.0073	2.79	.4974	.9974	.0026

TABLE III *(concluded)*

1	2	3	4	1	2	3	4
	Area from	Area from	Area from		Area from	Area from	Area from
z	Mean to z	$-\infty$ to z	z to $+\infty$	z	Mean to z	$-\infty$ to z	z to $+\infty$
2.80	.4974	.9974	.0026	3.05	.4989	.9989	.0011
2.81	.4975	.9975	.0025	3.06	.4989	.9989	.0011
2.82	.4976	.9976	.0024	3.07	.4989	.9989	.0011
2.83	.4977	.9977	.0023	3.08	.4990	.9990	.0010
2.84	.4977	.9977	.0023	3.09	.4990	.9990	.0010
2.85	.4978	.9978	.0022	3.10	.4990	.9990	.0010
2.86	.4979	.9979	.0021	3.11	.4991	.9991	.0009
2.87	.4979	.9979	.0021	3.12	.4991	.9991	.0009
2.88	.4980	.9980	.0020	3.13	.4991	.9991	.0009
2.89	.4981	.9981	.0019	3.14	.4992	.9992	.0008
2.90	.4981	.9981	.0019	3.15	.4992	.9992	.0008
2.91	.4982	.9982	.0018	3.16	.4992	.9992	.0008
2.92	.4982	.9982	.0018	3.17	.4992	.9992	.0008
2.93	.4983	.9983	.0017	3.18	.4993	.9993	.0007
2.94	.4984	.9984	.0016	3.19	.4993	.9993	.0007
2.95	.4984	.9984	.0016	3.20	.4993	.9993	.0007
2.96	.4985	.9985	.0015	3.21	.4993	.9993	.0007
2.97	.4985	.9985	.0015	3.22	.4994	.9994	.0006
2.98	.4986	.9986	.0014	3.23	.4994	.9994	.0006
2.99	.4986	.9986	.0014	3.24	.4994	.9994	.0006
3.00	.4987	.9987	.0013	3.30	.4995	.9995	.0005
3.01	.4987	.9987	.0013	3.40	.4997	.9997	.0003
3.02	.4987	.9987	.0013	3.50	.4998	.9998	.0002
3.03	.4988	.9988	.0012	3.60	.4998	.9998	.0002
3.04	.4988	.9988	.0012	3.70	.4999	.9999	.0001

TABLE IV
Critical Values of t

df	Level of Significance for One-Tailed Test					
	.10	.05	.025	.01	.005	.0005
	Level of Significance for Two-Tailed Test					
df	.20	.10	.05	.02	.01	.001
1	3.078	6.314	12.706	31.821	.63.657	.636.619
2	1.886	2.920	4.303	6.965	9.925	31.598
3	1.638	2.353	3.182	4.541	5.841	12.941
4	1.533	2.132	2.776	3.747	4.604	8.610
5	1.476	2.015	2.571	3.365	4.032	6.859
6	1.440	1.943	2.447	3.143	3.707	5.959
7	1.415	1.895	2.365	2.998	3.449	5.405
8	1.397	1.860	2.306	2.896	3.355	5.041
9	1.383	1.833	2.262	2.821	3.250	4.781
10	1.372	1.812	2.228	2.764	3.169	4.587
11	1.363	1.796	2.201	2.718	3.106	4.437
12	1.356	1.782	2.179	2.681	3.055	4.318
13	1.350	1.771	2.160	2.650	3.012	4.221
14	1.345	1.761	2.145	2.624	2.977	4.140
15	1.341	1.753	2.131	2.602	2.947	4.073
16	1.337	1.746	2.120	2.583	2.921	4.015
17	1.333	1.740	2.110	2.567	2.898	3.965
18	1.330	1.734	2.101	2.552	2.878	3.922
19	1.328	1.729	2.093	2.539	2.861	3.883
20	1.325	1.725	2.086	2.528	2.845	3.850
21	1.323	1.721	2.080	2.518	2.831	3.819
22	1.321	1.717	2.074	2.508	2.819	3.792
23	1.319	1.714	2.069	2.500	2.807	3.767
24	1.318	1.711	2.064	2.492	2.797	3.745
25	1.316	1.708	2.060	2.485	2.787	3.725
26	1.315	1.706	2.056	2.479	2.779	3.707
27	1.314	1.703	2.052	2.473	2.771	3.690
28	1.313	1.701	2.048	2.467	2.763	3.674
29	1.311	1.699	2.045	2.462	2.756	3.659
30	1.310	1.697	2.042	2.457	2.750	3.646
40	1.303	1.684	2.021	2.423	2.704	3.551
60	1.296	1.671	2.000	2.390	2.660	3.460
120	1.289	1.658	1.980	2.358	2.617	3.373
∞	1.282	1.645	1.960	2.326	2.576	3.291

From Fisher, R. A., & Yates, F.: *Statistical Tables for Biological, Agricultural and Medical Research, 6th ed.* London: Longman Group Ltd., 1974. (Previously published by Oliver and Boyd Ltd., Edinburgh.) Reprinted by permission of the authors and the publishers.

TABLE V

Critical Values of the Pearson r

df $(df = n - 2;$ n = number of pairs)	Level of Significance for One-Tailed Test			
	.05	.025	.01	.005
	Level of Significance for Two-Tailed Test			
	.10	.05	.02	.01
1	.988	.997	.9995	.9999
2	.900	.950	.980	.990
3	.805	.878	.934	.959
4	.729	.811	.882	.917
5	.669	.754	.833	.874
6	.622	.707	.789	.834
7	.582	.666	.750	.798
8	.549	.632	.716	.765
9	.521	.602	.685	.735
10	.497	.576	.658	.708
11	.476	.553	.634	.684
12	.458	.532	.612	.661
13	.441	.514	.592	.641
14	.426	.497	.574	.623
15	.412	.482	.558	.606
16	.400	.468	.542	.590
17	.389	.456	.528	.575
18	.378	.444	.516	.561
19	.369	.433	.503	.549
20	.360	.423	.492	.537
21	.352	.413	.482	.526
22	.344	.404	.472	.515
23	.337	.396	.462	.505
24	.330	.388	.453	.496
25	.323	.381	.445	.487
26	.317	.374	.437	.479
27	.311	.367	.430	.471
28	.306	.361	.423	.463
29	.301	.355	.416	.456
30	.296	.349	.409	.449
35	.275	.325	.381	.418
40	.257	.304	.358	.393
45	.243	.288	.338	.372
50	.231	.273	.322	.354
60	.211	.250	.295	.325
70	.195	.232	.274	.302
80	.183	.217	.256	.283
90	.173	.205	.242	.267
100	.164	.195	.230	.254

From Fisher, R. A., & Yates, F.: *Statistical Tables for Biological, Agricultural and Medical Research, 6th ed.* London: Longman Group Ltd., 1974. (Previously published by Oliver and Boyd Ltd., Edinburgh.) Reprinted by permission of the authors and the publishers.

TABLE VI
Critical values of F ($\alpha = .05$ lightface type; $\alpha = .01$ boldface type)

n_2	n_1, Degrees of Freedom for Numerator											
	1	2	3	4	5	6	7	8	9	10	11	12
1	161	200	216	225	230	234	237	239	241	242	243	244
	4,052	4,999	5,403	5,625	5,764	5,859	5,928	5,981	6,022	6,056	6,082	6,106
2	18.51	19.00	19.16	19.25	19.30	19.33	19.36	19.37	19.38	19.39	19.40	19.41
	98.49	99.00	99.17	99.25	99.30	99.33	99.34	99.36	99.38	99.40	99.41	99.42
3	10.13	9.55	9.28	9.12	9.01	8.94	8.88	8.84	8.81	8.78	8.76	8.74
	34.12	30.82	29.46	28.71	28.24	27.91	27.67	27.49	27.34	27.23	27.13	27.05
4	7.71	6.94	6.59	6.39	6.26	6.16	6.09	6.04	6.00	5.96	5.93	5.91
	21.20	18.00	16.69	15.98	15.52	15.21	14.98	14.80	14.66	14.54	14.45	14.37
5	6.61	5.79	5.41	5.19	5.05	4.95	4.88	4.82	4.78	4.74	4.70	4.68
	16.26	13.27	12.06	11.39	10.97	10.67	10.45	10.27	10.15	10.05	9.96	9.89
6	5.99	5.14	4.76	4.53	4.39	4.28	4.21	4.15	4.10	4.06	4.03	4.00
	13.74	10.92	9.78	9.15	8.75	8.47	8.26	8.10	7.98	7.87	7.79	7.72
7	5.59	4.74	4.35	4.12	3.97	3.87	3.79	3.73	3.68	3.63	3.60	3.57
	12.25	9.55	8.45	7.85	7.46	7.19	7.00	6.84	6.71	6.62	6.54	6.47
8	5.32	4.46	4.07	3.84	3.69	3.58	3.50	3.44	3.39	3.34	3.31	3.28
	11.26	8.65	7.59	7.01	6.63	6.37	6.19	6.03	5.91	5.82	5.74	5.67
9	5.12	4.26	3.86	3.63	3.48	3.37	3.29	3.23	3.18	3.13	3.10	3.07
	10.56	8.02	6.99	6.42	6.06	5.80	5.62	5.47	5.35	5.26	5.18	5.11
10	4.96	4.10	3.71	3.48	3.33	3.22	3.14	3.07	3.02	2.97	2.94	2.91
	10.04	7.56	6.55	5.99	5.64	5.39	5.21	5.06	4.95	4.85	4.78	4.71
11	4.84	3.98	3.59	3.36	3.20	3.09	3.01	2.95	2.90	2.86	2.82	2.79
	9.65	7.20	6.22	5.67	5.32	5.97	4.88	4.74	4.63	4.54	4.46	4.40
12	4.75	3.88	3.49	3.26	3.11	3.00	2.92	2.85	2.80	2.76	2.72	2.69
	9.33	6.93	5.95	5.41	5.06	4.82	4.65	4.50	4.39	4.30	4.22	4.16
13	4.67	3.80	3.41	3.18	3.02	2.92	2.84	2.77	2.72	2.67	2.63	2.60
	9.07	6.70	5.74	5.20	4.86	4.62	4.44	4.30	4.19	4.10	4.02	3.96

Reprinted by permission from Snedecor, G. W., and Cochran, W. C.:"Statistical Methods." 6th ed., © 1967 by the Iowa State University Press, Ames, Iowa.

TABLE VI (continued)

n_1 Degrees of Freedom for Numerator											
14	16	20	24	30	40	50	75	100	200	500	∞
245	246	248	249	250	251	252	253	253	254	254	254
6,142	6,169	6,208	6,234	6,258	6,286	6,302	6,323	6,334	6,352	6,361	6,366
19.42	19.43	19.44	19.45	19.46	19.47	19.47	19.48	19.49	19.49	19.50	19.50
99.43	99.44	99.45	99.46	99.47	99.48	99.48	99.49	99.49	99.40	99.50	99.50
8.71	8.69	8.66	8.64	8.62	8.60	8.58	8.57	8.56	8.54	8.54	8.53
26.92	26.83	26.69	26.60	26.50	26.41	26.35	26.27	26.23	26.18	26.14	26.12
5.87	5.84	5.80	5.77	5.74	5.71	5.70	5.68	5.66	5.65	5.64	5.63
14.24	14.15	14.02	13.93	13.83	13.74	13.69	13.61	13.57	13.52	13.48	13.46
4.64	4.60	4.56	4.53	4.50	4.46	4.44	4.42	4.40	4.38	4.37	4.36
9.77	9.68	9.55	9.47	9.38	9.29	9.24	9.17	9.13	9.07	9.04	9.02
3.96	3.92	3.87	3.84	3.81	3.77	3.75	3.72	3.71	3.69	3.68	3.67
7.60	7.52	7.39	7.31	7.23	7.14	7.09	7.02	6.99	6.94	6.90	6.88
3.52	3.49	3.44	3.41	3.38	3.34	3.32	3.29	3.28	3.25	3.24	3.23
6.35	6.27	6.15	6.07	5.98	5.90	5.85	5.78	5.75	5.70	5.67	5.65
3.23	3.20	3.15	3.12	3.08	3.05	3.03	3.00	2.98	2.96	2.94	2.93
5.56	5.48	5.36	5.28	5.20	5.11	5.06	5.00	4.96	4.91	4.88	4.86
3.02	2.98	2.93	2.90	2.86	2.82	2.80	2.77	2.76	2.73	2.72	2.71
5.00	4.92	4.80	4.73	4.64	4.56	4.51	4.45	4.41	4.36	4.33	4.31
2.86	2.82	2.77	2.74	2.70	2.67	2.64	2.61	2.59	2.56	2.55	2.54
4.60	4.52	4.41	4.33	4.25	4.17	4.12	4.05	4.01	3.96	3.93	3.91
2.74	2.70	2.65	2.61	2.57	2.53	2.50	2.47	2.45	2.42	2.41	2.40
4.29	4.21	4.10	4.02	3.94	3.86	3.80	3.74	3.70	3.66	3.62	3.60
2.64	2.60	2.54	2.50	2.46	2.42	2.40	2.36	2.35	2.32	2.31	2.30
4.05	3.98	3.86	3.78	3.70	3.61	3.56	3.49	3.46	3.41	3.38	3.36
2.55	2.51	2.46	2.42	2.38	2.34	2.32	2.28	2.26	2.24	2.22	2.21
3.85	3.78	3.67	3.59	3.51	3.42	3.37	3.30	3.27	3.21	3.18	3.16

(continued)

TABLE VI *(continued)*

n_2	n_1 Degrees of Freedom for Numerator											
	1	2	3	4	5	6	7	8	9	10	11	12
14	4.60	3.74	3.34	3.11	2.96	2.85	2.77	2.70	2.65	2.60	2.56	2.53
	8.86	6.51	5.56	5.03	4.69	4.46	4.28	4.14	4.03	3.94	3.86	3.80
15	4.54	3.68	3.29	3.06	2.90	2.79	2.70	2.64	2.59	2.55	2.51	2.48
	8.68	6.36	5.42	4.89	4.56	4.32	4.14	4.00	3.89	3.80	3.73	3.67
16	4.49	3.63	3.24	3.01	2.85	2.74	2.66	2.59	2.54	2.49	2.45	2.42
	8.53	6.23	5.29	4.77	4.44	4.20	4.03	3.89	3.78	3.69	3.61	3.55
17	4.45	3.59	3.20	2.96	2.81	2.70	2.62	2.55	2.50	2.45	2.41	2.38
	8.40	6.11	5.18	4.67	4.34	4.10	3.93	3.79	3.68	3.59	3.52	3.45
18	4.41	3.55	3.16	2.93	2.77	2.66	2.58	2.51	2.46	2.41	2.37	2.34
	8.28	6.01	5.09	4.58	4.25	4.01	3.85	3.71	3.60	3.51	3.44	3.37
19	4.38	3.52	3.13	2.90	2.74	2.63	2.55	2.48	2.43	2.38	2.34	2.31
	8.18	5.93	5.01	4.50	4.17	3.94	3.77	3.63	3.52	3.43	3.36	3.30
20	4.35	3.49	3.10	2.87	2.71	2.60	2.52	2.45	2.40	2.35	2.31	2.28
	8.10	5.85	4.94	4.43	4.10	3.87	3.71	3.56	3.45	3.37	3.30	3.23
21	4.32	3.47	3.07	2.84	2.68	2.57	2.49	2.42	2.37	2.32	2.28	2.25
	8.02	5.78	4.87	4.37	4.04	3.81	3.65	3.51	3.40	3.31	3.24	3.17
22	4.30	3.44	3.05	2.82	2.66	2.55	2.47	2.40	2.35	2.30	2.26	2.23
	7.94	5.72	4.82	4.31	3.99	3.76	3.59	3.45	3.35	3.26	3.18	3.12
23	4.28	3.42	3.03	2.80	2.64	2.53	2.45	2.38	2.32	2.28	2.24	2.20
	7.88	5.66	4.76	4.26	3.94	3.71	3.54	3.41	3.30	3.21	3.14	3.07
24	4.26	3.40	3.01	2.78	2.62	2.51	2.43	2.36	2.30	2.26	2.22	2.18
	7.82	5.61	4.72	4.22	3.90	3.67	3.50	3.36	3.25	3.17	3.09	3.03
25	4.24	3.38	2.99	2.76	2.60	2.49	2.41	2.34	2.28	2.24	2.20	2.16
	7.77	5.57	4.68	4.18	3.86	3.63	3.46	3.32	3.21	3.13	3.05	2.99
26	4.22	3.37	2.98	2.74	2.59	2.47	2.39	2.32	2.27	2.22	2.18	2.15
	7.72	5.53	4.64	4.14	3.82	3.59	3.42	3.29	3.17	3.09	3.02	2.96

TABLE VI (continued)

n_1 Degrees of Freedom for Numerator											
14	16	20	24	30	40	50	75	100	200	500	∞
2.48	2.44	2.39	2.35	2.31	2.27	2.24	2.21	2.19	2.16	2.14	2.13
3.70	3.62	3.51	3.43	3.34	3.26	3.21	3.14	3.11	3.06	3.02	3.00
2.43	2.39	2.33	2.29	2.25	2.21	2.18	2.15	2.12	2.10	2.08	2.07
3.56	3.48	3.36	3.29	3.20	3.12	3.07	3.00	2.97	2.92	2.89	2.87
2.37	2.33	2.28	2.24	2.20	2.16	2.13	2.09	2.07	2.04	2.02	2.01
3.45	3.37	3.25	3.18	3.10	3.01	2.96	2.89	2.86	2.80	2.77	2.75
2.33	2.29	2.23	2.19	2.15	2.11	2.08	2.04	2.02	1.99	1.97	1.96
3.35	3.27	3.16	3.08	3.00	2.92	2.86	2.79	2.76	2.70	2.67	2.65
2.29	2.25	2.19	2.15	2.11	2.07	2.04	2.00	1.98	1.95	1.93	1.92
3.27	3.19	3.07	3.00	2.91	2.81	2.78	2.71	2.68	2.62	2.59	2.57
2.26	2.21	2.15	2.11	2.07	2.02	2.00	1.96	1.94	1.91	1.90	1.88
3.19	3.12	3.00	2.92	2.84	2.76	2.70	2.63	2.60	2.54	2.51	2.49
2.23	2.18	2.12	2.08	2.04	1.99	1.96	1.92	1.90	1.87	1.85	1.84
3.13	3.05	2.94	2.86	2.77	2.69	2.63	2.56	2.53	2.47	2.44	2.42
2.20	2.15	2.09	2.05	2.00	1.96	1.93	1.89	1.87	1.84	1.82	1.81
3.07	2.99	2.88	2.80	2.72	2.63	2.58	2.51	2.47	2.42	2.38	2.36
2.18	2.13	2.07	2.03	1.98	1.93	1.91	1.87	1.84	1.81	1.80	1.78
3.02	2.94	2.83	2.75	2.67	2.58	2.53	2.46	2.42	2.37	2.33	2.31
2.14	2.10	2.04	2.00	1.96	1.91	1.88	1.84	1.82	1.79	1.77	1.76
2.97	2.89	2.78	2.70	2.62	2.53	2.48	2.41	2.37	2.32	2.28	2.26
2.13	2.09	2.02	1.98	1.94	1.89	1.86	1.82	1.80	1.76	1.74	1.73
2.93	2.85	2.74	2.66	2.58	2.49	2.44	2.36	2.33	2.27	2.23	2.21
2.11	2.06	2.00	1.96	1.92	1.87	1.84	1.80	1.77	1.74	1.72	1.71
2.89	2.81	2.70	2.62	2.54	2.45	2.40	2.32	2.29	2.23	2.19	2.17
2.10	2.05	1.99	1.95	1.90	1.85	1.82	1.78	1.76	1.72	1.70	1.69
2.86	2.77	2.66	2.58	2.50	2.41	2.36	2.28	2.25	2.19	2.15	2.13

(continued)

TABLE VI *(continued)*

n_2	n_1 Degrees of Freedom for Numerator											
	1	2	3	4	5	6	7	8	9	10	11	12
27	4.21	3.35	2.96	2.73	2.57	2.46	2.37	2.30	2.25	2.20	2.16	2.13
	7.68	5.49	4.60	4.11	3.79	3.56	3.39	3.26	3.14	3.06	2.98	2.93
28	4.20	3.34	2.95	2.71	2.56	2.44	2.36	2.29	2.24	2.19	2.15	2.12
	7.64	5.45	4.57	4.07	3.76	3.53	3.36	3.23	3.11	3.03	2.95	2.90
29	4.18	3.33	2.93	2.70	2.54	2.43	2.35	2.28	2.22	2.18	2.14	2.10
	7.60	5.42	4.54	4.04	3.73	3.50	3.33	3.20	3.08	3.00	2.92	2.87
30	4.17	3.32	2.92	2.69	2.53	2.42	2.34	2.27	2.21	2.16	2.12	2.09
	7.56	5.39	4.51	4.02	3.70	3.47	3.30	3.17	3.06	2.98	2.90	2.84
32	4.15	3.30	2.90	2.67	2.51	2.40	2.32	2.25	2.19	2.14	2.10	2.07
	7.50	5.34	4.46	3.97	3.66	3.42	3.25	3.12	3.01	2.94	2.86	2.80
34	4.13	3.28	2.88	2.65	2.49	2.38	2.30	2.23	2.17	2.12	2.08	2.05
	7.44	5.29	4.42	3.93	3.61	3.38	3.21	3.08	2.97	2.89	2.82	2.76
36	4.11	3.26	2.86	2.63	2.48	2.36	2.28	2.21	2.15	2.10	2.06	2.03
	7.39	5.25	4.38	3.89	3.58	3.35	3.18	3.04	2.94	2.86	2.78	2.72
38	4.10	3.25	2.85	2.62	2.46	2.35	2.26	2.19	2.14	2.09	2.05	2.02
	7.35	5.21	4.34	3.86	3.54	3.32	3.15	3.02	2.91	2.82	2.75	2.69
40	4.08	3.23	2.84	2.61	2.45	2.34	2.25	2.18	2.12	2.07	2.04	2.00
	7.31	5.18	4.31	3.83	3.51	3.29	3.12	2.99	2.88	2.80	2.73	2.66
42	4.07	3.22	2.83	2.59	2.44	2.32	2.24	2.17	2.11	2.06	2.02	1.99
	7.27	5.15	4.29	3.80	3.49	3.26	3.10	2.96	2.86	2.77	2.70	2.64
44	4.06	3.21	2.82	2.58	2.43	2.31	2.23	2.16	2.10	2.05	2.01	1.98
	7.24	5.12	4.26	3.78	3.46	3.24	3.07	2.94	2.84	2.75	2.68	2.62
46	4.05	3.20	2.81	2.57	2.42	2.30	2.22	2.14	2.09	2.04	2.00	1.97
	7.21	5.10	4.24	3.76	3.44	3.22	3.05	2.92	2.82	2.73	2.66	2.60
48	4.04	3.19	2.80	2.56	2.41	2.30	2.21	2.14	2.08	2.03	1.99	1.96
	7.19	5.08	4.22	3.74	3.42	3.20	3.04	2.90	2.80	2.71	2.64	2.58

TABLE VI *(continued)*

n_1 Degrees of Freedom for Numerator											
14	16	20	24	30	40	50	75	100	200	500	∞
2.08	2.03	1.97	1.93	1.88	1.84	1.80	1.76	1.74	1.71	1.68	1.67
2.83	2.74	2.63	2.55	2.47	2.38	2.25	2.21	2.16	2.16	2.12	2.10
2.06	2.02	1.96	1.91	1.87	1.81	1.78	1.75	1.72	1.69	1.67	1.65
2.80	2.71	2.60	2.52	2.44	2.35	2.30	2.22	2.18	2.13	2.09	2.06
2.05	2.00	1.94	1.90	1.85	1.80	1.77	1.73	1.71	1.68	1.65	1.64
2.77	2.68	2.57	2.49	2.41	2.32	2.27	2.19	2.15	2.10	2.06	2.03
2.04	1.99	1.93	1.89	1.84	1.79	1.76	1.72	1.69	1.66	1.64	1.62
2.74	2.66	2.55	2.47	2.38	2.29	2.24	2.16	2.13	2.07	2.03	2.01
2.02	1.97	1.91	1.86	1.82	1.76	1.74	1.69	1.67	1.64	1.61	1.59
2.70	2.62	2.51	2.42	2.34	2.25	2.20	2.12	2.08	2.02	1.98	1.96
2.00	1.95	1.89	1.84	1.80	1.74	1.71	1.67	1.64	1.61	1.59	1.57
2.66	2.58	2.47	2.38	2.30	2.21	2.15	2.08	2.04	1.98	1.94	1.91
1.98	1.93	1.87	1.82	1.78	1.72	1.69	1.65	1.62	1.59	1.56	1.55
2.62	2.54	2.43	2.35	2.26	2.17	2.12	2.04	2.00	1.94	1.90	1.87
1.96	1.92	1.85	1.80	1.76	1.71	1.67	1.63	1.60	1.57	1.54	1.53
2.59	2.51	2.40	2.32	2.22	2.14	2.08	2.00	1.97	1.90	1.86	1.84
1.95	1.90	1.84	1.79	1.74	1.69	1.66	1.61	1.59	1.55	1.53	1.51
2.56	2.49	2.37	2.29	2.20	2.11	2.05	1.97	1.94	1.88	1.84	1.81
1.94	1.89	1.82	1.78	1.73	1.68	1.64	1.60	1.57	1.54	1.51	1.49
2.54	2.46	2.35	2.26	2.17	2.08	2.02	1.94	1.91	1.85	1.80	1.78
1.92	1.88	1.81	1.76	1.72	1.66	1.63	1.58	1.56	1.52	1.50	1.48
2.52	2.44	2.32	2.24	2.15	2.06	2.00	1.92	1.88	1.81	1.78	1.75
1.91	1.87	1.80	1.75	1.71	1.65	1.62	1.57	1.54	1.51	1.48	1.46
2.50	2.42	2.30	2.22	2.13	2.04	1.98	1.90	1.86	1.80	1.76	1.72
1.90	1.86	1.79	1.74	1.70	1.64	1.61	1.56	1.53	1.50	1.47	1.45
2.43	2.40	2.28	2.20	2.11	2.02	1.96	1.88	1.84	1.78	1.73	1.70

(continued)

TABLE VI *(continued)*

n_2	n_1 Degrees of Freedom for Numerator											
	1	2	3	4	5	6	7	8	9	10	11	12
50	4.03	3.18	2.79	2.56	2.40	2.29	2.20	2.13	2.07	2.02	1.98	1.95
	7.17	5.06	4.20	3.72	3.41	3.18	3.02	2.88	2.78	2.70	2.62	2.56
55	4.02	3.17	2.78	2.54	2.38	2.27	2.18	2.11	2.05	2.00	1.97	1.93
	7.12	5.01	4.16	3.68	3.37	3.15	2.98	2.85	2.75	2.66	2.59	2.53
60	4.00	3.15	2.76	2.52	2.37	2.25	2.17	2.10	2.04	1.99	1.95	1.92
	7.08	4.98	4.13	3.65	3.34	3.12	2.95	2.82	2.72	2.63	2.56	2.50
65	3.99	3.14	2.75	2.51	2.36	2.24	2.15	2.08	2.02	1.98	1.94	1.90
	7.04	4.95	4.10	3.62	3.31	3.09	2.93	2.79	2.70	2.61	2.54	2.47
70	3.98	3.13	2.74	2.50	2.35	2.23	2.14	2.07	2.01	1.97	1.93	1.89
	7.01	4.92	4.08	3.60	3.29	3.07	2.91	2.77	2.67	2.59	2.51	2.45
80	3.96	3.11	2.72	2.48	2.33	2.21	2.12	2.05	1.99	1.95	1.91	1.88
	6.96	4.88	4.04	3.56	3.25	3.04	2.87	2.74	2.64	2.55	2.48	2.41
100	3.94	3.09	2.70	2.46	2.30	2.19	2.10	2.03	1.97	1.92	1.88	1.85
	6.90	4.82	3.98	3.51	3.20	2.99	2.82	2.69	2.59	2.51	2.43	2.36
125	3.92	3.07	2.68	2.44	2.29	2.17	2.08	2.01	1.95	1.90	1.86	1.83
	6.84	4.78	3.94	3.47	3.17	2.95	2.79	2.65	2.56	2.47	2.40	2.33
150	3.91	3.06	2.67	2.43	2.27	2.16	2.07	2.00	1.94	1.89	1.85	1.82
	6.81	4.75	3.91	3.44	3.14	2.92	2.76	2.62	2.53	2.44	2.37	2.30
200	3.89	3.04	2.65	2.41	2.26	2.14	2.05	1.98	1.92	1.87	1.83	1.80
	6.76	4.71	3.88	3.41	3.11	2.90	2.73	2.60	2.50	2.41	2.34	2.28
400	3.86	3.02	2.62	2.39	2.23	2.12	2.03	1.96	1.90	1.85	1.81	1.78
	6.70	4.66	3.83	3.36	3.06	2.85	2.69	2.55	2.46	2.37	2.29	2.23
1000	3.85	3.00	2.61	2.38	2.22	2.10	2.02	1.95	1.89	1.84	1.80	1.76
	6.66	4.62	3.80	3.34	3.04	2.82	2.66	2.53	2.43	2.34	2.26	2.20
∞	3.84	2.99	2.60	2.37	2.21	2.09	2.01	1.94	1.88	1.83	1.79	1.75
	6.64	4.60	3.78	3.32	3.02	2.80	2.64	2.51	2.41	2.32	2.24	2.18

TABLE VI *(concluded)*

n_1 Degrees of Freedom for Numerator											
14	16	20	24	30	40	50	75	100	200	500	∞
1.90	1.85	1.78	1.74	1.69	1.63	1.60	1.55	1.52	1.48	1.46	1.44
2.46	2.39	2.26	2.18	2.10	2.00	1.94	1.86	1.82	1.76	1.71	1.68
1.88	1.83	1.76	1.72	1.67	1.61	1.58	1.52	1.50	1.46	1.43	1.41
2.43	2.35	2.23	2.15	2.06	1.96	1.90	1.82	1.78	1.71	1.66	1.64
1.86	1.81	1.75	1.70	1.65	1.59	1.56	1.50	1.48	1.44	1.41	1.39
2.40	2.32	2.20	2.12	2.03	1.93	1.87	1.79	1.74	1.68	1.63	1.60
1.85	1.80	1.73	1.68	1.63	1.57	1.54	1.49	1.46	1.42	1.39	1.37
2.37	2.30	2.18	2.09	2.00	1.90	1.84	1.76	1.71	1.64	1.60	1.56
1.84	1.79	1.72	1.67	1.62	1.56	1.53	1.47	1.45	1.40	1.37	1.35
2.35	2.28	2.15	2.07	1.98	1.88	1.82	1.74	1.69	1.62	1.56	1.53
1.82	1.77	1.70	1.65	1.60	1.54	1.51	1.45	1.42	1.38	1.35	1.32
2.32	2.24	2.11	2.03	1.94	1.84	1.78	1.70	1.65	1.57	1.52	1.49
1.79	1.75	1.68	1.63	1.57	1.51	1.48	1.42	1.39	1.34	1.30	1.28
2.26	2.19	2.06	1.98	1.89	1.79	1.73	1.64	1.59	1.51	1.46	1.43
1.77	1.72	1.65	1.60	1.55	1.49	1.45	1.39	1.36	1.31	1.27	1.25
2.23	2.15	2.03	1.94	1.85	1.75	1.68	1.59	1.54	1.46	1.40	1.37
1.76	1.71	1.64	1.59	1.54	1.47	1.44	1.37	1.34	1.29	1.25	1.22
2.20	2.12	2.00	1.91	1.83	1.72	1.66	1.56	1.51	1.43	1.37	1.33
1.74	1.69	1.62	1.57	1.52	1.45	1.42	1.35	1.32	1.26	1.22	1.19
2.17	2.09	1.97	1.88	1.79	1.69	1.62	1.53	1.48	1.39	1.33	1.28
1.72	1.67	1.60	1.54	1.49	1.42	1.38	1.32	1.28	1.22	1.16	1.13
2.12	2.04	1.92	1.84	1.74	1.64	1.57	1.47	1.42	1.32	1.24	1.19
1.70	1.65	1.58	1.53	1.47	1.41	1.36	1.30	1.26	1.19	1.13	1.08
2.09	2.01	1.89	1.81	1.71	1.61	1.54	1.44	1.38	1.28	1.19	1.11
1.69	1.64	1.57	1.52	1.46	1.40	1.35	1.28	1.24	1.17	1.11	1.00
2.07	1.99	1.87	1.79	1.69	1.59	1.52	1.41	1.36	1.25	1.15	1.00

TABLE VII
Critical Values of the Dunn Multiple Comparison Test

Number of Comparisons (C)	α_{ew}	5	7	10	12	15	20	24	30	40	60	120	∞
2	.05	3.17	2.84	2.64	2.56	2.49	2.42	2.39	2.36	2.33	2.30	2.27	2.24
	.01	4.78	4.03	3.58	3.43	3.29	3.16	3.09	3.03	2.97	2.92	2.86	2.81
3	.05	3.54	3.13	2.87	2.78	2.69	2.61	2.58	2.54	2.50	2.47	2.43	2.39
	.01	5.25	4.36	3.83	3.65	3.48	3.33	3.26	3.19	3.12	3.06	2.99	2.94
4	.05	3.81	3.34	3.04	2.94	2.84	2.75	2.70	2.66	2.62	2.58	2.54	2.50
	.01	5.60	4.59	4.01	3.80	3.62	3.46	3.38	3.30	3.23	3.16	3.09	3.02
5	.05	4.04	3.50	3.17	3.06	2.95	2.85	2.80	2.75	2.71	2.66	2.62	2.58
	.01	5.89	4.78	4.15	3.93	3.74	3.55	3.47	3.39	3.31	3.24	3.16	3.09
6	.05	4.22	3.64	3.28	3.15	3.04	2.93	2.88	2.83	2.78	2.73	2.68	2.64
	.01	6.15	4.95	4.27	4.04	3.82	3.63	3.54	3.46	3.38	3.30	3.22	3.15
7	.05	4.38	3.76	3.37	3.24	3.11	3.00	2.94	2.89	2.84	2.79	2.74	2.69
	.01	6.36	5.09	4.37	4.13	3.90	3.70	3.61	3.52	3.43	3.34	3.27	3.19
8	.05	4.53	3.86	3.45	3.31	3.18	3.06	3.00	2.94	2.89	2.84	2.79	2.74
	.01	6.56	5.21	4.45	4.20	3.97	3.76	3.66	3.57	3.48	3.39	3.31	3.23
9	.05	4.66	3.95	3.52	3.37	3.24	3.11	3.05	2.99	2.93	2.88	2.83	2.77
	.01	6.70	5.31	4.53	4.26	4.02	3.80	3.70	3.61	3.51	3.42	3.34	3.26
10	.05	4.78	4.03	3.58	3.43	3.29	3.16	3.09	3.03	2.97	2.92	2.86	2.81
	.01	6.86	5.40	4.59	4.32	4.07	3.85	3.74	3.65	3.55	3.46	2.37	3.29
15	.05	5.25	4.36	3.83	3.65	3.48	3.33	3.26	3.19	3.12	3.06	2.99	2.94
	.01	7.51	5.79	4.86	4.56	4.29	4.03	3.91	3.80	3.70	3.59	3.50	3.40
20	.05	5.60	4.59	4.01	3.80	3.62	3.46	3.38	3.30	3.23	3.16	3.09	3.02
	.01	8.00	6.08	5.06	4.73	4.42	4.15	4.04	3.90	3.79	3.69	3.58	3.48
25	.05	5.89	4.78	4.15	3.93	3.74	3.55	3.47	3.39	3.31	3.24	3.16	3.09
	.01	8.37	6.30	5.20	4.86	4.53	4.25	4.1*	3.98	3.88	3.76	3.64	3.54
30	.05	6.15	4.95	4.27	4.04	3.82	3.63	3.54	3.46	3.38	3.30	3.22	3.15
	.01	8.68	6.49	5.33	4.95	4.61	4.33	4.2*	4.13	3.93	3.81	3.69	3.59
35	.05	6.36	5.09	4.37	4.13	3.90	3.70	3.61	3.52	3.43	3.34	3.27	3.19
	.01	8.95	6.67	5.44	5.04	4.71	4.39	4.3*	4.26	3.97	3.84	3.73	3.63
40	.05	6.56	5.21	4.45	4.20	3.97	3.76	3.66	3.57	3.48	3.39	3.31	3.23
	.01	9.19	6.83	5.52	5.12	4.78	4.46	4.3*	4.1*	4.01	3.89	3.77	3.66
45	.05	6.70	5.31	4.53	4.26	4.02	3.80	3.70	3.61	3.51	3.42	3.34	3.26
	.01	9.41	6.93	5.60	5.20	4.84	4.52	4.3*	4.2*	4.1*	3.93	3.80	3.69
50	.05	6.86	5.40	4.59	4.32	4.07	3.85	3.74	3.65	3.55	3.46	3.37	3.29
	.01	9.68	7.06	5.70	5.27	4.90	4.56	4.4*	4.2*	4.1*	3.97	3.83	3.72
100	.05	8.00	6.08	5.06	4.73	4.42	4.15	4.04	3.90	3.79	3.69	3.58	3.48
	.01	11.04	7.80	6.20	5.70	5.20	4.80	4.7*	4.4*	4.5*		4.00	3.89
250	.05	9.68	7.06	5.70	5.27	4.90	4.56	4.4*	4.2*	4.1*	3.97	3.83	3.72
	.01	13.26	8.83	6.9*	6.3*	5.8*	5.2*	5.0*	4.9*	4.8*			4.11

*Obtained by graphical interpolation.

Adapted from Tables 1 and 2 in Dunn, O.J.: Multiple comparisons among means. *Journal of the American Statistical Association,* 1961, *56,* 52–64. By permission of the American Statistical Association.

TABLE VIII
Critical Values of Chi-Square

df	\multicolumn{6}{c}{Level of Significance}
	.20	.10	.05	.02	.01	.001
1	1.64	2.71	3.84	5.41	6.63	10.83
2	3.22	4.61	5.99	7.82	9.21	13.82
3	4.64	6.25	7.82	9.84	11.34	16.27
4	5.99	7.78	9.49	11.67	13.28	18.46
5	7.29	9.24	11.07	13.39	15.09	20.52
6	8.56	10.64	12.59	15.03	16.81	22.46
7	9.80	12.02	14.07	16.62	18.48	24.32
8	11.03	13.36	15.51	18.17	20.09	26.12
9	12.24	14.68	16.92	19.68	21.67	27.88
10	13.44	15.99	18.31	21.16	23.21	29.59
11	14.63	17.28	19.68	22.62	24.72	31.26
12	15.81	18.55	21.03	24.05	26.22	32.91
13	16.98	19.81	22.36	25.47	27.69	34.53
14	18.15	21.06	23.68	26.87	29.14	36.12
15	19.31	22.31	25.00	28.26	30.58	37.70
16	20.46	23.54	26.30	29.63	32.00	39.25
17	21.62	24.77	27.59	31.00	33.41	40.79
18	22.76	25.99	28.87	32.35	34.81	42.31
19	23.90	27.20	30.14	33.69	36.19	43.82
20	25.04	28.41	31.41	35.02	37.57	45.32
21	26.17	29.62	32.67	36.34	38.93	46.80
22	27.30	30.81	33.92	37.66	40.29	48.27
23	28.43	32.01	35.17	38.97	41.64	49.73
24	29.55	33.20	36.42	40.27	42.98	51.18
25	30.68	34.38	37.65	41.57	44.31	52.62
26	31.80	35.56	38.89	42.86	45.64	54.05
27	32.91	36.74	40.11	44.14	46.96	55.48
28	34.03	37.92	41.34	45.42	48.28	56.89
29	35.14	39.09	42.56	46.69	49.59	58.30
30	36.25	40.26	43.77	47.96	50.89	59.70

From Fisher, R. A., & Yates, F.: *Statistical Tables for Biological, Agricultural and Medical Research, 6th ed.* London: Longman Group Ltd., 1974. (Previously published by Oliver and Boyd Ltd., Edinburgh.) Reprinted by permission of the authors and the publishers.

ANSWERS TO CHAPTER PROBLEMS

CHAPTER 2 **1.** 7

2. 15

3. 100

4. (a) 3   **(b)** 5   **(c)** 55   **(d)** 225   **(e)** 135   **(f)** 625

(g) $3 + 1 + 5 = 9$ **(h)** $\Sigma X + \Sigma Y = 15 + 25 = 40$

(i) $\Sigma(X^2 + 2XY + Y^2) = \Sigma X^2 + 2\Sigma XY + \Sigma Y^2 = 55 + 2(75) + 135 = 340$

(j) $28 + 18 + 4 + 15 + 10 = 75$ **(k)** $18 + 4 = 22$

5. (a) the median   **(b)** the mean

6. (a) mean   **(b)** median

CHAPTER 3 **1.**

X	f	cf
20	2	35
19	5	33
18	10	28
17	5	18
16	3	13
15	3	10
14	2	7
13	2	5
12	1	3
11	1	2
10	1	1

2.

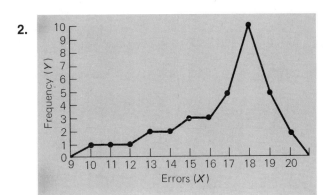

3. Unimodal

4. Yes; to the left.

5. $\bar{X} = \dfrac{\Sigma fX}{n} = \dfrac{580}{35} = 16.57$

6. $\bar{X} = \dfrac{\Sigma fX}{n} = \dfrac{3750}{50} = 75$

7. A histogram

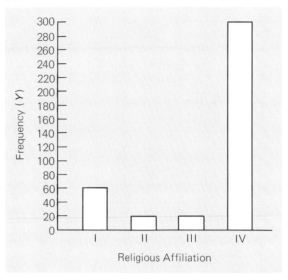

Religious Affiliation

8. Three

9.

(a)

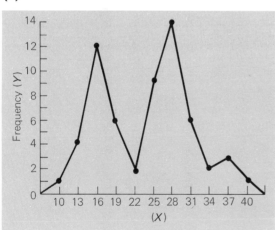

(b)

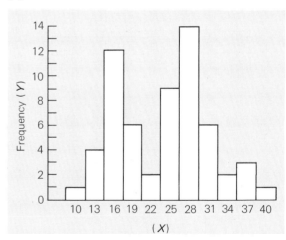

10. $\bar{X} = \dfrac{\Sigma fX}{n} = \dfrac{1434}{60} = 23.9$

11. (a) Range = 70.5 − 30.5 = 40   **(b)** 20   **(c)** 3
     (d) Any of the following three distributions is correct, in that the lowest and highest intervals contain the lowest and highest scores.

X	f
70–72	1
67–69	1
64–66	2
61–63	2
58–60	2
55–57	2
52–54	3
49–51	3
46–48	4
43–45	5
40–42	10
37–39	6
34–36	4
31–33	3

X	f
69–71	1
66–68	2
63–65	3
60–62	1
57–59	2
54–56	2
51–53	4
48–50	2
45–47	4
42–44	6
39–41	10
36–38	6
33–35	3
30–32	2

X	f
68–70	2
65–67	2
62–64	2
59–61	2
56–58	2
53–55	2
50–52	4
47–49	3
44–46	4
41–43	9
38–40	7
35–37	6
32–34	2
29–31	1

12.

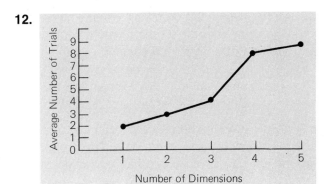

Note that the independent variable is on the X axis and the dependent variable is on the Y axis.

CHAPTER 4　**1.** PR(8) = 93
2. $P_{70} = 6$
3. PR(4) = 36
4. PR(10) = 1 (rounded from 1.25)
5. PR(20) = 12 (rounded from 11.67)
6. (a) Median $= P_{50} = 31$
　　(b) $P_{25} = 25.0$　(the first quartile)
　　　　$P_{75} = 34.6$　(the third quartile)

CHAPTER 5 **1.** $\sigma^2 = \dfrac{\Sigma X^2 - (\Sigma X)^2/n}{n}$

$$= \dfrac{120 - (20)^2/4}{4}$$

$$= 5$$

2. $\sigma = \sqrt{\dfrac{\Sigma X^2 - (\Sigma X)^2/n}{n}}$

$$= \sqrt{\dfrac{18 - (8)^2/4}{4}}$$

$$= \sqrt{.50}$$

$$= .71$$

3. $\sigma^2 = 6$. To obtain this answer, you need only square the standard deviation, given in the problem. There is no need to compute the variance using the raw scores. If you computed the variance from the raw scores, you may not understand that the variance really is the square of the standard deviation, and cannot possibly be anything else. (Of course, you may have known this but computed the variance with the raw scores just for practice.)

4. $\sigma^2 = 12.14$. As with the previous example, you should *not* have computed anything using the data. The two formulas in this problem are the defining formula and the computational formula. They are identical in meaning, and should give the same answer. Thus, knowing that one is 12.14, the other must also be 12.14.

5. $s = \sqrt{\dfrac{\Sigma X^2 - (\Sigma X)^2/n}{n - 1}}$

$$= \sqrt{\dfrac{146 - (20)^2/4}{3}}$$

$$= \sqrt{15.33}$$

$$= 3.92$$

6. (a) $\sigma^2 = \dfrac{\Sigma X^2 - (\Sigma X)^2/n}{n}$

(b) $\sigma = \sqrt{\dfrac{\Sigma X^2 - (\Sigma X)^2/n}{n}}$

(c) $s^2 = \dfrac{\Sigma X^2 - (\Sigma X)^2/n}{n-1}$

CHAPTER 6 **1. (a)** $z = \dfrac{60.5 - 50}{7} = 1.5.$

(b) $z = \dfrac{39.5 - 50}{7} = -1.5.$

(c)
$$\begin{array}{r} 64 \\ -50 \\ \hline 7|\quad 14 \\ 2 \end{array}$$
answer: 2σ.

(d) $z = \dfrac{64 - 50}{7} = 2.$

(e) A z score is the number of standard deviations from the mean.

2. (a) $X = 40 + 6(3)$
$= 58.$

(b) $X = 40 + 6(-2)$
$= 28.$

3. $\bar{X} = \dfrac{\Sigma X}{n}$

$= \dfrac{30}{7} = 4.29.$

$\sigma = \sqrt{\dfrac{158 - (30)^2/7}{7}}$

$= 2.05.$

$z = \dfrac{7.00 - 4.29}{2.05} = 1.32.$

CHAPTER 7 **1.** exclusive; point; events (or outcomes); complement; 1/3; 1/36

2. $\left(\dfrac{1}{3}\right)^4 = \dfrac{1}{81} = .0123.$

3. .25; .25; .25; .25 + .25 = .50.

467 Chapter 7

4. $(.60)^6 = .0467$.

5. (a) $(.30 + .15 + .05 + .20) = .70$.

(b) $1 - .70 = .30$.

6. In the answers to problem 6, (a–e), the letters R and W stand for the colors of the marbles (red and white), and the subscripts refer to the urn from which each outcome is obtained.

(a) $P(R_1) \cdot P(R_2) = (.2) \cdot (.1) = .02$.

(b) $P(R_1) \cdot P(W_2) = (.2) \cdot (.9) = .18$.

(c) $P(W_1) \cdot P(R_2) = (.8) \cdot (.1) = .08$.

(d) $[P(R_1) \cdot P(W_2)] + [P(W_1) \cdot P(R_2)] = .18 + .08 = .26$.

(e) $[P(R_1) \cdot P(W_2)] + [P(W_1) \cdot P(R_2)] + [P(R_1) \cdot P(R_2)]$
$= .18 + .08 + .02 = .28$.

Alternatively

$1 - [P(W_1) \cdot P(W_2)] = 1 - (.8)(.9) = 1 - .72 = .28$.

The explanation for the second solution is as follows. The complement of the probability of obtaining at least one red marble is the probability of obtaining no red marbles. The probability of obtaining no red marbles is the probability of obtaining two white marbles.

CHAPTER 8 **1.** 1. We must be able to dichotomize the outcome of every trial.
2. The probability of success must be constant over trials.
3. Each trial must be independent of every other trial.
4. There must be a specified number of trials.

2. 24

3. 1

4. 84

5. 10

6.

X	Probability
0	.16807
1	.36015
2	.30870
3	.13230
4	.02835
5	.00243

7. .03078

8. (a) .03078   **(b)** .03078, Type I error

9. The assumptions are incorrect.

10. (a) Yes, .0328   **(b)** No

11. (a) Yes   **(b)** Yes

12. 4

13. .6231

CHAPTER 9 **1. (a)** 3.59% (from column 4)
    (b) 2.87% (Because of symmetry, column 4 gives the probability of values below $z = -1.9$, as well as above $z = +1.9$.)
    (c) 97.13% (Because of symmetry, column 3 gives the probability of values below $z = +1.9$, as well as above -1.9.)
    (d) .72% (Column 2 gives the probability of a value between $z = 0$ and $z = 1.9$, as well as between $z = 0$ and $z = 1.8$. Subtracting the latter from the former yields the probability of a value between 1.8 and 1.9. Multiplication by 100 yields the percentage of scores between the two values.)
    (e) 92.82% (Column 2 supplies the answer when the tabled value is doubled and then converted to a percentage.)

2. The answers to problem 2 require that the raw scores be first converted to z scores. Here, $z = (X - 65)/5$. Then, Table III in Appendix B is used, similarly to the way it was used in problem 1.
    (a) 5.31%   **(b)** 7.40%   **(c)** 57.64%   **(d)** .35%   **(e)** 81.59%

3. The answers to problem 3 require converting the percentage to proportions (moving the decimal point two places), and then searching for the desired proportions in the body of Table III in Appendix B, to locate associated z values in column 1. Then Equation (9.4), $X = \mu + \sigma z$, is used to find each raw score. The range of scores for C are simply the scores between D and B.

    F 0–62,   D 63–66,   C 67–79,

    B 80–85,   A 86–100.

4. 6.68%: $z = (95 - 86)/6 = 1.5$. A z score of 1.5 is associated with a probability of .0668 in Column 4 of Table III.

5. 58.99%, or 58.66% (depending on decimal rounding to a z of .67 or .66). For problem 5, Column 2 is used, adding the values associated with the two z scores of .67 and -1.

6. 83.36, or simply 83. (Column 4 gives $z = .44$ as the z score that is equalled or surpassed by 33%. Thus, $z = -.44$ is the z score which equals or surpasses 33%.)

7. 93.32%

8. 30.85%

9. (a) The population mean for the ninth district is $\mu = 400$.
    (b) ± 1.96

(c) Convert her observed mean of $\bar{X} = 421$ to a z score.

(d) $z = \dfrac{421 - 400}{72/\sqrt{576}}$

$\qquad = 21/3$

$\qquad = 7.$

(e) She has statistical significance. Therefore, she will conclude that the new program is working to improve the performance on the competency test.

CHAPTER 10 **1.** $s_x = s/\sqrt{n}$

$$= \sqrt{\frac{1}{n}\left[\frac{\Sigma X^2 - (\Sigma X)^2/n}{n-1}\right]}$$

$$= \sqrt{\frac{1}{5}\left[\frac{86 - (20)^2/5}{4}\right]}$$

$$= \sqrt{.30}$$

$$= .55$$

2. (a) ± 2.306, for a two-tailed test at the .05 level.
(b) $t = -1.77^*$
(c) not significant
(d) There is no evidence of a difference in self-denial in the two populations represented by these two samples of children.
(e) 32

3. (a) ± 2.306, for a two-tailed test at the .05 level.
(b) $t = 1.66$
(c) not significant
(d) There is no evidence for concluding that the large state universities and small private colleges offer different intellectual populations.

The computing formula looks like:

---

*Since there were an equal number of subjects in each group, Equation (10.6) for t could have been used with either Equation (10.7) or Equation (10.11) for the standard error. The two choices would have looked like the following:

$$t = \frac{1.6 - 2.6}{\sqrt{(.30 + 1.30)/5}} \quad \text{or} \quad t = \frac{1.6 - 2.6}{\sqrt{\dfrac{14 + 39 - (8)^2/5 - (13)^2/5}{5 + 5 - 2}\left(\dfrac{10}{25}\right)}}$$

$$t = \frac{88.33 - 80}{\sqrt{\frac{47100 + 25800 - (530)^2/6 - (320)^2/4}{6 + 4 - 2}\left(\frac{10}{24}\right)}}.$$

4. (a) ± 3.182

(b) $t = 5.20$ (or -5.20, depending on the direction of subtraction in obtaining different scores.

(c) significant

(d) The study technique used during the second semester appears to be effective.

The computing formula looks like:

$$t = \frac{6}{\sqrt{[4(10) - 36]/3}}.$$

CHAPTER 11 1. (a) $r_{XY} = \dfrac{6(218) - (24)(50)}{\sqrt{[6(106) - (24)^2][6(460) - (50)^2]}}$

$= .86$

(b) $r_{XY}^2 = .74$

2. (a) $Y' = b_{YX}X + a_{YX}$

$b_{YX} = r_{XY}\dfrac{\sigma_Y}{\sigma_X}$

$= .86\dfrac{2.69}{1.29}$

$= 1.79$

$a_{YX} = \bar{Y} - b_{YX}\bar{X}$

$= 8.33 - 1.79(4)$

$= 1.17$

$Y' = 1.79X + 1.17$

(b) $X' = b_{XY}Y + a_{XY}$

$b_{XY} = r_{XY}\dfrac{\sigma_X}{\sigma_Y}$

$= .86\dfrac{1.29}{2.69}$

$= .41$

$a_{XY} = \bar{X} - b_{XY}\bar{Y}$

$= 4 - .41(8.33)$

$= .58$

$X' = .41Y + .58$

3. Call income Y, and IQ X.

$$Y' = b_{YX}X + a_{YX}$$

$$b_{YX} = \frac{n\Sigma XY - (\Sigma X)(\Sigma Y)}{n\Sigma X^2 - (\Sigma X)^2}$$

$$= \frac{5(13400) - (600)(110)}{5(72250) - (600)^2}$$

$$= .80$$

$$a_{YX} = \bar{Y} - b_{YX}\bar{X}$$
$$= 22 - .8(120)$$
$$= -74$$
$$Y' = .8(X) - 74$$
$$Y' = .8(123) - 74$$
$$= 24.4$$

The 24.4 is a reference to thousands, so the full answer is 24,400.

4. (a) $r_{XY} = \dfrac{n\Sigma XY - (\Sigma X)(\Sigma Y)}{\sqrt{[n\Sigma X^2 - (\Sigma X)^2][n\Sigma Y^2 - (\Sigma Y)^2]}}$

$$= \frac{5(13400) - (600)(110)}{\sqrt{[5(72250) - (600)^2][5(2580) - (110)^2]}}$$

$$= 1.0$$

(b) Perfect (errorless).

5. (a) Turn to Table V in Appendix B and see if the sampled correlation reaches (or exceeds) the tabled value.

(b) .95   **(c)** Yes

6. ✓ There is not sufficient evidence . . .

—

—

7. —

✓ There is sufficient evidence . . .

—

(This is only a sample obtained with 30 subjects, so we would not know the population correlation. Significance would only permit us to conclude that the population correlation is not zero.)

8. $r_{pb} = \dfrac{9(215) - 4(520)}{\sqrt{5 \cdot 4[9(30450) - (520)^2]}}$

$$= -.54$$

[X_1 is the sign group, and X_0 the no-sign group. Using Equation (11.14) yields the negative value. Calling the sign group X_0 would yield a positive value.]

$r_{pb}^2 = .29$, which is the proportion of variance in car speeds estimated to be associated with presence or absence of the sign.

CHAPTER 12 1. For coefficient alpha (Kuder–Richardson version) the formula is

$$r\alpha = \frac{k}{k-1}\left(1 - \frac{\Sigma p_i q_i}{\sigma_X^2}\right),$$

where k is the number of items (8) and $\Sigma p_i q_i$ is the sum of the variances of the individual test items. As indicated in the text, the variance for dichotomous items is the product of the proportion of ones times the proportion of zeros. These values are shown in the reproduction of the data matrix below at the bottom of the columns of responses to each item. Their sum, $\Sigma p_i q_i$, is also indicated. The value σ_X^2 is simply the variance of the score totals for each subject. The totals for each subject and the totals squared have been added to the data matrix as X and X^2 in the two last columns. These columns are used in computing σ_X^2.

				Items					Total	(Total)²
Subject	1	2	3	4	5	6	7	8	X	X²
1	1	1	1	1	0	1	1	1	7	49
2	0	1	1	1	1	1	0	1	6	36
3	0	0	0	0	1	0	0	0	1	1
4	0	1	0	0	0	1	0	0	2	4
5	1	0	1	0	0	1	1	0	4	16
6	0	0	0	1	0	0	0	1	2	4
$p_i q_i =$	$\frac{2}{6}\cdot\frac{4}{6}$	$\frac{3}{6}\cdot\frac{3}{6}$	$\frac{3}{6}\cdot\frac{3}{6}$	$\frac{3}{6}\cdot\frac{3}{6}$	$\frac{2}{6}\cdot\frac{4}{6}$	$\frac{4}{6}\cdot\frac{2}{6}$	$\frac{2}{6}\cdot\frac{4}{6}$	$\frac{3}{6}\cdot\frac{3}{6}$	$22 = \Sigma X$	$110 = \Sigma X^2$

$$\Sigma p_i q_i = \frac{8}{36} + \frac{9}{36} + \frac{9}{36} + \frac{9}{36} + \frac{8}{36} + \frac{8}{36} + \frac{8}{36} + \frac{9}{36}$$

$$= \frac{68}{36} = 1.89$$

$$\sigma_X^2 = \frac{\Sigma X^2 - (\Sigma X)^2/n}{n}$$

$$= \frac{110 - (22)^2/6}{6}$$

$$= 4.89$$

$$r_\alpha = \frac{k}{k-1}\left(1 - \frac{\Sigma p_i q_i}{\sigma_X^2}\right)$$

473 Chapter 12

$$= \frac{8}{7}\left(1 - \frac{1.89}{4.89}\right)$$

$$= .70$$

For the split-half reliability coefficient, two subtotals are needed for each subject. Call the subtotal of odd-numbered items X_1 and even-numbered items X_2. These two subtotals, along with X_1X_2, X_1^2, and X_2^2, have been added to the rearranged data matrix below.

Subjects	1 3 5 7	X_1 Sum, Odd Items	2 4 6 8	X_2 Sum, Even Items	X_1X_2	X_1^2	X_2^2
1	1 1 0 1	3	1 1 1 1	4	12	9	16
2	0 1 1 0	2	1 1 1 1	4	8	4	16
3	0 0 1 0	1	0 0 0 0	0	0	1	0
4	0 0 0 0	0	1 0 1 0	2	0	0	4
5	1 1 0 1	3	0 0 1 0	1	3	9	1
6	0 0 0 0	0	0 1 0 1	2	0	0	4
		$\Sigma X_1 = 9$		$\Sigma X_2 = 13$	$\Sigma X_1X_2 = 23$	23	41

$$r_{sh} = \frac{2r_{12}}{1 + r_{12}}$$

$$= \frac{2(.32)}{1 + .32}$$

$$= .48$$

$$r_{12} = \frac{n\Sigma X_1X_2 - (\Sigma X_1)(\Sigma X_2)}{\sqrt{[n\Sigma X_1^2 - (\Sigma X_1)^2][n\Sigma X_2^2 - (\Sigma X_2)^2]}}$$

$$= \frac{6(23) - (9)(13)}{\sqrt{[6(23) - (9)^2][6(41) - (13)^2]}}$$

$$= .32$$

CHAPTER 13 1.

SV	SS	df	MS	F
Between groups	27.00	2	13.50	4.46*
Within groups	45.50	15	3.03	
Total	72.50	17		

*$p < .05$.

2.

SV	SS	df	MS	F
Between groups	41.53	3	13.84	6.92*
Within groups	26.00	13	2.00	
Total	67.53	16		

*$p < .01$.

3. 2.71

2.82 (when exact df are not listed, use closest smaller value)

3.56

3.94

CHAPTER 14 **1.** $t_{crit}\sqrt{\dfrac{2MS_w}{n}} = 2.78\sqrt{\dfrac{2(.85)}{9}}$

$$= 1.21$$

$\bar{X}_{.2} - \bar{X}_{.1} = 1.22$

$\bar{X}_{.3} - \bar{X}_{.2} = 2.34$

$\bar{X}_{.4} - \bar{X}_{.3} = 0.77$

$\bar{X}_{.4} - \bar{X}_{.2} = 3.11$

$\bar{X}_{.4} - \bar{X}_{.1} = 4.33$

$\bar{X}_{.5} - \bar{X}_{.1} = 5.56$

All the comparisons except $\bar{X}_{.4} - \bar{X}_{.3}$ are significant.

2.

Comparison	Formula needed for the test
$\bar{X}_{.2} - \bar{X}_{.1}$	$= 0.42 \ngeqslant 2.94\sqrt{3.10(\tfrac{1}{3} + \tfrac{1}{4})} = 3.95$
$\bar{X}_{.3} - \bar{X}_{.2}$	$= 0.45 \ngeqslant 2.94\sqrt{3.10(\tfrac{1}{5} + \tfrac{1}{4})} = 3.47$
$\bar{X}_{.4} - \bar{X}_{.3}$	$= 4.30 \geqslant 2.94\sqrt{3.10(\tfrac{1}{5} + \tfrac{1}{4})} = 3.47$
$\bar{X}_{.4} - \bar{X}_{.2}$	$= 4.75 \geqslant 2.94\sqrt{\dfrac{2(3.10)}{4}} = 3.66$

The last two comparisons are the only significant ones.

3. $\dfrac{F - 1}{F - 1 + n} = \dfrac{3.60 - 1}{3.60 - 1 + 20}$

$$= .12,$$

which is the estimate of the proportion of the variance associated with treatment levels, using the intraclass correlation coefficient.

4. $\dfrac{(g - 1)(F - 1)}{(g - 1)(F - 1) + gn} = \dfrac{4(2.60)}{4(2.60) + 5(20)}$

$$= .09,$$

which is the estimate of the proportion of the variance associated with treatment levels using omega-squared.

CHAPTER 15 **1.** **(a)** and **(b)**

Five basic terms in the sums of squares:

$$\frac{\left(\sum\limits_{i}^{n}\sum\limits_{j}^{a}\sum\limits_{k}^{b} X_{ijk}\right)^2}{nab} = \frac{(441)^2}{7\cdot3\cdot4} = 2315.25.$$

$$\frac{\sum\limits_{j}^{a}\left(\sum\limits_{i}^{n}\sum\limits_{k}^{b} X_{ijk}\right)^2}{nb} = \frac{(119)^2 + (140)^2 + (182)^2}{7\cdot4} = 2388.75.$$

$$\frac{\sum\limits_{k}^{b}\left(\sum\limits_{i}^{n}\sum\limits_{j}^{a} X_{ijk}\right)^2}{na} = \frac{(105)^2 + (105)^2 + (42)^2 + (189)^2}{7\cdot3} = 2835.$$

$$\frac{\sum\limits_{j}^{a}\sum\limits_{k}^{b}\left(\sum\limits_{i}^{n} X_{ijk}\right)^2}{n} = \frac{(28)^2 + (28)^2 + (14)^2 + \cdots + (77)^2}{7} = 2933.$$

$$\sum\limits_{i}^{n}\sum\limits_{j}^{a}\sum\limits_{k}^{b} X^2_{ijk} = (4)^2 + (3)^2 + \cdots + (13)^2 = 3121.$$

SV	SS	df	MS	F	Omega-Squared
A	2388.75 − 2315.25 = 73.50	2	36.75	14.08*	.08
B	2835 − 2315.25 = 519.75	3	173.25	66.38*	.63
AB	2933 − 2388.75 −2835 + 2315.25 = 24.50	6	4.08	1.56	
Within cells	3121 − 2933 = 188.00	72	2.61		
Total	3121 − 2315.25 = 805.75	83			

*$p < .01$.

(c) Multiple comparisons on variable A, $\alpha_{pc} = .05$.

$$\bar{X}_{.1.} = 4.25,\ \bar{X}_{.2.} = 5.00,\ \bar{X}_{.3.} = 6.50.$$

$$\bar{X}_{.j.} - \bar{X}_{.j'.} \geq t_{crit}\sqrt{\frac{2MS_w}{nb}}$$

$$\geq t_{\alpha_{pc}}\sqrt{\frac{2(2.61)}{7.4}}$$

$$\geq 2.00\sqrt{.19}$$

$$\geq .86.$$

$\bar{X}_{.3.} - \bar{X}_{.2.} = 6.50 - 5.00$
$\qquad = 1.50 \qquad \geq .86.$

$\bar{X}_{.3.} - \bar{X}_{.1.} = 6.50 - 4.25$
$\qquad = 2.25 \qquad \geq .86.$

$\bar{X}_{.2.} - \bar{X}_{.1.} = 5.00 - 4.25$
$\qquad = .75 \qquad \nleq .86.$

Two of the comparisons are significant using the per-comparison criterion.

Multiple comparisons on variable A, $\alpha_{ew} = .05$. For three comparisons at $\alpha_{ew} = .05$, $t_{crit} = 2.47$. ($df_w = 72$ and the closest lower value in the table is 60 df, which indicates 2.47 for three comparisons.)

$$\bar{X}_{.j.} - \bar{X}_{.j'.} \geq t_{crit}\sqrt{\frac{2MS_w}{nb}}$$

$$\geq t_{\alpha_{ew}}\sqrt{\frac{2MS_w}{nb}}$$

$$\geq 2.47\sqrt{\frac{2(2.61)}{7.4}}$$

$$\geq 2.47\sqrt{.19}$$

$$\geq 1.07.$$

$\bar{X}_{.3.} - \bar{X}_{.2.} = 6.50 - 5.00$
$\qquad = 1.50 \qquad \geq 1.07.$

$\bar{X}_{.3.} - \bar{X}_{.1.} = 6.50 - 4.25$
$\qquad = 2.25 \qquad \geq 1.07.$

$\bar{X}_{.2.} - \bar{X}_{.1.} = 5.00 - 4.25$
$\qquad = .75 \qquad \not\geq 1.07.$

Two of the comparisons are significant using the experimentwise criterion. (The same two as with the per-comparison criterion.)

2. (a)

SV	SS	df	MS	F
A	$750 - 750 = 0$	1	0	0
B	$755 - 750 = 5$	2	2.50	1.11
AB	$790 - 750$ $-755 + 750 = 35$	2	17.50	7.78*
Within cells	$844 - 790 = 54$	24	2.25	
Total	$844 - 750 = 94$	29		

*$p < .01$.

(b)

Level of Test of A	Sum of Squares	df	Mean Squares	F
A at B_1	$\dfrac{(20)^2 + (30)^2}{5} - \dfrac{(50)^2}{10}$ $= 10$	1	10.00	4.44*
A at B_2	$\dfrac{(25)^2 + (30)^2}{5} - \dfrac{(55)^2}{10}$ $= 2.50$	1	2.50	1.11

Level of Test of A	Sum of Squares	df	Mean Squares	F
A at B_3	$\dfrac{(30)^2 + (15)^2}{5} - \dfrac{(45)^2}{10}$ $= 22.50$	1	22.50	10.00**
Within cells	54	24	2.25	

*$p < .05.$
**$p < .01.$

(c)

Level of Test of B	Sum of Squares	df	Mean Squares	F
B at A_1	$\dfrac{(20)^2 + (25)^2 + (30)^2}{5} - \dfrac{(75)^2}{15}$ $= 10$	2	5.00	2.22
B at A_2	$\dfrac{(30)^2 + (30)^2 + (15)^2}{5} - \dfrac{(75)^2}{15}$ $= 30$	2	15.00	6.67*
Within cells	54	24	2.25	

*$p < .01.$

Multiple comparisons on variable B at A_2, $\alpha_{ew} = .05$.

$$\bar{X}_{..k} - \bar{X}_{..k'} \geq t_{crit} \sqrt{\frac{2MS_w}{n}}$$

For three comparisons,

at $\alpha_{ew} = .05$, $t_{crit} = 2.58$.

$$\geq 2.58 \sqrt{\frac{2(2.25)}{5}}$$

$$\geq 2.45.$$

At level A_2 both comparisons with B_3 are significant, the remaining one, $B_2 - B_1$, is not significant. The same results are obtained with the per-comparison criterion, for which $t_{crit} = 2.06$ and $t_{crit} \sqrt{\dfrac{2MS_w}{n}} = 1.95$.

CHAPTER 16 **1. (a)** See upper left-hand corner of each cell.

Variable A

		I	II	III	IV	
	I	9 / 5	9 / 15	6 / 5	6 / 5	30
Variable B	II	9 / 0	9 / 10	6 / 10	6 / 10	30
	III	12 / 25	12 / 5	8 / 5	8 / 5	40
		30	30	20	20	N = 100

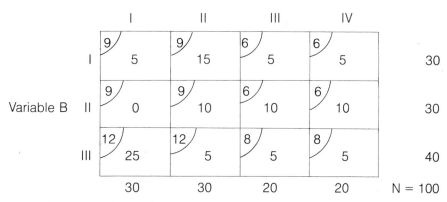

(b) $\chi^2 = 40.97$ **(c)** $(2)(3) = 6$ **(d)** 12.59   **(e)** Yes

(f) Cramer's phi $= \sqrt{\dfrac{40.97}{100(2)}} = \sqrt{.20} = .45$

2. (a) 16.30   **(b)** 1   **(c)** 3.84   **(d)** Yes

   (e) $\phi = \sqrt{\dfrac{16.30}{65}} = \sqrt{.25} = .50$

3. The answer again should be 16.30.

4. (a) $\chi^2 = 62.83$

   (b) $p < .001$. (The largest critical value at two degrees of freedom in the chi-square table is 13.82. This is for a probability of .001. The computed value of chi-square, 62.83, surpasses the tabled critical value of 13.82.)

   (c) The general conclusion is that the different social classes do not apply to the school in the same proportion as they are found in the general population.

GLOSSARY OF SYMBOLS

Scores, Sums, and Means

X Any individual score in a set of scores.

X_i The ith score in a set of scores.

Σ Sigma, the symbol for addition.

ΣX The sum of all of the scores in a set of scores.

$\sum_{i=1}^{k} X_i$ The sum of scores from $i = 1$ to $i = k$, which is only equivalent to ΣX when $k = n$, the total number of scores.

$\bar{X}$ A sample mean.

μ A population mean.

μ_z Mean of a population of z scores, always equal to one.

fX The frequency of the scores with a value of X, within a particular frequency distribution.

ΣfX The sum of the scores in a frequency distribution.

$\bar{Y}$ A sample mean, where the individual scores are symbolized by Y.

X_{ij} An individual score in a one-factor analysis of variance design (the ith score in the jth group).

$\sum_{i=1}^{n} \sum_{j=1}^{a} X_{ij}$ Sum of all the scores in a one-factor analysis of variance design.

$\bar{X}_{..}$ Grand mean, in a one-factor analysis of variance design.

X_{ijk} An individual score in a two-factor analysis of variance design (the ith score at the jth level of variable A and the kth level of variable B).

481

$$\sum_{i=1}^{n} \sum_{j=1}^{a} \sum_{k=1}^{b} X_{ijk}$$ The sum of all the scores in a two-factor analysis of variance design.

$\bar{X}_{...}$ Grand mean, in a two-factor analysis of variance design.

$\bar{X}_{.j}$ Mean of the jth group in a one-factor analysis of variance design.

$\bar{X}_{.j.}$ Mean of the jth level of variable A in a two-factor analysis of variance design. (The mean of the jth row of the scores in the matrix.)

$\bar{X}_{..k}$ Mean of the kth level of variable B in a two-factor analysis of variance design. (The mean of the kth column of the scores in the matrix.)

$\bar{X}_{.jk}$ Mean of the cell in the jth row, k^{th} column of the matrix in a two-factor analysis of variance design.

Variability

σ^2 Population variance.

σ Population standard deviation.

s^2 Sample estimate of the population variance.

s Sample estimate of the population standard deviation.

$\sigma_{\bar{x}}$ Standard error of a population.

$s_{\bar{x}}$ Sample estimate of the standard error of a population.

σ_z Standard deviation of a population of z scores, always equal to one.

$s_{\bar{x}_1 - \bar{x}_2}$ Standard error of the difference between two means.

$s_{\bar{D}}$ Standard error for a set of sampled difference scores.

σ_e^2 Variance of the error of estimate.

Statistical Tests for Significance

t t test, used to test for the difference from some hypothesized mean or for the difference between sampled means, when the variability in the population must be estimated.

F F test, which is a ratio of two variances. In the most common applications the two variances are called mean squares, and the test is an omnibus F test of whether the treatment variable is effective. Some examples of F ratios appear below.

$$F = \frac{MS_{between}}{MS_{within}}$$ Omnibus F test in a one-factor analysis of variance.

$$F = \frac{MS_{AB}}{MS_w}$$ F test for an interaction between two factors (A and B).

$$F = \frac{MS_{A_{bj}}}{MS_w}$$ F test for the simple effect of variable A at the jth level of variable B.

Mean squares are themselves ratios. For example:

$$MS_A = \frac{SS_A}{df_A}$$

SS_A = Sum of squares for variable A.

df_A = degrees of freedom for MS_A.

χ^2 Chi-square, the test with classified variables.

E_{jk} Expected value in the cell of the jth row of the kth column of the contingency table, used in a chi-square analysis.

rm_j Marginal of the jth row (sum of the frequencies in the row). Used in obtaining the expected value for a cell.

cm_k Marginal of the kth column (sum of the frequencies in the column). Used in obtaining the expected value for a cell.

Measures of Degree of Relationship

ρ_{xy} Pearson's product moment correlation coefficient, for a population of scores. (ρ is the Greek letter rho.)

r_{xy} Pearson's product moment correlation coefficient, estimated from a sample of scores. Also simply called Pearson's r.

r_{xy}^2 Square of the Pearson product moment correlation coefficient, which offers an estimate of the proportion of variance in Y associated with variability in X.

r_{pb} The point biserial correlation coefficient, a special version of the Pearson r that is conveniently used when one variable is dichotomous, and the other is continuous or wide ranging.

$r_{intraclass}$ Intraclass correlation coefficient. Estimate of the proportion of variance in the dependent variable associated with levels of the independent variable, computed with a significant F. (Used when drawing inferences beyond the randomly sampled levels of the independent variable.)

ω^2 Omega squared. Estimate of the proportion of variance in the dependent variable associated with levels of the independent variable, computed with a significant F. (Used when the conclusions are restricted to the levels of the independent variable appearing in the experiment.)

ϕ Phi coefficient. A measure of correlation between two dichotomized classified variables, computed from a significant chi-square. Equivalent in meaning to a Pearson r.

Cramer's ϕ Cramer's phi. A measure of correlation between two classified variables, computed from a significant chi-square, when the contingency table is greater than a 2×2. Varies between zero and one, but is not strictly equivalent to a Pearson r.

C Contingency coefficient. A measure of correlation between two classified variables, computed from a significant chi-square, when the contingency table is greater than a 2×2. Can have a maximum value less than one, so not strictly analogous to other measures of correlation.

Measures of Reliability

r_{new} Reliability of a test when the size of the test is changed by a factor of k.

r_{sh} Split half reliability.

r_{α} Coefficient alpha.

Prediction

Y' Predicted point on a linear prediction line predicting Y from (X).

b_{yx} Slope of a linear prediction line (predicting Y from X).

b_{xy} Slope of a linear prediction line (predicting X from Y).

a_{yx} Intercept of a linear prediction line (predicting Y from X).

a_{xy} Intercept of a linear prediction line (predicting X from Y).

Transformations

z z score, also called a standard score. It is a score reexpressed in terms of its distance from the mean, using the standard deviation as the unit of measurement. For example, a z score of 2 is two standard deviations above the mean.

PR(X) Percentile rank. This is the percentage of scores equaled or surpassed by X.

P_{perc} Percentile. A percentile is a score that occupies the percentile rank that is specified in the subscript. For example, P_{40}, the 40th percentile, is a score which has the 40th percentile rank. It is the score that equals or surpasses 40 percent of the scores.

Probability

S$_j$ The jth sample point. Given the simplest mutually exclusive definition of the complete set of possible outcomes in some situation, each such outcome is a sample point.

S Sample space. All of the potential outcomes in a given situation.

P(S$_j$) The probability of the occurrence of the jth sample point.

E$_j$ The jth event. An event is a subset of sample points containing one or more sample points.

P(E$_j$) The probability of the occurrence of the jth event.

P($\bar{E}_j$) The probability of event E$_j$ not occurring.

α Alpha error, the probability of a Type I error.

β Beta error, the probability of a Type II error.

α_{ew} Experimentwise Type I error probability.

α_{pc} Per-comparison Type I error probability.

B(x; n, p) The binomial distribution. The probability of x successes in n trials with dichotomous outcomes, one with a probability of p, and the other outcome with a probability of $(1 - p)$. The probability of x successes is $B(x; n, p) = \binom{n}{x}p^x(1 - p)^{n-x}$.

Mathematical Symbols

|X| Absolute value of X. (If X is a negative number the sign is ignored.)

< Less than. $X < Y$ means that X is less than Y.

≤ Less than or equal to. $X \leq Y$ means that X is less than or equal to Y.

> Greater than. $X > Y$ means that X is greater than Y.

≥ Greater than or equal to. $X \geq Y$ means that X is greater than or equal to Y.

± Plus or minus.

≈ Approximately equal to.

∞ Infinity.

$\binom{n}{x}$ The binomial coefficient. The number of ways that x successes could occur in n trials with dichotomous outcomes.

$$\binom{n}{x} = \frac{n!}{(n - x)!x!}$$

n! n factorial, where n can be any integer. $n! = n \cdot (n - 1) \cdot (n - 2) \cdots 1$

0! zero factorial, which is defined as 1.

INDEX

Degree of relationship summarized in a number (correlation), 233, *See also* Analysis of variance, one factor, intraclass correlation coefficient in, *and* omega-squared; Chi-square, degree of relationship from; Pearson product-moment correlation coefficient; Point biserial correlation coefficient

Degrees of freedom, 93–95, 207, 251–254. *See also* Analysis of variance, one factor, intraclass correlation coefficient in, *and* omega-squared; Analysis of variance, two factor, omega-squared

estimating statistics and, 207

t tests and, 207, 211, 215

Dependent variable, 6–7, 10–11

Descriptive statistics, 11

Deviant scores, 16–17

Dichotomous variables, 231, 248–249, 285–286, 384, 397–398

Directional hypotheses, 185–186

Distributions

alternative, 150–152, 187, 189, 218–220

bimodal, 41–42

binomial. *See* Binomial distribution

chi-square. *See* Chi-square distribution

continuous, 43–45, 163

probabilities for, 164–169

cumulative frequency. *See* Cumulative frequency distribution

empirical, 133

F, 296–297. *See also* Analysis of variance, one factor; Analysis of variance, two factor

frequency, 38

cumulative, 57–58

mean, computation of the, 39–40

modal peaks in, 41–42

frequency, grouped, 48

graphing data in a, 56

interval size of, 48–49, 50–55

mean, computation of the, 56–56

number of intervals for, 50–52

Distributions *(cont.)*

frequency, grouped *(cont.)*

open intervals in, 55–56

overt limits of intervals in, 49

purpose of, 52

range of, 50

real limits of intervals in, 49

unequal intervals in, 53–55

zero frequencies in, 53

frequency, regular, 48

monotonic decreasing, 58

monotonic increasing, 58

multimodal, 41

normal. *See* Normal distribution

null hypothesis, 135, 182–184, 187–188

rectangular, 41, 126

skewed, 42–43

t, 200–201, 204–205. *See also t* distribution

Theoretical probability, 135–137

uniform, 41

unimodal, 42

Double subscript notation, 297–299, 302

Dunn, O. J., 336n

Dunn table, 336–338, 367–369, **460**

Drake, R., 390n

E

Empirical distribution, 133

Empirical probabilities, 126–127, 133–134

Error (random) variance, 322

Events, 119–120

complementary, 122, 124

exhaustive listing of, 120–123

independent, 124

joint, 124–125

mutually exclusive, 120–124

Expected frequencies, 378–381

Expected values, 295

Experimental group, 4

Experimental manipulation, 5, 287–290

conclusions from, 289–290

Experimentwise Type I error probability, 335–338, 367–369

a 1
b 2
c 3
d 4
e 5
f 6
g 7
h 8
i 9